A European Introduction to Financial Accounting

A European Introduction to Financial Accounting

DAVID ALEXANDER
CHRISTOPER NOBES

PRENTICE HALL
New York   London   Toronto   Sydney   Tokyo   Singapore

First published 1994 by
Prentice Hall International (UK) Limited
Campus 400, Maylands Avenue
Hemel Hempstead
Hertfordshire, HP2 7EZ
A division of
Simon & Schuster International Group

© Prentice Hall International (UK) Limited 1994

All rights reserved. No part of this publication may be reproduced, stored in a retrieval system, or transmitted, in any form, or by any means, electronic, mechanical, photocopying, recording or otherwise, without prior permission, in writing, from the publisher.
For permission within the United States of America contact Prentice Hall Inc., Englewood Cliffs, NJ 07632

Typeset in 10/12 pt Times by
Mathematical Composition Setters Ltd, Salisbury, Wiltshire

Printed and bound in Great Britain by
Redwood Books Trowbridge, Wilts

Library of Congress cataloging-in-publication data

Nobes, Christopher.
    A European introduction to financial accounting / Christopher Nobes, David Alexander.
      p. cm.
    Includes bibliographical references and index.
    ISBN 0-13-030206-6
    1. Accounting—Europe. 2. Financial statements—Europe.
I. Alexander, David. II. Title.
HF5616.E8N63 1994
657′.094—dc20   93-37958
                                                                 CIP

British Library cataloguing in publication data

A catalogue record for this book is available from the British Library

ISBN 0-13-030206-6 (pbk)
---
1 2 3 4 5   97 96 95 94 93

Contents

Foreword	xi
Preface	xiii
Acknowledgements	xv

PART I **The context of accounting**   1

1 Introduction   3
- Objectives   3
- 1.1 Purposes and users of accounting   3
- 1.2 Accounting regulation and the accountancy profession   6
- 1.3 The path ahead   8
- 1.4 Excitement in accounting   8
- Exercises   9

2 Fundamental principles   11
- Objectives   11
- 2.1 Introduction   11
- 2.2 The balance sheet   11
- 2.3 The income statement   17
- 2.4 Applying and practising the thinking   23
- 2.5 Two simple equations   24
- Appendix: The 'Italian' method   24
- Summary   37
- Exercises   38

3 Conventions and framework   44
- Objectives   44
- 3.1 Introduction   44
- 3.2 Traditional financial accounting conventions   45
- 3.3 A coherent framework   49
- 3.4 Back to basics   50
- 3.5 A conceptual framework?   51

3.6	IASC Framework: introduction	51
3.7	IASC assumptions, etc	53
3.8	IASC elements of financial statements	58
3.9	IASC recognition of the accounting elements	60
Summary		61
Exercises		61

PART II Introduction to international aspects   63

4 International differences   65
Objectives   65
4.1 The international nature of the development of accounting   65
4.2 Causes of differences   66
4.3 Legal systems   67
4.4 Providers of finance   68
4.5 Taxation   70
4.6 The profession   73
4.7 Inflation   75
4.8 Theory   76
4.9 Accidents   76
4.10 Classification   77
Summary   84
References   85
Exercises   85

5 Common European rules   87
Objectives   87
5.1 Reasons for, obstacles to and measurement of harmonization   88
5.2 EC harmonization   91
5.3 The Fourth Directive examined   96
5.4 Unresolved problems and future harmonization   106
5.5 The International Accounting Standards Committee   107
5.6 Other international bodies   112
5.7 Dual standards   113
Summary   115
Appendix: Formats in the European Community   116
References   117
Exercises   117

PART III Issues in financial reporting   119

6 Valuation of fixed assets   121
Objectives   121
6.1 Framework   121
6.2 Fourth Directive and IASC rules   125

	6.3	Practice	126
	6.4	Investment properties	131
	6.5	Leasing	131
	6.6	Intangibles	134
	6.7	Investments	140
	Summary		141
	Exercises		141
7	**Depreciation of fixed assets**		143
	Objectives		143
	7.1	Terminology	143
	7.2	The basic concept	143
	7.3	Some rules	146
	7.4	What depreciation is not for	147
	7.5	Allocation methods	151
	7.6	Practicalities	154
	7.7	Criticisms of depreciation	156
	7.8	Practice	157
	Summary		160
	Exercises		160
8	**Inventory valuation**		162
	Objectives		162
	8.1	Introduction	162
	8.2	Counting inventory	164
	8.3	Valuation	165
	8.4	Historical cost as an input value	167
	8.5	Fourth Directive and IASC rules	170
	8.6	Practice	173
	8.7	Current value accounting	175
	Summary		177
	Exercises		177
	Appendix: Construction contracts		178
9	**Capital and liabilities**		184
	Objectives		184
	9.1	Introduction	184
	9.2	Definition and clarification	184
	9.3	Some detailed distinctions	186
	9.4	Implications for interpretation	189
	Summary		191
	Exercises		191
10	**Accounting and taxation**		192
	Objectives		192
	10.1	Introduction	192

10.2	Tax bases	195
10.3	Tax systems	199
10.4	Deferred tax theory	205
10.5	Deferred tax practice	212
Summary		212
Exercise		213

11 Accounting for price changes — 215

Objectives		215
11.1	The meaning and measurement of inflation	215
11.2	Effects of price changes on accounting	218
11.3	European disagreement	219
11.4	General or specific adjustment	220
11.5	General price-level adjusted systems	224
11.6	Current value accounting	224
11.7	Current cost accounting	226
11.8	Partial adjustments	229
Summary		231
References		232
Exercises		232

12 Group accounting — 236

Objectives		236
12.1	Background	236
12.2	Control	237
12.3	The parent company approach	239
12.4	Minority interests	243
12.5	Proportional consolidation	245
12.6	Investments in other non-controlled companies	246
12.7	Intercompany transactions	249
12.8	Merger (pooling of interest) accounting	249
12.9	Treatment of goodwill on consolidation	250
12.10	Flexibility in consolidated accounts	252
Summary		253
Exercises		253

13 Foreign currency translation — 257

Objectives		257
13.1	Issues and terms	257
13.2	Transactions	258
13.3	Translation of financial statements	260
13.4	A numerical illustration	262
13.5	Some rules	264
13.6	Practice	264

	Summary	264
	Exercises	267

PART IV Analysis of financial statements — 269

14 Profitability analysis — 271
	Objectives	271
14.1	Introduction	271
14.2	Ratios and percentages	272
14.3	Profit ratios	272
14.4	Profitability ratios	276
14.5	Finance ratios	278
14.6	Investment ratios	284
	Summary	289

15 Liquidity analysis — 290
	Objectives	290
15.1	Introduction	290
15.2	Liquidity ratios	290
15.3	Interest cover	292
15.4	Fund management ratios	292
15.5	Cash and funds flow statements	294
	Summary	301
	Exercises	304

16 Valuation and analysis — 310
	Objectives	310
16.1	Introduction	310
16.2	The balance sheet	310
16.3	Valuation through expectations	312
16.4	Valuation through market values	313
16.5	Accounting policies and financial appraisal	314
	Summary	319
	Exercises	319

17 International analysis — 324
	Objectives	324
17.1	Purposes and problems	324
17.2	Language	325
17.3	Financial culture	328
17.4	Interpretation difficulties	329
17.5	Help by multinationals	332
17.6	A benchmark for international comparisons	335
	Summary	338
	Exercises	339

Appendix: The EC Fourth Directive on company law 351
Glossary of terms 384
Annotated bibliography 402
Feedback on exercises 404

Index 455

Foreword

Accounting education today is either too national or too international. Most accounting students are educated on the basis of material which is entirely devoted to their national environment. When these students start their professional career they will be exposed immediately to the great variety of accounting rules and practices in other parts of the world. Unfortunately, they will not have been prepared for this. Some students will have had some exposure to the international scene through a course on international accounting. However, most books on international accounting lack a global approach and attach too much importance to the description of the same selected sample of accounting systems in the world.

This book is the first attempt to describe accounting outside the scope of a national environment. It is also different from the traditional books on international accounting because it does not describe the accounting system in a selected number of countries. The authors should be commended for this, because their product clearly responds to a need. It is, of course, much more difficult to try to identify the essential features of accounting which are present in the various national accounting systems. This is certainly the main reason why such an effort has not been undertaken before.

The authors have selected the EC Accounting Directives and the International Accounting Standards as their benchmark. This is logical because both sets of rules transcend the accounting environment of one particular country. As the authors note, there is a slight UK bias in the choice of some examples. Also, in some areas, the authors have selected US accounting terminology which is found in an IASC context. This possible source of confusion, is overcome through the very useful glossary of terms which is included in the Appendix and which allows the European reader to find the corresponding term in UK (European) terminology.

A disadvantage of using the EC Accounting Directives and the International Accounting Standards as a combined benchmark is that less attention is paid to the company law (legal capital maintenance) approach which is prevalent in the European Community and which does not receive the same attention in the IASC's conceptual framework, which is the basis for the International Accounting Standards.

The book might be read as suggesting that the EC Commission fulfils the role of an accouting standard setting body. However, as the book points out, the EC Commission is primarily the initiator of Community legislation. The decisions are taken by the Council of Ministers, in cooperation with the European Parliament. On the other hand, through its right of initiative, the EC Commission has played a major role in shaping the face of European accounting. This book shows very clearly that much needs to be done before we can say that the harmonization work is finished.

I hope that this first book to describe accounting outside the constraints of a national environment will be appreciated by lecturers as well as by students. It will certainly help students in accounting to be more prepared to face the challanges of a world which is by definition international.

K. Van Hulle
Head of Accounting
at the EC Commission

Preface

This book is intended to break new ground in the treatment of the exposition of financial accounting by using the context of the accounting rules of the European Community (EC) and the International Accounting Standards Committee (IASC) rather than any particular country's regulatory system. Further, when practices are discussed or illustrations given, a range of European countries and companies is drawn upon.

The book is designed for those with little or no previous financial accounting knowledge; it will also be suitable for readers in the countries of eastern Europe whose accounting training is related to a quite different context from western capitalism. It is intended to deal with sufficient material for the whole of a student's first course in financial accounting.

The principal reader groups will be those who are taught accounting in English, including:

(a) undergraduate students in the European Community where it seems appropriate to use a context broader than that of the home country or that provided by a UK-based or US-based text;
(b) undergraduates and others outside the European Community whose countries are intending to join or to liaise closely with EC countries commercially;
(c) postgraduate (e.g. MBA) students in European institutions where classes contain students from many nationalities.

In writing this book we have, of course, made use of our experience over many years of writing and teaching in an international context. Thus, in some places we have adapted and updated material that we have used elsewhere in more specialist books to which the intended readers of this book would not have easy access.

The book concentrates on the supranational accounting rules of the EC and the IASC. Where practical examples are useful, several major European countries and companies are used. Numerical examples are generally in European currency units (ecus). Nevertheless, non-UK readers may detect a UK bias in the choice of some examples, where we have found the information easier to discover or easier to use because it is already in English. We apologise for any such bias but hope that readers will agree that the bias is small compared with other introductory books written in a national context.

There are four additional sections which we hope readers will find useful. The Appendix reprints the EC Fourth Directive (the major basis for European accounting rules). There is also a glossary of terms in English, and a short bibliography of books in English that have some European accounting content. The book concludes with feedback relating to the exercises found at the end of the chapters.

In preparing this book, we have been greatly assisted by Cathy Peck and John Yates of Prentice Hall, by Carol Wright of the University of Reading and Carol Dean, Tracy Naylor and Sue Green of the University of Hull; and by many people throughout Europe who have read draft chapters and whose names are given in the following Acknowledgements pages. Of course, we remain responsible for any errors or omissions.

DAVID ALEXANDER
University of Hull

CHRISTOPHER NOBES
University of Reading

Acknowledgements

The book has benefited very much from the advice and critical evaluation of the following reviewers, whose comments throughout its preparation are greatly appreciated:

Ron Hodges, University of Nottingham
Professor Ann Jorissen, UFSIA (University of Antwerp)
Professor Arie de Koning, IMD, Lausanne
Dr Meziane Lasfer, City University
Professor Monique Meyer, Université Grenoble II
Eileen Roddy, Manchester Metropolitan University

We are also grateful to the following, whose responses to a questionnaire helped to shape the content and pedagogic layout of the book:

Paolo Andrei, University of Parma
Dr Wilfried Bechtel, Institut für Revisionswesen
Professor Dr Ignace de Beelde, University of Gent
Mick Broadbent, Sheffield Hallam University
Professor Bettina Campedelli, University of Bergamo
Keith Cornish, University of Derby
Drs H Carel Dekker, Nijenrode University
Eamon Fagan, University College Cork
Hilary J. Fortes, Middlesex University
Professor Giuseppe Galassi, University of Parma
Andrew Gray, University of Kent at Canterbury
Professor Martin Hoogendoorn, University of Amsterdam
Peter Hughes, Newcastle Business School
Professor Marc Jegers, Free University Brussels (VUB)
Associate Professor Niels L. Koefoed, Aalborg University Centre
Jose M. Moneva, University of Zaragoza
Professor Jan Mouritsen, Copenhagen Business School
Bahadur Najak, Durham University Business School
Associate Professor Helge Pedersen, Agder College

Professor Bernard Raffournier, University of Geneva
Professor Dr Carl Reyns, UFSIA (University of Antwerp)
Professor Titular Emiliano Ruiz Barbadillo, Business School Universidad Cadiz
Dr Bahram Soltani, University of Paris-Dauphine
Professor Dr Kyojiro Someya, Waseda University
Dr Joachim Tanski, Freie Universität Berlin
Professor Hilda Theunisse, University of Antwerp/RUCA
Hardy Thomas, University of Essex
Dr Anastassios Tsamis, Pantion University of Political and Social Science, Athens
John Young, University of Southampton

PART I

The context of accounting

CHAPTERS	
1 Introduction	3
2 Fundamental principles	11
3 Conventions and framework	44

CHAPTER 1

Introduction

OBJECTIVES

- To outline the scope and purposes of financial accounting
- To describe the role of national and supranational accountancy bodies
- To explain the aims and coverage of this book

1.1 Purposes and users of accounting

There is no single authoritative generally accepted definition of financial accounting, or of accounting in general. It began as a practical activity in response to perceived needs, and for most of its development it has progressed in the same way – adapting to meet changes in the demands made on it. Where the needs differed in different countries or environments, accounting tended to develop in different ways as a response to that environment, essentially on the Darwinian principle: useful accounting survived. If accounting developed in different ways it is likely that definitions suggested in different contextual surroundings will vary.

At a general level it is at least safe to say that accounting exists to provide a service. In Table 1.1 there are three definitions. These have all been taken from the same economic and cultural source (the United States) because that country has the longest history of attempting explicit definitions of this type. Note that each suggested definition seems broader than the previous one, and the last one, from 1970, does not restrict accounting to *financially* quantifiable information at all. Many would not accept this last point even in the US context and, as will be explored at length in this book, attitudes to accounting and its role differ substantially between European countries.

If information is to be useful, then some obvious questions arise: useful to whom and for what purposes? A moment of thought will suggest a number of different types of people likely to be dealing in some way with business organizations:

1. *Managers*. These are the people who have to take decisions, both day-to-day and

Table 1.1 **Some definitions of accounting.**

Accounting is the art of recording, classifying and summarizing in a significant manner and in terms of money, transactions and events which are, in part at least, of a financial character, and interpreting the results thereof.[1]

The process of identifying, measuring and communicating economic information to permit informed judgements and decisions by users of the information.[2]

Accounting is a service activity. Its function is to provide quantitative information, primarily financial in nature, about economic entities that is intended to be useful in making economic decisions, in making resolved choices among alternative courses of action.[3]

---

[1] 'Review and Resume', *Accounting Terminology Bulletin No. 1* (New York: American Institute of Certified Public Accountants, 1953), para. 5.

[2] American Accounting Association, *A Statement of Basic Accounting Theory* (Evanston, IL: American Accounting Association. 1966), p. 1.

[3] Accounting Principles Board, *Statement No. 4*, 'Basic Concepts and Accounting Principles Underlying Financial Statements or Business Enterprises' (New York: American Institute of Certified Public Accountants, 1970), paragraph 40.

strategic, about how the scarce resources within their control are to be used. They need information that will enable them to predict the likely outcomes of alternative courses of action. As part of this process, they will need feedback on the results of their previous decisions in order to extend successful aspects of the decisions, and to adapt and improve the unsuccessful aspects.

2. *Investors*. The providers of risk capital and their advisers are concerned with the risk inherent in, and return provided by, their investments. They need information to help to determine whether they should buy, hold or sell securities. Shareholders are also interested in information that enables them to assess the ability of the enterprise to pay dividends.
3. *Lenders*. Lenders (such as banks or debenture holders) are interested in information that enables them to determine whether loans, and the interest attaching to them will be paid when due.
4. *Employees*. Employees and their representative groups are interested in information about the stability and profitability of their employers. They are also interested in information that helps to assess the ability of the enterprise to provide remuneration, retirement benefits and employment opportunities.
5. *Suppliers and other trade creditors*. These creditors are interested in information that enables them to determine whether amounts owing will be paid when due. Trade creditors are likely to be interested in an enterprise over a shorter period than lenders unless they are dependent upon the continuation of the enterprise as a major customer.
6. *Customers*. Customers have an interest in information about the continuance of an enterprise, especially when they have a long-term involvement with, or are dependent on, the enterprise.

7. *Governments and their agencies* Governments and their agencies are interested in the allocation of resources and, therefore, the activities of enterprises. They also require information in order to regulate the activities of enterprises, collect taxation and as the basis for national income and similar statistics.
8. *Public* Enterprises affect members of the public in a variety of ways. For example, enterprises may make a substantial contribution to the local economy by employing many people and patronizing local suppliers. They may also pollute the atmosphere or despoil the countryside. Financial statements may assist the public by providing information about the trends and recent developments in the prosperity of the enterprise and the range of its activities.

This list leads to a very important distinction, that between financial accounting and management accounting. Management accounting is that branch of accounting concerned with the provision of information intended to be useful to management within the business. Financial accounting is the branch of accounting intended for users outside the business itself, i.e. Groups 2–8 above. The wording of Groups 2–8 is closely based on a document called 'Framework for the Preparation and Presentation of Financial Statements' issued by the International Accounting Standards Committee (IASC), discussed further in Chapter 3.

It is obvious from the previous paragraphs that the needs of users to whom financial accounting is addressed are very diverse, so it does not follow that the same information will be valid for all their purposes. Nevertheless, it is usually assumed that one set of financial statements in the public domain should be able to satisfy most needs. The IASC Framework goes on to say:

> While all of the information needs of these users cannot be met by financial statements, there are needs which are common to all users. As investors are providers of risk capital to the enterprise, the provision of financial statements that meet their needs will also meet most of the needs of other users that financial statements can satisfy.

This last sentence would certainly earn a fail mark on any course in logic or philosophy, but the view is widely followed in practice. Accepting, however, that the needs of different users are likely to be different, at least in relative if not in absolute terms, it is clear that different national environments (cultural, political and economic) are likely to lead to different accounting practices. Indeed accounting (as opposed to bookkeeping) is very much a social science. It therefore reflects the biases and norms, sometimes long term, sometimes transitory, of the societies in which it is embedded. This area is developed later in Part II.

Having distinguished financial accounting from management accounting, there are some further possible confusions to address. The function of external *auditing* is quite separate from that of financial accounting. Auditing is a control mechanism designed to provide an external and independent check on the activities of businesses and on the financial statements and reports published by those businesses. Financial reports on the state of affairs and the past results of businesses are prepared by accountants, and then their validity assessed by auditors. The wording used by auditors in their reports on financial statements varies considerably between countries, and the meaning and significance of the words which they use varies even more. There is inevitably some conflict between the necessity for an auditor to 'keep the client happy', and the provision of an 'expert and independent check'. A study of auditing is outside the scope of this book, but the reader from any particular country or jurisdiction should certainly not assume that the role, objectives and effectiveness of the audit function in other jurisdictions are comparable to his or her existing experience. For example, in Japan, the statutory auditors of most companies are not required to be either expert or independent. In some other countries, statutory auditors have to comply with stringent technical and independence requirements.

Another set of distinctions which must be made clear are those between finance, financial management and financial accounting. Very broadly, finance is concerned with the optimal means of *raising* money, financial management is concerned with the optimal means of *using* it, and financial accounting can then be thought of as reporting on the results from having used it. Finally, financial accounting must be carefully distinguished from bookkeeping. Bookkeeping is about recording the data, about keeping records of money and financially related movements. It is financial accounting which takes these raw data, and then chooses and presents them as appropriate. It is financial accounting which acts as the *communicating* process.

1.2 Accounting regulation and the accountancy profession

How should the provision of accounting information be controlled? Two extreme answers can be envisaged. The first is that it should be determined purely by market forces. A potential supplier of finance will be more willing to supply it if there is reliable information about how and by whom the finance will be used. So, a business providing a good quality and quantity of financial information will obtain more and cheaper finance. Therefore, business has its own market-induced incentive to provide accounting information which meets the needs of users.

The second extreme answer is that the whole process should be regulated entirely by the 'state', and some legal or bureaucratic body should specify what is to be reported and should provide an enforcement mechanism. Neither extreme is consistent with modern capitalist-based economies, but the balance adopted between the two varies quite sharply around (and beyond) Europe. The points mentioned so far in this section only consider the market and the state, but there is a third important force to consider, namely, the accountancy profession.

The accountancy profession in European countries is organized into professional associations under national jurisdictions. The European Community requires two types of organization: qualifying bodies (which set exams and might make technical rules) and regulatory bodies (which are under government control and which supervise statutory audit). In some countries, such as the United Kingdom, various accountancy bodies are allowed to fill both roles. In some other countries, such as France and Germany, the roles are filled by separate bodies of 'accountants' and 'auditors', e.g. in France by *experts comptables* and *commissaires aux comptes*, respectively. Professional bodies are responsible for monitoring the activities and standards of accounting and auditing, in terms of both general ethics and professional competence. However, in some countries the profession also takes on much of the role of *creating* the regulations under which its members will operate.

There is now widespread agreement within EC member states, and other European countries with similar economic attitudes, of the need for carefully thought out comprehensive regulation. This statement leaves open two important points of detail. The first is the extent to which comprehensive regulation needs to be flexible in detailed application, or on the other hand precise but inflexible. The second is the relative position and importance of state 'regulation' compared with professional 'regulation'. As will be seen later, differences in attitudes to both these questions can be significant in their effects on accounting practice in different jurisdictions.

The coordinating organization for the accountancy profession in Europe is the Fédération des Experts Comptables Européens (FEE), which formally began on 1 January 1987 and was formed by the merger of two earlier organizations, the Union Européenne des Experts Comptables, Economiques et Financiers (UEC), founded in 1951, and the Groupe d'Etudes des Experts Comptables de la CEE (Group d'Etudes), founded in 1966.

The main objectives of FEE have been stated as follows:

- to work generally towards the enhancement and harmonization of the practice of accountancy in the broadest sense;
- to represent the European accountancy profession at international level;
- to be the sole consultative organization of the European accountancy profession in relation to EC authorities.

The members of FEE are formally national professional bodies, some thirty-four of them, representing twenty-two countries including all twelve EC member states. FEE is gradually increasing its role and influence as the 'spokesperson' for European professional accountancy bodies, and therefore for European accountants. There is also a worldwide grouping, the International Federation of Accountants (IFAC); with an international membership (see below). FEE does not intend to act as a standard-setting body, but proposes to promote accounting harmonization in line with the policies of IFAC.

IFAC, like FEE, is independent of government or pseudo-government control. Its stated purpose is 'to develop and enhance a coordinated world-wide accountancy profession with harmonized standards'. IFAC was created in 1977. International auditing standards are produced by IFAC's International Auditing Practices Committee. An important aspect of IFAC has been its relationship with the

International Accounting Standards Committee (IASC). This was also created in 1973, and all member bodies of IFAC are automatically members of IASC.

IASC is independent and has total autonomy in the setting of international accounting standards. Its main objectives are:

- to formulate and publish in the public interest accounting standards to be observed in the presentation of financial statements, and to promote their world-wide acceptance and observance;
- to work generally for the improvement and harmonization of regulations, accounting standards and procedures relating to the presentation of financial statements.

The implications of diverse national backgrounds and attitudes, of diverse regulatory groupings, and of diverse attitudes to such factors as the role of law, professional independence, and so on, are a major underlying theme of this book.

1.3 The path ahead

The structure of the remainder of this book is as follows. The rest of Part I investigates the fundamental principles and conventions that form the basis of accounting thought and practice. For the reader with no accounting background it is essential to understand the thinking that underlies what accountants do. For the reader with previous accounting or possibly bookkeeping experience these two chapters (2 and 3) should still be regarded as essential reading, as they bring out the interrelationships between the various ideas and techniques.

Part II looks at the European and international dimensions at a general level, expanding, as a glance at the contents pages will show, on some of the issues touched on in this introductory chapter. Part III explores in some detail the major problem topics of financial reporting. Each aspect is considered from first principles. Practices in Europe are investigated, always with an eye to the comparative perspective. In many cases a variety of theoretical conclusions are possible, and a variety of different practices can be found in different countries. These are explored both for themselves and for their causes and implications. Finally, in Part IV techniques of analyzing financial statements are introduced and applied. In several senses this part should be seen as the culmination of what has gone before. Financial accounting is about communication, and study of the various influences on accounting in Part II and of the ways of tackling the problem issues in Part III should help in appreciating the real information content of accounting numbers – both what they do mean and, just as important, what they do not.

1.4 Excitement in accounting

Accounting is not universally regarded as an exciting and exhilarating area of activity or study, but it can be fascinating, in several ways:

- in itself, because it is a young, incomplete and rapidly evolving discipline and its study allows the interest of uncertainty and discovery;
- in application, because the theoretical ideas become intimately bound up with human attitude and human nature;
- in effects, because it has a major impact on financial decisions, share prices, etc;
- in the European and international sphere because of its integration with cultural, economic and political change.

At present, two further elements exist which further increase the interest of accounting. First, this is a time of great change both inside Europe and in influences affecting Europe. Closer cooperation and harmonization within the EC is in the air. Expansion of the European Community is steadily in train. The economies of vast areas of Eastern Europe are changing fast – dangerously fast in some cases. Accounting, involving the communication of information central to this whole economic and political process, is both changing rapidly itself and acting as an agent for change. Accounting affects people's lives.

The final reason that particularly relates to the authors, is that we are breaking new ground in textbook and educational terms. This book seeks to communicate the importance of accounting in a genuinely European rather than a national context. We hope that our work leads to greater understanding by readers (and between readers) whatever their background and starting point.

EXERCISES

1.1 Is financial accounting really necessary?

1.2 It can be suggested that eight different groups of users of accounting information can be distinguished, i.e.:

Managers
Investors
Lenders
Employees
Suppliers and other creditors
Customers
Governments and their agencies
Public

Considering either all these groups, or any number you care to choose, suggest the information they are likely to need from accounting statements and reports. Are there likely to be difficulties in satisfying the needs of all the groups you have considered with one set of common information?

1.3 Consider the relative benefits to accounts users of:
   (a) information about the past;
   (b) information about the present;
   (c) information about the future.

1.4 Do you think a single set of financial reports can be designed that will be reasonably adequate for all major users and their needs?

1.5 Do you think all users actually know what to ask for from their accountant or financial adviser?

1.6 In the context of your own national background, rank the seven 'external' user groups suggested in the text (i.e. omitting managers), in order of the priority which you think should be given to their needs. Explain your reasons.

1.7 If at all possible, compare your answer to Exercise 1.6 with the answers of students from different national backgrounds. Try to explore likely causes of any major differences which emerge, in terms of legal, economic and cultural environment.

CHAPTER 2

Fundamental principles

> **OBJECTIVES**
>
> - To explore the principles underlying the recording of financial data
> - To outline the form and properties of income statements and balance sheets
> - To introduce double entry thinking and demonstrate its logical connections with the accounting principles

2.1 Introduction

The first chapter looked at the role of accounting: what accounting is and why it exists. This chapter explores at some length the basic ideas of financial accounting: the way accounting actually *works*, the logic behind the double entry recording system and the accounting statements of balance sheet and income statement. As suggested in Chapter 1, it is essential to understand the thinking which underlies accounting practice, but for this it is not necessary to study in detail the techniques of bookkeeping.

2.2 The balance sheet

What is a balance sheet? A balance sheet is probably one of the most widely misunderstood products of the whole accounting operation. Students and practitioners of bookkeeping regard the balance sheet as the culmination of a long and complex recording process. If it does not balance then mistakes have definitely been made during the preparation process. They will have to be found, and more work is needed. The public at large tend to regard the balance sheet, which contains lots of big numbers and yet apparently magically arrives at the same figure twice, as proof of both the complicated nature of accountancy and of the technical competence and reliability of the particular accountants and auditors involved.

However, reduced to its simplest, a balance sheet consists of two lists. The first is a list of things owned or a list of *resources* which is under the control of the individual or organization concerned. It is a list of assets. To understand the second list, it is merely necessary to realize that everything must have come from somewhere, it is a list of where everything came from, i.e. of the *sources* from which the organization obtained its present stock of *resources*. Since those sources will require repayment or recompense in some way it follows that this second list can also be regarded as a list of *claims* against the resources. The organization will have to settle these claims at some time, and this second list can therefore be regarded as amounts due to others.

The first list could therefore, as a final link in this exposition, be regarded as the ways in which those sources have been applied at this point in time, that is, as a list of *applications*. These terms can be summarized in a way which simplifies the situation such as in Table 2.1.

The creation of a new business enterprise can be viewed in terms of Table 2.1. The enterprise has things, all of which must have come from somewhere. It has resources, all of which are claimed by some body outside the enterprise. The resources are owned and the claims are due to others. The assets are represented by the borrowings. The applications represent the current position of those items (no more and no less) which came from the sources. It therefore follows that the total of each list must be the same and that the balance sheet *must* balance.

A balance sheet is often defined as a statement of financial position at a point in time. It is a list of sources, of where everything came from, and a list of applications, of everything which the business has got. Since both lists relate to the same business at the same point in time, the totals of each list must be equal and the balance sheet must balance because it is defined and constructed so that it has to balance. It represents two ways of looking at the same situation.

Simple balance sheets

When creating a new business, the starting position is that there is no balance sheet

Table 2.1 **The contents of a balance sheet.**

First list	Second list
Things	Where they came from
Assets	Borrowings
Owned	Due to others
Resources	Claims
Applications	Sources

because there is no business. The new business will have to be owned by someone. This outside body will put some money into the business which is referred to as *capital*. Capital is the *source* of the money which the business now owns. The *application* which the business has made with what it obtained from this source is, so far, a store of money. So we can prepare our balance sheet, our two lists of sources and applications, as in Table 2.2.

Notice that the money is an asset, i.e. a resource, whereas the capital is a source. It represents a claim on the business by the owners. In a sense the capital is 'owed' by the business to the owners. Suppose that capital of 100,000 ecu is put in to begin the business. This gives the balance sheet as in Table 2.3.

Suppose the business is a retail shop which undertakes the following transactions:

1. Buys property for 50,000 ecu by means of a loan.
2. Buys inventory costing 30,000 ecu, paying cash.
3. Sells half of this inventory for 35,000 ecu, on credit (i.e with the customer agreeing to pay later).
4. Pays wages for the period, in cash, of 4,000 ecu.
5. Half of the money due from the customer is received.
6. Buys inventory costing 25,000 ecu, on credit.

It would be possible to prepare new balance sheets incorporating these transactions one at a time. These are shown in Tables 2.4–2.9. Follow these through carefully and note the following points. Transaction 1 creates an additional source of 50,000 ecu and this is immediately applied in buying property. Sources and applications both rise by 50,000 ecu. Transaction 2, however, does not involve any new or additional source, only a change in application: 30,000 ecu which had previously been applied as part of a store of money has now been changed to a different application, i.e. inventory. Total sources and total applications remain constant.

Table 2.2 The balance sheet.

Resources/Applications	Claims/Sources
Money	Capital

Table 2.3 Balance sheet of a new business.

Resources		Claims	
Money	100,000	Capital	100,000
	100,000		100,000

Table 2.4 The balance sheet after buying property.

Resources		Claims	
Money	100,000	Capital	100,000
Property	50,000	Loan	50,000
	150,000		150,000

Table 2.5 The balance sheet after buying inventory.

Resources		Claims	
Money	70,000	Capital	100,000
Property	50,000	Loan	50,000
Inventory	30,000		
	150,000		150,000

Table 2.6 The balance sheet after selling some inventory.

Resources		Claims	
Money	70,000	Capital	100,000
Property	50,000	Profit	20,000
Inventory	15,000	Loan	50,000
Debtor	35,000		
	170,000		170,000

Table 2.7 The balance sheet after paying wages.

Resources		Claims	
Money	66,000	Capital	100,000
Property	50,000	Profit	16,000
Inventory	15,000	Loan	50,000
Debtor	35,000		
	166,000		166,000

Table 2.8 **The balance sheet after receipt from debtor.**

Resources		Claims	
Money	83,500	Capital	100,000
Property	50,000	Profit	16,000
Inventory	15,000	Loan	50,000
Debtor	17,500		
	166,000		166,000

Table 2.9 **The balance sheet after further inventory purchase.**

Resources		Claims	
Money	83,500	Capital	100,000
Property	50,000	Profit	16,000
Inventory	40,000	Loan	50,000
Debtor	17,500	Creditor	25,000
	191,000		191,000

Transaction 3 is rather more complicated. There are some easy aspects. First, half the inventory has disappeared so the inventory figure must reduce from 30,000 to 15,000 ecu. Second, the customer has agreed to pay the business 35,000 ecu. This does not mean that the business *owns* the money, it does, however, own the *right* to receive the money. This is most certainly an additional resource of the business, an additional asset. The business owns something extra, namely, the valuable and useful right to receive this money: the 35,000 ecu, representing the debtor – the customer who has an obligation to pay and from whom the business has a right to receive – the additional asset. The conclusion so far as regards Transaction 3 is that one resource has fallen by 15,000 ecu, and a new resource has appeared in the amount of 35,000 ecu. This means that total resources have risen by 20,000 ecu. However, we cannot have a resource without a claim. What is the source of this extra resource of 20,000 ecu?

In intuitive terms it should be fairly clear what has happened. The business has sold something for more than it had originally paid for it. It has turned an asset of 15,000 ecu (i.e. half the inventory) into an asset of 35,000 ecu (i.e. the debtor) through its business operations. The business has made a profit. Numerically, in order to make the balance sheet balance, it is necessary to put this profit of 20,000 ecu on to the opposite side of the balance sheet, i.e. as a source and claim. Would this make sense in logical as well as numerical terms?

The answer is 'yes', as can be seen by looking back at the second list in Table 2.1. Extra 'things' have come from the profitable trading of the business. The profits made by the business are made for the ultimate benefit of the owners and therefore can be said to belong to the owners of the business. Since these profits have been made within the business and are still within the business, but belong to the owners, it follows that they can be regarded as claims against the business by the ownership group. Finally, what is the source of these extra applications? The answer is that the source is the successful result of the trading operation. Profits *are* a source.

So the balance sheet shown in Table 2.6 follows quite logically from the accounting thought processes being developed. The extra applications of 20,000 ecu are represented by extra sources of 20,000 ecu, namely, the profit which is an additional ownership claim on the business.

It should be obvious by now that each transaction, or more accurately each element of each transaction, will have two effects on the balance sheet position. Each number will be added or subtracted twice. So moving on to Transaction 4 (see above), what two numerical alterations are needed to the previous balance sheet in order to incorporate the new event?

First, the amount of money which the business owns as asset, resource or application goes down by 4,000 ecu. This sum of money has physically been paid out by the business so the amount remaining must be 4,000 ecu less than it was before. Has this 4,000 ecu been applied by being turned into some other resource, some other asset, some other possession available to the business to do things with? The answer seems to be 'no'. The wages relate to the past, and therefore they represent the reward given by the business for work, for labour hours *which have already been used*.

The wages represent services provided and already totally consumed by the business as part of the process of generating profit in the trading period, which we had previously recorded at 20,000 ecu. This therefore needs to be taken into account in calculating the overall profit or gain made by the business through the operations over this trading period. Thus 4,000 ecu needs to be deducted from the profit figure of 20,000 ecu brought forward in order to show the correct net profit from the operations of the business made for the benefit of the owners.

Transaction 5 is straightforward. The starting position is that there was a debtor, an asset, an amount owed to the business, of 35,000 ecu. Half of this money has now been received by the business. This tells us two things: first, the money figure must increase by the amount of this cash received, i.e. by 17,500 ecu; second, the business is no longer owed this 17,500 because it has already received it. The debtor therefore needs to be reduced by 17,500. In summary, we have an increase in the asset 'money' and a decrease in the asset 'debtors', both by the same amount. Total applications remain the same, and therefore total sources remain the same too. The business has in no sense borrowed money through this transaction and equally clearly there has been no effect on profit – nothing has been gained, all that has happened is that an earlier transaction has moved further towards completion.

The final transaction for consideration is the sixth. The business is buying more inventory for 25,000 ecu, so the inventory figure in the balance sheet, the resource or asset of inventory, rises by 25,000. This has not yet been paid for, so there is no corresponding reduction in any of the other resources. The total of resources therefore rises by 25,000 ecu – and so, of course, does the total claims. What is the particular claim on the business which increases by 25,000 to cause this increase in the total? The business owes the supplier money for the extra inventory and therefore the extra claim will be this liability, known as a creditor, as shown in Table 2.9.

This example has been explored at considerable length because it is useful to keep thinking in terms of source and application, of asset and liability, of resource and claim. Is a transaction changing one resource into another? Or is it getting more resources from somewhere – obviously from some source – and therefore increasing both lists, both sides, of the balance sheet? And if total sources do increase, is it through operating successfully and making a profit, or is it borrowing money or simply not paying for the resource you have acquired? Try Exercises 2.1 and 2.2 from the end of this chapter.

2.3 The income statement

It has been shown that any transaction, event or adjustment can be recorded in a given balance sheet to produce a new and updated balance sheet. Also, provided one follows the logic of the 'sources and applications' idea, the new balance sheet must inevitably balance.

It would be possible to carry on this process in the same way for ever, producing an endless series of instant balance sheets. This would not be very practicable and, more important, it would not be very useful. Users of accounting information may wish to see balance sheets monthly, half-yearly or yearly. They may also require current and ongoing information about the results of the operating activities of the business. It is necessary, to meet these requirements, to collect together and summarize those items which are part of the calculation of the profit figure for the particular period concerned. As already shown, profit will consist of two sets of elements, one positive and one negative. When the business makes a sale then the proceeds of the sale are a positive part of the profit calculation which is referred to as a *revenue*. On the other hand, this operating process involved the consumption of some business resources, an *expense*. In the example explored in detail earlier there were two such items. First, the resource of inventory was itself used, and so the cost of the used inventory was a negative component of the profit calculation. Second, some of the resource of money was itself used to pay the wages which had necessarily been incurred in the process of the business operations. The cost of these wages is also a negative component of the profit calculation. It is important to notice that the cost of wages became a necessary negative part in the profit calculation when labour was put into the operating activities of the business, i.e. when the work was done, not at the time payment for the wages was actually made.

Preparing the income statement

The logic of the income statement in relation to the balance sheet can be explored by reworking the transactions we used earlier, and by segregating out revenues and expenses. The way to think of this is that sources can be regarded as being of two types:

(a) claims relating to owners or lenders,
(b) revenues.

It has already been established that profits are a source, and since revenues have been defined as the positive component of profit, it follows that revenues can be regarded logically as a source, and numerically as on the same 'side' as the capital and liabilities. Similarly applications can also be thought of as being of two types:

(a) assets, resources available to the business,
(b) expenses.

Expenses have been defined as the negative component of profit and are therefore logically and numerically on the opposite 'side' to the revenues. Expenses represent the resources that have already been used.

We can set up a simple layout, a template, for recording our transactions under this four-way split, as shown in Table 2.10. The best way to proceed is to take a large sheet of paper and divide it into four, with the appropriate headings (see Table 2.10). Then record the effects of each transaction one at a time, as adjustments to the previous position, on the same sheet of paper. The first position will be a simple repeat of Table 2.3, as in Table 2.11. Transactions 1–6, as described earlier, can now be recorded again – for convenience these are produced below:

1. Buys property for 50,000 ecu by means of a loan.
2. Buys inventory costing 30,000 ecu, paying cash.
3. Sells half of this stock for 35,000 ecu, on credit (i.e. with the customer agreeing to pay later).

Table 2.10 **Applications and sources.**

Applications	Sources
Assets	Capital and Liabilities
Expenses	Revenues

Table 2.11 **The introduction of capital.**

Applications		Sources	
Assets		Capital and Liabilities	
Money	100,000	Capital	100,000
	100,000		100,000
Expenses		Revenues	
	0		0
	0		0
	100,000		100,000

4. Pays wages for the period, in cash, of 4,000 ecu.
5. Half of the money owed by the customer is received.
6. Buys inventory costing 25,000 ecu, on credit.

Transactions 1 and 2 should be very straightforward, as they do not involve the creation of any profit and therefore do not give rise to the existence of any revenues or expenses. The position after incorporating Transaction 1 is shown in Table 2.12 and the position after incorporating Transaction 2 is shown in Table 2.13. Compare these with Tables 2.4 and 2.5. Totals have been put in on each of these tables, both for each of the four quarters and for each of the two sides. This is just to prove at each stage that the system is working properly both logically and numerically. There is no need for you to do this on your large sheet of paper, and indeed since you are

Table 2.12 **Incorporating Transaction 1.**

Applications		Sources	
Assets		Capital and Liabilities	
Money	100,000	Capital	100,000
Property	50,000	Loan	50,000
	150,000		150,000
Expenses		Revenues	
	0		0
	0		0
	150,000		150,000

Table 2.13 **The position after Transaction 2.**

Applications		Sources	
Assets		Capital and Liabilities	
Money	70,000	Capital	100,000
Property	50,000	Loan	50,000
Inventory	30,000		
	150,000		150,000
Expenses		Revenues	
	0		0
	0		0
	150,000		150,000

Table 2.13a **Working paper after Transaction 2.**

Applications		Sources	
Assets		Capital and Liabilities	
Money 100,000 – 30,000 =	70,000	Capital	100,000
Property	50,000	Loan	50,000
Inventory	30,000		
Expenses		Revenues	

recording the adjustments cumulatively you would find it very messy to try to do so. Your sheet of paper should at this point look like Table 2.13a.

Transaction 3 is more interesting. This gives rise to a revenue because some inventory has been sold for 35,000 ecu, and therefore puts a plus 35,000 sales figure into the revenues section of our table. As some of the resources have now been used, i.e. some of the assets have become expenses, an amount of 15,000 ecu needs to be removed from the assets figure for inventory and added to the expenses figure. We might call it the cost of goods sold. On the other hand an extra resource has been created, an extra asset. The business is now owed 35,000 ecu which it was not owed before and this new item, this debtor of 35,000 ecu, needs to be added to the assets section. When you have incorporated these adjustments on to your sheet of paper, in terms of pluses and minuses, you should arrive at the end position shown in Table 2.14.

Transaction 4 involves the payment of the wages bill for the period. Two points need to be recognized here: (a) the asset or resource of money has gone down by

FUNDAMENTAL PRINCIPLES

Table 2.14 The position after Transaction 3.

Applications		Sources	
Assets		Capital and Liabilities	
Money	70,000	Capital	100,000
Property	50,000	Loan	50,000
Inventory	15,000		
Debtor	35,000		
	170,000		150,000
Expenses		Revenues	
Cost of goods sold	15,000	Sales	35,000
	15,000		35,000
	185,000		185,000

4,000 ecu; and (b) 4,000 ecu of resources have been *used* in the operating process of the business, i.e. 4,000 has now become an expense. This 4,000 expense needs to be matched against the sales proceeds as part of the overall profit calculation for the trading period. This thinking leads to the position shown in Table 2.15.

Neither Transaction 5 nor Transaction 6 involves the creation of any additional revenues or expenses. Transaction 5 increases the asset of money and reduces the

Table 2.15 After wages have been paid.

Applications		Sources	
Assets		Capital and Liabilities	
Money	66,000	Capital	100,000
Property	50,000	Loan	50,000
Inventory	15,000		
Debtor	35,000		
	166,000		150,000
Expenses		Revenues	
Cost of goods sold	15,000	Sales	35,000
Wages	4,000		
	19,000		35,000
	185,000		185,000

asset of debtor by the same amount. Money is now being *received*, but it arises from an earlier revenue. The money now received was earned at an earlier date and it is the act of earning, not the act of receiving, which determines the revenue. With Transaction 6 there is an additional source into the business, from the granting of credit to the business by the supplier. The application of this extra amount is in the possession of extra inventory. Incorporation of Transaction 5 and then Transaction 6 leads to the positions in Tables 2.16 and 2.17 respectively.

When you work out all the pluses and minuses on your sheet of paper, you should arrive at the final position as shown in Table 2.17 – but what does it mean? The bottom half of Table 2.17, the revenues and expenses quarters, is in effect an income statement. It contains all the positive parts of the profit calculation (the revenues) and all the negative parts of the profit calculation (the expenses). One can extract the bottom half from Table 2.17 and present this as the detailed profit calculation – a detailed statement of the result of trading for the period. In total the revenues are 35,000 ecu and the expenses are 19,000 ecu. The profit is the difference between the two, i.e. 16,000 ecu.

Table 2.17 may be looked at in the following manner at first. The profit (the excess of revenues over expenses) is clearly a *source*. Since at all times the sources into the business must equal the applications by the business, it follows that the income statement (the whole of the bottom half of Table 2.17) can be replaced by the single profit number of 16,000 ecu on the sources side in the top half of the table. This half of the table is, of course, the balance sheet. Replacing the revenues and expenses parts of Table 2.17 by the single profit figure in the balance sheet as a claim, leads us exactly to Table 2.9 (check back for yourself). This profit, as shown earlier, represents an additional ownership claim on the business.

Table 2.16 **Incorporating Transaction 5.**

Applications		Sources	
Assets		Capital and Liabilities	
Money	83,500	Capital	100,000
Property	50,000	Loan	50,000
Inventory	15,000		
Debtor	17,500		
	166,000		150,000
Expenses		Revenues	
Cost of goods sold	15,000	Sales	35,000
Wages	4,000		
	19,000		35,000
	185,000		185,000

Table 2.17 After Transaction 6.

Applications		Sources	
Assets		Capital and Liabilities	
Money	83,500	Capital	100,000
Property	50,000	Loan	50,000
Inventory	40,000	Creditor	25,000
Debtor	17,500		
	191,000		175,000
Expenses		Revenues	
Cost of goods sold	15,000	Sales	35,000
Wages	4,000		
	19,000		35,000
	210,000		210,000

Second, one could look at Table 2.17 and think purely *numerically*. The bottom half, the income statement half, has an excess of 16,000 ecu on the right-hand side. The top half, the balance sheet half, has an excess of 16,000 ecu on the left-hand side. How can each part balance out? The answer, in purely numerical terms, is that 16,000 can be put into the left-hand side of the bottom half, and be called profit. Then 16,000 can be put into the right-hand side of the top half, and be called profit. The bottom half can now be dropped away altogether (as it consists of an equal number of pluses and minuses), leaving a balance sheet that balances.

The logical interrelationship can be summarized as follows:

Applications	= Sources
Assets + Expenses	= Sources
Capital + Liabilities + Revenues	= Applications
Assets + Expenses	= Capital + Liabilities + Revenues
Assets	= Capital + Liabilities + Revenues − Expenses
Assets	= Capital + Liabilities + Profit

2.4 Applying and practising the thinking

It is important that you are able to follow and to apply the logic behind this system. A number of carefully graded exercises are given at the end of this chapter. Exercises 2.3–2.5 have suggested solutions and discussion of the adjustments required given in the Feedback section at the end of the book. These introduce a number of terms and concepts that may be new to you, in which case you will be learning from the exercises as well as deepening your command over what has already been done. Make sure that you do not lose sight of the basics in attempting to master the additional new detail. At all times think in terms of sources and applications, of the resources and claims of the balance sheet, of the earnings (revenues) and usage (expenses) of the income statement, and of the interrelationships involved within the mechanism and within the logic as a whole.

2.5 Two simple equations

The logic of the balance sheet structure can be expressed in a simple equation:

$$\text{assets} = \text{liabilities} + \text{capital}$$

This is often referred to as the balance sheet equation. Rearranged, it becomes:

$$\text{capital} = \text{assets} - \text{liabilities}$$

That is, the net wealth of the business is equal to the capital invested in it at that point in time. In this model, there are only two factors that can affect capital and cause it to change over time. These are first, that the business will operate and make a profit (or it could, of course, make a loss), and second, that the owners will take some profits out of the business by way of drawings (or they could invest extra capital into the business). Thus if profit $= P$ and drawings $= D$, then the increase in capital is $P - D$. So,

$$C_1 - C_0 = P_1 - D_1$$

and

$$C_0 + P_1 - D_1 = C_1$$

This is our second simple equation.

The important point about these equations is the generality of their truth and application. To illustrate this generality consider the classic schoolroom problem of the tank of water containing a given number of litres. A tap is pouring water in at the top at a given rate per hour, and water is leaking out of the bottom at a given rate per hour. Clearly, (opening water) + (water in) − (water out) = (closing water). If we know any three of these items, we can find the fourth. Further, it does not matter how the water is measured, provided it is measured in the same way all the time, i.e. consistency must be applied.

Appendix: The 'Italian' method

This appendix explores the application and extension of the ideas of this chapter into the practical double entry bookkeeping system used in the real world. This does not, of course, mean that you need to be expertly trained bookkeepers, but it is necessary for you to have a clear basic understanding of the way the system works. The

FUNDAMENTAL PRINCIPLES 25

mechanics and terminology of simple bookkeeping principles will be used wherever necessary in later parts of the text.

If bookkeeping is new to you then you should study this appendix carefully. If you have done a lot of bookkeeping before, then you should still read this appendix in order to ensure that you see fully how it relates to the earlier arguments.

Double entry: explanation and justification

It has been pointed out that any transaction has at least two effects. For example, when a 5,000 ecu building is bought for cash, the asset records show an increase of 5,000 ecu and the cash records show a decrease of 5,000 ecu. It has also been shown that a credit sale of 300 ecu inventory for 500 ecu will give rise to three effects on the balance sheet (see Table 2A.1). In practice it will usually be very difficult to tell how much inventory (at cost) has been disposed of in a sale, particularly if several types of material and labour have been combined to make a product. Therefore, it will also be difficult to calculate the profit on every small sale. So, as the chapter points out, accountants wait until the end of an accounting period to calculate profit. At that point the inventory used is taken to be the purchases during the period, adjusted for the fact that there was some inventory handed on at the beginning of the period and that there remains some inventory at the end.

Meanwhile, sales and purchases of inventory are recorded without adjusting profit figures. That is, sales transactions do not give rise to the effects in the above balance sheets on a daily basis. When a business makes a 500 ecu credit sale, the sales records show a 500 ecu increase and the debtors also show a 500 ecu increase (see Table 2A.2). When there are 200 ecu of purchases for cash, the purchases records show a 200 ecu increase and the cash records show a 200 ecu decrease.

Table 2A.1

Balance sheet			
Inventory	− 300	Profit	+ 200
Debtor	+ 500		

Table 2A.2

Profit calculation:		Sales
		+ 500 (i.e. inventory + profit)
Balance sheet:	Debtor + 500	

Table 2A.3 contains some more examples of these and other types of transactions. Each transaction can be said to have an effect on what the business *owns* and an equal effect on the claims against it. All the items in the 'Effect A' column can be said to represent increases in what the business owns or decreases in the claims against it. That is,

1 and 3	it owns more cash
2	it owns more debt
4	it owns more assets
5	it 'owes' less to its owners in profit (because of expenses)
6	it owes less to outside creditors

All items in the 'Effect B' column can be understood as decreases in things owned or increases in what is owed by the business. That is,

1 and 2	it 'owes' more to the owners as profit (because of revenues)
3	it owes more to lenders
4 and 6	it owns less cash
5	it owes more to outside creditors

For reasons discussed below, each of the effects in Column A is called a *debit* and each in Column B is called a *credit*. So, at the end of a period during which accounts are run, the total of all debits equals the total of all credits. The system is self-balancing.

There is no stigma attached to 'debit' nor congratulatory connotation attached to 'credit'; they are merely labels to describe two groupings of transactions. It can be seen that 'debit' is by no means synonymous with plus or with minus; it means an increase in owning or a decrease in claims, as summarized in Table 2A.4.

The chapter has already shown that this is a further consequence of the accounting equation: assets plus expenses equals liabilities (including capital) plus revenues. This can be expressed as:

$$\Sigma A + \Sigma E = \Sigma L + C + \Sigma R$$

where A is assets, E is expenses, L is liabilities, C is capital, R is revenues, and Σ indicates the summation.

Table 2A.3

Transaction	Value (ecu)	Effect A	Effect B
1. Cash sale	50	+ Cash	+ Sales
2. Credit sale to X	80	+ Debtors	+ Sales
3. Loan raised from Y	2,000	+ Cash	+ Lenders
4. Asset bought	1,000	+ Assets	− Cash
5. Electricity bill received	100	+ Expenses	+ Creditors
6. Electricity bill paid	100	− Creditors	− Cash

FUNDAMENTAL PRINCIPLES

Table 2A.4 **The meaning of 'debit' and 'credit'.**

Debits	Credits
Increases in owning	Decreases in owning
Decreases in claims	Increases in claims
+ Assets	− Assets
+ Expenses	− Expenses
− Liabilities	+ Liabilities
− Capital	+ Capital
− Revenues	+ Revenues

The words 'debit' and 'credit' have their origins in early Italian accounting, which particularly concerned itself with debts to and from persons. The derivations of the words will be clear to those who are familiar with any Latin-based language. 'Debit' means *he ought* (to pay us); a debit on a person's account means that he must pay the business at some future date. Similarly, 'credit' means *he trusts* (us to pay him). From these basic entries all the others fall into place, as in Table 2A.4.

In practice most accountants would not work out whether, for example, any particular transaction involved a debit to cash or a credit to cash but would know by reflex. Many might not be able easily to work out from first principles which entry should be made. The system is merely a convention that is fairly easily learned and works well.

Let us follow the six transactions of Table 2A.3 into some accounts, performing double entry. An 'account' is just a piece of paper (or perhaps a card or a space on a computer disk) that stores all the information relating to one type of asset, one type of expenses, and so on. The convention is that the debits are stored on the left of an account and the credits on the right. So, Transaction 1 (a cash sale) will be recorded on two accounts as shown in Figure 2A.1.

The cash account records a debit to show that the business now owns 50 ecu more cash (due to sales). The sales account records a credit to show that there have been revenues of 50 ecu (due to cash receipts).

Cash account		Sales account	
Debits	Credits	Debits	Credits
Sales 50			Cash 50

Figure 2A.1

Transaction 2 (an 80 ecu sale on credit to X) will give rise to an entry on the personal account of X and an extra entry on the sales account. No cash changes hands, so that there will be no effect on the cash account (see Figure 2A.2). Notice that by looking at one entry we can find out where the other related entry is. The third transaction will give rise to two entries, shown in Figure 2A.3, and Transaction 4 will cause two extra entries (with asterisks in Figure 2A.4). Transaction 5 (receiving a bill but not paying it) is entered as in Figure 2A.5. While Transaction 6 (paying the bill later) will give the two new entries with asterisks shown in Figure 2A.6.

As the business year continues, more transactions will occur and give rise to double entries each time. Every sale (whether for cash or on credit terms) will be recorded on the right-hand side of the sales account as a credit. Every receipt of

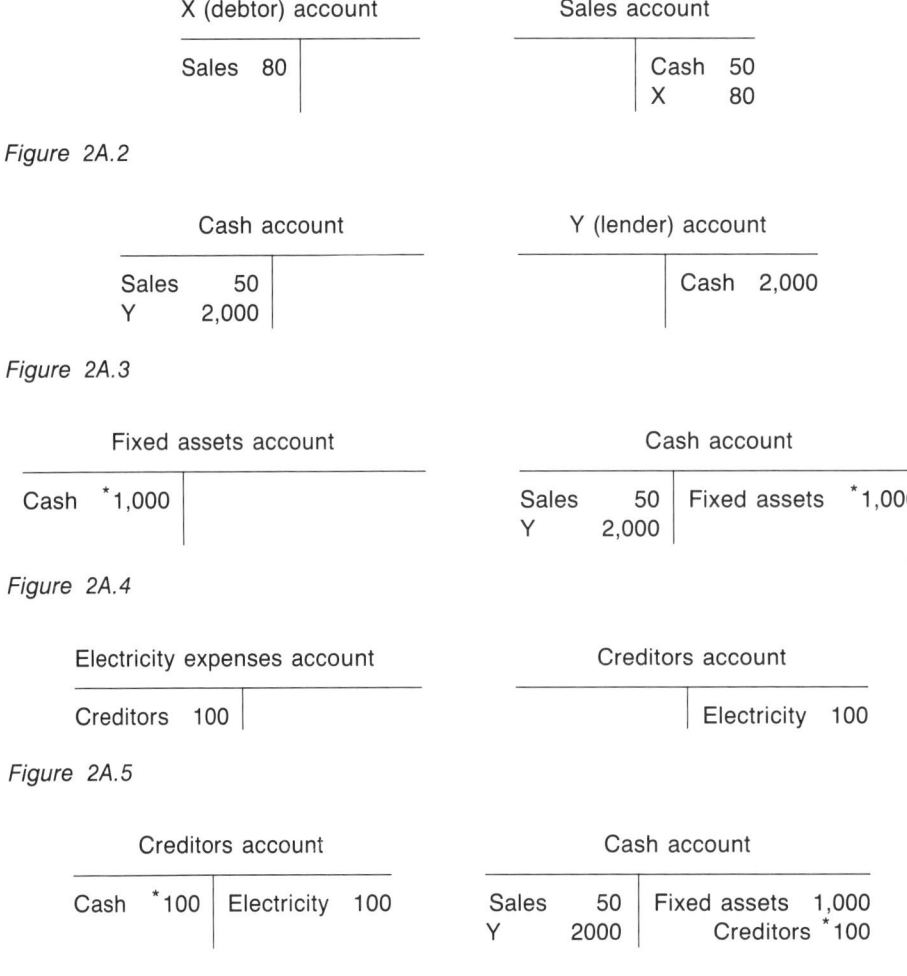

Figure 2A.2

Figure 2A.3

Figure 2A.4

Figure 2A.5

Figure 2A.6

cash, for whatever reason, will be recorded on the left-hand side of the cash account as a debit. There is no theoretical limit to the number of accounts that can be used. The accountant must strike a balance between the need for detail and the desire to avoid unnecessary work.

We have seen that it is possible to redraw a balance sheet each time that any transaction occurs. In a normal business involving thousands of transactions in a year this would be time-consuming and unproductive. Therefore, accounts (such as those above) are kept throughout the year, using double entry in order that the balance sheet need only be redrawn periodically. It is assumed here that the balance sheet is drawn up annually. In practice businesses may do this more frequently.

Those accounts that record assets or liabilities or capital, which are accumulating entries throughout the year, are totalled at the end of the year to provide the asset, liability and capital figures for the balance sheet. Those accounts that record expenses and revenues are combined together to form a profit and loss account for the year. The profit or loss is transferred to the capital account, which is recorded on the balance sheet. We shall look at examples of this later in this appendix.

The advantages of double entry

There are several important advantages to be gained from using a double entry system. First, since there are clearly two effects from each transaction, it is useful to record them both. Before double entry, a cash sale would have been recorded only in the cash book, which contained all other transactions affecting cash. This meant that in order to find a total of recorded sales it was necessary to look through all cash transactions picking out those relating to sales. For a large trader this would have been very laborious for even one day's sales, let alone one year's. So, double entry allows an easy totalling of sales, cash, electricity bills, wages, fixed assets, and so on. Without these totals, balance sheets and profit and loss accounts would be impossible to produce.

Totalling is made particularly easy because the accounts are two-sided, allowing positive and negative effects to be stored separately on the same account. This enables quick balancing of any accounts. For example, in the accounts on the last few pages (which, of course, will normally have many more entries on them), the total of cash in hand can be worked out to be 950 ecu (i.e. 2,050 − 1,100). Table 2A.5 gives the balanced account.

Double entry has been maintained by creating a brought-forward debit of equal size to the balancing credit of 950 ecu. At the start of the next accounting period the cash account will already show 950 ecu, which is correct. Clearly, it will be a good idea to check the cash and the bank account to see if there is 950 ecu. If there is not, an investigation into shortages of cash or errors in the records should be carried out. The fact that all cash entries are on one account, that only cash entries are on it and that the entries are separated into cash-in (debit, left-hand side) and

Table 2A.5 Cash account of example in Figure 2A.6.

Sales	50	Fixed assets	1,000
by	2,000	Creditors	100
		Balance carried down	950
	2,050		2,050
Balance brought forward	950		

cash-out (credit, right-hand side) aid quick totalling. The same applies to all accounts of whatever sort.

Another significant advantage is that it is known that the whole system should be self-balancing. When the end-of-year balancing act is performed, it is very unusual for the accounts of businesses of any substantial size to balance straight away. That is, when all the debits are added together, they probably do not equal all the credits as they should. This is due to inevitable errors of recording and analyzing the entries in the accounts. Any lack of balance warns the accountant that errors should be searched for. Also, since each entry is cross-referenced to its equal and opposite entry, it is fairly easy to understand the origin of any entry.

At this point, it should be said that accounting entries always carry a date in order to make it easier to understand them if they need to be checked in the future. For example, if Transaction 1 (the cash sale) occurred on 3 November 19X9, it might be recorded as in Figure 2A.7. (Dates will only be used in accounts in this book when they are necessary for clarity.)

Several of these factors make it more difficult fraudulently to manipulate items in the accounts. It has been mentioned that checking is fairly easy. It is helped by the fact that balancing is impossible if the totals of only one account are manipulated, and adjustments of more than one account may entail the alteration of a figure that is regularly checked (e.g. the cash balance).

It has been said that at the end of the accounting period (we have been considering it to be a year), the revenue and expense accounts are combined to calculate profit. This is performed using double entry too. The revenue and expense accounts already met are shown in Figure 2A.8 after year-end balancing and closing-off procedures have occurred (new entries have asterisks). The reasons for positioning these entries in the incomplete profit and loss account should become clear in the next section. Notice that the expense and revenue accounts have now been closed down by

Cash account	Sales account
3 Nov.X9 Sales 50	3 Nov.X9 Cash 50

Figure 2A.7

FUNDAMENTAL PRINCIPLES

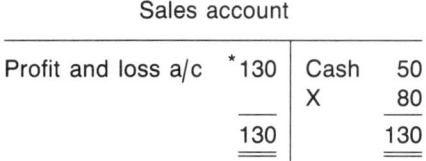

Sales account				
Profit and loss a/c	*130	Cash		50
		X		80
	130			130

Electricity expense account			
Creditors	100	Profit and loss a/c	100*
	100		100

Trading and profit and loss account			
		Sales	130*
Electricity	100*		

Figure 2A.8

transferring their balances to the profit and loss account. They start the next year with no balances, apart from the exceptions noted below.

The trading account: gross profit

Conventionally, in many countries, there are two important subtotals in the calculation of profit: gross profit and net profit. The trading account collects together the revenue and expense entries relating to the main trading activities of the business and leads to the calculation of gross profit. The trading and profit and loss accounts are part of the system of double entry.

Let us look at some more transactions specifically related to trading. For simplicity, consider the transactions of a new business called Ropa (Table 2A.6). Each of these entries will be recorded on the appropriate side of the appropriate account. The accounts specifically connected with trading will look like Figure 2A.9 (the other halves of the double entries being in other accounts, as noted in the table). If these were the only trading entries in the accounting period, the trading account would be made up by closing down the above accounts and transferring the balances as shown in Figure 2A.10.

This does not seem to be a very healthy trading position, but it must be remembered that not all the purchases will have been turned into sales. That is, there is usually some closing inventory remaining at the end of an accounting period. If stocktaking shows that there are 3,500 ecu worth of marble and paint left, the trading account will look like Table 2A.7. Notice that double entry is being maintained. The gross profit entries balance each other. The closing inventory (and opening inventory) entries will be discussed later.

Table 2A.6 **Transactions of Ropa.**

Transaction	Debit		Credit	
1. Purchase 3,000 worth of marble on credit from C	Purchases a/c	3,000	C (creditor) a/c	3,000
2. Sell 1,000 worth of marble for cash to D	Cash a/c	1,000	Sales a/c	1,000
3. Purchase 2,000 worth of paint for cash from E	Purchases a/c	2,000	Cash a/c	2,000
4. Sell 500 worth of paint on credit to F	F (debtor) a/c	500	Sales a/c	500
5. Sell 800 worth of marble for cash to G	Cash a/c	800	Sales a/c	800
6. Return of 100 worth of paint by F	Sales a/c	100	F (debtor) a/c	100

Figure 2A.9

```
        Purchases account              Sales account
1. C      3,000                 6. F    100  | 2. Cash  1,000
3. Cash   2,000                              | 4. F       500
                                             | 5. Cash    800
```

Figure 2A.10

```
        Purchases account                      Sales account
C      3,000 | Trading a/c 5,000     D            100 | Cash   1,000
Cash   2,000 |                       Trading a/c 2,200| D        500
                                                      | Cash     800
       ─────   ─────                              ─────  ─────
       5,000   5,000                              2,300  2,300
```

```
                Trading account
        Purchases   5,000 | Sales   2,200
```

Table 2A.7 **Trading account of Ropa for the period ending 31 December.**

Purchases	5,000	Sales	2,200
less Closing inventory	3,500		
	1,500		
Gross profit c/d	700		
	2,200		2,200
		Gross profit b/f	700

The profit and loss account

The next account is the profit and loss account, which leads on from the trading account and contains all other revenues and expenses that are not raw trading transactions. Suppose that the only extra transactions in this accounting period of Ropa are those shown in Table 2A.8. The revenue and expense account halves of these transactions will thus appear as Figure 2A.11 (the other halves are in the cash account and G account, as noted in the table). These accounts have been shown already closed off. The other halves of the double entry for each of the asterisked items are in the income statement in Table 2A.9, which combines the trading and profit and loss accounts.

Table 2A.8 **Further transactions of Ropa.**

Transactions	Debit		Credit	
7. Wages of 100 ecu paid	Wages a/c	100	Cash a/c	100
8. Rent for the period of 150 ecu (not yet paid to the landlord)	Rent a/c	150	G (landlord) a/c	150
9. Advertising bill for the period, paid 30 ecu	Advertising a/c	30	Cash a/c	30
10. Stationery bought for 20 ecu	Stationery a/c	20	Cash a/c	20
11. More wages paid, 80 ecu	Wages a/c	80	Cash a/c	80
12. Rent received from subletting part of the premises, 40 ecu	Cash a/c	40	Rent received a/c	40

Figure 2A.11

Wages account				Rent (expenses) account			
7. Cash	100	Profit and loss a/c	*180	8. G	150	Profit and loss a/c	*150
11. Cash	80						
	180		180		150		150

Advertising account				Stationery account			
9. Cash	30	Profit and loss a/c	*30	10. Cash	20	Profit and loss a/c	*20
	30		30		20		20

Rent (revenues) account			
Profit and loss a/c	*40	12. Cash	40
	40		40

Table 2A.9 **Income statement of Ropa for the period ending 31 December.**

Purchases	5,000	Sales	2,200
less Closing inventory	3,500		
	1,500		
Gross profit c/d	700		
	2,200		2,200
Wages	*180	Gross profit b/f	700
Rent	*150	Rent received	*40
Advertising	*30		
Stationery	*20		
Total expenses	380		
Net profit c/d	360		
	740		740
		Net profit b/f	360

As before, the double entry system is strictly maintained. What happens to the net profit brought forward depends on the type of business. The rent received is not in the trading account because it does not result from its main trading activities. It is, of course, on the credit side, just like other revenues.

The order of the expense items is not very critical, although it seems sensible to start with the most important. Often, expenses are organized into groups (e.g. 'administrative', 'finance' and 'marketing'). Consistency from year to year will make comparisons easier. Note that the heading of the account includes the words 'for the period ending'. This emphasizes the fact that the profit and loss account deals with flows over time. The wording is often 'for the year ending', 'for the quarter ending', and so on.

Inventory, accruals and prepayments

During the year it is usual for no entries to be made in the inventory account. The business would be well advised to keep records of inventory movements and levels, but these will not be part of the double entry system. The inventory account is only needed at the end of the accounting period, which is naturally the beginning of the next. Let us assume that a business has been left 2,000 ecu of inventory from the previous year. Therefore, at the start of the year the inventory account appears as in Figure 2A.12.

FUNDAMENTAL PRINCIPLES

Inventory account

Opening inventory 2,000	

Figure 2A.12

At the end of the year, the inventory may be valued at 5,500 ecu. The accounting entries to record (a) the removal of the old inventory, and (b) the arrival of the new inventory figure are:

(a) trading a/c *debit* 2,000; inventory a/c *credit* 2,000; and
(b) inventory a/c *debit* 5,500; trading a/c *credit* 5,500.

This will give the asterisked entries of Figure 2A.13.

The normal presentation, as in the previous trading account, is different from this because it makes for better presentation to show the closing inventory as a negative figure on the left rather than as a positive figure on the right. It should be very clear by now that in all these manipulations we are adhering not to naturally occurring laws that have been discovered but to conventions that have been invented and adopted because they work well.

There are other items apart from inventory that can be passed from one year to another. For example, below there are two accruals and two prepayments for a business whose accounting period ends on 31 December.

1. Rent is paid half-yearly in arrears (500 ecu per half-year). Last payment was 30 September; next payment is due 31 March.
2. Telephone bill is paid quarterly. Next bill is expected 31 January (always about 120 ecu per quarter).
3. Property taxes are paid half-yearly in advance (200 ecu per half-year). Last payment was 1 October; next payment is due 1 April.
4. Yearly insurance premium of 180 ecu is paid on 1 November each year.

It has been explained that, in order to arrive at the profit figure, the payments *relating* to a period (i.e. the expenses), not the payments made in a period, are those included. This is the accruals convention (explained further in Chapter 3). Let us imagine that the business started on 1 January with expenses to pay for several

Inventory account

Opening	2,000	Trading a/c	*2,000
	2,000		2,000
Closing	*5,500		

Trading account

Opening	*2,000	Closing	*5,500

Figure 2A.13

premises. Without taking the above points into account, the total bills paid in the year may have been:

Rent	1,500
Telephone	800
Property tax	1,000
Insurance	500

The above four points imply that at 31 December:

(a) rent is in arrears by 250 ecu;
(b) telephone bill is in arrears by 80 ecu;
(c) property taxes are paid in advance by 100 ecu; and
(d) insurance is paid in advance by 150 ecu.

The expenses accounts for the year ended 31 December, taking all this into account, will look like Figure 2A.14.

Thus, the actual charges in the profit and loss account are increased by amounts owing that relate to the present accounting year and decreased by amounts paid on behalf of next year. Notice that next year's accounts have already been credited or debited with the appropriate amounts because of double entry. For example, when the 500 ecu rent bill arrives and is paid at the end of March next year and debited

Rent account

Cash	1,500	Profit and	*1,750
Accruals c/d	250	loss a/c	
	1,750		1,750
		Accruals b/f	250

Telephone account

Cash	800	Profit and	880
Accruals c/d	80	loss a/c	
	880		880
		Accruals b/f	80

Property taxes account

Cash	1,000	Prepayment c/d	100
		Profit and loss a/c	900
	1,000		1,000
Prepayment b/f	100		

Insurance account

Cash	500	Prepayment c/d	150
		Profit and loss a/c	350
	500		500
Prepayment b/f	150		

Profit and loss account

Rent	1,750	Gross profit	x,xxx
Property tax	900		
Telephone	880		
Insurance	350		

Figure 2A.14

Rent account	
Cash 500	Accruals b/f 250

Figure 2A.15

to the rent account (the cash account being credited with 500 ecu at the same time), the account will show a net charge of 250 ecu (i.e. 500 − 250) so far. This is correct for one quarter (Figure 2A.15).

The balance sheet

The observant reader may have noticed that the process of transferring various items of revenue and expense from their accounts to the profit and loss account has left a number of accounts with balances remaining on them. These accounts are asset, liability or capital accounts (including the profit and loss account which now also has a balance remaining). The total of all the credit balances should still equal the total of all the debit balances because double entry has been maintained throughout, even in the profit and loss account. When all the balances are collected together on a balance sheet (or sheet of balances), we have a picture of what is owned by and owed to the business at that moment in time.

The debit or credit balances on the asset, liability or capital accounts are *not being transferred* to the balance sheet; they are carried forward to the next period, as indeed are the real assets and liabilities that they represent. The balances are merely *recorded* on a balance sheet in order to show the financial position of the business at the end of the accounting period. That is, the balance sheet represents stocks, not flows. Therefore, it will have '*as at* December 93', for example, in its title.

SUMMARY

This chapter has explored and applied the fundamental principles behind the recording of financial data for business activities. The dual aspects of any transaction, and the relationship between resources and claims, underlie the logic of the double entry system, the interrelationship between income statement and balance sheet, and the interconnections between their major constituent elements of asset, liability, capital, expense and revenue.

EXERCISES

2.1 The following information relates to F company which started business on 1 January 19X3 when 150,000 ecu was paid in as share capital.

	31 Dec. 19X4	31 Dec. 19X3
Cash at bank	36,000	19,000
Inventory of goods	29,000	32,000
Freehold shop	135,000	135,000
Wages owed to staff	750	800
Amounts owed to supplier	21,250	26,500
Amounts owed by customers	34,000	35,000
Loans	50,000	50,000
Cash in till	2,000	500
Delivery vans	10,000	10,000

What is the missing item?
(a) Convert the above information into balance sheets at the end of the two years.
(b) What conclusion can you draw about the performance of F company during 19X3 and 19X4?
(c) Would your conclusion be affected if you knew the business had paid dividends of 15,000 ecu during 19X3?
(d) Does the figure for Delivery vans at 31 December 19X4 surprise you? If so, why?

2.2 G company has a hardware business. The balance sheet at the beginning of the financial year showed the following position (in ecu):

		(a)	(b)	(c)	(d)	(e)	(f)	(g)	(h)
Shares	50,000								
Retained profit	7,000								
Creditors	12,000								
	69,000								
Premises	20,000								
Equipment	9,000								
Vehicle	7,000								
Inventory	15,500								
Debtors	2,500								
Bank	14,700								
Cash	300								
	69,000								

FUNDAMENTAL PRINCIPLES

Show the adjustments for each of the following transactions:

(a) Goods were sold for 4,000 ecu (cash sales 3,000, credit sales 1,000) which were included in the inventory at 2,800.
(b) An invoice for van expenses of 400 ecu was received and paid immediately by cheque.
(c) Cheques of 8,000 ecu were written and sent to creditors. The 3,000 ecu from cash sales was paid into the bank.
(d) The vehicle was sold at book value for 7,000 ecu cash which was paid into the bank immediately.
(e) Cash 500 ecu and cheques 2,000 ecu were received from debtors.
(f) Office equipment (recorded in the books at 400 ecu) was sold for 700 ecu cash.
(g) The premises were revalued at 32,000 ecu.
(h) G company then announced that it would pay a dividend of 1,000 ecu in one month's time, after the balance sheet for the year had been finalized.

2.3 Kings Cross Company

	ecu		ecu
Land and buildings	110,000	Share capital	150,000
Machinery	50,000	Retained profits	5,000
Vehicles	25,000	Loans (10%)	20,000
Inventory at end of year	30,000	Creditors	50,000
Debtors	35,000		
Cash at bank	10,000		
	260,000		225,000
Cost of goods sold	90,000	Sales	160,000
Wages	20,000		
Rent, insurance, sundry expenses	15,000		
	125,000		160,000

The above information has been taken from the company's books as at 31 December 19X4, but the following have not yet been allowed for:

(a) Rent owing but not yet paid amounting to 1,000 ecu.
(b) Insurance paid includes 3,000 ecu which relates to next year.
(c) Audit fees not yet included and not yet paid are 1,500 ecu.
(d) Machinery and vehicles are to be depreciated by 10%.
(e) Land and buildings had been revalued at 150,000 ecu.
(f) Interest on the loans has not yet been paid.
(g) A dividend is to be proposed of 50% of the year's profits.

Record the appropriate adjustments on the quadrant and draw up the balance sheet and income statement.

2.4 Kings Happy Company

Sales	147,500
Land and buildings	60,000
Plant and machinery	40,000
Purchases	50,000
Wages and salaries	41,000
Salesmen's commission	6,000
Vehicles	30,000
Share capital	150,000
Inventory at start of year	20,000
Debtors	20,000
Rent, insurance, sundry expenses	8,500
Cash discounts allowed	1,500
Shares in listed company	40,000
Cash at bank and in hand	25,500
Creditors	37,000
Retained profits	6,000
Dividends received from listed investment	2,000

The above information has been taken from the company's books as at 31 December 19X4, but the following has not been allowed for:

(a) Inventory at the end of the year is 25,000.
(b) Audit fees owing amounted to 500.
(c) Machinery and vehicles are to be depreciated by 10% and 20% respectively.
(d) A dividend is to be proposed of 20% of the share capital.

Satisfy yourself that total sources equal total applications before making adjustments for (a)–(d). Then draw up the balance sheet and income statement.

2.5 Kingsad Company

Land and buildings	100,000
Share capital	100,000
Plant and machinery	50,000
Retained profits at 1 January 19X4	46,000
Purchases	70,000
Sales	150,000
Inventory at 1 January 19X4	30,000
Wages and salaries	40,000
Sales returned by customers as unacceptable	1,000
General expenses	10,000
Debtors	25,000
Creditors	30,000

This information has been taken from the company's books as at 31 December 19X4, but the information below has not been allowed for:

(a) Inventory at 31 December 19X4 is 20,000 ecu.
(b) Plant and machinery is to be depreciated by 10%.
(c) Land and buildings is to be revalued to 150,000 ecu.
(d) General expenses includes an insurance charge of 1,000 ecu covering the period 1 July 19X4 to 30 June 19X5.
(e) A debtor for 1,000 ecu has gone bankrupt.
(f) A dividend of 5,000 ecu is to be proposed.

Using the quadrant format, incorporate the additional information, and prepare the closing balance sheet and income statement.

2.6 The following is a summary of the payments for rent and property taxes made by a retailer for his business premises:

19X0		ecu
Nov. 13	Property taxes paid for 6 months to 31st March 19X1	160
Dec. 21	Rent paid for 3 months to 31st Dec. 19X0	100
19X1		
March 31	Rent paid for 3 months to 31st March 19X1	100
April 22	Property taxes paid for 6 months to 30th September 19X1	180
July 2	Rent paid for 3 months to 30th June 19X1	100
Oct. 4	Rent paid for 3 months to 30th September 19X1	100
Nov. 5	Property taxes paid for 6 months to 31st March 19X2	180
19X2		
Jan. 4	Rent paid for 3 months to 31st December 19X1	100

Write up separate accounts for (a) rent and (b) property taxes, showing within the accounts the amounts that should be entered in the income statement for the year ended 31st December 19X1. Show the appropriate entries in the balance sheet at that date.

2.7 The following is the trial balance at 30th September, 19X2 of company M (in ecu).

Trial Balance of Company M at 30th September 19X2

	Dr	Cr
Capital, 1st October 19X1	—	12,920
Office furniture	2,816	—
Creditors	—	2,829
Bank overdraft	—	323
Land and buildings	7,700	—
Equipment	1,400	—
Vehicles	1,500	—
Inventory, 1st October 19X1	4,400	—
Debtors	2,926	—
Purchases	21,435	—
Sales	—	31,219
Rent received from subtenant	—	500
Wages	4,304	—
Insurances	274	—
Light and heat	185	—
Sundry administrative expenses	319	—
Selling expenses	532	—
	47,791	47,791

The following additional information is to be taken into consideration:

(a) Balance owing for wages for the last few days of the accounting year is 95 ecu.
(b) Insurance premium prepaid is 32 ecu.
(c) The inventory at 30th September 19X2 is valued at 7,200 ecu.

Prepare an income statement and balance sheet for the financial year to 30th September 19X2, showing clearly in the accounts the cost of goods sold and the net trading profit.

2.8 The following trial balance was extracted from the books of a trader, at 31st December, 19X7 (in ecu).

Capital	—	24,447
Office furniture	2,148	—
Debtors and creditors	7,689	5,462
Sales	—	81,742
Purchases	62,101	—
Rent and property taxes	880	—
Lighting and heating	246	—
Salaries and wages	8,268	—

Inventory 31st December 19X6	9,274	—
Insurance	172	—
General expenses	933	—
Bank balance	1,582	—
Motor vans at cost	8,000	—
Motor expenses	1,108	—
Freehold premises at cost	10,000	—
Rent received	—	750
	112,401	112,401

The following matters are to be taken into account:

(a) Inventory at 31st December 19X7 was 9,884 ecu.
(b) Property taxes paid in advance at 31st December 19X7 were 40 ecu.
(c) Rent receivable due at 31st December 19X7 was 250 ecu.
(d) Lighting and heating due at 31st December 19X7 was 85 ecu.
(e) Included in the amount for insurance is an item of 82 ecu for motor insurance, and this amount should be transferred to motor expenses.

Prepare an income statement for 19X7 and a balance sheet at 31st December 19X7.

CHAPTER 3

Conventions and framework

OBJECTIVES

- To outline the traditional conventions applied in financial reporting, and to consider them individually and collectively.
- To define the major classes of items appearing in financial statements.
- To describe the attempt by the International Accounting Standards Committee (IASC) to relate the fundamental ideas of financial accounting and reporting into a coherent framework.

3.1 Introduction

In the previous chapter, the balance sheet and profit and loss were investigated and illustrated with a number of common types of transaction. The accounting system is extremely powerful, and is capable of variation. Any particular transaction involving the business can be incorporated into the model. Also, any consistently applied measurement technique can be used, as will be examined in detail in Part III. What ideas, assumptions and conventions do accountants traditionally choose to follow within this apparently wide-ranging flexibility, which they hope will provide the useful information that was seen in Chapter 1 as the main purpose of accounting?

Twelve separate conventions, will be considered as follows: business entity, duality, monetary measurement, cost, realization of revenue, matching, accounting period, continuity (going concern), conservatism (prudence), consistency, materiality and objectivity. Other writers might suggest longer or shorter lists of conventions.

3.2 Traditional financial accounting conventions

Business entity

This convention holds that the business has an identity and existence distinct from its owners. To the accountant, whatever the legal position, the business and the owner(s) are considered completely separately. Thus the accountant can speak of the owner having claims against the business. Think of the basic business balance sheet as in Figure 3.1.

A properly prepared balance sheet can always be relied upon to balance. This is because capital is the balancing figure. Capital is the amount of wealth invested in the business by the owner, or the amount of money obtained by the business from the owner, or the amount the business 'owes' the owner. None of these three statements could be made unless the accountant is treating the business as separate from the owner. Another balance sheet could always exist, namely, for the owner as an individual. This would contain his investment in the business, shown as one of the owner's personal assets.

Duality

This may be regarded as a formalization of the basis of double entry. It states that in relation to any one economic event, two aspects are recorded in the accounts, namely:

(a) the source of wealth;
(b) the form it takes (i.e. its application).

In the simplest of terms, (a) is 'where it comes from', and (b) is 'what it is'. The source from where it came will still have a claim on it. So, again in balance sheet terms, we can say that the balance sheet shows the array of resources at a point in time (assets), and the claims on those resources (capital and liabilities).

Monetary measurement

The accountant's job is to deal with *financial* information. This convention states that the accountant only records those facts that can be expressed in money terms.

Assets	Capital
	Liabilities
Total	Total

Figure 3.1 The basic business balance sheet.

It is often said that the greatest asset that an effective and efficient business possesses is its workforce. So why does the workforce not appear on a business balance sheet? The short answer is that it would be extremely difficult to 'put a figure on' the workforce, i.e. to express this asset, this resource, in money terms.

Cost

This convention states simply that resources acquired by the business are generally recorded at their original purchase price. It follows from the previous convention in that it tells us *how* the item is to be measured. This is the well known historical cost convention.

Accounting period

This very simple convention recognizes that profit occurs over time, and we cannot usefully speak of profit until we define the length of the period. The maximum length normally used is one year. This does not, of course, preclude the preparation of accounts for shorter periods as well, though the formal 'published accounts' period is nearly always one year.

Realization of revenue

It has been established that an asset acquired by the business is usually recorded at the original purchase price. It is thus based on a market transaction. It is obvious that at some point (at the latest, when the asset is disposed of by the business) the actual disposal price must be recorded. So if inventory is bought for 30 ecu, 30 ecu cash has to be recorded as having gone, and inventory of 30 has to be recorded as being present. If the inventory is then sold for 50 ecu then 50 ecu cash must be recorded as being present, and inventory has to be removed from the accounts. Thus an asset of 30 ecu has been replaced by an asset of 50 ecu, giving a profit of 20 ecu. Once the 50 ecu cash is physically received, there is no other possibility than to record an asset of 50. However, is there a possibility of recognizing an asset of 50 before, i.e. earlier than, the physical arrival of the money? Suppose the inventory is sold on 1 December and the money received on 10 December. When did assets of 30 ecu turn into assets of 50 ecu? Was it on receipt of the money or when the business acquired the expectation – indeed the right – to receive the money?

More importantly, perhaps, what are the *criteria* to be used to answer this question? On what *grounds* can the accountant decide when the total asset figure increased, i.e. when the profit was made?

The usual (conventional) answer is:

Revenue is recognized as soon as it is allocated to the period in which:

(a) it is capable of objective measurement; and
(b) the asset value receivable in exchange is reasonably certain.

This seems all very well, but how can a phrase like 'reasonably certain' have any *exact* meaning at all? The usual practical interpretation of this statement is that the revenue should be recognized as soon as the goods are made available to the customer in exchange for some valuable consideration – normally the creation of a debt which is legally enforceable. Technically this should be the date when the sale is agreed, but it may be the date of physical transfer of the goods, or in practice the invoice date.

Matching

Looking back over the conventions discussed so far, there have been decisions on:

(a) the basic characteristics of the recording system (**business entity** and **duality**);
(b) how to record items entering the business's control (**monetary measurement** and **cost**); and
(c) how to record the proceeds from the disposal of such items (**revenue recognition**).

The essential item missing is clearly the mechanism for recording the actual loss of the item – its removal from the financial statements of the business. The question was asked above: when did assets of 30 ecu turn into assets of 50 ecu? It is intuitively clear that whenever this did happen (and the revenue recognition convention tells us when), a profit of 20 ecu was made. If the revenue, the benefit, is 50 ecu, then the expense, the amount used or lost, is 30 ecu. The matching convention covers this final stage in the process of profit calculation. It states that:

Income (or profit) determination is a process of matching against revenue the expenses incurred in earning that revenue.

When an asset gets used, it becomes recorded as an expense. The question in effect is: at precisely what point does the accountant regard an asset as being 'used'? The answer is: at the point when the related revenue is recognized. First, determine the point at which the revenue is to be recognized. Second, *match* the expense *against* the revenue. So if the revenue from selling the item of inventory is recognized on 29 December as 50 ecu then the expense of 30 ecu is also recognized on 29 December. Accounts prepared on 31 December include profit of 20 ecu, and an asset of 50 ecu (debtors or cash). However, if the revenue from selling the inventory is recognized on 2 January, then the expense is also recognized on 2 January. Accounts prepared on 31 December include an asset of 30 ecu (inventory), no revenue and no expense, and therefore no profit or loss from this transaction.

The **matching convention** is often referred to as the **accruals convention**. The essence of the accruals convention is that the time when an item of benefit should be recognized and recorded by the accountant is determined by the *generation* of the benefit – not by the date of the *receipt* of the benefit in cash. Similarly, the time when an item of expense should be recognized and recorded as such is determined by usage of the item, not by the date of the acquisition of the item or of the *payment* in cash for the item. The process of profit calculation consists of relating (matching) together the revenues with the expenses. It is not concerned with relating together cash receipts and cash payments.

Continuity (going concern)

This important convention states that in the absence of evidence to the contrary, it is assumed that the business will continue for the foreseeable future. This convention has a major influence on the assumptions made when evaluating particular items in the balance sheet. The convention allows the assumption that stock will eventually be sold in the normal course of business, i.e. at normal selling prices. It allows for the principle of depreciation. If the business depreciates an item of plant over ten years, then it is assuming that the plant will have a useful life *to the business* of ten years. This assumption can only be made by first assuming that the business will continue – or keep going – for at least ten years.

Conservatism (prudence)

This convention refers to the accounting practice of recognizing all possible losses, but not anticipating possible gains. This will tend to lead to an understatement of profits and to an understatement of asset values with no corresponding understatement of liability.

The accounts are trying to give an indication of the current position (the balance sheet), and of the degree of success achieved through the accounting period (the income statement or profit and loss account). Recognizing that a number of estimates are involved in accounting, the accountant, according to this convention, should ensure the avoidance of overstatement by deliberately setting out to achieve a degree of understatement. This requires that similar items, some of which are positive and some of which are negative, should not be treated symmetrically.

Consistency

This is the practice of applying the same accounting rules, methods or procedures in each similar case. This convention should avoid manipulation of reported results, and facilitate comparisons within the firm over different accounting periods.

Consistency can, of course, never overrule the requirements of proper and useful reporting. However, the convention does certainly support the argument that where several alternative treatments or approaches are acceptable, the business should make a decision and then stick to it year by year for all similar items. Of course, this does not necessarily enable comparison between different businesses, which may be consistently using different procedures from each other. That is, there may be a lack of 'uniformity'.

Materiality

This implies that insignificant items should not be given the same emphasis as significant items. The insignificant items are by definition unlikely to influence decisions or provide useful information to decision-makers, but they may well cause complication and confusion to the user of accounts. Immaterial items do not need separate disclosure and may not need to be accounted for strictly correctly. What is 'insignificant' in any particular context may be a highly subjective decision.

Objectivity

Accounting measurements and information should permit qualified individuals working independently to develop similar measures or conclusions from the same evidence. Accounting information should be verifiable. Two schools of thought seem to have arisen in recent years over the full implications of this. One school of thought argues that the desire for objectivity implies as much factual content as possible. Facts, e.g. the actual cost figure specified in a contract, are easily verifiable. This idea surely corresponds with the everyday meaning of objectivity, i.e. the avoidance of subjectivity, the avoidance of personal opinion.

The second school of thought argues that the degree of objectivity can be indicated not by the amount of formal (factual) verifiability, but the degree of consensus achieved by several independent opinions. Objectivity would then mean a lack of bias, both in the sense that the personality of the preparer does not affect the result, and in the sense that the information prepared is not biased in favour of one particular user at the expense of the others.

3.3 A coherent framework

How do the above conventions relate together? Are they 'coherent' or consistent with each other?

One of the most problematic conventions is that of prudence, or conservatism. At its most basic, it derives from the obviously sensible belief that it is important not to encourage the users of accounts to spend money or to consume resources they have not got. Also, it might act as a restraint on over-confident managers or promoters. Consideration of this convention, together with several of the other conventions, gives rise to considerable difficulties. For example:

1. *Prudence and going concern.* The going concern convention assumes that the firm will 'keep going', e.g. that it will not be forced out of business by competition or bankruptcy. This may be a likely and rational assumption, but it is not necessarily prudent – in certain circumstances it could be decidedly risky.
2. *Prudence and matching.* The matching convention, building on the going concern convention, allows us to carry forward assets into future periods on the grounds that they will be used profitably later. This obviously makes major assumptions about the future that may not be at all prudent. The tension between these two conventions is one of the major problems of accounting practice, and it underlies many of the more problematic issues, discussed in Part III.
3. *Prudence and objectivity.* Objectivity implies certainty and precision, it implies freedom from personal opinion, freedom from bias. Prudence, quite explicitly, implies that the accountant *should* bias information in a certain direction.

3.4 Back to basics

It is worth remembering the purpose of all this: to provide accounting information that will communicate some understanding of a complex real-life economic situation. This is an extraordinarily complicated task. This book has been exploring simple ideas and simple situations, and yet it is clear that a wide variety of methods of presentation are possible. Furthermore, the typical business organization is far from being a 'simple situation'. One cannot hope to present and communicate the complete reality in all its complexity and uncertainty.

This leads to the idea that since the picture that can be given through accounting information and accounting statements is inevitably incomplete, it is necessary to make sure that the omissions do not distort the general impression of the economic totality which the reader of the accounts receives. If one cannot present the total position one must ensure that the incomplete picture is compatible with the total position. This is often referred to as the need for 'fair presentation'. In the United Kingdom the 'true and fair view' concept is widely regarded as leading to this 'fair presentation'. However, this belief is not necessarily justified. This concept, now of general European importance because of its inclusion in the EC Fourth Directive, is discussed at length in Chapter 5.

It is important to realize that this accounting idea of aiming to present a fair but approximate picture of a complicated economic and financial reality is not likely to be very attractive to the legal profession or to the legal mind. It could be argued that accounts should be designed above all else to give a report on the legal position of a business both in isolation and as it affects and is affected by other parties. Since a balance sheet is a statement of resources and claims, how can it be other than a document derived from and fully consistent with legal rights? This tension, of economic *substance* against legal *form*, permeates much accounting debate. As we noted in Chapter 1, attitudes and traditional views on the appropriate balance between these arguments differ significantly in Europe. The extent to which 'substance over form' is regarded as an acceptable or desirable accounting axiom is an issue met many times in later pages.

3.5 A conceptual framework?

Chapter 1 outlined the role of accounting and the people it seeks to serve. Chapter 2 looked at the mechanics of financial statements. This chapter looks at some of the concepts used, noting some of the uncertainties and flexibility.

Out of the various possible ways of valuing, measuring and presenting information, is it possible to analyze the whole situation on broadly scientific lines and produce an agreed theory? In the United States the Financial Accounting Standards Board (FASB) set up its Conceptual Framework project in the 1970s, in an attempt to do just this. FASB defined a conceptual framework as:

> A constitution, a coherent system of interrelated objectives and fundamentals that can lead to consistent standards and that prescribes the nature, function and limits of financial accounting and financial statements.

This project was not fully successful, but since that time a number of other attempts have been made, both by individual academics and by accounting bodies, to establish not an agreed theory, so much as a broadly coherent and integrated framework. The idea is not to establish a watertight theoretical structure but a set of carefully defined pathways designed to lead through any particular given situation to arrive at a logical and defensible conclusion.

3.6 IASC Framework: introduction

This chapter continues with a detailed look at the attempt to create such a framework produced by the International Accounting Standards Committee. This is one of the most authoritative attempts made in recent years. It is also, of course, important in its own right because of the position of the IASC itself.

The IASC Framework, after earlier appearance in Exposure Draft form, was published in July 1989. The full document, 'Framework for the Preparation and Presentation of Financial Statements', is published in the International Accounting Standards Committee Book of International Accounting Standards (IASC, London, regular editions). It is not itself a Standard and indeed its exact status is rather unclear.

Its declared purposes are to:

(a) assist the Board of IASC in the development of future International Accounting Standards and in its review of existing International Accounting Standards;
(b) assist the Board of IASC in promoting harmonization of regulations, accounting standards and procedures relating to the presentation of financial statements by providing a basis for reducing the number of alternative accounting treatments permitted by International Accounting Standards;
(c) assist national standard-setting bodies in developing national standards;
(d) assist preparers of financial statements in applying International Accounting Standards and in dealing with topics that have yet to form the subject of an International Accounting Standard;
(e) assist auditors in forming an opinion as to whether financial statements conform with International Accounting Standards;
(f) assist users of financial statements in interpreting the information contained in financial statements prepared in conformity with International Accounting Standards; and
(g) provide those who are interested in the work of IASC with information about its approach to the formulation of International Accounting Standards.

The overall scope of the document covers:

(a) the objective of financial statements;
(b) the qualitative characteristics that determine the usefulness of information in financial statements;
(c) the definition, recognition and measurement of the elements from which financial statements are constructed; and
(d) concepts of capital and capital maintenance.

The Framework first of all outlines the users of accounting information as discussed in Chapter 1. It notes that:

> While all of the information needs of these users cannot be met by financial statements, there are needs which are common to all users. As investors are providers of risk capital to the enterprise, the provision of financial statements that meet their needs will also meet most of the needs of other users that financial statements can satisfy.

This last proposition is open to question! The Framework then goes on to summarize the overall objectives of financial statements:

> 12. The objective of financial statements is to provide information about the financial position, performance and changes in financial position of an enterprise that is useful to a wide range of users in making economic decisions.
> 13. Financial statements prepared for this purpose meet the common needs of most users. However, financial statements do not provide all the information that users may need to make economic decisions since they largely portray the financial effects of past events and do not necessarily provide non-financial information.

CONVENTIONS AND FRAMEWORK

15. The economic decisions that are taken by users of financial statements require an evaluation of the ability of an enterprise to generate cash and cash equivalents and of the timing and certainty of their generations. This ability ultimately determines, for example, the capacity of an enterprise to pay its employees and suppliers, meet interest payments, repay loans and make distributions to its owners. Users are better able to evaluate this ability to generate cash and cash equivalents if they are provided with information that focuses on the financial position, performance and changes in financial position of an enterprise.

Next the Framework discusses the various 'assumptions and characteristics' of accounting statements. These correspond closely to ideas already discussed, but they are arranged in a series of subgroups with various headings and subheadings that give interesting nuances of relative significance and importance. In order to give the full flavour, the Framework is quoted here at some length, and should be read carefully.

3.7 IASC assumptions, etc

UNDERLYING ASSUMPTIONS

Accrual Basis

22. In order to meet their objectives, financial statements are prepared on the accrual basis of accounting. Under this basis, the effects of transactions and other events are recognised when they occur (and not as cash or its equivalent is received or paid) and they are recorded in the accounting records and reported in the financial statements of the periods to which they relate. Financial statements prepared on the accrual basis inform users not only of past transactions involving the payment and receipt of cash but also of obligations to pay cash in the future and of resources that represent cash to be received in the future. Hence, they provide the type of information about past transactions and other events that is most useful to users in making economic decisions.

Going Concern

23. The financial statements are normally prepared on the assumption that an enterprise is a going concern and will continue in operation for the foreseeable future. Hence, it is assumed that the enterprise has neither the intention nor the need to liquidate or curtail materially the scale of its operations; if such an intention or need exists, the financial statement may have to be prepared on a different basis and, if so, the basis used is disclosed.

QUALITATIVE CHARACTERISTICS OF FINANCIAL STATEMENTS

24. Qualitative characteristics are the attributes that make the information provided in financial statements useful to users. The four principal qualitative characteristics are understandability, relevance, reliability and comparability.

Understandability

25. An essential quality of the information provided in financial statements is that it is readily understandable by users. For this purpose users are assumed to have a reasonable knowledge of business and economic activities and accounting and a willingness to study the information with reasonable diligence. However,

information about complex matters that should be included in the financial statements because of its relevance to the economic decision-making needs of users should not be excluded merely on the grounds that it may be too difficult for certain users to understand.

Relevance

26. To be useful, information must be relevant to the decision-making needs of users. Information has the quality of relevance when it influences the economic decisions of users by helping them evaluate past, present or future events or confirming, or correcting, their past evaluations.
27. The predictive and confirmatory roles of information are interrelated. For example, information about the current level and structure of asset holdings has value to users when they endeavour to predict the ability of the enterprise to take advantage of opportunities and its ability to react to adverse situations. The same information plays a confirmatory role in respect of past predictions about, for example, the way in which the enterprise would be structured or the outcome of planned operations.
28. Information about financial position and past performance is frequently used as the basis for predicting future financial position and performance and other matters in which users are directly interested, such as dividend and wage payments, security price movements and the ability of the enterprise to meet its commitments as they fall due. To have predictive value, information need not be in the form of an explicit forecast. The ability to make predictions from financial statements is enhanced, however, by the manner in which information on past transactions and events is displayed. For example, the predictive value of the income statements is enhanced if unusual, abnormal and infrequent items of income or expense are separately disclosed.

Materiality

29. The relevance of information is affected by its nature and materiality. In some cases, the nature of information alone is sufficient to determine its relevance. For example, the reporting of a new segment may affect the assessment of the risks and opportunities facing the enterprise irrespective of the materiality of the results achieved by the new segment in the reporting period. In other cases, both the nature and materiality are important, for example, the amounts of inventories held in each of the main categories that are appropriate to the business.
30. Information is material if its omission or misstatement could influence the economic decisions of users taken on the basis of the financial statements. Materiality depends on the size of the item or error judged in the particular circumstances of its omission or misstatement. Thus, materiality provides a threshold or cut-off point rather than being a primary qualitative characteristic which information must have if it is to be useful.

Reliability

31. To be useful, information must also be reliable. Information has the quality of reliability when it is free from material error and bias and can be depended upon by users to represent faithfully that which it either purports to represent or could reasonably be expected to represent.
32. Information may be relevant but so unreliable in nature or representation that its recognition may be potentially misleading. For example, if the validity and amount of a claim for damages under a legal action are disputed, it may be inappropriate

for the enterprise to recognise the full amount of the claim in the balance sheet, although it may be appropriate to disclose the amount and circumstances of the claim.

Faithful Representation

33. To be reliable, information must represent faithfully the transactions and other events it either purports to represent or could reasonably be expected to represent. Thus, for example, a balance sheet should represent faithfully the transactions and other events that result in assets, liabilities and equity of the enterprise at the reporting date which meet the recognition criteria.

34. Most financial information is subject to some risk of being less than a faithful representation of that which it purports to portray. This is not due to bias, but rather to inherent difficulties either in identifying the transactions and other events to be measured or in devising and applying measurements and presentation techniques that can convey messages that correspond with those transactions and events. In certain cases, the measurement of the financial effects of items could be so uncertain that enterprises generally would not recognise them in the financial statements; for example, although most enterprises generate goodwill internally over time, it is usually difficult to identify or measure that goodwill reliably. In other cases, however, it may be relevant to recognise items and to disclose the risk of error surrounding their recognition and measurement.

Substance over Form

35. If information is to represent faithfully the transactions and other events that it purports to represent, it is necessary that they are accounted for and presented in accordance with their substance and economic reality and not merely their legal form. The substance of transactions or other events is not always consistent with that which is apparent from their legal or contrived form. For example, an enterprise may dispose of an asset to another party in such a way that the documentation purports to pass legal ownership to that party; nevertheless, agreements may exist that ensure that the enterprise continues to enjoy the future economic benefits embodied in the asset. In such circumstances, the reporting of a sale would not represent faithfully the transaction entered into (if indeed there was a transaction).

Neutrality

36. To be reliable, the information contained in financial statements must be neutral, that is, free from bias. Financial statements are not neutral if, by the selection or presentation of information, they influence the making of a decision or judgement in order to achieve a predetermined result or outcome.

Prudence

37. The preparers of financial statements do, however, have to contend with the uncertainties that inevitably surround many events and circumstances, such as the collectability of doubtful receivables, the probable useful life of plant and equipment and the number of warranty claims that may occur. Such uncertainties are recognised by the disclosure of their nature and extent and by the exercise of prudence in the preparation of the financial statement. Prudence is the inclusion of a degree of caution in the exercise of the judgements needed in making the estimates required under conditions of uncertainty, such that assets or income are not overstated and liabilities or expenses are not understated. However, the exercise of

prudence does not allow, for example, the creation of hidden reserves or excessive provision, the deliberate understatement of assets or income, or the deliberate overstatement of liabilities or expenses, because the financial statements would not be neutral and, therefore, not have the quality of reliability.

Completeness

38. To be reliable, the information in financial statements must be complete within the bounds of materiality and cost. An omission can cause information to be false or misleading and thus unreliable and deficient in terms of its relevance.

Comparability

39. Users must be able to compare the financial statements of an enterprise through time in order to identify trends in its financial position and performance. Users must also be able to compare the financial statements of different enterprises in order to evaluate their relative financial position, performance and changes in financial position. Hence, the measurement and display of the financial effect of like transactions and other events must be carried out in a consistent way throughout an enterprise and over time for that enterprise and in a consistent way for different enterprises.

40. An important implication of the qualitative characteristic of comparability is that users be informed of the accounting policies employed in the preparation of the financial statements, any changes in those policies and the effects of such changes. Users need to be able to identify differences between the accounting policies for like transactions and other events used by the same enterprise from period to period and by different enterprises. Compliance with International Accounting Standards, including the disclosure of the accounting policies used by the enterprise, helps to achieve comparability.

41. The need for comparability should not be confused with mere uniformity and should not be allowed to become an impediment to the introduction of improved accounting standards. It is not appropriate for an enterprise to continue accounting in the same manner for a transaction or other event if the policy adopted is not in keeping with the qualitative characteristics of relevance and reliability. It is also inappropriate for an enterprise to leave its accounting policies unchanged when more relevant and reliable alternatives exist.

42. Because users wish to compare the financial position, performance and changes in financial position of an enterprise over time, it is important that the financial statements show corresponding information for the preceding periods.

Constraints on Relevant and Reliable Information

Timeliness

43. If there is undue delay in the reporting of information it may lose its relevance. Management may need to balance the relative merits of timely reporting and the provision of reliable information. To provide information on a timely basis it may often be necessary to report before all aspects of a transaction or other events are known, thus impairing reliability. Conversely, if reporting is delayed until all aspects are known the information may be highly reliable but of little use to users who have had to make decisions in the interim. In achieving a balance between relevance and reliability, the overriding consideration is how best to satisfy the economic decision-making needs of users.

Balance Between Benefit and Cost
44. The balance between benefit and cost is a pervasive constraint rather than a qualitative characteristic. The benefits derived from information should exceed the cost of providing it. The evaluation of benefits and costs is, however, substantially a judgmental process. Furthermore, the costs do not necessarily fall on those users who enjoy the benefits. Benefits may also be enjoyed by users other than those for whom the information is prepared; for example, the provision of further information to lenders may reduce the borrowing costs of an enterprise. For these reasons, it is difficult to apply a cost–benefit test in any particular case. Nevertheless, standard-setters in particular, as well as the preparers and users of financial statements, should be aware of this constraint.

Balance Between Qualitative Characteristics
45. In practice a balancing, or trade-off, between qualitative characteristics is often necessary. Generally the aim is to achieve an appropriate balance among the characteristics in order to meet the objective of financial statements. The relative importance of the characteristics in different cases is a matter of professional judgment.

True and Fair View/Fair Presentation
46. Financial statements are frequently described as showing a true and fair view of, or as presenting fairly, the financial position, performance and changes in financial position of an enterprise. Although this framework does not deal directly with such concepts, the application of the principal qualitative characteristics and of appropriate accounting standards normally results in financial statements that convey what is generally understood as a true and fair view of, or as presenting fairly such information.

It is worth studying the above with some care. It should be compared with lists and discussions given earlier in this chapter. In the IASC Framework not only are some further ideas introduced but the ideas are carefully given different levels of importance. There are said to be two underlying assumptions, the accrual basis and the going concern assumption. We then have four qualitative characteristics: understandability, relevance, reliability and comparability. Relevance was not included in our earlier list of traditional assumptions, but it is in a sense obvious. Notice carefully that materiality is suggested here as a sub-characteristic of relevance, i.e. at a lower level of logical importance. Observe the importance of reliability and, in particular, the possibility that relevant information may be unreliable, and that reliable information may be irrelevant, i.e. there could well be conflict between the two.

Reliability has no less than five sub-characteristics: faithful representation, substance over form, neutrality, prudence and completeness. There are two points to emphasize here. The first is the importance of substance over form. This idea has come into great prominence in recent years, though more in some countries than in others. Where there is difference or conflict the accountant could, and arguably should, look behind the legal description and deduce the economic reality, the real financial position and implications. The IASC suggests that it is this economic reality that should form the basis of the accountant's reports, even if this appears to be in direct conflict with the legal position.

The second point worthy of emphasis is that the characteristic of prudence is just one of the series of sub-characteristics of reliability. This contrasts sharply with the situation in many countries (in past or present), where prudence is regarded in practice as an overriding attitude to take. It is put firmly in its place by the IASC: it is one of a number of equal influences, sub-characteristics, which together help to determine the reliability of accounting information.

After discussing the fourth qualitative characteristic, that of comparability, there is a brief discussion of constraints on relevant and reliable information. These are timeliness, the importance of a proper balance between cost and benefit as regards the preparation of any particular package of accounting information, and finally, but importantly, the explicit recognition that in any particular situation a balance between the various qualitative characteristics is required, that they are often in conflict, and that subjective judgement is required in achieving an effective resolution.

Finally, in this part of the Framework there is a brief comment on the concept of true and fair view, of fair presentation (paragraph 46). This will be considered in more detail in Chapter 4.

3.8 IASC elements of financial statements

The first stage of the 'elements' part of the Framework is concerned with definitions. Notice that the substance over form concept permeates them and their interpretation.

Assets and liabilities

49. (a) An *asset* is a resource controlled by the enterprise as a result of past events and from which future economic benefits are expected to flow to the enterprise.
    (b) A *liability* is a present obligation of the enterprise arising from past events, the settlement of which is expected to result in an outflow from the enterprise of resources embodying economic benefits.
    (c) *Equity* is the residual interest in the assets of the enterprise after deducting all its liabilities.
50. The definitions of an asset and a liability identify their essential features but do not attempt to specify the criteria that need to be met before they are recognised in the balance sheet. Thus, the definitions embrace items that are not recognised as assets or liabilities in the balance sheet because they do not satisfy the criteria for recognition discussed in paragraphs 82 to 98. In particular, the expectation that future economic benefits will flow to or from an enterprise must be sufficiently certain to meet the probability criterion in paragraph 83 before an asset or liability is recognised.

51. In assessing whether an item meets the definition of an asset, liability or equity, attention needs to be given to its underlying substance and economic reality and not merely its legal form.

It is worth exploring the concepts of assets and liabilities in a little more detail. There are three elements involved in determining the existence of an asset. Thus an asset should:

(a) give probable future benefit;
(b) be possessed by or controlled by the business;
(c) have arisen from some earlier transaction or event.

So, for example:

1. A heap of rusty metal worth 10 ecu as scrap but costing 20 ecu to transport to the scrap dealer is not an asset (no probable future benefit).
2. A community welfare centre outside the factory that substantially improves the overall working conditions of a firm's employees is not an asset (not possessed or controlled by the business).
3. The benefits probably to be derived from next year's sales are not an asset (no earlier transaction or event).

Assets are always divided into **fixed assets** and **current assets**. A fixed asset is an asset that the firm intends to use within the business, over an extended period, in order to assist its daily operating activities. A current asset, on the other hand, is one not intended for continuing use. A current asset is an asset likely to change its form, i.e. likely soon to undergo some transaction, usually within 12 months. Consider two firms, A and B. Firm A is a motor trader. It possesses some motor vehicles that it is attempting to sell, and it also possesses some desks used by the salesmen, management and so on. Firm B is a furniture dealer. It possesses some desks that it is attempting to sell, and it also possesses some motor vehicles used by salesmen and for delivery purposes. In the accounts of A, the motor vehicles are current assets and the desks are fixed assets. In the accounts of B, the motor vehicles are fixed assets and the desks are current assets. By convention a fixed asset which, after several years' use, is about to be sold for scrap, remains in a fixed asset part of the accounts even though it is about to be sold.

A liability may also be said to have three parts to the definition. A liability should:

(a) involve probable future sacrifice;
(b) arise from present obligations to act in the future;
(c) be a result of past transactions or events.

So, for example, a firm will have a liability if it has given promises to pay future pensions. However, the firm does not have a liability, today, to pay for next week's purchases or for next week's wages. This is because next week's work has also not been done. The important 'event' is the doing of the work, which is a future event, not the signing of the employee's contract – which was a past event.

Liabilities are usually divided into current liabilities and long-term liabilities. Here the distinction is simply one of time. Current liabilities are those likely to be settled within 12 months. Long-term liabilities are those items regarded as long-term sources of finance for the business.

Income and expenses

Income and expenses are defined in the Framework as follows:

70. (a) *Income* is increases in economic benefits during the accounting period in the form of inflows or enhancements of assets or decreases of liabilities that results in increases in equity, other than those relating to contributions from equity participants.
    (b) *Expenses* are decreases in economic benefits during the accounting period in the form of outflows or depletions of assets or incurrences of liabilities that result in decreases in equity, other than those relating to distributions to equity participants.
74. The definition of income encompasses both revenue and gains. Revenue arises in the course of the ordinary activities of an enterprise and is referred to by a variety of different names including sales, fees, interest, dividends, royalties and rent.
75. Gains represent other items that meet the definition of income and may, or may not, arise in the course of the ordinary activities of an enterprise. Gains represent increases in economic benefits and as such are no different in nature from revenue. Hence, they are not regarded as constituting a separate element in this framework.
76. Gains include, for example, those arising on the disposal of non-current assets. The definition of income also includes unrealised gains; for example, those arising on the revaluation of marketable securities and those resulting from increases in the carrying amount of long term assets. When gains are recognised in the income statements, they are usually displayed separately because knowledge of them is useful for the purpose of making economic decisions. Gains are often reported net of related expenses.
81. The revaluation or restatement of assets and liabilities gives rise to increases or decreases in equity. While these increases or decreases meet the definition of income and expenses, they are not included in the income statement under certain concepts of capital maintenance. Instead these items are included in equity as capital maintenance adjustments or revaluation reserves.

This last paragraph is explained more fully in the chapter on accounting for price changes.

3.9 IASC recognition of the accounting elements

Once it is established that an element exists within the above definitions, it is then necessary to decide whether to recognize it, i.e. whether to record it in the accounting system and in the financial statements:

An item that meets the definition of an element should be recognized if:

(a) it is probable that any future economic benefit associated with the item will flow to or from the enterprise; and
(b) the item has a cost or value that can be measured with reliability.

As regards the final state in this logical process, that of deciding what figure to use to record the recognition of the elements, the Framework is brief and purely descriptive. It outlines historical cost and other valuation bases but does not come to a choice. These issues are explored in Chapter 11.

SUMMARY

This chapter has looked at the usual conventions that are said to apply to accounting practice. They were considered individually, and then some of their interrelationships were explored.

A number of more formal attempts have been made to consider the interrelationships of accounting ideas and conventions, and to produce coherent definitions as key elements in financial statements. This chapter explored the IASC thinking on this by looking at their suggested 'Framework'.

EXERCISES

3.1 (a) Which accounting conventions do you regard as most important to accountants, and why?
    (b) Which accounting conventions do you regard as most useful from the viewpoint of the readers of financial statements, and why?
    (c) Explain any difference between your answers to (a) and (b) above.

3.2 Is the traditional historical cost balance sheet objective?

3.3 The money measurement convention imposes a restriction which makes the completeness convention impossible to follow. Discuss.

3.4 (a) How do accountants decide when to recognize revenue?
    (b) When do accountants usually recognize revenue?
    (c) Do your answers to (a) and (b) satisfy the objectivity convention?

3.5 Explain the relationship between revenue recognition and asset valuation.

3.6 'The historical cost convention looks backwards but the going concern convention looks forwards'.
  (a) Explain clearly what is meant by:
    (i) the historical cost convention;
    (ii) the going concern convention.
  (b) Does traditional financial accounting, using the historical cost convention, make the going concern convention unnecessary? Explain your answer fully.
  (c) Which do you think a shareholder is likely to find more useful: a report on the past or an estimate of the future? Why?

3.7 On 21 December 19X1, your client paid 10,000 ecu for an advertising campaign. The advertisements will be heard on local radio stations between 1 January and 31 January 19X2. Your client believes that as a result sales will increase by 60% in 19X2 (over 19X1 levels) and by 40% in 19X3 (over 19X1 levels). There will be no further benefits.
  Write a memorandum to your client explaining your views on how this item should be treated in the year-end accounts for the three years. Your answer should include explicit reference to relevant traditional accounting conventions, and to the requirements of users of published financial accounts.

3.8 Explain, in a way understandable to a non-accountant, the following terms:
  (a) Asset.
  (b) Fixed asset.
  (c) Liability.
  (d) Revenue.
  (e) Expense.
  (f) Capital.

3.9 Equity investors are major users of financial statements. Identify the general nature of the 'information needs' of this group of users. Describe the likely specific uses of company financial information by investors, and give examples of information which may be relevant to each of these uses.

3.10 'Neutrality is about freedom from bias. Prudence is a bias. It is not possible to embrace both conventions in one coherent framework.' Discuss.

3.11 'What is relevant to investors is information about the future. Since this is not objective, financial accountants give them irrelevant information instead.' Discuss.

3.12 'Substance over form is a recipe for failing to achieve comparability between accounting statements for different businesses.' Discuss.

3.13 'The nature of accounting statements means that any attempt at a coherent overall framework is bound to fail.' Discuss.

PART II

Introduction to international aspects

CHAPTERS

4 International differences	65
5 Common European rules	87

CHAPTER 4

International differences

OBJECTIVES

- To alert readers to the scale of international differences in accounting
- To examine the major causes of difference
- To uncover some important institutions that affect accounting in various countries
- To set out the usefulness of grouping countries by accounting similarities
- To propose an international classification of countries by accounting practices

4.1 The international nature of the development of accounting

Different countries have contributed to the development of accounting over the centuries. When archaeologists uncover remains in the Middle East, almost anything with writing or numbers is a form of accounting: expenses of wars or feasts or constructions; lists of taxes due or paid. It is now fairly well documented that the origins of written numbers and written words are closely associated with the need to keep account and render account. More recently, the Romans developed sophisticated forms of single entry accounting from which, for example, farm profits could be calculated.

Later, the increasing complexity of business in late Medieval northern Italy led to the emergence of double entry; the existence of a wealthy merchant class and the need for large investment for major projects led to public subscription of share capital in seventeenth century Holland; the growing separation of ownership from management raised the need for audit in nineteenth century Britain. Many European countries have contributed: France led in the development of legal control over accounting; Scotland gave us the accountancy profession; Germany gave us standardized formats for financial statements.

From the late nineteenth century onwards, the United States has given us consolidation, management accounting, capitalization of leases and deferred tax accounting. The United Kingdom contributed the 'true and fair view' that has been rounded out with the American 'substance over form'.

The common feature of all these international influences on accounting is that commercial developments have led to accounting advances. Not surprisingly, leading commercial nations in any period are the leading innovators in accounting. So, in the late twentieth century, Japan has contributed greatly to managerial accounting and control.

However, although international influences and similarities are clear, there are also great differences, particularly within Europe. This chapter investigates the causes of international accounting differences and tries to put countries into groups.

4.2 Causes of differences

It is not possible to be *sure* that the factors discussed below cause the financial reporting differences, but a relationship can be established and reasonable deductions made. There seems to be consensus, on the whole, about which factors are involved in shaping financial reporting. Some researchers have used their estimates of such causes as a means of differentiating between countries (Mueller, 1967). Other researchers have studied whether perceived differences in accounting practices correlate with perceived causal factors (Frank, 1979). Factors which are seen as influencing accounting development include the nature of the legal system, the prevalent providers of finance, the influence of taxation and the strength of the accountancy profession.

On a world-wide scale, factors such as language or geography have been referred to by the above-mentioned researchers. To the extent that these do have some explanatory power, it seems more sensible to assume that this results from auto-correlation. That is, the fact that Australian accounting bears a marked resemblance to accounting in New Zealand might be 'confirmed' by language and geographical factors. However, most of their similarities were probably not caused by these factors, but by their historical connection with the United Kingdom, which passed on both accounting and language, and was colonizing most parts of Australasia in the same period.

If one wanted to encompass countries outside the developed Western world, it would be necessary to include factors concerning the state of development of their economy and the nature of their political economy. Of course, to some extent a precise definition of terms might make it clear that it is impossible to include some of these countries. For example, if our interest is in the financial reporting practices of listed corporations, those countries with few or no such corporations will have to be excluded. Fortunately, as our main purpose concerns Europe and developed countries elsewhere, there is a reasonable degree of uniformity in such countries concerning the presence of developed economies, democratic governments, listed companies, qualified accountants, and so on. For our purposes, the following seven factors may constitute an explanation for financial reporting differences: legal systems, providers of finance, taxation, the accountancy profession, inflation, theory, and the accidents of history. These are now considered in turn.

4.3 Legal systems

Most continental European countries have a system of law that is based on the Roman *jus civile* as compiled by Justinian in the sixth century and developed by European universities from the twelfth century. Here rules are linked to ideas of justice and morality; they become doctrine. The word 'codified' may be associated with such a system, in which company law or commercial codes establish rules in detail for accounting and financial reporting. Both the nature of regulation and the type of detailed rules to be found in a country are affected. For example, in Germany, company accounting is to a large extent a branch of company law.

In France, Belgium, Spain, Portugal and Greece, much of the detail of accounting rules is found in 'accounting plans' (e.g. the French *plan comptable général*) which are run by government committees. In Italy and several of the countries already mentioned, commercial codes contain many legal instructions on accounting. In many such countries, the codes date back to Napoleon, who adopted and adapted the Roman legal system. Japan introduced a commercial legal system similar to that of Germany in the second half of the nineteenth century.

By contrast, many other countries use a version of the English legal system that relies upon a limited amount of statute law. This is then interpreted by courts, which build up large amounts of case law to supplement the statutes. Such a 'common law' system was formed in England primarily after the Norman Conquest (1066) by judges acting on the king's behalf. It is less abstract than codified law; a common

Table 4.1 **Legal systems (some examples).**

Common law	*Codified Roman law*
England and Wales	France
Ireland	Italy
United States	Germany
Canada	Spain
Australia	Netherlands
New Zealand	Portugal
Hong Kong	Japan (commercial)

Note: The laws of Scotland, Israel, South Africa, Quebec, Louisiana and the Philippines embody elements of both systems.

law rule seeks to provide an answer to a specific case rather than to formulate a general rule for the future. This common law system may be found in similar forms in many countries influenced by England. Thus, the federal law of the United States, the laws of Ireland, India, Australia, and so on, are to a greater or lesser extent modelled on English common law. This naturally influences company law, which traditionally does not prescribe a large number of detailed all-embracing rules to cover the behaviour of companies and how they should publish their financial statements. To a large extent (at least up until the British Companies Act 1981), accounting within such a context is not dependent upon law, but is an independent discipline.

Table 4.1 illustrates the way in which some developed countries' legal systems fall into these two categories.

4.4 Providers of finance

In some countries, a major source of corporate finance for two centuries has been share capital and loan capital provided by large numbers of private investors. This has been the predominant mode of raising finance in the United States and the United Kingdom. Although it is increasingly the case that shares in these countries are held by institutional investors rather than by individual shareholders, this still contrasts with state, bank or family holdings (see below). Indeed, the increased importance of institutional investors is perhaps a reinforcement for the following hypothesis: 'in countries with a widespread ownership of companies by shareholders who do not have access to internal information there will be a pressure for disclosure, audit and "fair" information'. Institutional investors hold larger blocks of shares and may be better organized than private shareholders, so they should increase this pressure. However, they may also be able to press successfully for more detailed information than is generally available to the public.

By contrast, in France and Italy, capital provided by the state or by banks is very significant, as are family businesses. In Germany, the banks, in particular, are important owners of companies as well as providers of debt finance. A majority of shares in some public companies are owned directly or controlled through proxies by banks, particularly by the Deutsche, Dresdner and Commerz banks. In such countries the banks or the state will, in many cases, nominate directors and thus be able to obtain private information and to affect decisions. If it is the case that many companies in continental countries are dominated by banks, governments or families, the need for published information is much smaller. This also applies to audit because this is designed to check up on the managers in cases where the owners are 'outsiders'. Examples of this are:

- The large German listed public company, Daimler-Benz AG is 28% owned by the Deutsche Bank. That bank and three others are represented on the supervisory board (*Aufsichtsrat*) of Daimler-Benz. The banks therefore obtain private information and exercise long-run direction over the company. The majority of shares are held by long-run shareholders of this sort, and so a New York or London-style take-over bid is not possible.

- The largest Italian car maker is Fiat SpA in which the Agnelli family have a large shareholding. Many other large Italian companies are majority-owned by government holding companies. The results are as for Daimler-Benz above.

Evidence of the two-way characterization of countries may be found by looking at their numbers of listed companies. Table 4.2 shows the numbers of domestic listed companies on Stock Exchanges where there are over 200 such companies. The comparison between the United Kingdom and Germany or France is instructive. A two-group categorization of these countries is almost as obvious as that for legal systems in Table 4.1 (taking account of size of economy or population). Incidentally, the country with the longest history of 'public' companies is the Netherlands. Although it has a fairly small stock exchange, many multinationals

Table 4.2 **Stock Exchanges with over 200 domestic[a] listed companies.**

Region	Exchange	Count
Europe:	Barcelona	364
	Copenhagen	240
	Germany	413
	Italy	220
	London	1,701
	Madrid	427
	Paris	443
Americas:	American	679
	Mid-West	2,020
	Montreal	628
	New York	1,469
	Rio de Janeiro	612
	Sao Paolo	579
	Toronto	1,127
Asia, Africa:	Australian	1,043
	Hong Kong	224
	Johannesburg	732
	Korea	669
	Kuala Lumpur	265
	Osaka	1,138
	Tokyo	1,627

[a] There are also a number of non-domestic companies listed on these exchanges. The numbers given exclude investment funds.
Source: *Statistiques*, Fédération Internationale des Bourses de Valeurs, Paris, 1990.

(such as Unilever, Philips, Royal Dutch) are listed on it. It seems reasonable, then, to place the Netherlands with the English-speaking world in a 'shareholder' group as opposed to a 'bank/state/family' group.

'Fair' was mentioned above, as it has been in previous chapters. It is a concept related to the existence of a large number of outside owners who require unbiased information about the success of a business and its state of affairs. Although reasonable prudence will be expected, these shareholders are interested in comparing one year with another and one company with another; thus the accruals concept and some degree of realism will be required. This entails judgement, which entails experts. This expertise is also required for checking financial statements by auditors. In countries like the United Kingdom, the United States and the Netherlands, this can, over many decades, result in a tendency to require accountants to work out their own technical rules. This is acceptable to governments because of the influence and expertise of the accountancy profession, which is usually running ahead of the interest of the government (in its capacity as shareholder, protector of the public interest or collector of taxation). Thus generally accepted accounting principles control accounting. To the extent that governments intervene, they impose disclosure, filing or measurement requirements and those tend to follow best practice rather than create it.

In most continental European countries, the traditional paucity of 'outsider' shareholders has meant that external financial reporting has been largely invented for the purposes of governments, as tax collectors or controllers of the economy. This has not encouraged the development of flexibility, judgement, fairness or experimentation.

Nevertheless, even in such countries as Germany, France or Italy, where there are comparatively few listed companies, governments have recognized the responsibility to require public or listed companies to publish detailed, audited, financial statements. There are laws to this effect in the majority of such countries, and the governments in France and Italy have also set up bodies specifically to control the securities markets: in France the *Commission des Opérations de Bourse* (COB), and in Italy the *Commissione Nazionale per le Società e la Borsa* (CONSOB). These bodies are to some extent modelled on the Securities and Exchange Commission (SEC) of the United States. They have been associated with important developments in financial reporting, generally in the direction of Anglo-American practice. This is not surprising, as these stock exchange bodies are taking the part otherwise played by private and institutional shareholders who have, over a much longer period, helped to shape Anglo-American accounting systems.

4.5 Taxation

Although it is possible to make groupings of tax systems in a number of ways, only some of them are of relevance to financial reporting. For example, it is easy to divide EC countries into those using 'classical' and those using 'imputation' systems of corporation tax (see Chapter 10). However, this distinction does not affect financial reporting. What is much more relevant is the degree to which taxation regulations determine accounting measurements. To some extent this is seen in a negative way by studying the problem of deferred taxation, which is caused by timing differences between tax and accounting treatments. In the United Kingdom, the Netherlands and the United States, for example, the problem of deferred tax has caused much controversy and a considerable amount of accounting standard documentation.

Turning to France or Germany, it is found that the problem has traditionally not really existed; for in these countries, it is to a large extent the case that the tax rules are the accounting rules. In Germany, the tax accounts (*Steuerbilanz*) should be the same as the commercial accounts (*Handelsbilanz*). There is even a word for this idea: the *Massgeblichkeitsprinzip*.

One obvious example of the areas affected by this difference is depreciation (which is discussed further in Chapter 7). In the United Kingdom, for example, the amount of depreciation charged in the published financial statements is determined according to custom established over the last century and influenced by the accounting standard SSAP 12. The standard points out that:

> Depreciation should be allocated to accounting periods so as to charge a fair proportion of the cost or valuation of the asset to each accounting period expected to benefit from its use. (para. 1)
>
> Management should select the method regarded as most appropriate to the type of asset and its use in the business so as to allocate depreciation as fairly as possible. (paragraph 8).

The injunctions contained in the standard are of a fairly general nature, and their spirit is quite frequently ignored. Convention and pragmatism, rather than exact rules or even the spirit of the standard, also determine the method of judging the scrap value and the expected length of life.

The amount of depreciation for tax purposes in the United Kingdom is quite independent of these figures. It is determined by capital allowances, which are a formalized scheme of tax depreciation allowances designed to standardize the amounts allowed and to act as investment incentives. Because of the separation of the two schemes, there can be a complete lack of subjectivity in tax allowances, but full room for judgement in financial depreciation charges.

At the opposite extreme, in countries like Germany, the tax regulations lay down maximum depreciation rates to be used for particular assets. These are generally based on the expected useful lives of assets. However, in some cases, accelerated depreciation allowances are available: for example, for industries producing energy-saving or anti-pollution products or for certain regions. In the past, the allowances applied in West Berlin or other areas bordering East Germany; now they apply in the new German *länder*. If these allowances are to be claimed for tax purposes (which would normally be sensible), they must be charged in the financial accounts. Thus, the charge against profit would be said by the UK accountant not to be 'fair', even though it could certainly be 'correct' or 'legal'. This influence is felt even in the details of the choice of method of depreciation, where a typical German note to a company's balance sheet might read: 'Plant and machinery are depreciated over a useful life of ten years on a declining-balance basis: straight-line depreciation is adopted as soon as this results in a higher charge'.

A second example of the overriding effect of taxation on accounting measurement is the valuation of fixed assets in France. During the inflationary 1970s and before, French companies were allowed to revalue assets. However, this would have entailed extra taxation due to the increase in the post-revaluation balance sheet total compared to the previous year's. Consequently, except in the special case of merger by *fusion*, when tax-exempt revaluation is allowed, revaluation was not practised. However, the Finance Acts of 1978 and 1979 made revaluation obligatory for listed companies and for those which solicit funds from the public; it was optional for others. The purpose was to show balance sheets more realistically. The revaluation was performed by use of government indices relating to 31 December 1976. The credit went to an undistributable revaluation reserve. As a result of this, for depreciable assets, an amount equal to the extra depreciation due to revaluations is credited each year to profit and loss and debited to the revaluation account. Thus the effect of revaluation on profit (and tax) is neutralized. This move from no revaluations to compulsory revaluations was caused by the tax rules.

Similar tax-exempt revaluations occurred in the 1980s in Italy, Spain and Greece, although tax depreciation was allowed to rise in these cases. Further examples of tax effects are easy to find: bad debt provisions (determined by tax laws in many continental countries), pension expenses (amounts charged in accounts often follow those allowed for tax purposes), or various provisions related to specific industries.

The effects of all this are to reduce the room for operation of the accruals convention (which is the driving force behind such practices as depreciation) and to reduce 'fairness'. Until the legislation following the EC's Fourth Directive, the importance of this effect was not disclosed in published accounts. With some variations, this *Massgeblichkeitsprinzip* operates in Germany, France, Belgium, Italy, Spain and many other countries. It is perhaps due partly to the pervasive influence of codification in law, and partly to the predominance of taxation as a cause of accounting. Nevertheless, by the late 1980s, there were clear moves away from this in some countries. For example, the Spanish accounting law of 1989 reduces the influence of tax and increases disclosures of the remaining tax effects. France also has substantially liberated consolidated accounts from tax rules.

The alternative approach, exemplified above by the United Kingdom, the United States and the Netherlands, is found in countries with an older tradition of published accounting, where commercial rules have come first. The countries on the left in Table 4.1 are, in varying degrees, like this. In most cases, there is not the high degree of separation between tax and financial reporting that is found in the United Kingdom in the shape of capital allowances. However, in all such countries the taxation authorities have to adjust the commercial accounts for their own purposes, after exerting only minor influence directly on them. There is a major exception to this in the use of last-in, first-out (LIFO) inventory valuation in the United States, largely for tax reasons (see Chapter 8 for a description of LIFO).

4.6 The profession

The power, size and competence of the accountancy profession in a country may follow, to a large extent, from the various factors outlined above and from the type of financial reporting they have helped to produce. For example, the lack of a substantial body of private shareholders and public companies in some countries means that the need for auditors is much smaller than it is in the United Kingdom or the United States. However, the nature of the profession also feeds back into the type of accounting that is practised and could be practised. For example, a 1975 Decree in Italy (not brought into effect until the 1980s), requiring listed companies to have extended audits similar to those operated in the United Kingdom and the United States, could only be brought into effect initially because of the substantial presence of international accounting firms.

This difference in professional bodies constitutes a considerable obstacle to any attempts at significant and deep harmonization of accounting between some countries. The need for extra auditors was a controversial issue in Germany's implementation of the EC's Fourth Directive (see Chapter 5).

The scale of the difference is illustrated in Table 4.3 which lists the bodies whose members may audit the accounts of companies (but see below for an explanation of the French and German situations). These remarkable figures need some interpretation. For example, let us compare more carefully the German and the British figures. In Germany, there is a separate, though overlapping, profession of tax experts (*Steuerberater*), which is larger than the accountancy body. However, in the United Kingdom the accountants' figure is inflated by the inclusion of many who specialize in or occasionally practise in tax. Second, a German accountant may only be a member of the *Institut* if he is in practice, whereas at least half of the British figure represents members in commerce, industry, government, education, and so on. Third, the training period is much longer in Germany than it is in the United Kingdom. It normally involves a four-year relevant degree course, six years' practical experience (four in the profession), and a professional examination consisting of oral and written tests plus a thesis. This tends to last until the aspiring accountant is 30–35 years old. Thus, many of the German 'students' would be counted as part of the qualified figure if they were in the British system. Fourth, in the 1980s, as part of the preparation for more audits, a second-tier body of *Vereidigte Buchprüfer* was established, whose members may audit certain private companies (GmbHs).

These four factors help to explain the differences. However, there is still a very substantial residual difference which results from the much larger number of companies to be audited and the different process of forming a judgement on the 'fair' view. The differences are diminishing as auditing is extended to many private

Table 4.3 Public accountancy bodies, age and size.

Country	Body	Founding date*	Approx no.s (000s) 1991/2
United States	American Institute of Certified Public Accountants	1887	301
United Kingdom	Institute of Chartered Accountants in England & Wales	1880 (1870)	97
	Institute of Chartered Accountants of Scotland	1951 (1854)	13
	Chartered Association of Certified Accountants	1939 (1891)	38
	Institute of Chartered Accountants in Ireland	1888	8
Australia	Australian Society of Accountants	1952 (1887)	62
	Institute of Chartered Accountants in Australia	1928 (1886)	23
Netherlands	Nederlands Instituut van Registeraccountants	1895	8
France	Ordre des Experts Comptables et des Comptables Agréés	1942	12
Germany	Institut der Wirtschaftsprüfer	1932	6
Spain	Instituto de Censures Jurados de Cuentas de España	1945	6
	Registro de Economistas Auditores	1982	4
Japan	Japanese Institute of Certified Public Accountants	1948	10

a Dates of earliest direct predecessor bodies in brackets.

companies in EC countries. Also, it is possible that the requirement for small company audit may be abolished in the United Kingdom, with the encouragement of the European Community.

It is interesting to note a further division along Anglo-American versus Franco-German lines. In the former countries, governments or government agencies do require certain types of companies to be audited, and put certain limits on who shall be auditors, with government departments having the final say. However, in

Table 4.4 **Accountancy and auditing bodies in France and Germany.**

	Private professional body	State auditing body
France	Ordre des Experts Comptables	Compagnie Nationale des Commissaires aux Comptes
Germany	Institut der Wirtschaftsprüfer	Wirtschaftsprüferkammer

general, membership of the private professional accountancy bodies is the method of qualifying as an auditor. On the other hand, in France and Germany there is a dual set of accountancy bodies. Those in Table 4.3 are not the bodies to which one must belong to qualify as an auditor of companies, though to a large extent the membership of these professional bodies overlaps with that of the auditing bodies, and membership of the former permits membership of the latter. The auditing bodies are shown in Table 4.4. The professional bodies set exams, consider ethical matters, belong to the international accounting bodies, and so on. The auditing bodies are run by the state. The *Compagnie Nationale* is responsible to the Ministry of Justice; the *Wirtschaftsprüferkammer* to the Federal Minister of Economics.

The Eighth EC Directive on company law (see Chapter 5) requires this arrangement throughout the European Community; but the United Kingdom and the Netherlands, for example, have largely retained their former structures, in substance.

4.7 Inflation

Section 4.5 noted the effect of government-induced, tax-based revaluations of assets in several European countries. These were carried out partly to adjust balance sheet values for changing prices. Further detail is given in the chapter on asset valuation (Chapter 6). By contrast, accountants in the English-speaking world have proved remarkably immune to inflation when it comes to decisive action. However, there are some countries where inflation has been overwhelming. In several South American countries, the most obvious feature of accounting practices is the use of methods of general price-level adjustment (see Chapter 11). The use of this comparatively simple method is probably due to:

(a) the reasonable correlation of inflation with any particular specific price changes when the former is in hundreds of per cent per year;
(b) the objective nature of government published indices; and
(c) the paucity of well-trained accountants.

Without reference to this factor, it would not be possible to explain accounting differences in several countries severely affected by it.

4.8 Theory

In a few cases, accounting theory has strongly influenced accounting practice, perhaps most obviously in the case of microeconomics in the Netherlands. Accounting theorists there (notably Theodore Limperg, Jr) had advanced the case that the users of financial statements would be given the fairest view of the performance and state of affairs of an individual company by allowing accountants to use judgement, in the context of that particular company, to select and present accounting figures. In particular, it was suggested that replacement cost information might give the best picture. The looseness of law and tax requirements, and the receptiveness of the profession to microeconomic ideas (partly due, no doubt, to their training by the academic theorists) led to the present diversity of practice, the emphasis on 'fairness' through judgement, and the experimentation with and practice of replacement cost accounting.

In most other countries, the influence of accounting theory on accounting practice seems slight. In the English-speaking world, accounting is a practical, commercial discipline in which the rules are largely made up piecemeal in response to specific problems of the moment. The development of conceptual frameworks (see Chapter 3) is recent. In most continental countries, accounting rules are closely connected to the collection of tax or the control of the economy, and no specifically accounting theoretical framework is obvious as a single basis for the practice of accounting.

4.9 Accidents

Many other influences have been at work in shaping accounting practices. Some are not indirect and subtle like the type of ownership of companies, but direct and external to accounting like the framing of a law in response to economic or political events. For example, the economic crisis in the United States in the late 1920s and early 1930s produced the Securities and Exchange Acts which have diverted US accounting from its previous course by introducing extensive disclosure requirements and control (usually by threat only) of accounting standards. Other examples include the introduction into Italy of Anglo-American accounting principles by choice of the government, and the introduction into Luxembourg of consolidation and detailed disclosure as a result of EC Directives – both against all previous trends there. In Spain, the 'artificial' adoption of the accounting plan from France follows the latter country's adoption of it after influence by the occupying Germans in the early 1940s. Perhaps most obvious and least natural is the adoption of various British Companies Acts or International Accounting Standards by developing countries with a negligible number of the sort of public companies or private shareholders that have given rise to the financial reporting practices contained in these laws or standards. In its turn, the United Kingdom in 1981 adopted uniform formats derived from the 1965 *Aktiengesetz* of Germany because of EC requirements. For their part, Roman law countries are now having to grapple with the 'true and fair view' (see Chapter 5).

4.10 Classification

So far, this chapter has discussed the causes of differences in financial reporting practices in Europe. From this it is clear that, although no two countries have identical rules and practices, some countries seem to form pairs or larger groupings with reasonably similar influences on financial reporting. If this is so, it may be possible to establish a classification. Such an activity is a basic step in many disciplines. Before attempting a European accounting classification, it may be useful to make short surveys of classification in other disciplines, of the normal rules for classifications, of the purposes of classifications, and of previous attempts in accounting.

Classification is one of the basic tools of a scientist. The Mendeleev table of elements and the Linnaean system of classification are fundamental to chemistry and biology. Classification should sharpen description and analysis. It should reveal underlying structures and enable prediction of the properties of an element based on its place in a classification.

Different types of classification are possible, from the simplest form of dichotomous grouping (e.g. things black versus things white) or rank ordering (e.g. by height of students in a class) to more complex dimensioning (such as the periodic table of chemical elements) or systematizing (such as the Linnaean system).

It may now be useful to examine traditional methods of classification in areas close to accounting. There have been classifications of political, economic and legal systems. For example, political systems have been grouped into political democracies, tutelary democracies, modernizing oligarchies, totalitarian oligarchies and traditional oligarchies. Economic systems have been divided into capitalism, socialism, communism and fascism. A more recent classification is: traditional economies, market economies and planned economies.

One set of authors, while classifying legal systems, has supplied practical criteria for determining whether two systems are in the same group. Systems are said to be in the same group if 'someone educated in . . . one law will then be capable, without much difficulty, of handling [the other]' (David and Brierley, 1978). Also, the two systems must not be 'founded on opposed philosophical, political or economic principles'. The second criterion ensures that systems in the same group not only have similar superficial characteristics, but also have similar fundamental structures and are likely to react to new circumstances in similar ways. Using these criteria a four-group legal classification was obtained: Romano-Germanic, common law, socialist and philosophical-religious.

In all the above examples, the type of classification used was rudimentary, involving no more than splitting systems into a few groups. The groups within the classifications were sometimes not precisely defined nor exhaustive. Also, the method used to determine and fill the groups was little more than subjective classification based on personal knowledge or descriptive literature. These shortcomings are very difficult to avoid because of the complexity and 'greyness' in the social sciences.

In accounting, classification should facilitate a study of the logic of and the difficulties facing international harmonization. Classification should also assist in the training of accountants and auditors who operate internationally. Further, a developing country might be better able to understand the available types of financial reporting, and which one would be most appropriate for it, by seeing which other countries use particular systems. Also, it should be possible for a country to predict the problems that it is about to face and the solutions that might work by looking at other countries in its group.

Early classifications

Early attempts at classification and more recent descriptions of different national systems form the background to modern classifications. Of the former, there is evidence for a three-group classification (United Kingdom, United States and Continental) being used from the beginning of the twentieth century (Hatfield, reprinted 1966). More recent descriptions and analyses like those by Price Waterhouse (surveys of 1973, 1975 and 1979) and the AICPA (surveys of 1964 and 1975) provide the raw material for classification.

Professor Gerhard Mueller broke new ground in 1967 by preparing a suggested classification of accounting systems into four patterns of development. This was a simple grouping which is not accompanied by an explanation of the method used to obtain it. However, the 'range of four is considered sufficient to embrace accounting as it is presently known and practised in various parts of the globe' (Mueller, 1967, p. 2). Each group was illustrated by one or two examples. It may well be that it is not reasonable to expect a more sophisticated classification, particularly in a pioneering work, and that Mueller's informed judgement was one of the best methods of classification available.

Mueller stresses that the types of accounting rules which exist in a country are a product of economic, political and other environments that have determined the nature of the system. This also suggests that other countries' rules would not be appropriate to that country and that rules must be chosen to fit a country's needs. Consequently, doubt is cast on the possibility and usefulness of harmonization.

Mueller's four patterns of development are as follows:

1. *Accounting within a macroeconomic framework.* In this case, accounting has developed as an adjunct of national economic policies. We might expect such financial accounting to stress value-added statements, to encourage income smoothing, to be equivalent to tax accounting and to include social responsibility accounting. Sweden is said to be an example.

2. *The microeconomic approach.* This approach can prosper in a market-oriented economy which has individual private businesses at the core of its economic affairs. The influence of microeconomics has led accounting to try to reflect economic reality in its measurement and valuations. This means that accounting rules must be sophisticated but flexible. Developments like replacement cost accounting will be accepted most readily in such systems. The Netherlands is suggested as an example.
3. *Accounting as an independent discipline.* Systems of this sort have developed independently of governments or economic theories. Accounting has developed in business, has faced problems when they arrived, and has adopted solutions which worked. Theory is held in little regard and turned to only in emergencies or used *ex post facto* in an attempt to justify practical conclusions. Expressions such as 'generally accepted accounting principles' are typical. Mueller recognized the accounting systems of the United Kingdom and the United States as examples.
4. *Uniform accounting.* Such systems have developed where government have used accounting as a part of the administrative control of business. Accounting can be used to measure performance, allocate funds, assess the size of industries and resources, control prices, collect taxation, manipulate sectors of business, and so on. It involves standardization of definitions, measurements and presentation. France is cited as an example.

Mueller was not classifying financial reporting systems directly, on the basis of differences in *practices*, but indirectly, on the basis of differences in the importance of economic, governmental and business factors in the development of particular systems. However, one might expect that systems that have developed in a similar way would have similar accounting practices.

Nevertheless, there are a few problems with Mueller's classification. The fact that there are only four exclusive groups and no hierarchy reduces the usefulness of the classification. In effect, the Netherlands is the only country in one of the groups and the classification does not show whether Dutch accounting is closer to UK accounting than it is to Swedish accounting. Similarly, the classification cannot include such facts as whether German accounting exhibits features that remind one of macroeconomic accounting as well as of uniform accounting.

Classifications using clustering

Other researchers have used the 1973 and the 1975 Price Waterhouse surveys of practices. For example, one set of researchers (Nair and Frank, 1980) divide the 1973 survey's financial reporting characteristics into those relating to measurement and those relating to disclosure. This is a very useful differentiation, particularly because of the effect it has on the classification of countries like Germany which have advanced disclosure requirements. Using disclosure and measurement characteristics,

Germany is classified in a 'US group'. However, by using 'measurement' characteristics only, it is possible to classify Germany in the continental European group. Table 4.5 represents the classification using measurement characteristics. As yet there is no hierarchy, but the overall results do seem very plausible and fit well with the analysis in this chapter. The suggestion is that, in a world-wide context, much of continental Europe can be seen as using the same system. However, the United Kingdom, Ireland and the Netherlands are noticeably different.

Another approach

It would be possible to criticize the classifications discussed above for:

(a) lack of precision in the definition of what is to be classified;
(b) lack of a model with which to compare the statistical results;
(c) lack of hierarchy which would add more subtlety to the portrayal of the size of differences between countries; and
(d) lack of judgement in the choice of 'important' discriminating features.

Can these problems be remedied? One of the authors attempted to solve them in the following ways (see Nobes, 1983).

Table 4.5 Classification based on 1973 measurement practices.

British Commonwealth model	Latin American model	Continental European model	United States model
Australia	Argentina	Belgium	Canada
Bahamas	Bolivia	France	Japan
Eire	Brazil	Germany	Mexico
Fiji	Chile	Italy	Panama
Jamaica	Columbia	Spain	Philippines
Kenya	Ethiopia	Sweden	United States
Netherlands	India	Switzerland	
New Zealand	Paraguay	Venezuela	
Pakistan	Peru		
Singapore	Uruguay		
South Africa			
Trinidad and Tobago			
United Kingdom			
Zimbabwe			

Source: Nair and Frank (1980), p. 429.

INTERNATIONAL DIFFERENCES 81

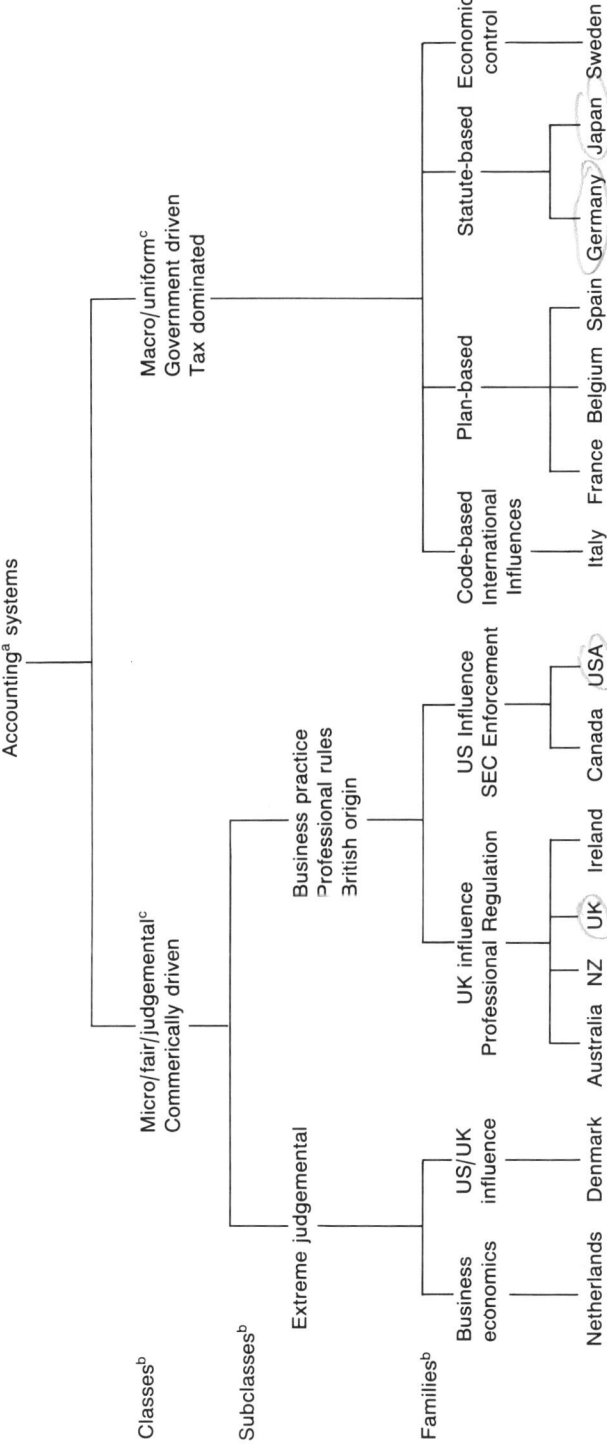

[a] This is an abbreviated term for corporate financial reporting.
[b] These terms, while borrowed from biology, should be interpreted merely as loose labels.
[c] The terms at these and other branching points are merely labels to be used as shorthand to try to capture some of the attributes of the members of the accounting systems below them. This classification has been prepared by a UK researcher and may contain usage of terms that will mislead those from other cultures.

Figure 4.1 Groupings of some major countries.

The scope of the work is defined as the classification of some Western countries by the financial reporting practices of their *public companies*. It was carried out in the early 1980s. The reporting practices are those concerned with *measurement and valuation*. It is public companies whose financial statements are generally available and whose practices can be most easily discovered. It is the international differences in reporting between such companies that are of main interest to shareholders, creditors, auditing firms, taxation authorities, managements and harmonizing agencies. Measurement and valuation practices were chosen because these determine the size of the figures for profit, capital, total assets, liquidity and so on. The result is Figure 4.1.

The figure suggests that there are two main types of financial reporting 'system' in Europe: the micro/professional and the macro/uniform. The former involves accountants in individual companies striving to present fair information to outside users, without detailed constraint of law or tax rules but with professional guidelines. The latter type has accounting mainly as a servant of the state, particularly for taxation purposes.

The micro/professional side contains the Netherlands, the United Kingdom, Ireland, Denmark, the United States, Australia, New Zealand and Canada. The Netherlands is even more free of rules than are the United Kingdom and Ireland, although the influence of microeconomic theory has led to use of replacement cost information to varying degrees. Denmark rearranged its accounting system after World War II, and it now looks somewhat like the United Kingdom or the United States.

The macro/uniform side contains all other European countries and Japan. However, they can be divided into subgroups. For example, accounting plans are now the predominant source of detailed rules in France, Belgium, Spain and Greece. In Germany, company law is the major authority and there is much stricter observance of historical cost values. In Italy, Luxembourg and Portugal, tax rules are also a vital determinant of detailed practices. Other rules come from commercial codes rather than from accounting plans. In Sweden, the predominant influence seems to be the government as economic planner and tax collector.

The purpose of the figure is to organize countries into groups by similarities of financial reporting measurement practices. This means that a knowledge of one country enables inferences to be drawn about others. The 'distance' between two countries is suggested by how far back up the classification it is necessary to go to reach a common point. This should be useful for those accountants and auditors who have to deal with financial reports from several countries or who have to work in more than one country.

Such a classification can be borne in mind while studying detailed accounting practices in Part III. Table 4.6 summarizes some of the typical differences between countries on a two-group basis.

Change from 1980

The classification of Figure 4.1 and Table 4.6 was originally drawn up in the early

Table 4.6 **A two-group classification (traditional[a] practices).**

Anglo-Saxon	Continental
Background	
'English' common law	Roman law
Large, old, strong profession	Small, young, weak profession
Large stock exchange	Small stock exchange
General accounting features	
Fair	Legal
Shareholder-orientation	Creditor-orientation
Disclosure	Secrecy
Tax rules separate	Tax-dominated
Substance over form	Form over substance
Professional standards	Government rules
Specific accounting features	
Percentage of completion method	Completed contract method
Depreciation over useful lives	Depreciation by tax rules
No legal reserves	Legal reserves
Finance leases capitalized	No lease capitalization
Funds flow statements	No funds flow statements
Earnings per share disclosed	No earnings per share disclosures
No secret reserves	Secret reserves
No tax-induced provisions	Tax-induced provisions
Preliminary expenses expensed	Preliminary expenses capitalizable
Taking gains on unsettled foreign currency monetary items	Deferring gains on unsettled foreign currency monetary items
Some examples of countries	
United Kingdom	France
Ireland	Germany
United States	Austria
Canada	Sweden
Australia	Spain
New Zealand	Italy
Hong Kong	Portugal
Singapore	Japan
Denmark	Belgium
The Netherlands	Greece

[a] From the late 1980s in particular, accounting practices in several countries made significant shifts to the left. For example, many French sets of group accounts capitalized leases; and this is now required in Spain for finance leases.

1980s, before the EC harmonization programme and before extensive globalization of capital markets. In the 1980s major changes occurred in several countries. For example, many sets of group accounts from France have been substantially liberated from tax influences (see Chapters 5 and 12). In a sense, this moves France to the left in these classifications. Some movement in that direction is also clear from Italy, Spain and Sweden. By contrast, Britain introduced many accounting rules into law in the 1980s and, for example, has standardized its formats of accounts. This is a move in a rightward direction. Consequently, Figure 4.1 and Table 4.6 are too simple to reflect the real world of the 1990s.

SUMMARY

This chapter has discussed some of the influences on the development of financial reporting practices. The importance of the mix of users of accounting information seems clear; it has a major part to play in the emergence of the dominant source of rules for accounting practice. In many continental European countries, the importance of governments as collectors of taxation or controllers of the economy has led to the dominance of company law, commercial codes and tax regulations. In other countries, the effective control of financial reporting practice has been exercised by the accountancy profession. This was first seen as a vague corpus of 'best' or 'accepted' practices, and has since been refined in the publication of detailed accounting standards. However, these standards are still loosely drawn documents that permit considerable flexibility and the use of judgement. The interests of private shareholders as users of financial statements have been a continuing background pressure on the profession as it develops standard practice.

As a result of international harmonization, much of it caused directly by the European Community, many European countries are finding 'fairness' and audit thrust upon them; and the United Kingdom, Ireland and the Netherlands are receiving many detailed financial reporting rules into their laws. This development cuts across the fundamental causes of differences that we have been looking at. However, it was certainly the case, at least before this influence was widely felt, that the same countries were generally found together under most of the factors discussed above. This observation leads on to the thought of classification of countries.

Classification is of fundamental importance to natural scientists, and has also been used in many social sciences. It seems reasonable that we might gain from a classification exercise in comparative international accounting, and that similar rules of classification to those used by scientists might be appropriate. In accounting, such classification may aid understanding and training, and may help to chart the need for, and progress of, harmonization.

There have been many attempts at classification in international accounting, and there has been much description and data gathering. Mueller's four-group classification of practices and later classification of environments were useful preliminary works. However, the classification of practices needs a hierarchy. Other attempts have been made to construct morphologies and to identify zones of influence.

Most recently, attempts have been made to classify using the Price Waterhouse Survey data of 1973-9. The results seem to vary in their plausibility, and there are doubts about the suitability of the data. An alternative classification has been proposed here, which has a detailed hierarchy and has been tested in a number of ways.

References

R. David and J. E. C. Brierley (1978), *Major Legal Systems in the World Today*, Stevens, London.
W. G. Frank (1979), 'An empirical analysis of international accounting principles', *Journal of Accounting Research*, Autumn.
H. R. Hatfield (1966), 'Some variations in accounting practices in England, France, Germany and the US', *Journal of Accounting Research*, Autumn.
G. G. Mueller (1967), *International Accounting*, Part I, Macmillan, New York.
R. D. Nair and W. G. Frank (1980), 'The impact of disclosure and measurement practices on international accounting classifications', *Accounting Review*, July.
C. W. Nobes (1983), 'A judgmental international classification of financial reporting practices', *Journal of Business Finance and Accounting*, Spring.

EXERCISES

4.1 Seven factors have been suggested as related to financial reporting differences, i.e. legal systems, providers of finance, taxation, the accountancy profession, inflation, theory, and accidents of history.
   (a) Within your knowledge and experiences, which factors do you believe to be the most important, and why?
   (b) To what extent do you think your views on (a) above have been influenced by your own national environment?

4.2 'International differences in financial reporting are related to the relative importance of the different user groups in different countries.' Discuss.

4.3 'International accounting classification systems are, by their very nature, simplistic.' Discuss.

4.4 By reference to any countries in Figure 4.1 with which you are familiar, comment on the apparent validity of the groupings. Make notes of points for and against the particular positions of the countries concerned. Be ready to update these notes as you read later chapters.

4.5 Do you think Roman law or common law provide a better context in which financial reporting can achieve its objectives?

CHAPTER 5

Common European rules

> **OBJECTIVES**
>
> - To examine the purposes and problems of international harmonization of accounting
> - To look at the major players in world or regional harmonization, particularly the IASC and the European Community
> - To study the contents of major EC accounting Directives
> - To chart the progress of harmonization

The preceding chapter makes it clear that there are major differences in the financial reporting practices of companies in different countries. This leads to great complications for those preparing, consolidating, auditing and interpreting published financial statements. Since the preparation of internal financial information often overlaps with the preparation of published information, the complications spread further. To combat this, several organizations throughout the world are involved in attempts to harmonize or standardize accounting.

'Harmonization' is a process of increasing the compatibility of accounting practices by setting bounds to their degree of variation. 'Standardization' appears to imply the imposition of a more rigid and narrow set of rules. However, within accounting, these two words have almost become technical terms, and one cannot rely upon the normal difference in their meanings. Harmonization is a word which tends to be associated with the transnational legislation being promulgated in the European Communities;[1] standardization is a word often associated with the International Accounting Standards Committee. In practical effect, the 'harmonization' of the European Community has been more powerful than the 'standardization' of the IASC, and many accounting standards at the national or international level are far from rigid or narrow.

---

[1] In November 1993, the European Community was absorbed into an expanded set of institutions known as the European Union.

This chapter starts by looking at the purposes of and obstacles to harmonization or standardization. The bulk of the chapter concerns the nature and progress of harmonization in the European Community. There follow sections on the work of the IASC and other international bodies.

5.1 Reasons for, obstacles to and measurement of harmonization

Reasons

It is increasingly the case that the products of accounting in one country are used in various other countries. Consequently, some of the reasons that make national accounting standards desirable also apply internationally. The pressure for international harmonization comes from those who regulate, prepare and use financial statements. We will now look at their interests more closely.

1. *Investors and financial analysts* need to be able to understand the financial statements of foreign companies whose shares they might wish to buy. They would like to be sure that statements from different countries are reliable and comparable, or at least to be clear about the nature and magnitude of the differences. They also need confidence in the soundness of the auditing.

2. *The United Nations and the European Community*. For the above reason, various intergovernmental transnational bodies from the EC Commission to the United Nations (UN) are interested, among other things, in protecting investors within their spheres of influence. Also, in cases where foreign shares are quoted on the domestic stock exchange of an investor, that stock exchange will often demand financial statements that are consistent with domestic practices. In addition, those companies that wish to issue new shares more widely than on their domestic markets will see the advantages of standardized practices in the promotion of their issues.

3. *Multinationals*. These pressures will also be felt by companies that do not operate multinationally. However, for multinationals, the advantages of harmonization are much more important. The great effort of financial accountants to prepare and consolidate financial statements would be much simplified if statements from all round the world were prepared on the same basis. Similarly, the task of preparing comparable internal information for the appraisal of the performance of subsidiaries in different countries would be made much easier. Many aspects of investment appraisal, performance evaluation and other decision-making uses of management accounting information would benefit from harmonization. The appraisal of foreign companies for potential take-overs would also be greatly facilitated. Multinational companies would also find it easier to transfer accounting staff from one country to another.

4. *Accountancy firms*. A fourth group that would benefit from harmonization are the international accountancy firms. Many of the clients of the large accountancy firms have at least one foreign subsidiary or branch. The preparation, consolidation

and auditing of these companies' financial statements would become less onerous if accounting practices were harmonized. Also, the accountancy firms would benefit from the added mobility of staff.

5. *Tax authorities* throughout the world have their work greatly complicated when dealing with foreign incomes by differences in the measurement of profit in different countries. It should be admitted, however, that revenue authorities have caused many of the differences, for example, the influence of tax on much of continental European accounting and the use of LIFO in the United States (see Chapter 4).

6. *Other groups*. Governments in developing countries might find it easier to understand and control the operations of multinationals if financial reporting were harmonized, particularly as this would imply greater disclosure in some cases. International credit grantors like the World Bank must also face the difficulties of comparison. Other organizations that would benefit from greater international comparability of company information are labour unions who face multinational employers. All these groups might benefit from harmonization.

Obstacles

The most fundamental of obstacles to harmonization is the size of the present differences between the accounting practices of different countries. Using the type of classifications of accounting systems discussed in Chapter 4, there are several significant differences even within the Anglo-Saxon class, let alone between that class and the Franco-German. These latter differences go to the root of the reasons for the preparation of accounting information. The general dichotomy between shareholder/fair-view presentation and creditor/tax/conservative presentation is an obstacle that cannot be overcome without major changes in attitudes and law.

Indeed, it is not clear that it *should be* overcome. If the predominant purposes of financial reporting vary by country it seems reasonable that the reporting should vary. However, harmonization is concerned with similar users who receive information from companies in different countries. That is, harmonization seems necessary within a single market. Perhaps the relevant companies should be required to produce two sets of financial statements: one for domestic and another for international consumption. This is discussed further in Section 5.7.

Another obstacle is the lack of strong professional accountancy bodies in some countries. This means that any body such as the IASC, which seeks to operate through national accountancy bodies, will not be effective in all countries. The alternative to this, a world-wide enforcement agency, is also lacking. The EC Commission may prove to be such an agency for one part of the world, as is discussed in the second half of this chapter.

A further problem is nationalism. This may show itself in an unwillingness to accept compromises that involve changing accounting practices towards those of other countries. This unwillingness may exist on the part of accountants and companies or on the part of states who may not wish to lose their sovereignty.

Another manifestation of nationalism may be the lack of knowledge or interest in accounting elsewhere. A rather more subtle and acceptable variety of this is the concern that it would be difficult to alter internationally set standards in response to a change of mind or a change of local or international circumstances.

These are the major general obstacles to international harmonization. The following sections look at the progress of several organizations in overcoming them. Many harmonizing agencies have already been discussed in this chapter, and discussion of a few more will follow. Before launching into further detail, it will be useful to classify agencies by authority and by geographical scope, as in Table 5.1. This table is not exhaustive; as we shall see, there are other regional bodies.

Measurement

It is possible to distinguish between *de jure* harmonization (that of rules, standards, etc.) and *de facto* harmonization (that of corporate financial reporting practices). For any particular topic or set of countries it is possible to have one of these two forms of harmonization without the other. For example, countries or companies may ignore the harmonized rules of standard-setters or even law-makers. By contrast, market forces persuade many companies in Sweden, Switzerland or Spain to produce English-language financial reports that approximately follow Anglo-American practice.

Mutual recognition

A related issue is mutual recognition whereby, for example, the stock exchange authorities of two countries would accept each other's accounting (or auditing) rules for prospectuses or annual reports of each other's companies. The United States and Canada have achieved this, but they have very similar rules.

The EC Commission and particularly German multinationals are keen on this route. For example, until 1993, no German company was listed on the New York

Table 5.1 Classification of some accounting harmonizers.

	World	Regional
Government	UN, OECD	EC
Professional	IASC	FEE

Stock Exchange because they were unwilling to obey the accounting rules and to provide the disclosures demanded by the Securities and Exchange Commission. A number of companies from other European countries are New York listed and have to provide supplementary information according to US rules. In 1993, Daimler-Benz reached an agreement with the SEC, and will now be listed after changing some accounting practices and providing some extra disclosures.

The problem with mutual recognition is that it pretends that the accounting differences are not important. It is a political 'solution' to a serious technical problem. To the extent that mutual recognition proceeds without prior harmonization of rules, then the former is the enemy of harmonization because it reduces the commercial pressure for it from multinational companies.

5.2 EC harmonization

Reasons for and obstacles to EC harmonization

The objects of the Treaty of Rome (1957) include the establishment of the free movement of persons, goods and services, and capital. This involves the elimination of customs duties, the imposition of common tariffs to third countries and the establishment of procedures to permit the coordination of economic policies. More specifically, the ECs Common Industrial Policy (1970) calls for the creation of a unified business environment, including the harmonization of company law and taxation, and the creation of a common capital market.

The reasoning behind these objectives includes the fact that the activities of companies extend beyond national frontiers, and that shareholders and others need protection throughout the European Community. In order to achieve this and to encourage the movement of capital, it is necessary to create a flow of reliable homogeneous financial information about companies from all parts of the European Community. Further, since companies in different EC countries exist in the same form and are in competition with each other, it is argued that they should be subject to the same laws and taxation.

The obstacles to harmonization of financial reporting and company law have been discussed earlier in this chapter. Of particular importance here are the fundamental differences between the various national accounting systems in the European Community. They include the differences between creditor/secrecy in the Franco-German systems and investor/disclosure in the Anglo-Dutch systems; between law/tax-based rules and professionally set standards. These large differences have contributed towards the great variations in the size and strength of the profession. The smaller and less influential professional bodies in Franco-German countries would be an obstacle to movements towards accounting and auditing of an Anglo-Dutch type (see Chapter 4).

Directives and Regulations

The EC Commission achieves its harmonizing objectives through two main instruments: Directives, which must be incorporated into the laws of member states; and Regulations, which become law throughout the European Community without the need to pass through national legislatures. The concern of this section will be with the Directives on company law and with two Regulations. These are listed in Table 5.2 with a brief description of their scope. The company law Directives of most relevance to accounting are the Fourth and Seventh (see also Chapter 12 for the latter). The Fourth Directive will be discussed in more detail below, after an outline of the procedure for setting Directives. In addition to the Directives listed in Table 5.2, there are several others of relevance to accounting, e.g. the special versions of the Fourth Directive for banks and for insurance companies.

First, the Commission, which is the EC permanent civil service, decides on a project and asks an expert to prepare a report. In the case of the Fourth Directive, this was the Elmendorff Report of 1967. Then an *avant projet* or discussion document is prepared. This is studied by a Commission working party and may lead to the issue of a draft Directive which is commented on by the European Parliament (a directly elected assembly with limited powers) and the Economic and Social Committee (a consultative body of employers, employees and others). A revised proposal is then submitted to a working party of the Council of Ministers. The Council, consisting of the relevant ministers from each EC country, decide whether a Directive or Regulation is to be adopted. In the case of a Directive, member states are required to introduce a national law within a specified period, though they often exceed it, as discussed below in the case of the Fourth Directive.

The Fourth Directive

The exact effects of any Directive on a particular country will depend upon the laws passed by national legislatures. For example, there are dozens of provisions in the Fourth Directive which begin with such expressions as 'member states may require or permit companies to...'. Given this flexibility, the effects on the accounting of different countries have been included in the relevant topic chapters of Part III. However, it seems appropriate to consider here the general outline of the Directive and the process whereby it took its ultimate form. The content of the Directive is considered in more detail in the following section. The complete Directive is reprinted in the appendix to this book.

The Directive covers public and private companies in all EC countries. Its articles include those referring to valuation rules, formats of published financial statements and disclosure requirements. It does not cover consolidation, which is left to the Seventh Directive. The Fourth Directive's first draft was published in 1971, before the United Kingdom, Ireland and Denmark (let alone Greece, Spain or Portugal)

Table 5.2 EC Directives and Regulations relevant to corporate accounting (to mid-1993).

Directives on company law	Draft dates	Date adopted	Topic
First	1964	1968	*Ultra vires* rules
Second	1970, 1972	1976	Separation of public companies, minimum capital, distributions
Third	1970, 1973, 1975	1978	Mergers
Fourth	1971, 1974	1978	Formats and rules of accounting
Fifth	1972, 1983		Structure, management and audit of companies
Sixth	1978	1982	De-mergers
Seventh	1976, 1978	1983	Consolidated accounting
Eighth	1978	1984	Qualifications and work of auditors
Ninth	—		Links between public company groups
Tenth	1985		International mergers of public companies
Eleventh	1986	1989	Disclosures about branches
Twelfth	1988	1989	Single member company
Thirteenth	1989		Take-overs
Vredeling	1980, 1983		Employee information and consultation
Regulations			
Societas Europea	1970, 1975, 1989		European company subject to EC laws
European Economic Interest Grouping	1973, 1978	1985	Business form for multinational joint ventures

had entered the European Community or had representatives on the *Groupe d'Etudes*. This initial draft was heavily influenced by German company law, particularly the *Aktiengesetz* of 1965. Consequently, for example, valuation rules were to be conservative, and formats were to be prescribed in detail. Financial statements were to obey the provisions of the Directive.

The influence of Anglo-Saxon thinking on the EC Commission, Parliament and Groupe d'Etudes was such that a much amended draft was issued in 1974. This introduced the concept of the 'true and fair view'. Another change by 1974 was that some flexibility of presentation had been introduced. This process continued and, by the promulgation of the finalized Directive, the 'true and fair view' was established as a predominant principle in the preparation of financial statements (Article 2, paragraph 2–5). In addition, the four basic principles (accruals, prudence, consistency and going concern) were made clearer than they had been in the 1974 draft (Article 31).

More rearrangement and summarization of items in the financial statements were made possible (Article 4). There were also calls for more notes in the 1974 draft than the 1971 draft, and more in the final Directive than in the 1974 draft (Articles 43–46). Another concern of Anglo-Dutch accountants has been with the effect of taxation on Franco-German accounts. The extra disclosures called for by the 1974 draft about the effect of taxation are included in the final Directive (Articles 30 and 35).

The fact that member states may permit or require a type of inflation accounting is treated in more detail than in the 1974 draft (Article 33). As a further accommodation of Anglo-Dutch opinion, a 'Contact Committee' of EC and national civil servants is provided for. This was intended to answer the criticism that the Directive will give rise to laws that are not flexible to changing circumstances and attitudes. The Committee looks at practical problems arising from the implementation of the Directive, and makes suggestions for amendments (Article 52). In 1991, a Forum of EC accounting rule-makers was established by the Commission to investigate amendments or extensions to Directives.

The Fourth Directive was supposed to be enacted in member states by July 1980 and to be in force by January 1982. No country managed the former date, as may be seen in Table 5.3. Dates of effects on annual reports are, of course, somewhat later than the dates of implementation as law. For example, for companies with 31 December year ends, the Fourth Directive came into force for annual reports of 1984 in France, 1987 in Germany, 1990 in Spain and 1993 in Italy.

The next section looks at some detailed examples of the content of the Directives.

Other Directives

The Second Directive concerns a number of matters connected with share capital and the differences between public and private companies. For example, the Directive requires all member states to have separate legal structures for public and

Table 5.3 Implementation of accounting Directives as laws.

	Fourth	Seventh
Denmark	1981	1990
United Kingdom	1981	1989
France	1983	1985
Netherlands	1983	1988
Luxembourg	1984	1988
Belgium	1985	1990
West Germany	1985	1985
Greece	1986	1987
Ireland	1986	1992
Portugal	1989	1991
Spain	1989	1989
Italy	1991	1991

private companies and to have separate names for the companies. Table 5.4 shows the company names in the European Community. A public company, in this context, is one that is legally allowed to have a market in its securities, although it does not need to have. For example, many PLCs, SAs or AGs are not listed. It is important to note that 'public' in this sense means neither listed nor anything to do with government. The implementation of the Directive led to the creation of the BV in the Netherlands and to the invention of the label 'PLC' in the United Kingdom.

The draft Fifth Directive and the draft Vredeling Directive concern attempts by the Commission to improve the involvement of employees in companies. There are proposals for informing employees and consulting them on important matters, and for employee involvement in the management of public companies. The Seventh Directive concerns consolidated accounting, and is considered in Chapter 12. The Eighth Directive was watered down from its original draft which might have greatly affected the training patterns and scope of work of accountants. However, its main effect now is to decide on who is allowed to audit accounts in certain countries that have small numbers of accountants, such as Germany.

Regulations

One of the draft Regulations shown in Table 5.2 concerns a totally new type of company that will be registered as an EC company and will be subject to EC laws. It will be called the *Societas Europea* (SE). However, despite continued pressure from the Commission, progress has been very slow, partly because member states may not wish to lose sovereignty over companies operating in their countries, and

Table 5.4 EC company names.

	Private	Public
Denmark	Anspartsselkab (ApS)	Aktieselskab (AS)
Belgium, France, Luxembourg	Société à responsibilité limitée (Sarl)	Société anonyme (SA)
Germany	Gesellschaft mit beschränkter Haftung (GmbH)	Aktiengessellschaft (AG)
Greece	Etairia periorismenis efthynis (EPE)	Anonymos etairia (AE)
Italy	Societá a responsibilità limitata (SRL)	Società per azioni (SpA)
Netherlands, Belgium	Besloten vennootschap (BV)	Naamloze vennootschap (NV)
Portugal	Sociedade por quotas (Lda)	Sociedade anónima (SA)
Spain	Sociedad de responsibilidad limitada (SRL)	Sociedad anónima (SA)
United Kingdom, Ireland	Private limited company (Ltd)	Public limited company (PLC)

partly because member states have found it difficult to agree upon a company structure with respect to worker participation on boards of directors.

It was easier to agree upon proposals for a form of joint venture organization for EC companies. The Regulation on the 'European Economic Interest Grouping' is based on the successful French business form, the *groupement d'intérêt économique* – as used, for example, by Airbus Industrie. It provides a corporate organization which can be smaller and of shorter duration than the SE. Members of a Grouping are autonomous profit-making entities, whereas the Grouping itself provides joint facilities or enables a combination for a specific purpose.

5.3 The Fourth Directive examined

Survey of contents

Article 1 states that the directive relates to public and private companies throughout the European Community, except that member states need not apply the provisions to banks, insurance companies and other financial institutions (for whom a special version of the Fourth Directive has been prepared). Article 2 defines the annual accounts to which it refers as the balance sheet, profit and loss account, and notes. Reference to cash flow or funds flow statements, which are standard in the United Kingdom and some other countries, is omitted. The accounts 'shall be drawn up clearly and in accordance with the provisions' of the directive, except that the need to present a 'true and fair view' may require extra information or may demand a departure from the provisions of the directive. Such departures must be disclosed. The Directive is intended to establish minimum standards, and 'Member States may authorize or require' extra disclosure.

Articles 3–7 contain general provisions about the consistency and detail of the formats for financial statements. There is a specified order of items, and some items cannot be combined or omitted. Corresponding figures for the previous year must be shown. Articles 8–10 detail two formats for balance sheets, one or both of which may be allowed by member states. The Articles allow some combination and omission of immaterial items, but the outline and much detail will be standard.

Articles 11 and 12 allow member states to permit small companies to publish considerably abridged balance sheets. 'Small companies' are those falling below two of the following limits: balance sheet total, 1m units of account (UA); turnover, 2m UA; employees, 50. There is also the possibility of lesser reductions for medium-sized companies (see Articles 27 and 47). These size limits are capable of being raised, and this happened in 1984 and 1990. Articles 13 and 14 concern details of disclosure, particularly of contingent liabilities, which were shown in the United Kingdom but not in some other countries. Articles 15–21 concern the definition and disclosure of assets and liabilities. It is useful that 'value adjustments' must be disclosed (Article 15(3)(a)); this might make clearer the comparatively conservative revaluations that are common in Franco-German systems.

Articles 22–26 specify four formats for profit and loss accounts, which member states may allow companies to choose between. Two of these classify expenses and revenues by nature, and the other two classify them by stage of production. There are two in each case because vertical or two-sided versions may be chosen. (There is a discussion on formats later.) However, Article 27 allows member states to permit medium-sized companies to avoid disclosure of the items making up gross profit. In this case the limits were: balance sheet total, 4m UA; turnover, 8m UA; employees, 250. Articles 28–30 contain some definitions relating to the profit and loss accounts.

Articles 31 and 32 set out general rules of valuation. The normal principles of accounting (including the accruals convention) are promulgated. Article 33 is a fairly lengthy series of member state options on accounting for inflation or for specific price changes. Whatever happens, member states must ensure that historical cost information is either shown or can be calculated using notes to the accounts. However, member states may permit or require supplementary or main accounts to be prepared on a replacement value, current purchasing power or other basis. Revaluation of assets would entail a balancing revaluation reserve; there are detailed requirements relating to this.

Articles 34–42 relate to detailed valuation and disclosure requirements for various balance sheet items. Again the point about the disclosure of 'exceptional value adjustments' is made, this time with specific reference to taxation-induced writings down (Articles 35(1)(d) and 39(1)(e)). The periods over which research and development expenditure and goodwill are written off are to be standardized (Article 37).

Articles 43–46 concern the large number of disclosures that are obligatory in the annual report, including the notes to the accounts. 'Small companies' (as in Article 11) may be partially exempted. Articles 47–51 relate to the audit and publication of accounts. In general, procedures for these matters may remain as they were under different national laws. Member states may exempt 'small companies' from publishing profit and loss accounts (Article 47(2)(b)) and from audit (Article 51). This would mean that they would only produce unaudited abridged balance sheets. Article 47(3) allows members states to permit 'medium-sized companies' (as in Article 27) to abridge their balance sheets and notes. However, this abridgement is not as extensive as that for 'small companies', and audit and profit and loss accounts are necessary.

Articles 52–62 deal with the implementation of the directive and with transitional problems, particularly those relating to consolidation, which awaited the Seventh Directive. A 'Contact Committee' was to be set up to facilitate the application of the Directive and to advise on amendments or additions. Article 55 called for member states to pass the necessary laws within two years of the July 1978 notification, and then to bring these into force within a further 18 months.

The example of formats

As an example of the evolution and effect of the Fourth Directive's provisions, the formats of financial statements will be examined here.

Compared with traditional Anglo-Dutch accounting, the most obvious feature of the *Aktiengesetz*, and thus of the Fourth Directive and hence the UK Companies Act 1981 and Dutch 1983 Act, is the prescription of uniform formats. Understanding the evolution of the Fourth Directive must involve a study of previous German law. German state intervention, as opposed to Anglo-Dutch *laisser-faire*, has been established for many years and covers accounting and company law. Perhaps because of the importance of banks and creditors, and the lack of importance of individual shareholders, German interest in accounting has been concentrated on the protection of creditors and on cost accounting, not on published financial statements for shareholders.

Some of the German history of uniform formats has been examined in Chapter 4. This had its culmination in the *Aktiengesetz* (AktG) of 1965 which laid down formats in its sections 151 and 157. The AktG offered no choice between formats, nor any substantial flexibility within a format. As might have been expected, there was considerable difficulty in arriving at agreed formats for the first draft of the Fourth Directive, even among the six member states belonging to the European Community in 1971. This shows itself in the inclusion in the Directive of two balance sheet formats and four profit and loss account formats. These remained largely unaltered in the second draft and the final Directive. (Incidentally, the English version of the Directive uses the normal British term 'profit and loss account' rather than 'income statement'.)

Looking first at the balance sheet, AktG § 151 was reproduced with slight amendment as Article 8 of the 1971 draft of the Fourth Directive (see Table 5.5). This is a two-sided (or horizontal) balance sheet with assets on the left. The only significant change between the 1971 draft and those of 1974 and 1978 (in the latter it becomes Article 9) is in the classification of reserves. (The Fourth Directive is reprinted in the Appendix.) The AktG and the 1971 draft Directive show profits as the last item on the *credit* side of the balance sheet, and losses as the last item on the *debit* side. Such a treatment of profits fits better with a creditor's or entity view rather than a proprietor's view: 'it contains no implications that ... the proprietors possess any particular lien' (Edwards, 1981). This had been the presentation shown in the British 1856 Act, and was common in Britain before the Second World War. Perhaps 'it reflects the mechanical approach to accounts construction then prevailing' (Edwards, 1981).

In the final Directive, however, a more Anglo-Dutch approach to reserves is adopted. Format 2 of the UK 1981 (and now 1985) Act (see Table 5.5) follows that of the Directive, except for permitted deletions such as formation expenses, which was a necessary heading for practice in some countries. Table 5.5 illustrates the gradual and slight changes in the formats over the sixteen-year period. It shows only the first two levels of headings. A third level of subheadings is omitted here, but does exist for each case.

However, it should not be supposed that balance sheets throughout the European Community look like the expanded version of this format. There are several reasons why this is not the case. First, the Directive contains another format (Article 9 of the 1971 and 1974 drafts, which became Article 10 in the 1978 version). The British version of this is shown in Table 5.6, and is a vertical or statement form of the format in Table 5.5. Member states are allowed to adopt one format or to permit companies to make the choice, as long as they are consistent. The UK and Dutch Acts do the latter, and present the vertical form as 'Format 1' and 'Format A' respectively, presumably on the grounds that this format corresponded much more closely with existing UK and Dutch practice for published accounts (at least those of large companies). However, the French revised *plan comptable* (for individual company accounts) and the German law of 1985 allow only the horizontal format. The vertical format contains broadly the same headings, subheadings and sub-subheadings as the horizontal format, except that current liabilities are shown separately and positioned so as to enable a calculation of net current assets and then net assets.

Second, there are several ways in which flexibility is allowed. The AktG in § 151 permitted:

(a) different classifications for particular trades,
(b) extra detail to be added, and
(c) empty headings to be omitted.

Table 5.5 The evolution of the balance sheet (abbreviated versions).

AktG (§ 151)	1971 Draft (Art. 8)	1981 British Act (Format 2)
Assets (shown on left)		
I. Unpaid capital	(A) Unpaid capital	(A) Unpaid capital
—	(B) Formation expenses	—
II. Fixed and financial (A) Fixed and intangible (B) Financial	(C) Fixed assets I. Intangible II. Tangible III. Participations	(B) Fixed assets I. Intangible II. Tangible III. Investments
III. Current assets (A) Stocks (B) Other current	(D) Current assets I. Stocks II. Debtors III. Securities	(C) Current assets I. Stocks II. Debtors III. Investments IV. Cash
IV. Deferred charges	(E) Prepayments	(D) Prepayments
V. Accumulated losses	(F) Loss I. For the year II. Brought forward	—
Liabilities and capital (shown on right)		
I. Share capital	(A) Subscribed capital	(A) Capital and reserves I. Called-up capital
II. Disclosed reserves	(B) Reserves	II. Share premium III. Revaluation reserve IV. Other reserves V. Profit and loss
III. Provisions for diminutions	(C) Value adjustments	—
IV. Provisions for liabilities	(D) Provisions for charges	(B) Provisions for liabilities and charges
V. Liabilities (4 years +)	(E) Creditors	(C) Creditors
VI. Other liabilities	—	—
VII. Deferred income	(F) Accruals	(D) Accruals
VIII. Profit	(G) Profit I. For the year II. Brought forward	—

Table 5.6 **Balance sheet format 1 from the British Companies Act 1985.**

(A) *Called-up share capital not paid*

(B) Fixed Assets
  I. Intangible assets
     1. Development costs
     2. Concessions, patents, licences, trade marks and similar rights and assets
     3. Goodwill
     4. *Payments on account*
  II. Tangible assets
     1. Land and buildings
     2. Plant and machinery
     3. Fixtures, fittings, tools and equipment
     4. *Payments on account and assets in course of construction*
  III. Investments
     1. *Shares in group companies*
     2. *Loans to group companies*
     3. *Shares in related companies*
     4. *Loans to related companies*
     5. Other investments other than loans
     6. Other loans
     7. *Other shares*

(C) Current assets
  I. Stocks
     1. Raw materials and consumables
     2. Work in progress
     3. Finished goods and goods for resale
     4. *Payments on account*
  II. Debtors
     1. Trade debtors
     2. *Amounts owed by group companies*
     3. *Amounts owed by related companies*
     4. Other debtors
     5. Called-up share capital not paid
     6. Prepayments and accrued income
  III. Investments
     1. *Shares in group companies*
     2. *Own shares*
     3. Other investments
  IV. Cash at bank and in hand

(D) *Prepayments and accrued income*

(E) Creditors: amounts falling due within one year
  1. Debenture loans
  2. Bank loans and overdrafts
  3. Payments received on account
  4. Trade creditors
  5. Bills of exchange payable
  6. *Amounts owed to group companies*
  7. *Amounts owed to related companies*
  8. Other creditors including taxation and social security
  9. Accruals and deferred income

(F) Net current assets (liabilities)

(G) Total assets less current liabilities

(H) Creditors: amounts falling due after more than one year
  1. Debenture loans
  2. Bank loans and overdrafts
  3. Payments received on account
  4. Trade creditors
  5. Bills of exchange payable
  6. *Amounts owed to group companies*
  7. *Amounts owed to related companies*
  8. Other creditors including taxation and social security
  9. Accruals and deferred income

(I) Provision for liabilities and charges
  1. Pensions and similar obligations
  2. Taxation, including deferred taxation
  3. Other provisions

(J) *Accruals and deferred income*

(K) Capital and reserves
  I. Called-up share capital
  II. Share premium account
  III. Revaluation reserve
  IV. Other reserves
     1. Capital redemption reserve
     2. Reserve for own shares
     3. Reserves provided for by the articles of association
     4. Other reserves
  V. Profit and loss account

The Directive contains these provisions, and also allows arabic number headings to be combined where the amounts are separately immaterial or where this would lead to greater clarity (in this latter case, the information must be shown by note) (Article 4).

Third, more flexibility exists within the Directive's formats, which was not present in the AktG. This takes the form of several alternative presentations of particular items, in addition to the deletions of empty headings mentioned above (e.g. formation expenses in the United Kingdom). For example, referring to Table 5.6, unpaid capital (A) may be (and, in the United Kingdom, is) shown under debtors (C,II,5). Similarly, prepayments (D) may be shown under debtors (C,11,6), and accruals (J) may be shown under creditors (E,9 and H,9). Indeed, unless this latter option which involves showing 'current' accruals under 'current' creditors is taken, either the balance sheet will not articulate arithmetically (i.e. F will not equal $C + D - E$) or the total F will not be equal to net current assets. This is a good illustration of the uneasy results of compromising away from the original pure format of the AktG.

As an example of national implementation, taking the most British options and assuming that certain items will be immaterial or may be removed to notes, might mean that the italicized items in Table 5.6 will not appear in many UK balance sheets. Naturally, the letters and numerals will also be omitted. Also, given that one is concerned with a consolidated balance sheet, further items have been italicized; but a heading would need to be inserted for 'minority interests'. The lack of references to, or suitable headings for, consolidation in the Directive can only be explained by referring back to continental Europe where consolidation had traditionally been rare; although it was demanded for German AG companies for domestic subsidiaries in the AktG. The implementation of the Seventh Directive changes this.

Another feature that may require explanation for Anglo-Dutch accountants is the omission of proposed dividends (as current liabilities in the balance sheet, and as appropriations 'below the line' in the profit and loss account). Again, the explanation lies in the predominant, 'legal' continental view of proposed dividends as amounts not established at the balance sheet date because they require the later approval of the shareholders. In the case of the United Kingdom, the Companies Act specifically requires companies to adjust the profit and loss account for this. There is no specific instruction to adjust the balance sheet. Thus, proposed dividends may be shown separately under creditors or may be included under some other headings.

The appendix to this chapter examines national choices of balance sheet formats in the European Community.

Turning now to the profit and loss account, there was one format only in the AktG (§ 157), but four in each of the versions of the Directive. The format in the AktG contains thirty-two headings, whereas the nearest to it (Article 20 in 1971 and 1974, Article 23 in 1978) contains about twenty headings (see the Directive in the appendix to this book, and a discussion of national practice in the appendix to this chapter). These are statement formats, which combine together expenses and revenues by their financial accounting nature, for example, all salaries together and all depreciation together. In French, these formats are called *par nature*. They might be called 'total output' formats, as this could be a label for the total of lines 1 to 3.

This Germanic format might also be said to be production-oriented; it compares input with output (not sales with cost of sales), and this is perhaps more the view of a business economist than an accountant. Thus, the turnover is adjusted for changes in stocks and for the construction of fixed assets. The effect is reminiscent of a value-added statement, and might seem attractive to some users as a compromise between that and a traditional profit and loss account. This is called 'format E' in the Netherlands and 'format 2' in the British Act; it is also used in two-sided form for individual French accounts; and is one of the options in the 1985 Act in Germany.

The alternative that is the most popular in the United Kingdom is shown in the Directive as Article 24. This is also a vertical statement format and is identical to the *par nature* version from line 7, but is sales-oriented and combines expenses by stage of production. This is called 'format F' in the Netherlands, and is allowed in Germany. It is called *par destination* in French, and might be called a gross profit format. The remaining two formats in the Directive are two-sided versions with charges (i.e. *debits*) on the left and income (i.e. *credits*) on the right.

The provisions relating to flexibility are the same as for the balance sheet, and one might note that all the headings in the profit and loss accounts are preceded by arabic numbers. In the United Kingdom, the law requires the inclusion of items for dividends, movements on reserves and pretax profit. Other items, like 'minority's share of profit' may be added. Overall, profit and loss accounts in most countries have become much more detailed, with the disclosure of the constituent parts of gross profit. A summary of formats for some EC countries is shown in the appendix to this chapter.

The example of accounting 'principles'

Anglo-Dutch financial reporting has traditionally been free of legal constraints in the area of principles of valuation and measurement, whether from company law, tax law or accounting plan. However, this is far from the case in some other EC countries, especially Germany whose 1965 *Aktiengesetz* was a major source of the Fourth Directive. There are three levels of principle in the AktG, in the Directive and in the resulting laws of member states. The first and 'vaguest' level consists of a statement of the overriding purpose of the financial statements. In the AktG (§ 149), this overriding purpose was to obey the provisions of the law. By the final 1978 version of the Directive, the overriding purpose had become to give a true and fair view. The evolution of this may be seen in Table 5.7. Pressure from Anglo-Dutch countries had caused its insertion in the 1974 draft and its dominance in the

Table 5.7 'True and fair' in the Fourth Directive.

1965 Aktiengesetz (§ 149)

1. The annual financial statements shall conform to proper accounting principles. They shall be clear and well set out and give as sure a view of the company's financial position and its operating results as is possible pursuant to the valuation provisions.

1971 Draft (Art 2)

1. The annual accounts shall comprise the balance sheet, the profit and loss account and the notes on the accounts. These documents shall constitute a composite whole.
2. The annual accounts shall conform to the principles of regular and proper accounting.
3. They shall be drawn up clearly and, in the content of the provisions regarding the valuation of assets and liabilities and the lay-out of accounts, shall reflect as accurately as possible the company's assets, liabilities, financial position and results.

1974 Draft (Art 2)

1. (As 1971 Draft)
2. The annual accounts shall give a true and fair view of the company's assets, liabilities, financial position and results.
3. They shall be drawn up clearly and in conformity with the provisions of this directive.

1978 Final (Art 2)

1. (As 1971 Draft)
2. They shall be drawn up clearly and in accordance with the provisions of this Directive.
3. The annual accounts shall give a true and fair view of the company's assets, liabilities, financial position and profit or loss.
4. Where the application of the provisions of this Directive would not be sufficient to give a true and fair view within the meaning of paragraph 3, additional information must be given.
5. Where in exceptional cases the application of a provision of this Directive is incompatible with the obligation laid down in paragraph 3, that provision must be departed from in order to give a true and fair view within the meaning of paragraph 3. Any such departure must be disclosed in the notes on the accounts together with an explanation of the reasons for it and a statement of its effect on the assets, liabilities, financial position and profit or loss. The Member States may define the exceptional cases in question and lay down the relevant special rules.
6. The Member States may authorize or require the disclosure in the annual accounts of other information as well as that which must be disclosed in accordance with this Directive.

Directive in special circumstances. It should be noted that neither the concept nor the special circumstances are defined.

Implementation of the 'true and fair' concept has been interpreted in different ways in different countries, both linguistically and philosophically.

1. *Language.* The expression 'true and fair view' (TFV) has found its way into the laws of the twelve EC member states in the way shown in Table 5.8. Four countries have an apparently dual concept (e.g. true *and* fair), whereas eight have a unitary concept (following the French *fidèle* and Dutch *getrouw*). Recent investigation (Parker and Nobes, 1991) in the United Kingdom suggests that financial directors of large companies see TFV as unitary, whereas their auditors see it as dual: approximately, 'truth' is taken to mean that the accounts are in accordance with the facts, and 'fairness' that they are not misleading.

In all languages, except Greek, the indefinite article is used, leading to the conclusion that a number of different financial statements could all give *a* true and fair view of any particular state of affairs or profit or loss. It is not clear that the British parliament intended this nor that the Greek one intended the opposite.

2. *Philosophy.* Accountants and lawyers in continental countries were, of course, aware of the forthcoming need to implement the TFV from at least the publication of the draft Directive of 1974. It was a topic of conversation at international meetings and even of specific European conferences in the 1970s and 1980s. The idea that law should be departed from as a result of the opinion of directors and auditors is hard to accept; even for 'English' lawyers let alone for 'Roman' lawyers.

Table 5.8 **True and fair view.**

UK (1947) Ireland (1963)	true and fair view
Netherlands (1970) Belgium (1985)	getrouw beeld
Denmark (1981)	retvisende billede
France (1983) Luxembourg (1984) Belgium (1985)	image fidèle (getrouw beeld)
Germany (1985)	ein den tatsächlichen Verhältnissen entsprechendes Bild
Greece (1986)	pragmatiki ikona
Spain (1989)	imagen fiel
Portugal (1989)	imagem verdadeira e apropriada
Italy (1991)	in modo veritiero e corretto

The national stances towards the implementation of the Directive may also be classified into five types:

Case I TFV is used by directors/auditors in interpreting the law and standards or where there is no law or standard, and sometimes to override the law or standards. TFV can also be used by standard-setters to make rules that override details of the law. (UK, Ireland)

Case II TFV (and 'insight') is used by directors/auditors as the basic principle in interpreting the law and guidelines. It can be used by them to override guidelines and, potentially, in exceptional cases, the law. It is also used by guideline-setters to make rules but not to override the law. (Netherlands)

Case III The arrival of TFV was used by law-makers to allow some change towards 'substance' rather than 'form'. It may be used by directors/auditors to interpret governmental requirements or when there are none and, in principle, to override them in exceptional cases. (France, Spain)

Case IV TFV may be used by directors/auditors to interpret government requirements or in cases where there are no requirements. In very exceptional cases, which in practice will probably not arise, it could be used to depart from the law. (Italy)

Case V Either (a) as for the first sentence only of Case IV; or (b) TFV relates only to notes. (Germany)

5.4 Unresolved problems and future harmonization

Despite all the harmonizing work of the EC Commission and the substantial implementation programmes of most member states, much of the problem of different accounting practices remains after implementation of the Fourth Directive. Some examples follow. These can be supplemented by differences in group accounting as examined in Chapter 12.

1. *Publication and audit.* The prevalence of the requirement to publish accounts and to have external audit still varies throughout the European Community. For example, in the United Kingdom audit is universal for active limited companies, whereas it is restricted to the minority of larger companies in most EC countries.
2. *Formats and terminology.* The different national degrees of choice allowed for formats, and the resulting differences in predominant formats, may make analysis more difficult. To some extent this may seem a trivial problem, but the formats are not convertible into each other in the case of the two styles of profit and loss account (see appendix to this chapter). Terminology may also seem a trivial problem, but only a few large companies produce translations, and even these may be misleading. For untranslated accounts, added difficulties are raised for most analysts.

3. *Fixed asset valuation.* Despite the Fourth Directive, the European variations in asset valuation remain great. In the United Kingdom and the Netherlands, there is a mixture of historical and current values. In France, Italy and Spain, there are government-induced revaluations at intervals. In Germany, there is strict historical cost. This makes it difficult to compare net assets, total assets, shareholders' funds or ratios based on these.
4. *Conservatism.* Apart from fixed asset valuation, there are also other general differences in bias which have survived harmonization. For example, there is greater conservatism in German than in UK accounting.
5. *Taxation and fairness.* Dispute between tax-based values and commercial values is central to accounting, and to international comparisons. In much of continental Europe, taxation is a dominant influence on accounting numbers. This is not the case in the United Kingdom and the Netherlands, and need not be the case for French group accounts.
6. *Future EC harmonization.* In 1990 the EC Commission announced that there would be no more major Directives on accounting. This is partly in recognition of the slowness of the programme (e.g. see Table 5.3) and partly that the resulting laws are inflexible to economic and other developments.

At the same time, an EC Forum was established to discuss remaining major differences. Topics such as leasing, long-term contracts and currency translation were examined in the early 1990s. However, the Forum has unclear purposes and effects.

There is also a Contact Committee set up by the Fourth Directive. However, it too seems unlikely to lead to changes in the Directives or to any other practically important result. Consequently, future change in the European Community may be driven by commercial pressures, perhaps aided by the IASC.

5.5 The International Accounting Standards Committee

History and purpose of the IASC

Of the many bodies working for international standardization looked at in this chapter, the IASC is perhaps the most important and the most successful (apart from the EC bodies which operate in a more restricted area). The IASC was founded in 1973 and has a small secretariat based in London. The original members were the accountancy bodies of nine countries: Australia, Canada, France, Japan, Mexico, the Netherlands, the United Kingdom and Ireland,[1] the United States and West Germany. Most of these, plus three other countries make up the main board of IASC (Table 5.9). In 1993, there were about 100 member accountancy bodies from about 80 countries.

---

[1] As one 'country'.

Table 5.9 **Board members of IASC, 1993.**

Australia	Netherlands
Canada	Nordic Federation of Public Accountants
France	
Germany	South Africa
India	United Kingdom
Italy	United States
Japan	International Coordinating Committee of Financial Analysts Associations
Jordan	

The aim of the IASC is 'to formulate and publish in the public interest accounting standards to be observed in the presentation of financial statements and to promote their worldwide acceptance and observance' (IASC, 1982;[2] the word 'basic' preceded the words 'accounting standards' in the original 1973 version). The member bodies of IASC agree to support the standards and to use 'their best endeavours' to ensure that published financial statements comply with the standards; to ensure that auditors enforce this; and to persuade governments, stock exchanges and other bodies to back the standards.

The standards

A list of IASC standards is shown in Table 5.10. These are preceded by exposure drafts prepared by subcommittees of the board. In order to be published, an exposure draft must be approved by a two-thirds majority of the board. A subsequent standard must be approved by a three-quarters majority.

It is the countries influenced by the Anglo-American tradition that are most familiar with setting accounting standards and are most likely to be able to adopt them professionally. It is not surprising, then, that the working language of the IASC is English, that its secretariat is in London, that nearly all the chairmen[3] and secretaries-general have been from countries using Anglo-American or Dutch accounting, and that most standards closely follow or compromise between US and UK standards.

Consequently, the IASCs standards generally allow a range of practices, and are therefore more flexible than the standards of many countries. For example, research and development expenditure may be carried forward according to IAS 9 under

---

[2] 'Preface to Statements of International Accounting Standards'.
[3] There was a French chairman for part of the 1980s and a Japanese one for part of the 1990s, but these were both partners in Arthur Andersen, the Big-Six firm which is the most clearly US-dominated.

Table 5.10 **IASC standards (to early 1994).**

Preface (revised January 1983).

Objectives and Procedures (including the constitution; revised October 1982).

IAS	1	Disclosure of accounting policies
IAS	2	Valuation and presentation of inventories in the context of the historical cost system
IAS	3	Consolidated financial statements (superseded by IASs 27 and 28)
IAS	4	Depreciation accounting
IAS	5	Information to be disclosed in financial statements
IAS	6	Accounting responses to changing prices (superseded by IAS 15)
IAS	7	Statement of changes in financial position
IAS	8	Unusual and prior period items and changes in accounting policies
IAS	9	Accounting for research and development activities
IAS	10	Contingencies and events occurring after the balance sheet date
IAS	11	Accounting for construction contracts
IAS	12	Accounting for taxes on income
IAS	13	Presentation of current assets and current liabilities
IAS	14	Reporting financial information by segment
IAS	15	Information reflecting the effects of changing prices
IAS	16	Accounting for property, plant and equipment
IAS	17	Accounting for leases
IAS	18	Revenue recognition
IAS	19	Accounting for retirement benefits in the financial statements of employers
IAS	20	Accounting for government grants and disclosure of government assistance
IAS	21	Accounting for the effects of changes in foreign exchange rates
IAS	22	Accounting for business combinations
IAS	23	Capitalization of borrowing costs
IAS	24	Related party disclosures
IAS	25	Accounting for investments
IAS	26	Accounting and reporting by retirement benefit plans
IAS	27	Consolidated financial statements and accounting for investments in subsidiaries
IAS	28	Accounting for investments in associates
IAS	29	Financial reporting in hyperinflationary economies
IAS	30	Disclosure in the financial statements of banks
IAS	31	Financial reporting of interests in joint ventures

similar conditions to those in SSAP 13 in the United Kingdom, whereas such expenditure cannot be carried forward under SFAS 2 in the United States. Similarly, IAS 12 allows partial allocation for deferred tax, like the UK's SSAP 15, whereas APB 11 in the United States requires comprehensive allocation.

The original intention of the IASC was to avoid complex detail and to concentrate on basic standards. However, the list of standards includes some, like *Related Party Disclosures*, which might not be thought to be 'basic'. Further, the contents of some standards could be criticized as being unnecessarily detailed. For example, details for the ascertainment of net realizable value (paragraphs 28–31 of IAS 2) could be thought excessive in the context of the great diversity of practice on much more fundamental matters within inventory valuation. However, in the authors' opinion, these are exceptions, and the standards in general are commendably clear in their presentation.

Important moves to reduce the options in IASC standards were begun in 1989 and are discussed below.

Enforcement

The success of member accountancy bodies' 'best endeavours' to promote the work of the IASC varies to some degree. The problem is one of enforcement. The IASC has no authority of its own and therefore must rely on that of its member professional bodies. It has been seen in Chapter 4 that the influence of professional accountancy bodies in the formulation of national accounting rules also varies widely between countries.

1. *France and Germany*. In France and Germany, for example, the *Ordre* and the *Institut* have little room (and inadequate authority) to influence accounting practice because of the strength and detail of company law and the *plan comptable*. More powerful bodies like the *Conseil national de la comptabilité* or the *Commission des opérations de bourse* are not members of the IASC.

2. *The United Kingdom*. At the other extreme, in the United Kingdom, Ireland, New Zealand and Canada, accounting standards were, until 1990, set by the professional bodies that belong to the IASC. Consequently it has been possible for the IASC standards to be introduced. Taking the United Kingdom and Ireland as an example, standards are brought into line with IASC standards wherever possible. Standards either state that compliance automatically ensures compliance with the IASC standard, or outline the differences.

3. *Italy*. There is probably some IASC influence in continental European countries. The most obvious example is in Italy, where listed companies (a small but important group) are required to follow IASC standards. This is part of a major change towards Anglo-Saxon types of financial reporting and auditing for listed and state companies in Italy.

4. *The United States of America*. In between these two extremes is the United States. The two bodies most directly concerned with the setting and enforcement of domestic standards, the FASB and the SEC, are not members of the IASC. However, the AICPA, which is the US representative on the IASC is influential. Also, the FASB is sympathetic to the work of the IASC, though it does not directly

take the IASC views into account. The FASB and the EC Commission have joined the IASCs Consultative Group.

One tell-tale sign of the problems of enforcement is the gradual weakening of the commitments required from member bodies. At one stage, members were required to use their best endeavours to ensure that companies who broke international standards would disclose this fact. Now the IASC Preface calls for companies that *observe* the standards to disclose this fact. In the case of the United Kingdom and Ireland, the professional bodies have moved away from the idea of audit qualifications for breaches of IASC standards or even for lack of disclosure of breaches. It is probably the case that most accountants are not very conversant with the content or status of IASC standards.

Further IASC benefits

There has also been IASC influence in the move towards consolidated accounting in continental Europe (see Chapter 12). Anglo-Dutch consolidation practices are clearly predominant in the European Community's Seventh Directive on Company Law, which requires consolidation. However, it was useful to be able to point to the internationally agreed IAS 3 on the subject; and countries such as France have enthusiastically moved towards adoption of consolidation on that basis, whereas they might have found it more difficult if this were seen as 'following the United Kingdom'. More generally, there may be great long-run benefit from bringing together senior accountants from major countries to discuss technical and theoretical problems. The enhanced level of understanding of each other's practices should assist harmonization eventually, perhaps via a different agency such as the EC Commission.

Developing countries

There is a second major area where we may look for IASC achievements towards the underlying aim of harmonization. For those developing countries that did not have accounting standards, a ready-made IASC set has proved attractive. It can be adapted to local conditions, as necessary. Kenya, Malaysia, Nigeria, Pakistan, Singapore and Zimbabwe fit into this category. It is obviously preferable for them to adopt (in whole or part) an internationally recognized set of standards, from a body to which they belong, rather than to follow the standards of any one country. However, the six countries above have one feature in common: they have inherited a British legal and commercial structure. This makes it less surprising that IASC standards seem suitable to them; perhaps they would have followed similar UK standards anyway, though that path might have been slower and less comfortable for them. An important point in this context is whether IASC standards are suitable for such countries at this stage.

The IASC in the 1990s

In the late 1980s, the IASC began a project (published as E 32, and completed in 1993) to reduce options within its standards. This was part of a major campaign to increase the IASC's influence. The SEC and the International Organization of Securities Commissions (IOSCO) had given the IASC some encouragement that they might support its standards for use by foreign registrants on national stock exchanges, but only if IASC standards became more precise. Since the options in IASs had been put in in order to enable international agreement, the process of removing them is painful. Furthermore, many observers doubt whether the SEC would ever relax its own regulations, especially for the much less detailed IASs. Nevertheless, it is clear that the IASC is increasingly important in the eyes of stock exchanges, IOSCO and the EC Commission.

5.6 Other international bodies

This section looks at the nature and importance of some other bodies concerned with international aspects of accounting.

Fédération des Experts Comptables Européens (FEE)

The FEE started work at the beginning of 1987, taking over from two earlier European bodies: the Groupe d'Etudes (formed in 1966) and the Union Européenne des Experts Comptables. FEE is based in Brussels and has member accountancy bodies throughout Europe. Its interests include auditing, accounting and taxation. It studies international differences and tries to contribute to their removal. Much of its work is connected with the European Community, and it advises the EC Commission on company law and accounting harmonization. If FEE can arrive at a consensus of European accountants this gives it a powerful voice in Brussels, particularly if governments are disagreeing. One of FEE's predecessors (the Groupe d'Etudes) seems to have accepted the dominance of 'true and fair' and the need for consolidation; this may have helped in the acceptance of these concepts by the Commission.

International Federation of Accountants (IFAC)

This body came into being in 1977 after the Eleventh International Congress of

Accountants. It aims to develop a coordinated international accountancy profession. A predecessor body, called the International Coordination Committee for the Accountancy Profession, which had been formed in 1972 after the Tenth Congress, was wound up in favour of the IFAC.

The IFAC has a full-time secretariat in New York and comprises an assembly of the same accountancy bodies as belong to the IASC. Its work includes the setting of international guidelines for auditing (via the International Auditing Practices Committee), ethics, education and management accounting; involvement in education and technical research; and organizing the international congress about every five years.

Non-accounting bodies

One of the factors that drives accountants and their professional bodies towards better national and international standards is the possibility that other bodies will intervene or gain the initiative. At present, with the regional exception of the EC Commission, such international bodies have influence rather than power. The Organisation for Economic Co-operation and Development (OECD) has researched and adopted recommendations for accounting practice: the *Guidelines for Multinational Enterprises*. This mainly concerns disclosure requirements. It is voluntary, but it may influence the behaviour of large and politically sensitive corporations. Since 1976, there has been a survey of accounting practices, but no agreement as to how to achieve harmonization.

It seems clear that part of the OECD's aim in this area is to protect developed countries from any extreme proposals that might have come from the United Nations, which is interested in the regulation of multinational businesses. In 1977, the UN published a report in this area which proposed very substantial increases in disclosure of financial and non-financial items by transnational corporations. The UN went further and set up an 'Intergovernmental Group on International Accounting Standards and Reporting' which intended to publish standards for multinational companies. However, progress has been slow, perhaps partly because of differences of stance towards multinationals between host and parent countries.

5.7 Dual standards

Some connected worries about the process of international harmonization should be mentioned. First, are the IASC standards (which are largely based on the Anglo-Saxon model) suitable for the majority of businesses in continental Europe or in developing countries? The standards have developed in the context of loose company law, large stock exchanges, widely held share ownership and large, well-trained bodies of auditors. It is not at all obvious that British accounting would be more suitable for the bulk of German companies than German accounting is! It is quite possible that a standardized system such as the French *plan comptable* might be more suitable than Anglo-Saxon accounting for developing countries with few listed companies, sophisticated shareholders or highly qualified accountants. The same may apply at present to several of the economies of Eastern Europe.

For the above reason, it may be sensible (as well as easier) to direct harmonization attempts at listed companies. These are an easily defined set that has many shareholders and is most involved in international trade and capital raising. For this set, Anglo-Saxon accounting may seem the appropriate system upon which to harmonize, because it stresses matters of relevance in large free capital markets: the true and fair view, substance over form, independent audit, consolidation, shareholder orientation, and so on. This leads to the possibility of dual standards. The primary set of financial statements would obey the accounting standards most suitable for the majority of users in their own country. A secondary set would be prepared using other accounting standards more appropriate for intended users in other countries. Alternatively, there could be an internationally agreed set of standards (perhaps the IASC's) which would be used in all countries when preparing secondary accounts for international uses.

In practice, dual standards already exist to some extent. This has been formally the case in Italy, as has been mentioned; but it is also the practice in Scandinavia for large companies to volunteer to prepare Anglo-Saxon-style financial reports. Similarly, many large companies that wish to raise money in London or New York volunteer to have Anglo-Saxon audits and to prepare world-wide consolidations even when their local regulations do not demand this. IASC standards would be a very suitable, neutral basis for any formal adoption of this idea. Such harmonization would be easier to implement than that discussed in the earlier parts of this chapter. Many of the obstacles would become irrelevant, and clear advantages would flow from having the most suitable financial statements for domestic and, separately, for international comparative purposes.

The above arguments may be illustrated with the aid of Figure 5.1. Country A is an Anglo-Saxon country, Country B is not. The two-headed arrow at the top of the figure represents the main object of harmonization. However, it is difficult to see how Multinational B could adopt international standards unless *either* other listed companies in Country B did so as well, or dual standards were implemented. Otherwise, various listed companies in the same country would be obeying different rules. Furthermore, precisely what constitutes a 'multinational' is hard to define. By an extension of this argument, it appears to be the IASC view that *all* companies in Countries A and B should be targets for harmonization. However, the arguments in the above paragraph might lead to the alternative conclusion that the companies within the dotted line should harmonize on IASC standards, leaving the bulk of the companies in Country B unaffected, at least initially.

Whether the listed companies in Country B should prepare additional financial statements using domestic rules would be a matter for Country B. The Italian answer (until 1994) seems to have been that consolidated accounts can follow only international rules and individual accounts can follow only domestic rules; and to

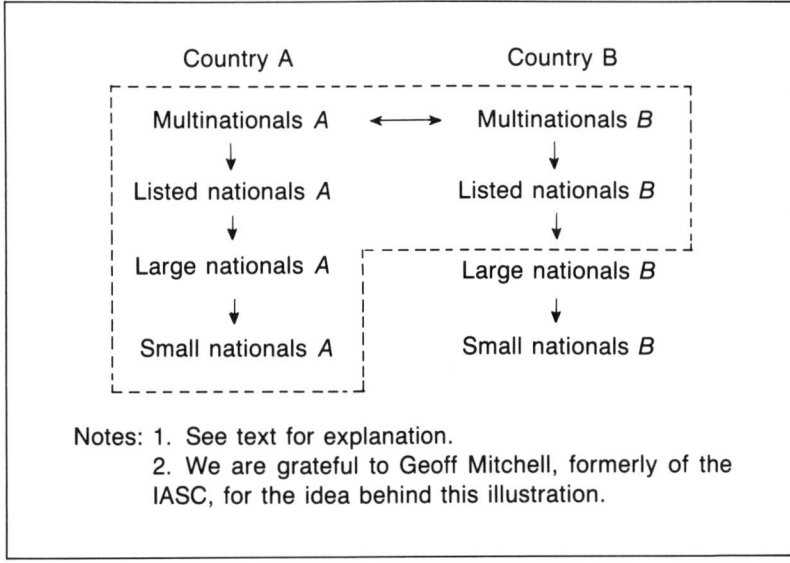

Figure 5.1 Dual standards.

some extent this could be the case in other continental countries where large, public or listed companies have special financial reporting rules. Perhaps surprisingly, this also approximately describes the case of the United States, where the minority of companies that are SEC-registered have much greater reporting and audit requirements than the majority of companies.

SUMMARY

Many parties might benefit from international harmonization: shareholders, stock exchanges, multinational companies, accounting firms, trade unions and tax authorities. The scope for harmonization is great because the international variations in practice are very large. However, the obstacles are important, too. The fundamental causes of differences remain and these are backed up by nationalistic inertia. At present, the lack of an international enforcement agency is crucial.

However, a number of bodies are working for harmonization of accounting rules and disclosure, notably the IASC which has rapidly published a substantial list of international standards. These are heavily influenced by practices in the United Kingdom and the United States. Enforcement in other areas of the world is difficult because of underdeveloped accountancy professions or because the rules for financial reporting are made by governments. However, there are significant effects in developing countries. It may be that the development of dual standards for domestic and foreign reporting would be an easier solution, which would preserve differences in accounting that result from national differences of an economic, social and legal nature. The IASC is reducing options in the 1990s.

There are other bodies concerned with harmonization on a world-wide or regional basis. However, the most powerful source of change towards harmonization among leading countries in world accounting has been the EC Commission. Harmonization of accounting is one of the many aims of the Commission as part of its overall objective to remove economic barriers within the EC.

Harmonization is being achieved through EC Directives and Regulations. It is particularly the Fourth and the Seventh Directives on company law which have been affecting accounting in Europe. The Fourth Directive has caused important changes in most EC countries in formats of accounts or disclosure or valuation procedures. The Seventh Directive has harmonized consolidation practices. However, partly because of differing opinions among the member states, there are no detailed requirements concerning valuation rules. This will restrict the degree of harmonization.

Appendix: Formats in the European Community

The two balance sheet formats and the four profit and loss account formats available in the Fourth Directive may be seen in Sections 3 and 5 of the Directive (see Appendix to this book).

The balance sheets may be described as horizontal, *en tableau* (Article 9) and vertical, *en liste* (Article 10). In terms of member state laws, most countries require the horizontal format, although Denmark, Ireland, Luxembourg, the Netherlands and the United Kingdom allow both. Only in the United Kingdom and Ireland is the vertical format the normal one.

Profit and loss accounts come in four types in the Directive: a horizontal and vertical version of two different approaches to the categorization of costs: by type (*par nature*) and by stage of production (*par destination*). The laws of the member states allow the following:

Belgium	*Par nature* only, but all allowed for groups
Denmark	All
France	*Par nature* only, but all allowed for groups
Germany	Both vertical types
Greece	*Par destination* both formats
Ireland	All
Italy	*Par nature* vertical

Luxembourg   All
Netherlands   All
Portugal   *Par nature* horizontal
Spain   *Par nature* horizontal (e.g. see Figure 6.2 in the next chapter)
United Kingdom All

Difficulties of interpretation arise, for example, between the horizontal *par nature* format of Spain and the predominant vertical *par destination* format of the United Kingdom. There is not enough information in a Spanish annual report to calculate the 'cost of sales' and 'gross profit' that UK analysts use.

References

J. R. Edwards, (1981), *Company Legislation and Changing Patterns of Disclosure in British Company Accounts, 1900–1940*, ICAEW, London, p. 17.

R. H. Parker and C. W. Nobes, (1991), 'Auditors' view of true and fair', *Accounting and Business Research*, Autumn.

EXERCISES

5.1 (a) Outline the objectives and achievements of the European Community in the area of financial reporting.
    (b) Outline the objectives and achievements of the IASC in the area of financial reporting.
    (c) Are the European Community and the IASC working in the same direction?

5.2 'European Directives and International Accounting Standards both contain far too many options to be useful.' Discuss.

5.3 'Dual standards would enable accounting harmonization, with all its difficulties, to be concentrated where it matters, i.e. on listed companies.' Explain and discuss.

PART III

Issues in financial reporting

CHAPTERS

6	Valuation of fixed assets	121
7	Depreciation of fixed assets	143
8	Inventory valuation	162
9	Capital and liabilities	184
10	Accounting and taxation	192
11	Accounting for price changes	215
12	Group accounting	236
13	Foreign currency translation	257

CHAPTER 6

Valuation of fixed assets

OBJECTIVES

- To explain the basic valuation methods that could be used for the presentation of fixed assets in balance sheets
- To look at the European Community and IASC rules on this
- To examine some European practices in this area
- To look at the special treatments of leased assets, investment properties, intangibles and investments

---

6.1 Framework

This chapter is not about the valuation of a business (see Chapter 16) but about the basic valuation method for individual fixed assets to be presented on a balance sheet. The topic of depreciation is also not covered here, but left to the following chapter. A number of conventions of valuation have already been discussed in Part I, such as prudence and going concern. It should also be remembered that, to be credible, balance sheets need independent expert appraisal, which requires some objectivity of valuation. Relevance has been contrasted with reliability in Part I. It is clear that prudence, objectivity and some other conventions lead to the loss of potentially relevant information. For example, when it comes to actual rules and practice, 'assets' such as the loyalty of customers tend not to be separately recognized in balance sheets (unless this is bought as part of goodwill), and values based on future income streams or estimated sale proceeds tend to be ignored in favour of depreciated historical costs.

Before examining present rules and practice in Europe, this chapter briefly looks at the theoretical possibilities for valuation. There are two main categories into which methods of valuing assets may be put: *historical cost* and *current cost*. The historical cost system uses valuations that rest upon recordable facts about prices paid for assets in the past or amounts agreed to be owing to, or owed by, a business.

There are some problems in defining when assets have been bought or sold or when they can be agreed to have risen in value, but these are usually resolved by relying on the evidence of actual external transactions. This way of adding up the assets has been used with variations over the past centuries, because it is usually simple, objective and prudent.

Current value accounting is a more recent idea and more complicated. However, it addresses many of the problems associated with historical cost accounting, particularly in times of inflation. The main asset valuation bases used within current value accounting are *replacement cost*, *net realizable value* (i.e. expected sale receipts less costs involved in a sale) and *economic value* (i.e. the discounted net present value of the expected net cash flows from the particular asset). It can easily be seen that, although these values may be more relevant and current than past values, they involve much more subjectivity than historical cost valuations. In practice, as will be shown, it is possible to introduce some conventions to narrow the range of choice. Also, some systems of accounting involve a choice of basis depending on circumstances. (This whole area is discussed in more detail in Chapter 11.) The alternatives mentioned in this section are summarized diagrammatically in Figure 6.1.

The choice of valuation method may also depend on who requires the valuation. Owners and prospective buyers will want the most realistic estimate of the worth of the business as a going concern. On the other hand, lenders may want a much more conservative valuation, based on the lowest likely valuation of the individual assets in the event that the business has to be closed down. Managers will, of course, also be interested in accounting information, but this book is mainly concerned with information presented to outsiders, for example, in the form of published annual reports of companies.

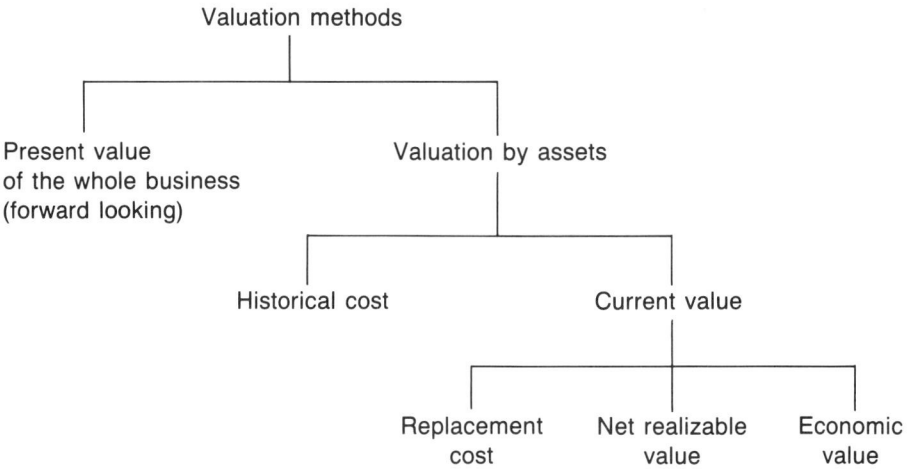

Figure 6.1 Valuation methods.

The predominant method of valuation in Europe (and elsewhere) has been historical cost. However, particularly in times of inflation, other methods have been discussed or experimented with. This is the case, for example, in Germany in the 1920s, in the United Kingdom and France in the 1970s, and in South America for several decades (see Chapter 11). In the Netherlands, accounting theory has centred on the use of replacement costs as values, and this has affected the practice of some companies. These precedents explain why the EC Fourth Directive was based mainly on strict historical cost but had to include optional revaluation methods for some member states.

Even the comparatively simple concept of 'cost' is not totally straightforward. What exactly is the 'cost' of a fixed asset? The answer is that cost should include not only the invoice price of the asset but also all costs involved in getting the asset into a location and condition where it can be productive. So, this will include delivery charges, sales taxes and installation charges in the case of plant and machinery. For land and buildings, cost will include legal fees, architect's fees, clearing the land and so on, as well as the builder's bill and the cost of the land.

If the company has used its own labour or materials, these should not be treated as current expenses but as items which increase the cost of the fixed asset; that is, they are *capitalized*. It is also possible to capitalize the interest cost on money borrowed to create fixed assets. Where labour or material are capitalized, certain formats of the income statement (described as *par nature* in the Appendix to Chapter 5) show this item as revenue. This is because all the labour and materials used have been charged in the income statement. However, the items capitalized do not relate to current operations, so they are added back as revenue. In the example of Figure 6.2 (CEPSA of Spain), the 1,411m pta. of capitalized expenses are a partial credit for the expenses shown on the debit side.

Which expenditures after purchase are of a capital nature and should be treated as an increase in 'cost' and thus depreciation? The answer is often unclear but, in general, repairs and maintenance are treated as current expenses, whereas improvements are capitalized. So, a new engine for a company vehicle will usually be treated as an expense, since it keeps it in running order rather than improving it, whereas the painting of advertising signs on the company's fleet of vans may well be treated as a capital item.

Obviously, the accountant needs to consider whether the amounts are material enough to capitalize them. He tends to treat as much as possible as expense, since this is the prudent and administratively more convenient method. If the inspector of taxes can be convinced that items are expenses this will also speed up their tax deductibility.

The depreciation treatment of the new engine mentioned above will depend on the depreciation 'units' that the accountant works on. Normally, the whole vehicle will be the unit, and so the new engine will be a current expense. If the vehicle and the engine were separate units for depreciation, the new engine would be a capital item.

Debit		Credit	
Expenses:		Revenues:	
Procurements	224,914	Net sales	313,740
Decrease in finished product and work-in-process inventories	3,174	Increase in finished product and work-in-progress inventories	—
Personnel expenses	17,207	Capitalized expenses of in-house work on fixed assets	1,411
Period depreciation and amortization	6,225	Other operating revenues	72
Variation in operating provisions	6,674		
Other operating expenses	44,357		
	302,551		315,223
Operating income	12,672		
Financial expenses on debt to Group and associated companies	2,862	Revenues from shareholdings	7,418
Financial expenses on debt to third parties and similar expenses	4,489	Revenues from marketable securities and loans to Group and associated companies	546
Variation in financial investment provisions	10	Revenues from other marketable securities and loans	120
Exchange losses	1,883	Other interest and similar revenues	3,627
		Exchange gains	—
	9,244		11,711
Financial income	2,467		
Ordinary income	15,139		
Variation in fixed asset provisions	1,753	Gains on fixed asset disposals	25
Losses on fixed assets	663	Capital subsidies transferred to income for the year	284
Extraordinary expenses	258	Extraordinary revenues	370
Prior years' expenses	—	Prior years' revenues	—
	2,674		679
Extraordinary income	0	Extraordinary loss	1,995
Income before taxes	13,144		
Corporate income tax	1,418		
Net income for the year	11,726		

Figure 6.2 Income statement of CESPA, 1991 (millions of pesetas).

6.2 Fourth Directive and IASC rules

This section and the three following deal with tangible fixed assets (i.e. those with physical existence). After that, intangibles and investments are considered. Depreciation of tangible assets is examined in the following chapter.

The balance sheet layouts prescribed in Articles 9 and 10 of the Fourth Directive require separate disclosure of the following tangible fixed assets:

C. **Fixed assets**
  ...
  II. *Tangible assets*
    1. Land and buildings.
    2. Plant and machinery.
    3. Other fixtures and fittings, tools and equipment.
    4. Payments on account and tangible assets in course of construction.

Article 15 of the Fourth Directive states that:

1. Whether particular assets are to be shown as fixed assets or current assets shall depend upon the purpose for which they are intended.
2. Fixed assets shall comprise those assets which are intended for use on a continuing basis for the purposes of the undertaking's activities.

According to IAS 16, 'Accounting for Property, Plant and Equipment', tangible fixed assets:

(a) are held by an enterprise for use in the production or supply of goods and services, for rental to others, or for administrative purposes and may include items held for the maintenance or repair of such assets;
(b) have been acquired or constructed with the intention of being used on a continuing basis, and
(c) are not intended for sale in the ordinary course of business.

The Fourth Directive states in Article 32 that, in general, the valuation of the items shown in the annual accounts shall be based on the principle of purchase price or production cost. There are also provisions in Article 35 relating to value adjustments and depreciation (see Chapter 7) and to the meaning of cost (see Article 35 in Appendix). Article 33 allows member states to use current cost valuation (subject to disclosure of method and some other requirements):

1. The Member States may declare to the Commission that they reserve the power, by way of derogation from Article 32 and pending subsequent coordination, to permit or require in respect of all companies or any classes of companies:
   (a) valuation by the replacement value method for tangible fixed assets with limited useful economic lives and for stocks;
   (b) valuation by methods other than that provided for in (a) which are designed to take account of inflation for the items shown in annual accounts, including capital and reserves;
   (c) revaluation of tangible fixed assets and financial fixed assets.

As mentioned, tangible fixed assets are addressed by the IASC in IAS 16, 'Accounting for Property, Plant and Equipment'. The 1990 Statement of Intent, 'Comparability of Financial Statements', proposed amendments to IAS 16. In the Statement of Intent, the benchmark for measurement of fixed assets is historical cost. The alternative treatment is measurement by reference to revaluation. Other changes included in the statement deal with the measurement issue in the case of an exchange of assets and with the recognition of upward revaluation relating to a previous downward revaluation. The changes were approved in 1993 and are in line with the Fourth Directive requirements.

There will be occasions when fixed assets need to be revalued downwards, below historical cost. Of course, there is normal wear or obsolescence, which is accounted for by depreciation, examined in the next chapter. However, there may be other permanent diminutions in value, due to unusual and substantial economic or physical events leading to rapid obsolescence, damage or other value loss. Such permanent diminutions in value will be expected not to reverse. An example might be the physical collapse of part of a building. The Fourth Directive, in Article 35, covers this case in 1. (c) (aa):

1. (a) Fixed assets must be valued at purchase price or production cost, without prejudice to (b) and (c) below.
   (b) The purchase price or production cost of fixed assets with limited useful economic lives must be reduced by value adjustments calculated to write off the value of such assets systematically over their useful economic lives.
   (c) (aa) Value adjustments may be made in respect of financial fixed assets, so that they are valued at the lower figure to be attributed to them at the balance sheet date.
   (bb) Value adjustments must be made in respect of fixed assets, whether their useful economic lives are limited or not, so that they are valued at the lower figure to be attributed to them at the balance sheet date if it is expected that the reduction in their value will be permanent.
   (cc) The value adjustments referred to in (aa) and (bb) must be charged to the profit and loss account and disclosed separately in the notes on the accounts if they have not been shown separately in the profit and loss account.
   (dd) Valuation at the lower of the values provided for in (aa) and (bb) may not be continued if the reasons for which the value adjustments were made have ceased to apply.

Note that the diminutions in value must be charged to the profit and loss account.

6.3 Practice

Table 6.1 shows the variation in valuation practices for land and buildings in European balance sheets. Historical cost can be seen to predominate in Germany and revaluations in the United Kingdom. For the Netherlands, there is some evidence of replacement costs. In France and Spain, the 'other' is an indexed

VALUATION OF FIXED ASSETS

Table 6.1 Valuation basis for land and buildings.

	Bel	Den	Fra	Ger	Gre	Ire	Ita	Lux	Net	Spa	Swe	Swi	UK	Total
Sample size	50	32	40	49	30	38	30	12	40	30	9	11	50	421
Evidence of land and buildings	38	29	33	48	27	35	27	12	39	27	8	11	50	384
Valuation basic used for land:[a]														
Cost, purchase price	5	5	28	1	25	8	4	4	6	7	7	4	—	104
Cost, purchase price less amortization	—	—	—	—	—	3	—	—	1	—	—	—	—	4
Replacement value	1	—	—	—	—	—	—	—	2	—	—	—	—	3
Independent expert valuation	—	—	—	—	—	4	—	—	1	—	—	—	—	5
Other	—	1	16	—	2	—	1	—	1	5	1	3	—	30
No separate disclosure of valuation basis for land	4	2	1	1	—	4	—	—	2	1	—	—	—	15
Valuation basis used for buildings:														
Cost, purchase price	2	1	—	—	—	1	11	—	2	5	7	6	—	35
Cost, purchase price less amortization	4	4	28	3	24	10	—	3	11	2	—	—	—	89
Cost, production cost (less amortization or not)	—	1	4	—	—	—	3	—	—	—	1	2	—	11
Replacement value less amortization	—	—	—	—	—	—	—	—	2	—	—	—	—	2
Independent expert valuation	—	—	—	—	—	4	—	—	1	—	—	—	—	5
Other	—	—	20	1	2	4	—	1	2	7	3	3	—	37
No separate disclosure of valuation basis for buildings	1	2	—	1	—	4	—	1	1	—	—	—	—	10
Valuation basis used for land and buildings:[a]														
Cost, purchase price	—	3	—	9	—	5	15	1	1	6	—	3	—	43
Cost, purchase price less amortization	14	13	1	39	—	7	—	5	13	—	—	1	14	106
Cost, production cost (less amortization or not)	2	2	—	34	—	—	5	—	1	—	—	1	1	46
Replacement value (less amortization or not)	—	—	—	—	—	—	—	—	8	—	—	—	—	8
Independent expert value (less amortization or not)	—	1	—	—	—	14	1	—	1	2	—	—	35	54
Other	4	4	2	1	—	5	—	1	2	8	—	3	—	30
No disclosure of valuation basis for land and buildings	10	3	1	2	—	—	1	1	2	4	—	—	—	22

[a] More than one answer possible.
Source: adapted from FEE *European Survey of Published Accounts 1991*, Routledge, London, 1991.

method of valuation caused by government-induced tax-exempt revaluations in 1978 (France) and 1983 (Spain). See Chapter 11 for more details.

Table 6.2 shows the figures for plant and machinery. The pattern is similar to that of Table 6.1 except that voluntary revaluations are less frequent for these shorter-lived assets.

Some illustrations of the practices of particular companies are given in Examples 6.1–6.3.

EXAMPLE 6.1

Olivetti shows the effects of several Italian revaluations.

Revaluation reserves
As of 31 December 1991 and 1990, revaluation reserves consisted of the following:

(in billions of lire)	1991	1990
Revaluation of assets under Law No. 576, 2 December 1975 and Law No. 72, 19 March 1983	284.8	284.8
Revaluation of assets under Law No. 413, 30 December 1991, net of related taxation at 16%	80.9	—
Gains arising from spin-offs and other organizational changes, as allowed by relevant laws	64.1	64.1
Other revaluations, net of amounts allocated to the other reserves	102.3	97.8
TOTAL	532.1	446.7

As of 31 December 1991, the parent company and certain Italian subsidiaries revalued their property as required by Law No. 413 of 30 December 1991. As a result, the net book value of property increased by Lire 102.9 billion. The revaluation surplus of Lire 80.9 billion, stated net of taxation and minority interests, had been credited to a specific equity reserve.

The revaluation reserves of the parent company and Italian subsidiaries are not presently taxable, and will not become so unless distributed to the shareholders or, in the case of spin-off gains, following sale of the revalued assets. No deferred taxes have been provided for these reserves since, at the present time, the events which would give rise to such taxation are not expected to occur.

Consequences

The revaluation reserve amounts to about 17% of shareholders' funds and 33% of fixed assets. Compared with most countries, where historical cost is used, these aggregates might be said to be overstated by these percentages. Of course, another way of putting it is that Olivetti's figures are more up to date.

Table 6.2 Valuation basis for plant and machinery.

	Bel	Den	Fra	Ger	Gre	Ire	Ita	Lux	Net	Spa	Swe	Swi	UK	Total
Sample size	50	32	40	49	30	38	30	12	40	30	9	11	50	421
Evidence of plant and machinery	45	32	32	46	30	33	30	11	32	27	9	11	47	385
Valuation basis used for plant and machinery[a]														
Cost, purchase price less amortization	31	29	32	41	30	29	5	9	22	11	9	10	44	302
Cost, production cost less amortization	8	—	11	44	—	—	—	—	2	3	—	3	2	73
Replacement value less amortization	—	—	—	—	—	1	—	—	8	—	—	2	—	11
Other	3	1	9	2	—	2	24	1	3	12	—	—	1	58
No disclosure of valuation basis for plant and machinery	8	2	—	—	—	1	1	1	—	4	—	—	—	17

[a] More than one answer possible.
Source: adapted from FEE, *European Survey of Published Accounts 1991*, Routledge, London, 1991.

EXAMPLE 6.2

Philips is an example of the minority Dutch practice of using current value.

Current value
The calculation of net income and the valuation of tangible fixed assets and inventories are based on current value. In order to maintain continuity, the current value of a tangible fixed asset is considered to be equivalent to its replacement value. In certain instances, however, the lower business value or net realizable value is regarded as the current value

Note what a large proportion the revaluation (illegal in several other countries) represents of the shareholders' funds.

Note 22: STOCKHOLDERS' EQUITY

	1990	1989
Issued, paid-up capital	2,972	2,765
Share premium account	2,637	2,494
Revaluation surplus	10,512	10,094
Retained earnings	6,341	10,335
Goodwill	−1,995	−1,168
Foreign exchange translation differences	−9,302	−7,632
	11,165	16,888

Consequences

Adjusting back to a historical cost basis, it could be said that 94% of Philips' shareholders' funds would disappear. This would have an appalling effect on gearing. Also, it might be said that Philips' fixed assets are overstated by 46%, compared to the historical cost basis.

EXAMPLE 6.3

ELCO (1991) show that some Swiss companies value at other than historical cost.

Land and buildings are valued between their historic purchase price and market value. This is based on a conservative estimate by independent experts less valuation tolerance. Furthermore, half the theoretical deferred property tax is deducted directly, and the value added is directly credited to Group reserves. Operational depreciation of buildings is calculated using the straight line method based on the value determined in this way.

Consequences

Such is the lack of detail in some Swiss accounts, that the effects of this revaluation policy are not quantifiable. The notes show only the increase in revaluation reserve in the year. Nevertheless, compared to many companies, ELCO will be showing overvalued assets and larger depreciation.

6.4 Investment properties

In most countries, investment properties are treated in the same way as other properties. However, in the United Kingdom and Ireland, another approach is taken. Because this illustrates apparent conflict between the Fourth Directive and national standards, a brief discussion is useful here.

The British and Irish accounting standard, SSAP 19, defines investment properties as those not owner-occupied; for example, offices owned by a company but let out to another company. Since they are held for value and might be sold at any moment, their current value is even more interesting than it would be for other properties. SSAP 19 therefore requires that, in order to give a true and fair view, investment properties should be revalued annually to net realizable values (NRV). This is held to be consistent with the British Companies Act's interpretation of Article 33 of the Directive (see Section 6.2).

However, when assets are valued at NRV, the concept of systematic depreciation makes no sense because it is a system of allocation of historical cost (or current cost). Therefore, the SSAP requires that there should be no depreciation, except in the sense that downward valuation adjustments would be recorded. This lack of depreciation appears inconsistent with the Directive and national laws (see Chapter 7), so the SSAP has to resort to the claim that only its requirements will give a true and fair view, thus the detail of the law must be departed from.

Other EC countries do not take this view of investment properties, and might not envisage such a flexible interpretation of the law.

6.5 Leasing

A company may decide to acquire the use of fixed assets without buying them. There may be tax or liquidity advantages in doing this. For example, if an industrial company has little taxable income, it may not be able currently to use the tax depreciation allowances on the purchase of plant and machinery. However, if a financial company buys the assets and hires them to an industrial company, the former can gain the tax allowances, thus enabling an attractive rental charge.

In the case of certain long-term legal arrangements between the financial company (the lessor) and the industrial company (the lessee), the situation is very much as though the lessee has bought the plant. For example, the lessee may expect to keep the asset for the whole of its useful life, and there may be an option to purchase the plant at a future date at a low price from the lessor. In such cases, it can be argued that the commercial substance of the lessee's arrangements is that he has bought the asset and has contracted obligations which are liabilities. This, of course, is not the legal form of the arrangements, because the lessor is still the owner, although the lessee has the exclusive right to use the assets.

For example, consider Company A and Company B. The former has borrowed 10m ecu and bought machines with the money. Company B has borrowed no money, but has long-leased machines that would have cost 10m ecu to buy. The balance sheets will be affected as shown in Figure 6.3. If Company B accounts only for the legal form of the arrangement, its financial statements will look unfairly better than Company A's. That is, B will have a better return on assets and a better gearing.

Accountants in the United States were the first to adjust for this problem by capitalizing certain leases, by adjusting Company B's balance sheet to the position on the right of Figure 6.3. By the 1980s, this had also become standard procedure in some other countries; for example, in the United Kingdom (SSAP 21) and the Netherlands (Guideline 1.05, etc.). By the late 1980s, many large French groups were capitalizing in their consolidated accounts, but not in their individual company accounts (because of tax effects). The Spanish law of 1989, which implemented the Fourth Directive, required the capitalization of certain leases. Interestingly, although in most countries capitalized leases are included under tangible fixed assets, in Spain they are shown under intangibles. This recognizes the legal point that what the company owns is the right to the assets, not the assets themselves. In some countries, the conceptual framework is such that lease obligations fall naturally within the definition of 'liabilities'. In some others, the appropriate accounting rules require that these should be recorded as liabilities anyway.

In countries with a more exact interpretation of legal requirements, such as Germany and Italy, either leases are not capitalized or the definition of capitalizable leases is such that leases are rarely capitalized in practice. Of course, even in 'substance'-oriented countries, the criteria for lease capitalization are subject to manipulation by directors, who may seek to avoid lease capitalization that makes

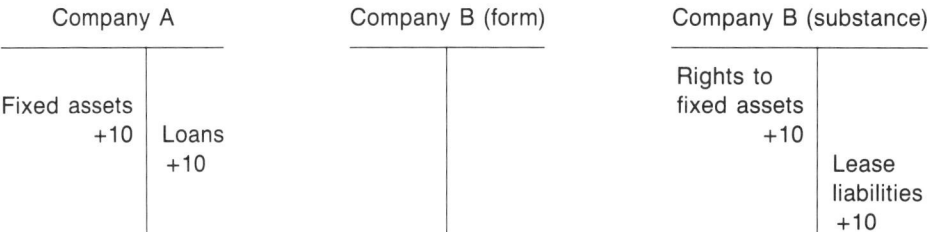

Figure 6.3 Capitalized leases.

their financial statements look worse. In terms of the classification of countries suggested in Figure 4.1 of Chapter 4, the micro countries tend to exhibit capitalization and the macro countries do not.

As an example of a criterion, the rules in the IAS 17 are that leases should be capitalized when the lease: 'transfers substantially all the risks and rewards incident to ownership of an asset'. In the UK, SSAP 21 adds:

> It should be presumed... if at the inception of a lease the present value of the minimum lease payments... amounts to substantially all (normally 90 per cent or more) of the fair value of the leased asset. (para. 15)

Such leases are called 'finance' or 'capitalizable' leases. The capitalized asset is depreciated over its legal or economic life. The lease payments to the lessor are treated as partly a reduction in lease liability and partly a finance expense. The latter is made to decline each year as the recorded lease liability declines. Other, non-capitalizable leases are called 'operating' leases (e.g. a short-term car-leasing arrangement). These are accounted for by recording the lease rental payments. That is, the double entries for the lease payments are:

Finance leases: Dr. Finance charge
                     Dr. Lease liability
                     Cr. Cash
Operating leases: Dr. Lease expense
                     Cr. Cash

So, for finance leases, expenses for both depreciation and finance charges will be recorded.

The Fourth Directive does not specifically mention leases, except to require disclosures of information concerning them. The International Accounting Standard (IAS 17) proposed the capitalization approach as discussed above.

Of course, whether or not leases are capitalized can have a major effect on published financial statements. For example, suppose an analyst were comparing the accounts of two similar large French groups both of which had substantial amounts of long-term leased assets. One group decided to capitalize and one not. The capitalizing group would show larger fixed assets and loans, and larger depreciation and finance expenses but smaller rental expenses. This would adversely affect gearing and return on assets calculations (see Part IV of this book for more detail on analysis). Example 6.4 is an illustration of this.

EXAMPLE 6.4

Total Oil (1990) is still noting (below) the effect of revaluation in 1978 and 1976 prices. It also notes the capitalization of certain leases. This is possible in France in group accounts only.

Tangible assets
These are carried in the consolidated balance sheet at their purchase cost. Fixed assets acquired by French companies before 1976 are recorded at the amounts derived from the legal revaluation at that time as stated in their own financial statements, and revaluations by foreign companies (excluded from their own accounts) are treated similarly. Assets are depreciated on a straightline basis over their estimated useful lives.

Fixed assets of significant value which are held under lease finance agreements are capitalized and depreciated on a straight line basis.

The corresponding commitment is recorded as a liability.

Consequences

It is not possible to tell from Total's notes how important the 1978 revaluation still is in the 1990 accounts. However, compared with most oil companies in the world (which use historical costs), the assets would be overvalued. However, the depreciation has already been corrected back to historical cost.

It appears from the notes that about 10% of 'processing plants and buildings' are capitalized leases (about 7% of fixed assets). Some other French groups will not have adopted this practice, so Total's fixed assets might be considered to be too high.

A further implication is that the same asset may appear in two balance sheets, e.g. those of a German lessor and a Dutch lessee, or it may appear in no balance sheet in the case of a Dutch lessor and a German lessee.

For lessor companies, the mirror-image arrangements are proposed, i.e. where lessees capitalize, lessors should not show the asset in their balance sheets, but should show finance receivables instead.

6.6 Intangibles

This section deals with intangible assets as purchased by individual companies. The complex problem of goodwill and of the purchase of other intangibles on acquisitions of businesses is left to Chapter 12.

In principle, there is no convincing reason to account for intangibles differently from tangible assets. That is, using criteria discussed earlier in this book, intangibles should be recorded where they are controlled by the enterprise, bring future benefits and where cost or value is determinable with reasonable reliability.

The Fourth Directive foresees the following intangibles in its balance sheet formats (Article 9):

C. Fixed assets

  I. *Intangible assets*
  1. Costs of research and development, in so far as national law permits their being shown as assets.
  2. Concessions, patents, licences, trade marks and similar rights and assets, if they were:
     (a) acquired for valuable consideration and need not be shown under C (I) (3); or
     (b) created by the undertaking itself, in so far as national law permits their being shown as assets.
  3. Goodwill, to the extent that it was acquired for valuable consideration.
  4. Payments on account.

National law may also provide for formation expenses to be shown as the first item under 'Intangible assets' according to Articles 9 and 10.

Let us apply the above asset recognition criteria to patents, licences and trade marks. Where these are acquired in specific transactions, it should be clear enough what the cost is, and whether there is control and future benefits. As with most other fixed assets, such intangibles wear out and should be depreciated. In the case of patents, etc., there are often legal lives over which depreciation can be charged.

For the formation expenses of a company (e.g. *frais d'établissement* in France), it is not clear what the asset is or how long it lasts. Consequently, it is illegal to capitalize such expenses in some countries (e.g. the United Kingdom). However, the Fourth Directive allows such expenses to be capitalized, and it is common to see this happen in several continental countries, typically with a five-year amortization period.

Research and development

Apart from goodwill, the most controversial intangible is probably research and development (R&D) costs. IAS 9 defines such costs:

> *Research* is original and planned investigation undertaken with the hope of gaining new scientific or technical knowledge and understanding.
> *Development* is the translation of research findings or other knowledge into a plan or design for the production of new or substantially improved materials, devices, products, processes, systems or services prior to the commencement of commercial production.

The argument for capitalizing such costs as intangible assets is the matching or accruals convention which would suggest that the costs should be matched against the future revenues that will result. The R&D could then be an asset because, in some cases, there is control, future benefit and cost measurement. Consequently, the Fourth Directive allows capitalization, followed by amortization (see below).

However, the argument against capitalizing is that the future benefit is uncertain, so that it would be imprudent. This is the attitude taken in the United States (in SFAS 2) and in Germany. The International Accounting Standard (IAS 9, as amended in 1993) requires research costs to be currently expensed but certain development costs to be capitalized:

> The development costs of a project should be recognized as an asset when all of the following criteria are met:
> (a) the product or process is clearly defined and the costs attributable to the product or process can be separately identified and measured reliably;
> (b) the technical feasibility of the product or process can be demonstrated;
> (c) the enterprise intends to produce and market, or use, the product or process;
> (d) the existence of a market for the product or process, or, if it is to be used internally rather than sold, its usefulness to the enterprise can be demonstrated; and
> (e) adequate resources exist, or their availability can be demonstrated to complete the project and market the product or process (para. 17)

The UK rules are similar to IAS 9, except that capitalization is an option; some development expenditures are capitalized by companies with important R&D efforts (e.g. aerospace companies). In France and Spain, research is sometimes capitalized as well as development. Table 6.3 illustrates some European practices in this area.

When R&D has been capitalized as an asset, it is necessary to charge it as expenses against future revenue. Article 34 of the Fourth Directive requires a maximum write-off period of five years, but Article 37 also allows Member states to amend this. For example, in the United Kingdom, R&D assets are expensed in line with the policy in IAS 9 (para. 21) which requires allocation on a systematic basis over the period of sale or use of the product or process that results from the R&D expenses. Table 6.4 shows some evidence of the periods chosen in practice.

As with tangible fixed assets, intangibles such as R&D should be written down if ever there is a permanent diminution in value below book value.

Brands

Particularly in the United Kingdom, it became popular in the late 1980s for certain companies to capitalize brand names, titles of publications and similar intangibles. The newspaper and food sectors contained several examples of this. Some companies restricted themselves to capitalizing brand names on purchase, others looked back into the past and capitalized internally generated brands. This practice

Table 6.3 R&D accounting.

Sample size	Bel 50	Den 32	Fra 40	Ger 49	Gre 30	Ire 38	Ita 30	Lux 12	Net 40	Spa 30	UK 50	Total 401
Evidence of R&D activity	9	15	16	38	4	10	7	1	14	7	23	144
Evidence of capitalized R&D costs	9	5	4	—	4	1	7	—	5	7	1	43
Valuation basis used:												
Cost	—	1	—	—	—	—	—	—	—	1	—	2
Cost less amortization	7	2	2	—	4	1	6	—	4	2	1	29
Other	1	—	—	—	—	—	—	—	—	—	—	1
No valuation basis disclosed for capitalized R&D costs	1	2	2	—	—	1	1	—	1	4	—	11
Cost recognized as R&D[a]												
Applied research costs	—	—	1	—	—	—	1	—	1	3	—	6
Development costs related to projects/products	—	1	1	—	—	1	6	—	2	2	1	14
Development costs for projects where revenues are foreseeable	—	2	—	—	—	—	—	—	—	—	—	3
Other	1	—	—	—	—	—	—	—	1	—	—	2
No disclosure of costs recognized	8	3	3	—	4	—	1	—	1	4	—	24

[a] More than one answer possible.
Source: adapted from FEE, *European Survey of Published Accounts 1991*, Routledge, London, 1991.

Table 6.4 **Write-off of R&D.**

	Bel	Den	Fra	Ger	Gre	Ire	Lux	Net	UK	Total
Sample size	50	32	40	49	30	38	12	40	50	341
Evidence of charge to income statement for R&D	9	15	16	38	4	10	1	14	23	130
Basis used for charge: Amortization with period of:										
Greater than five years	—	—	—	—	—	1	—	—	1	2
Five years	1	2	1	—	1	—	—	—	—	5
Less than five years	5	2	1	—	—	—	—	2	—	10
Other	—	—	—	—	—	—	—	—	—	—
Basis not specified	1	—	1	—	—	1	—	3	—	6
Whole cost expensed in year in which incurred	—	9	12	20	—	7	1	5	21	75
No disclosure of basis	2	2	1	18	3	1	—	4	1	32

Source: adapted from FEE, *European Survey of Published Accounts 1991*, Routledge, London, 1991.

was much to do with trying to fill the hole in the balance sheet left by the immediate writing off of goodwill on consolidation (see Chapter 12). Because the rules in the United Kingdom did not clearly cover brands, practice was varied and, in particular, amortization was unusual. Thus companies could show an asset without showing an amortization expense.

Illustrations

Some illustrations related to intangibles are given in Examples 6.5–6.7.

EXAMPLE 6.5

ENDESA (1991) reports the following intangible treatment, which is fairly typical for Spain.

(a) *Intangibles*
Expenses attributable to start-up of utility plants, loan formalization and other similar items are expensed as incurred.

Research and development expenses are recorded initially under the 'Intangibles' caption and, depending on the final viability of the project, are transferred to the 'Utility Plant' caption or are expensed. These expenses are being amortized over a maximum period of five years.

Consequences

There is not enough detail in the accounts to quantify the effect of this. However, continental European capitalization of research expenditures leads to higher assets than UK/US practice, and postponed expenses. Some of the assets would not be thought to be reliable by UK/US criteria.

EXAMPLE 6.6

Saint-Gobain (1990) reports differently. Note the opposite treatment of start-up costs and R&D in the Spanish and French companies.

> *Research and development expenses*
> Research and development expenses are charged to income when incurred.
> *Deferred charges*
> Deferred charges include start-up costs for major projects which are deferred and amortized over 5 years.
> *Other intangible assets*
> Other intangible assets are mainly represented by trademarks, patents and computer software. Trademarks are amortized over a period not exceeding 40 years using the straight-line method. A provision for depreciation of other intangible assets is made when there is any impairment in value. Patents and computer software are amortized over their estimated useful lives using the straight-line method.

Consequences

Deferred charges, which would generally be expensed in the United Kingdom, are treated as assets by Saint-Gobain to the extent of FF 826m. However, in this case, that is only 3% of tangible assets.

EXAMPLE 6.7

Sandoz (1991) illustrates the possible Swiss practice of writing off all intangibles (not only goodwill) immediately against reserves:

> *Intangible assets*
> Both intangible assets and any amount paid for goodwill in excess of the intrinsic values of an acquisition are charged to reserves in the year of acquisition.

Consequences

In 1991, the reserves were hit with intangible write-offs of SF 170m and goodwill write-offs of SF 400m. This is in the context of fixed assets (including investments) of SF 5bn, and reserves of SF $6\frac{1}{2}$ bn. In France, these items would generally be shown as assets. In the United Kingdom the intangibles probably would be, but the goodwill not.

6.7 Investments

Investments can be divided into fixed and current, on the same basis as other assets, i.e. depending on whether they are intended for continuing use in the business. In an individual company's balance sheet, typical fixed asset investments would be shares in subsidiaries or associated companies. Typical current asset investments would be marketable securities held as a temporary store of value. In the Fourth Directive's balance sheet formats, fixed asset investments are shown after intangibles and tangibles, and current asset investments after inventories and debtors.

The rules of fixed asset valuation examined earlier in this chapter apply to fixed asset investments. That is, they are normally valued at cost, less any permanent diminutions in value. It is possible to revalue fixed asset investments upwards in some countries, but this is unusual.

In the Netherlands, shares in subsidiaries and associated companies are not held at cost but by using the equity method. This is the normal method for holding associates in *group* accounts in other countries. This is discussed in Chapter 12.

For current asset investments, as for other current assets, the Fourth Directive generally requires valuation at 'the lower of cost and net realizable value' (see Chapter 8). However, as quoted earlier, Article 33 allows replacement value to be used. It is normal practice for financial institutions in several countries (e.g. the United Kingdom and the Netherlands) to use 'marking to market' for the valuation of current asset marketable securities. This means that such assets are held at current market values at the balance date, and any gains or losses are taken immediately to the profit and loss account.

The argument for doing this is that the securities *could* be sold on the balance sheet date and then bought back again a few minutes later. That would achieve 'marking to market' in reality. Companies that do not make the sale and purchase are no worse off in substance than companies that do. Therefore, they should account in the same way.

Banks and insurance companies have their own special versions of the Fourth Directive, and it seems that 'marking to market' is more difficult to achieve for ordinary companies within the rules of the Fourth Directive, particularly because of the question of which profits are realized.

VALUATION OF FIXED ASSETS

SUMMARY

Fixed assets could potentially be valued in several different ways on balance sheets. In particular, historical cost or several types of current valuation are possible. If rule-makers are trying to choose between these, then the basic objectives of accounting need to be borne in mind. In practice historical cost has been the dominant method. However, variations from this are allowed by the EC Fourth Directive and in several countries' rules; and the practical application of this varies internationally. In countries where taxation and accounting are closely linked, the revaluation of assets has tax effects. For certain assets, current values may seem particularly relevant. This has led to a requirement to show investment properties at current values in some countries.

Depending on the definition of assets and on the rules for their recognition in balance sheets, certain items may be recorded in some countries but not others. For example, certain leased machines might be considered to be, in commercial substance, the assets of the lessee and not of the lessor. This has tax and legal implications. Some intangible assets seem to fit the criteria for asset recognition, and are recorded in balance sheets. Other intangibles show varied treatment internationally. For example, research and development is capitalized in some countries, but in others the law allows only research to be capitalized or the rules prohibit capitalization of both research and development.

There are also some particular rules for the valuation of investments. In some countries, there have been moves towards the current valuation of certain current asset investments.

EXERCISES

6.1 (a) Provide, and explain, a definition of an asset.
   (b) What are the essential criteria to distinguish a fixed asset from other assets?

6.2 Costa Co. uses three identical pieces of machinery in its factory. These were all acquired for use on the same date by the following means:
   (a) machine 1 rented from Brava Co. at a cost of 250 ecu per month payable in advance and terminable at any time by either party;
   (b) machine 2 rented from Blanca Co. at a cost of eight half-yearly payments in advance at 1,500 ecu;
   (c) machine 3 rented from Sol Co. at a cost of six half-yearly payments in advance of 1,500 ecu;
   (d) the cash price of these machines is 8,000 ecu each and their estimated lives four years.
   Are the above machines rented by operating lease or by finance lease according to IASC rules?

6.3 For each of machines 1, 2 and 3 in the previous exercise, outline the effect on reported profits, and on the balance sheet, as included in the published financial statements.

6.4 'The idea of "substance over form" supports the recording of a finance lease as an asset, even though there is no legal ownership. This suggests that the idea of substance over form is a dangerous one.' Discuss.

6.5 'Research expenditure, by its nature, gives no reasonable expectation of future related revenues, and must be treated as an expense under the prudence convention. Development expenditure which satisfies the five criteria suggested in Section 6.6, on the other hand, clearly gives a reasonable expectation of future related revenues and must be treated as an asset, and amortized, under the matching convention.' Discuss.

CHAPTER 7

Depreciation of fixed assets

> **OBJECTIVES**
>
> - To examine the meaning and purpose of depreciation in accounting
> - To look at the rules for depreciation in the European Community and elsewhere
> - To study different methods of calculating depreciation
> - To note the practical and theoretical problems with depreciation accounting
> - To present some data on European practices

7.1 Terminology

Particularly in an international context, the terminology surrounding depreciation can lead to confusion. This chapter concerns depreciation in the sense of systematic allocations of the cost of a fixed asset as expenses to the profit and loss account. In North America, the word 'amortization' is used to describe depreciation of intangible fixed assets; and this is sometimes the case in English-speaking countries elsewhere. We follow this practice here.

Some continental European companies use the word 'depreciation' in English translations to mean downward valuation adjustments of fixed assets, including investments. This book does not do that. Such value adjustments are discussed in Chapter 6.

7.2 The basic concept

If a business buys goods or services (e.g. materials, electricity or labour) that are to be used up in the current year in the process of earning profit, they are charged to the profit and loss account. The amount charged in the accounting year is not the amount paid in the year but the amount that relates to the year. This is a practical working out of the accruals convention examined in Part I.

A further result of the accruals convention relates to cases where a company buys goods of significant value that are *not* to be used up in the current year. In such cases the cost should be treated as a capital purchase, not as a current expense. The difference in effect can be seen on the balance sheets of Figure 7.1.

However, it would be unreasonable to charge nothing against profit for the use of the machine. If it were hired, there would be a charge. So, if the asset is owned and is wearing out there will be a charge too. If the machine will last for ten years, the cost is spread over ten years rather than charged totally to the year of purchase or not charged at all.

Also, just as it is reasonable to charge for the services provided, so it seems reasonable to consider that the fixed asset is used up because it has provided the services. The asset may be used up or become less useful for a variety of reasons, which can be divided into two categories:

(a) *physical reasons*: deterioration or wearing out with use; the expiration of a lease or patent; the exhaustion of a mine;
(b) *economic reasons*: the obsolescence of the asset or the product that it makes; a change in company policy leading, for example, to the hiring of machines; expansion of the business causing an asset to be inadequate in size or performance.

So, accountants allocate the cost to expense over the life of the asset and recognize that the asset is being used up. The 'life' in question is the *useful economic life* to the present owner, which takes into account the fact that a machine may be obsolete before it is worn out or vice versa. The expense is labelled 'depreciation'.

For example, suppose that a 10,000 ecu machine is estimated to last ten years and to be worthless at the end. An obvious and simple method of depreciation would

(1) Expenses of 10,000:

Assets	Liabilities and capital
Current assets: −10,000 cash	Capital: −10,000 profit

(2) Capital purchase of 10,000:

Assets	Capital and liabilities
Fixed assets: +10,000 machine Current assets: −10,000 cash	

Figure 7.1 Showing goods that are not used up in the current year on the balance sheet.

be to allocate 1,000 ecu of the cost as an expense for each of the ten years. For example:

    1 January 1995   Purchase: machine + 10,000
                                                          cash   − 10,000
    31 December 1995   Depreciation recognized: machine − 1,000
                                                           profit   − 1,000

So the machine stands at 10,000 − 1,000 = 9,000 in the balance sheet. This 9,000 is the amount of the cost not yet treated as an expense. It is sometimes called the net book value (NBV) or the written-down value (WDV), although it is not, of course, a 'value' in any market sense. This method of depreciation is called the straight-line or fixed instalment or constant charge method. It is illustrated in Figure 7.2. If a scrap value (residual value) of 3,000 ecu were estimated and life were

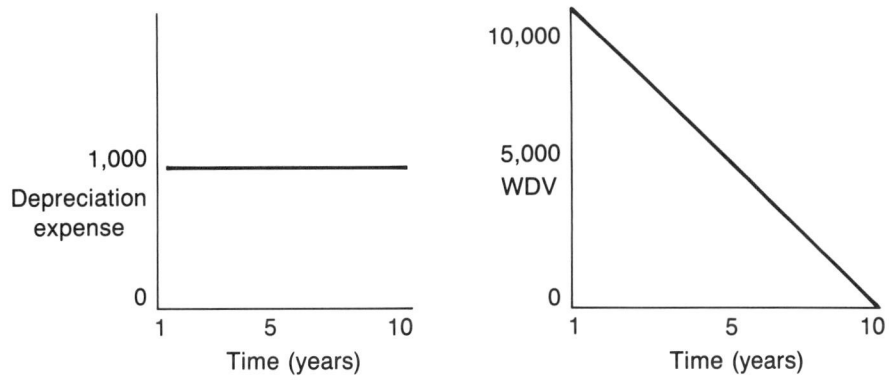

Figure 7.2 Straight-line depreciation.

Table 7.1 **Straight-line depreciation of net cost.**

End of year	Depreciation charge recognized	WDV
0	—	10,000
1	1,000	9,000
2	1,000	8,000
3	1,000	7,000
4	1,000	6,000
5	1,000	5,000
6	1,000	4,000
7	1,000	3,000

expected to be seven years, the depreciation charge would again be 1,000 ecu as in Table 7.1. At the end of year 6 in the example of Table 7.1, the balance sheet or the notes would show:

	ecu
Fixed asset: Cost	10,000
Cumulative depreciation	6,000
Written down value	4,000

7.3 Some rules

The Fourth Directive requires systematic depreciation of fixed assets over their useful economic lives (see Article 35 as reprinted in Chapter 6). This means that assets without limited lives, such as land, are not depreciated, unless they are being used up, as a gold mine is. Buildings with very long lives, such as castles or palaces may also not be depreciated because they are expected to be maintained, in effect, for ever. How far one can take this 'maintenance' argument is discussed later.

The International Accounting Standard (IAS 4) defines depreciation as:

the allocation of the depreciable amount of an asset over its estimated useful life. (para. 2)

Similarly, a statement by the American Institute of Certified Public Accountants (AICPA) says that depreciation accounting is a system of accounting that aims to distribute the cost or other basic value of tangible capital assets, less salvage value (if any), over the estimated useful life of the unit (which may be a group of assets) in a systematic and rational manner. It is a process of allocation, not of valuation.

The UK SSAP 12 states that:

depreciation is a measure of the wearing out, consumption or other reduction in the useful economic life of a fixed asset whether arising from use, effluxion of time or obsolescence through technological or market changes. Depreciation should be allocated so as to charge a fair proportion of cost or valuation of the asset to each accounting period expected to benefit from its use. (para. 3)

A major international difference is that depreciation in some countries has been closely linked with taxation. At first sight, this might seem inevitable in all countries. However, in Anglo-Saxon countries there have always been differences between tax depreciation and accounting depreciation. At the extreme, in the United Kingdom, the depreciation expenses charged in the profit and loss account are not allowable at all as tax deductible expenses for the calculation of taxable income. The tax calculations are done quite separately, and 'capital allowances', which are depreciation for tax purposes, are allowed instead. For example, for 1993/94, UK capital allowances are as shown in Table 7.2. In the United States, the separation

Table 7.2 **Main UK capital allowances, 1993/4.**

Plant and machinery	25% p.a. on reducing balance
Industrial buildings	4% p.a. on cost
Commercial buildings	0%

between tax and accounting depreciation is not so clear, but differences are common (leading to deferred taxation; see Chapter 9). The same applies in a few continental countries, for example, the Netherlands.

However, in most continental countries, there is a close relationship between tax and accounting depreciation. Technically, in the majority of those countries, the tax figures should be based on the accounting figures, rather than the other way round. For example, in Germany, the *Steuerbilanz* should be based on the *Handelsbilanz*; this is the authoritative principle or the *Massgeblichkeitsprinzip* (as mentioned in Chapter 4). In practice, in these countries, since the tax rules will allow only certain maximum charges for tax purposes, the accounting depreciation charges are chosen to coincide with these maxima. So, the accounting figures end up being based on tax rules. These are often more generous than accountants might have chosen on grounds of 'fairness'.

In many countries, governments offer accelerated tax depreciation in order to encourage investment in certain types of assets or certain regions. For example, this applies to the Mezzogiorno in Italy, to certain Greek islands, to the Highlands of Scotland, and to West Berlin (until the end of the 1980s). In certain cases, such accelerated depreciation must be recorded in the financial statements in order to be allowable for tax purposes. In general, partly as a result of the implementation of EC Directives, these effects should be disclosed in the notes or shown separately in the financial statements. An example of the latter is the requirement of the Spanish law of 1989.

7.4 What depreciation is not for

Having examined the basic concept and some definitions of depreciation, it is useful now to make clear what depreciation is not for. This is because many non-accountants misunderstand this.

Valuation

First, depreciation is not supposed to be a valuation technique. Although provisions for depreciation are deducted from the cost of fixed assets in order to show a net book value (NBV) on a balance sheet, that NBV is not supposed to represent the net realizable value of the assets at the balance sheet date. The NBV is merely the cost that has so far not been allocated as an expense to the profit and loss account. In some countries, attempts have been made to adjust NBVs so that they do more closely represent current values (see Section 7.6 and Chapter 11). However, this is done at the risk of mixing up values with costs, and ending up with an incoherent balance sheet.

In principle, of course, it would be possible to allocate depreciation on the basis of declining market values. However, this leads to the problems that result from having to make estimations; for example, expense of valuations, unreliability and difficulty of auditing. Furthermore, some assets decline in value very rapidly and it is not clear that allocation of cost over useful lives should be based on that process. For example, specialized assets such as power stations or telephone exchanges may be effectively unmarketable, and motor cars lose a large proportion of value in the first month. Although they lose value rapidly, they do not become less useful to the business so rapidly.

Another approach would be to abandon the allocation of cost altogether, and to measure depreciation directly as the loss of value for a period. One could take the view that the value of the asset to the firm is not the market value but the discounted expected net revenue contributions from the asset. One needs to identify the net revenues of the company with and without the asset in order to measure the net contributions of the asset.

The net contributions of the asset will be called R_1 in year 1, R_n in year n and so on. It has been briefly mentioned in Chapter 6 that future revenues need to be discounted in order to assess their present values. The value of an asset (PV_0) can therefore be said to be:

$$PV_0 = \frac{R_1}{1+r} + \frac{R_2}{(1+r)^2} + \cdots + \frac{R_n}{(1+r)^n}$$

where n is the life of the asset and r is the appropriate discount rate. This rate may be the cost of capital or the rate of return on funds (see Section 16.3). The above equation can be restated as:

$$PV_0 = \sum_{t=1}^{t=n} \frac{R_t}{(1+r)^t}$$

where t is the year. One year later the asset's value (PV_1) will be given by:

$$PV_1 = \sum_{t=2}^{t=n} \frac{R_t}{(1+r)^{t-1}}$$

and the depreciation for the year will be $PV_0 - PV_1$.

There are, of course, great practical difficulties in isolating the net revenues or cost savings of an asset after purchase. However, if it could be done it would lead to a justifiable current measure of the using up of the asset's value during the year, taking into account repairs and maintenance or deterioration in performance caused by lack of them. However, this would not be the allocation of cost, and would not fit with the conventional workings of accounting.

Replacement

The second potential misunderstanding about depreciation is that it is a mechanism for providing funds for the replacement of the depreciating asset. The double entry for depreciation is, of course:

Dr. Depreciation expense
Cr. Provision for depreciation

This shows that there is no direct effect on cash or investments. Unless amounts of cash that are equivalent to the depreciation charges are put into a tin box or another easily accessible store (e.g. an investment fund), an amount equalling the cost may not be available in liquid form at the end of the asset's life. Even if cash is available, inflation will probably have caused the price of a replacement asset to rise, and so it will be insufficient. Also, in many cases the company will not want to buy a similar asset but one that is technologically more advanced, bigger or concerned with the production of completely different goods.

Nevertheless, depreciation may help with replacement because it may help to maintain the original capital (in terms of historical money), because depreciation reduces profit available for distribution. So, less cash may be distributed, and this will build up in the company, perhaps converted into a variety of different assets such as debtors, stock and even fixed assets.

Let us look at an example of how charging depreciation may aid replacement in the extreme cases where either:

(a) no depreciation is charged (Company A) or
(b) depreciation *is* charged, and the assets that are consequently undistributed are kept as current assets (Company B).

The two companies are identical in other ways, and both distribute all their profits. They start by buying a fixed asset for 10,000 ecu, which will last for ten years and have no scrap value. There are also 10,000 ecu of current assets. Table 7.3 shows the situation after the first year. If this continues for another nine years, Company A will have a worthless fixed asset and 10,000 ecu current assets, and will see that its capital is only 10,000 ecu. Company B will have a worthless fixed asset but 20,000 ecu current assets due to distributing 10,000 ecu less 'profits' than Company A did. So, Company B can purchase another fixed asset and continue business with its capital intact. Company A will have a serious financial problem. In essence, depreciation assists replacement by ensuring that profit is only measured or distributed after some form of maintenance of capital.

A well-run business has an overall cash and funds plan for future months and years. Included in this is the expected need to replace assets. The assets that will be bought as replacements may be identical but more expensive or they may be entirely different. It would be unusual, and probably commercially unwise, for a business to set aside amounts of money in liquid or time-matched investments in order to be prepared for the replacement of assets. These funds could be better used elsewhere

Table 7.3 The effect on assets of not charging depreciation.

	Company A				Company B		
Gross profit	5,000			Gross profit	5,000		
less Expenses	3,000			less Expenses	3,000		
				less depreciation	1,000		
Net profit	2,000 distributed			Net profit	1,000 distributed		
Balance sheet				*Balance sheet*			
Fixed assets	10,000	Capital	20,000	Fixed assets	10,000	Capital	20,000
		Profit	2,000	less Depreciation	1,000	Profit	1,000
Current assets	10,000	less Distribution	2,000		11,000	less Distribution	1,000
	20,000		20,000	Current assets	20,000		20,000

in the business, and it is not until the time for replacement approaches that a good impression of the type and cost of replacement assets is obtainable.

7.5 Allocation methods

The straight-line method of allocation was used earlier in the chapter for a basic illustration of depreciation. Using the AICPA terminology (see Section 7.3), one can see that straight-line allocation is 'systematic', but is it 'rational'? In order to answer this question, it is necessary to recall why depreciation is being charged. Depreciation is a charge designed to recognize the loss of services that an asset has suffered in any year. As has been said, it is an example of the results of using the accruals or matching convention. Let us look at different types of assets with this in mind.

1. Leases, patents and some buildings can be said to require depreciation because of the effluxion of time. In this case straight-line depreciation seems to be satisfactory.
2. Other assets have increasing repairs and maintenance. So, if straight-line depreciation is used, the total expense per year relating to an asset increases over its life. Therefore, if a reasonably constant total charge for an asset's services is to be put to the profit and loss account, a declining depreciation charge may be appropriate.
3. Some assets wear out in proportion to their use.

Declining charge methods

It may, then, be rational to have a declining depreciation charge for some sorts of assets. There are several ways of producing this systematically. The reducing balance (or constant percentage on reducing balance) method is one of them. With 20 per cent depreciation this would give a situation as shown in Table 7.4.

So, the written-down value at the end of the third year will be 5,120 and the charge in the third year will be 1,280. How many years will it take to write down the asset to zero? The answer, inconveniently, is that it will take an infinite number of years. However, if there is a scrap value, it will not. If there is no scrap value, a small figure to which the asset will be written down may be chosen. The residual at that point will be an extra depreciation charge for the final year.

To find the appropriate percentage to use for a given net cost and a given useful life, a formula may be used:

$$r = 1 - \sqrt[n]{\frac{S}{K}}$$

where r is the depreciation rate, n is the life of the asset, S is the scrap value and K is the gross cost. This formula may be simply derived as in Table 7.5.

Table 7.4 **The reducing balance method.**

	Cost	10,000
Year 1	less 20% depreciation	2,000
	WDV	8,000
Year 2	less 20% depreciation	1,600
	WDV	6,400
Year 3	less 20% depreciation	1,280
	WDV	5,120

Table 7.5 **The reducing balance formula.**

End of year	WDV	Standardized form of WDV
0	K	$K(1-r)^0$
1	$K - Kr$	$K(1-r)^1$
2	$(K - Kr) - (K - Kr)r$	$K(1-r)^2$
3	etc.	etc.

Therefore, at the end of the asset's life, $S = K(1 - r)^n$ which thus gives the above equation.

As an example, let us use the asset costing 10,000, which will have a scrap value of 3,000 and a life of seven years. Applying the above formula,

$$r = 1 - \sqrt[7]{\frac{3{,}000}{10{,}000}} = 0.158 \text{ or } 15.8\%$$

The results of this are tabulated in Table 7.6, repeating the straight-line results for comparison. It can be seen that more depreciation is charged in the earlier years using the reducing balance method. This helps to stabilize the total charge (of depreciation plus maintenance) for the contribution of the machine to earning profits.

Another way of producing systematically declining charges for depreciation is to use the sum of digits method. For this, one merely adds up the digits of the number of years of useful life. For example, for a useful life of six years the sum of digits is 21 (i.e. $6 + 5 + 4 + 3 + 2 + 1$). The charge for year 1 will be 6/12, that for year 2 will be 5/12 and so on. Another method that can be used to obtain a declining charge is the double declining-balance method. Here, the straight-line depreciation rate is worked out and then doubled and applied on a reducing balance basis.

One of these three declining charge methods may be appropriate for assets that are expected to have considerable repair and maintenance costs in later years. The

Table 7.6 **Depreciation methods contrasted.**

	Straight line		Reducing balance	
Year	Charge	WDV	Charge	WDV
0	—	10,000	—	10,000
1	1,000	9,000	1,580	8,420
2	1,000	8,000	1,330	7,090
3	1,000	7,000	1,120	5,970
4	1,000	6,000	940	5,030
5	1,000	5,000	790	4,240
6	1,000	4,000	670	3,570
7	1,000	3,000	570 [a]	3,000

[a] Adjusted for rounding differences.

total amount allocated will, of course, be the same in all these declining charge methods and, for that matter, in the straight-line method.

It may be that the market value of most machines actually declines in a way that is more similar to the result of declining charge depreciation than of straight-line depreciation. However, this is not really an argument in favour of a declining charge method, since the main aim is to get a fair yearly allocation of cost against profit over the whole life of the asset. Nevertheless, if the business is very uncertain about the useful life of the asset or the date of sale, there is an argument for rapid depreciation and for keeping the written-down value fairly close to the market value at all times rather than just at the estimated end of life. In these cases a declining charge method may be more suitable.

Usage methods

Assets that come to the end of their useful lives owing mainly to wearing out through use may more rationally be depreciated on the basis of use. According to the usage method, if the asset concerned is expected to produce 100,000 units or to run for 20,000 hours, the depreciation charge for the year will be that proportion of the original cost that the usage of the year bears to the total expected usage. For example, in the case of a machine costing 20,000 ecu which is expected to produce 100,000 units, the usage may turn out to be as given in Table 7.7.

The revaluation method

Some assets are difficult to depreciate by using any of the above methods (i.e.

Table 7.7 **The usage method.**

Accounting year	Units produced	Depreciation charge (ecu)
1	15,000	3,000
2	35,000	7,000
3	20,000	4,000
4	20,000	4,000
5	10,000	2,000
	100,000	20,000

straight-line, declining charge and usage). These assets are such things as tools, crates and livestock, for which it may be inappropriate or unnecessary to keep item-by-item records.

In the case of tools and crates, the assets may be capable of a long life, but in practice their lives are short because of damage, breakage, theft, loss and so on. In addition, their individual values are immaterial in the context of the whole company. Therefore it would be inefficient to record the purchase, the yearly depreciation charges, the disposal and adjustments to depreciation on disposal. In such instances, depreciation is charged using the revaluation method. This method involves valuing the set of similar assets at the beginning of the year, adding assets purchased and deducting a valuation of the set at the year end. This gives a measure of the using-up of the type of asset, which is charged to the profit and loss account as depreciation. The year-end valuation is recorded as a fixed asset in the balance sheet.

7.6 Practicalities

Assuming that depreciation is being calculated as an allocation of the historical cost of the asset, measurements or estimations will need to be made. Some of these are necessary where depreciation is, in effect, based on tax rules or where, at the other extreme, depreciation is based on replacement costs or other current values.

Useful economic life

The causes of wearing out were mentioned earlier. IAS 4 gives some guidance on determining depreciable life:

> The useful life of a depreciable asset for an enterprise may be shorter than its physical life. In addition to physical wear and tear, which depends on operational factors such

as the number of shifts for which the asset is to be used and the repair and maintenance programme of the enterprise, other factors need to be taken into consideration. These include obsolescence arising from technological changes or improvements in production, obsolescence arising from a change in the market demand for the product or service output of the asset, and legal limits such as the expiry dates of related leases. (para. 6)

Clearly, the estimation of useful lives involves considerable judgement, which is likely to turn out to be wrong in any particular case. IAS 4 requires reviews of lives, followed by adjustments to depreciation to correct for errors in estimates. In practice, mis-estimation (or use of tax-based lives) often leads to the continued ownership and use by a business of fully depreciated assets. Strictly, the lack of any continued depreciation charge for them must mean that earlier charges were unfairly high and present charges (i.e. zero) are unfairly low.

Residual value and disposal

If there is a residual value, the asset should gradually be written down to this, rather than being written down to zero. That is, the *net* cost (i.e. cost less residual value) should be allocated over the useful life of the asset. In practice, estimates of residual value are difficult, and it is often assumed that there will be no residual value. The first sentence of IAS 4's guidance on the subject hints at this:

> The residual value of an asset is often insignificant and can be ignored in the calculation of the depreciable amount. If the residual value is likely to be significant, it is estimated at the date of acquisition, or the date of any subsequent revaluation of the asset, on the basis of the realisable value prevailing at that date for similar assets which have reached the end of their useful lives and have operated under conditions similar to those in which the asset will be used. The gross residual value in all cases is reduced by the expected costs of disposal at the end of the useful life of the asset. (para. 7)

Given that estimates of useful life and scrap value often turn out to be wrong, an amount that is smaller or larger than the net cost will have been allocated over the actual life of the asset. The implication is that previous years' depreciation charges have been incorrect. Because of the practical difficulties of correcting previous years, usually the correction occurs in the year of disposal. It will be shown separately in the notes to the profit and loss account if it is important. For example, on disposal there will be a loss or an extra depreciation charge of 1,000 ecu if the cash received for an asset is 5,000 ecu but the written-down value is 6,000 ecu.

Mid-year purchases

What depreciation should be charged on an asset bought during the accounting year? There are two possibilities: either the appropriate proportion (perhaps by month) of one year's depreciation is charged in the years of acquisition and disposal, or a whole year's depreciation is charged for only those assets that are on hand at the end of the year. As long as the second method is used consistently, it should only lead to significant distortion when the business has few assets or has just acquired or disposed of a very valuable asset.

Revaluation

Under strict historical cost accounting, any increases in value of a depreciable asset are deemed not to be relevant. They do not affect the allocation of the historical cost. IAS 4 makes it clear that, for companies using strict historical cost, such value changes should not even affect the estimation of residual value, which should be based on prices at the time of the purchase of the asset.

In countries such as the Netherlands and the United Kingdom, *ad hoc* revaluation of fixed assets is fairly common. Recommended practice is to base subsequent depreciation charges on the revalued amounts. Consequently, the total depreciation expense over the life of the asset will be a mixture of allocation of cost and amounts higher than cost. It is normal to ensure that the depreciation *provision* is adjusted so that it represents the appropriate proportion of useful life used up.

7.7 Criticisms of depreciation

Estimates

As can be seen from the above section, the calculation of depreciation can be criticized on different grounds for two different types of country:

1. Tax-based countries, where some depreciation charges have little relationship to economic reality but are maximized within the tax rules.
2. Non-tax-based countries, where depreciation charges involve so many estimates that they may be subject to large errors or manipulations.

Certainly profits and values are affected even by policy choices. For example, higher depreciation charges (and lower profits) and lower asset values will result in the early years of an asset's life by choosing reducing balance depreciation, a short life estimate and a low scrap value.

Some have argued that depreciation relies on so many estimates and choices and is so far removed from being a real cost of the year that it should not be charged. This, of course, could be part of a more general attack on accruals accounting. In practice, some analysts of accounts do add back depreciation charges to profits because of the arbitrary and non-cash nature of these expenses.

DEPRECIATION OF FIXED ASSETS

Lack of realism

Earlier in this chapter, there was a brief discussion of depreciation based on valuation rather than cost. Although the former does not fit well into conventional accounting, there certainly are problems with cost when prices are rising (see Chapter 11). In particular, depreciation charges will look increasingly unrealistic as prices rise and as the time since purchase increases.

A realistic cost of using up one-tenth of an asset bought several years ago is very unlikely to be one-tenth of its historical cost if prices have been changing in the interim. Consider again the asset bought for 10,000 ecu that will last ten years with no scrap value. After five years the replacement cost of the asset might be 20,000 ecu. It seems more reasonable to base depreciation on the 20,000 ecu rather than the 10,000 ecu, for it is a proportion of a machine that currently costs 20,000 that is currently being used up. This would be one possible approach to the recognition of the effects of price changes. The effect of basing depreciation on historical costs in inflationary periods is, in a sense, to overstate profit, particularly in companies with many old fixed assets.

7.8 Practice

The straight-line method of depreciation is the most frequently found in Europe, and most of the rest of the world. Table 7.8 shows that it is the normal basis for buildings, although the reducing balance method is also used in Germany when certain legal conditions are fulfilled. For plant and machinery, the same remarks apply (see Table 7.9). In Germany, not only is the reducing balance method common, but companies might start depreciation of an asset with reducing balance and then swap to straight line when this gives a larger charge. This is illustrated by Example 7.1.

EXAMPLE 7.1

Daimler-Benz note the following:

> *Intangible costs and fixed assets* are valued at acquisition costs which are reduced by scheduled depreciation allowances. The opportunities for special tax-deductible depreciation allowances are fully utilized.
>
> Scheduled fixed asset depreciation allowances are calculated generally using the following useful lives: 20 to 40 years for buildings, 10 to 20 years for site improvements, 3 to 10 years for technical facilities and machinery, other facilities as well as factory and office equipment.
>
> Buildings are depreciated using straight-line depreciation rates and – where allowable under the Tax Code – declining rates. Movable property with a useful life of four years and more is depreciated using the declining-balance-method. We change from the

Table 7.8 Depreciation of land and buildings.

Sample size	Bel 50	Den 32	Fra 40	Ger 49	Gre 30	Ire 38	Lux 12	Net 40	Swe 9	UK 50	Total 350
Evidence of land and buildings	38	29	33	48	27	35	12	39	8	50	319
Basis used for depreciation[a]											
Land:											
Depreciation	1	—	4	—	—	4	—	1	—	—	10
Basis not specified	2	—	2	—	—	—	—	2	—	—	6
No income effect	19	11	22	—	27	21	5	3	—	—	108
Buildings:											
Straight line	22	14	28	18	26	23	3	18	7	—	159
Reducing balance	2	1	3	7	—	—	—	—	—	—	13
Other or not specified	3	1	1	—	—	3	—	1	—	—	9
Land and buildings:											
Straight line	5	14	2	17	—	6	7	21	1	49	122
Reducing balance	1	—	—	10	—	—	—	—	—	—	11
Other or not specified	2	—	—	8	—	1	1	1	—	—	13
No income effect	—	—	—	—	—	3	—	—	—	1	4
Basis not disclosed	7	—	1	4	—	—	—	—	—	—	12

[a] More than one answer possible.
Source: adapted from FEE, *European Survey of Published Accounts 1991*, Routledge, London, 1991.

Table 7.9 Depreciation of plant and machinery.

Sample size	Bel 50	Den 32	Fra 40	Ger 49	Gre 30	Ire 38	Lux 12	Net 40	Swe 9	UK 50	Total 350
Evidence of charge to the income statement for depreciation of plant and machinery	45	32	32	46	30	33	11	32	9	47	317
Basis for depreciation:[a]											
Amortization											
Straight line	30	29	28	36	30	29	11	30	9	47	279
Reducing balance	3	3	15	32	—	2	1	—	—	—	56
Other	4	—	1	6	—	2	—	2	—	—	15
Other	—	1	1	4	—	—	—	—	—	—	6
Basis not disclosed	8	—	2	—	—	—	—	—	—	—	10

[a] More than one answer possible
Source: adapted from FEE, *European Survey of Published Accounts 1991*, Routledge, London, 1991.

declining-balance method to the straight-line method of calculating depreciation when the equal distribution of the remaining net book value over the remaining useful life leads to higher depreciation amounts.

Scheduled depreciation and special tax depreciation amount to DM 130 million and DM 29 million, respectively (pursuant to Section 6b of the Income Tax Act).

The net profit for the year was DM 1942 million, so depreciation was a significant expense.

The directors of some British companies have used various arguments to avoid depreciation charges, particularly on large assets such as buildings. For example, it might be claimed that certain hotels or shops have to be maintained in at least as good a condition as when they were purchased. Therefore they do not wear out during their life with the present owner; so there should be no depreciation charges (see Example 7.2).

EXAMPLE 7.2

Marks & Spencer's note illustrates the common UK procedure for stores groups:

> Depreciation is provided to write off the cost or valuation of tangible fixed assets by equal annual instalments at the following rates:
> Freehold and leasehold land and buildings over 50 years – 1 per cent (see *a* below),
> Leasehold land and buildings under 50 years – over the remaining period of the lease,
> Fixtures, fittings and equipment – $6\frac{2}{3}$ to $33\frac{1}{3}$ per cent according to the estimated life of the asset.
> *a* Depreciation is not provided on freehold and long leasehold properties where, in the opinion of the directors, the residual values of those properties are such that any depreciation charge would be immaterial.
> *b* Depreciation is charged on all additions to depreciating assets in the year of purchase.

An alternative argument, for investment properties, is that they are being held for value, and so they ought to be shown at current valuation, thereby absorbing any depreciation. Indeed, as mentioned in the previous chapter, the UK accounting standard (SSAP 19) does make investment properties an exception: they must be annually revalued and not depreciated.

Intangibles

The depreciation of certain intangible fixed assets was discussed in Chapter 6. In general straight-line depreciation and short amortization periods are found.

However, some intangibles in some countries are not amortized. as mentioned in that chapter. Goodwill and its amortization is considered in Chapter 12.

SUMMARY

The accounting concept of depreciation is concerned with the allocation of the historical cost of a fixed asset over its useful life in a systematic and rational manner. The amounts allocated are charged against profit in the appropriate year, with the intention that the fairest estimate of profit will be made, although in some countries there is an influence of tax rules on the size of depreciation.

There are many causes that contribute towards the limited life of the asset (e.g. the passing of time, the use of the asset, escalating repair expenses, and technical obsolescence of the machine or its product). If these causes can be identified and quantified, it should be possible to decide which method of depreciation would allocate the cost most fairly over the asset's life.

The methods in use include the straight-line, declining charge, usage and revaluation methods. Whichever method is used, depreciation does not provide cash for replacement (although it may mean that less cash is distributed), and it does not lead to the written-down value being an estimate of market value (except at the end of the asset's life, by which time it will usually be found that estimates of life and scrap value are inaccurate).

There are several practical problems (e.g. estimating the life and the scrap value of the assets). A further difficulty is the effect of inflation. If depreciation charges are calculated using current replacement costs, the charges are more realistic and larger, thus suggesting a smaller profit figure.

Around Europe the straight-line method based on historical cost is the most frequently found.

EXERCISES

7.1 The following payments have been made during the year in relation to a fixed asset bought at the beginning of the year:

		ecu
Cost as in supplier's list	12,000	
Less agreed discount	1,000	
		11,000
Delivery charge		100
Erection charge		200
Maintenance charge		400
Additional component to increase capacity		500
Replacement parts		600

What cost figure should be used as the basis for the depreciation charge for the year and why?

7.2 The following actual and estimated figures are available:

          Cost   12,000 ecu
          Useful life   4 years
          Scrap value   2,000 ecu

(a) Calculate annual depreciation under the straight-line method.

(b) Calculate the depreciation charge for each of the four years under the reducing balance method using a depreciation percentage of 40%.

(c) If the estimated scrap value turns out to be correct and the asset is sold on the first day of year 5, list and contrast the effect on reported profit for each of the five years under each method.

7.3 Provide in your own words:
(a) an explanation of what depreciation is;
(b) an explanation of the net book value (NBV) of a partially depreciated fixed asset.

7.4 A company borrows money at 12% interest in order to finance the building of a new factory. Suggest arguments for and against the proposition that the interest costs should be capitalized and regarded as part of the 'cost' of the factory. Which set of arguments do you prefer?

7.5 Outline three different depreciation methods, and appraise them in the context of the definition and objectives of depreciation.

7.6 Is depreciation either too subjective, or too arbitrary, to be useful?

CHAPTER 8

Inventory valuation

OBJECTIVES

- To clarify the important effects of inventory valuation on profit and balance sheet figures
- To examine the elements of arriving at an inventory figure: counting and valuing
- To note the several possible bases of valuation, and the several meanings of cost
- To outline the rules on inventories in EC and IASC documents
- To survey the practices in several European countries

8.1 Introduction

As discussed in Part I of this book, conventional accounting is generally based on the recording of transactions rather than on valuations. Consequently, when calculating the depreciation of assets as analyzed in the previous chapter, greater attention is paid to the meaning of the depreciation charge in the income statement than to the resulting effects on the written-down value of the depreciated asset in the balance sheet. The written-down value is not supposed to represent the sale value of the asset at the balance sheet date.

Like depreciation, the valuation of inventory[1] also directly affects the income statement and the balance sheet. However, in this case, because inventory is a current asset that will soon be sold (usually for debtors or cash), its realistic valuation is of greater importance than for most fixed assets. Inventory valuation affects the apparent liquidity of the company, as measured by various ratios (see Part IV).

---

[1] In certain countries the word 'stock' is used, but this is confusing for those who are used to American English. For more details, see the end of this section and Section 17.2.

INVENTORY VALUATION

It should be clear that the valuation of inventory on hand at the end of an accounting period is directly related to the profit figure. For example, for a retail company with no opening inventory, the gross profit might be:

Sales for the period	1,000
− Purchases for the period	− 800
+ Closing inventory at the end of period	+ 50
= Gross profit	= 250

This can be rearranged as:

Sales for the period		1,000
Purchases	800	
− Closing stock	50	
Cost of sales		750
Gross profit		250

Purchases of materials in the period are all treated initially as expenses (see Part I). However, the materials are not all used up in the accounting period; so, in order to take account of the existence of closing inventory, it is necessary to make an adjustment that reduces the expenses. Although the total profit of all accounting periods is not affected by the valuation of inventory (because one year's closing inventory is the next year's opening inventory), the profit of any individual year *is* affected.

Since the concern is with finding a fair figure for profit for the year, there must be an attempt to match the charge for inventory used against the sales that relate to it. There are many ways of valuing the remaining inventory, some of which cause fairer charges for the inventory used than others. The example in Table 8.1 should make it clear that any overvaluation of closing inventory by 1 ecu leads to an overstatement of profit by 1 ecu in the year in question. Naturally, such an overstatement would also make next year's opening inventory too large, and therefore next year's profit too small.

Table 8.1 **The relation between inventory valuation and profit.**

Sales (revenue)		2,000
Opening inventory	800	
Purchases	1,600	
	2,400	
less Closing inventory	950	
Cost of sales (expense)		1,450
Gross profit		550

Table 8.2 **Comparative usage of 'stock'.**

United States	United Kingdom
Inventory	Stock
Work-in-process	Work-in-progress
Stock	Shares
Common stock	Ordinary shares

Inventory is usually split into categories, typically:

- raw materials
- work-in-progress
- finished goods

A manufacturing business may have all three types, whereas a retail business may have only the last.

A language point is worth making here. The word 'inventory' is used in North America and some other English-speaking areas of the world. It is the word found in IASC statements. It is also used in many translated annual reports of continental European companies, who tend to use a mid-Atlantic version of English. However, in the United Kingdom and Ireland and some other English-speaking countries, the word 'stock' is used instead. This can lead to particular confusion, because 'stock' in US terminology means 'share'. A short comparative glossary for this point is shown as Table 8.2.

8.2 Counting inventory

Before *valuing* the inventory it is necessary to know how much there is. It is also useful to know what type of inventories there are. Inventories are often divided into raw materials, work-in-progress and finished goods. Looking at the process of counting, let us consider first a simple case where a business owns finished goods only, because it runs a wholesale warehouse. Even here, there are several ways of estimating the quantity of inventory on hand at a year end.

Stock-takes (or periodic counts)

The warehouse staff, perhaps assisted by administrative staff, physically count and record all items of inventory on the premises. The auditors will probably wish to advise on procedures, attend the count and check the results for a few types of inventory. Adjustments have to be made for goods on the premises that do not belong to the firm and for goods off the premises that do. Also, there will be adjustments for inventory movements if the actual count is done on a day that is not the accounting year end, perhaps because a weekend is more convenient.

Continuous stock-taking (or perpetual inventory)

Using this method a record is kept by item of all inventory movements as they occur. Therefore, a figure for the amount of inventory of each type on hand at any moment should be easy to calculate. This is supplemented by occasional counts of selected items to see if the inventory records are accurate. This avoids a massive and disruptive effort at the year end.

In practice many inventory control systems are run by computers, which record sales and purchases and produce invoices and lists of debtors. They can also report current inventory figures, slow-moving lines, reorder possibilities, and so on. The running of a perpetual inventory is much easier in these circumstances.

Comparing these two methods, it is clear that the latter will discover pilferage more quickly and help in signalling that a reorder of inventory is necessary. Note that the periodic count gives a figure for usage during the year by residual, which obscures any pilferage and breakages. On the other hand, the perpetual inventory method counts up usage during the year but leaves closing inventory as a residual figure. The physical figures must always be those used for profit measurements, if available. The accounting records must be adjusted to the actual physical inventory in cases of discrepancy.

8.3 Valuation

Now consideration can be given to potential alternative bases of valuation: *output values* and *input values*. These alternatives are the application to inventory of issues discussed in Part I.

Output values

The use of output values would rely on the proposition that the value of the inventory to the firm is the future receipts that will arise from it. There are several ways that could be used to measure this output value:

1. *Discounted money receipts* can be used when there is a definite amount and time of receipt. This will seldom be the case except for contracts of supply.
2. *Current selling prices* may be used when there is a definite price and no significant selling costs or delays. For example, inventories of gold may be valued in this way.

3. *Net realizable value* is the estimated selling price in the ordinary course of business, *less* costs of completion and *less* costs to be incurred in marketing, distributing and selling but without deduction for general administration or profit.

There seem to be grounds for using net realizable value when sales prices and other costs are known, particularly for inventories in an advanced state of completion. It can be argued that, if 90% of the work has been done, then to take all the profit before sale is better ('fairer') than taking none. However, conventional accounting is not disposed towards a consistent use of this valuation method, because profit would then be taken before the inventory was sold.

Input values

The alternatives to output values are input values, of which two will be considered. In each case the value will include those costs which contribute towards bringing the inventory to its present location and condition. For financial accounting purposes, these costs should usually include the appropriate proportion of production overheads (as illustrated below). However, other overheads (e.g. administration and selling) can be included in some countries.

Let us look at a simple example of overhead absorption:

Direct cost: Labour	3 ecu per unit
Materials	2 ecu per unit
Direct overheads (specific supervisors and machines)	40,000 ecu
Indirect overheads (rates, factory managers, etc.)	60,000 ecu
Administrative overheads of the rest of the company	80,000 ecu
Selling overheads	20,000 ecu

If the year's production were 20,000 units and this type of production used $\frac{1}{3}$ of the factory, the cost per unit for goods that had fully passed through production would be 8 ecu; that is:

	ecu units	
Direct costs	5	
Direct production overheads	2	(i.e. 40,000 ecu ÷ 20,000)
Indirect production overheads	1	(i.e. 60,000 ecu × $\frac{1}{3}$ ÷ 20,000)
Other overheads	—	
	8	

This 'cost' of 8 is used for financial accounting purposes. For management accounting, other methods of calculating costs might be used, e.g. concentrating on direct costs only, or including all overheads. Activity-based costing (ABC) does not alter the principle of this issue concerning treatment of overheads, but it will tend to lead to a higher proportion of direct overheads and a lower proportion of indirect ones.

The two input values considered in this chapter are historical cost and current replacement cost. The former has been the usual method of valuation for centuries. The latter (considered in Section 8.7) would be the normal method of valuation under some systems of current value accounting.

8.4 Historical cost as an input value

The historical cost of inventory can be measured by aggregating the net payments made in the past to bring the inventory to its present condition and location. This will include the original cost of materials and delivery, and normal costs of production. Abnormal costs (e.g. unusually great wastage or idle time) or unintended costs (e.g. inefficient buying or pilferage) are not costs of production but losses.

The advantages of an historical cost basis are that it is relatively objective and that it is usable where selling prices and extra costs to completion are volatile or uncertain. However, when prices are changing, the valuation may soon become out of date, and there will be the problem that inventories bought at different times that are still on hand will be added together at original cost, although they are not really comparable. Also, it will usually be necessary to allocate to the inventory in question the costs incurred jointly for it and other inventories.

There are several different assumptions about the flow of inventories that can be used for the historical cost basis. These are necessary because, having counted a particular item of inventory, it is not always clear what the historical cost is. This is because of lack of knowledge as to which particular identical units of inventory bought at varying prices throughout the year, are those on hand. Very often it is physically impossible to tell which units are still held (e.g. in the case of a tank full of oil), or it may be economically unjustifiable to find out (e.g. in the case of large inventories of small items). Even if the exact initial costs and production costs of each unit can be determined, there are reasons for ignoring this and assuming another sort of inventory flow for accounting purposes. This will be discussed further below.

A simple example of the problem will help to illustrate this. Suppose that the transactions listed in Table 8.3 occur. Which, for accounting purposes, are the five units that were sold, and which are the five that remain? The answers will determine the size of profit and the balance sheet valuation of inventory. Let us look at various possible assumptions.

Specific or unit cost

This method can be used when the items of inventory are large enough to be readily identifiable. Here it is assumed that each unit is a specific venture, that specific costs and revenues should be matched and that specific costs should be carried in

Table 8.3 **Example of inventory purchases.**

Transaction date	Purchases	Cost of sales charged to profit	Inventory at cost
1 January	10 at 3 ecu		10 at 3 ecu = 30 ecu
11 January		6 at 3 ecu	4 at 3 ecu = 12 ecu
21 January	6 at 4 ecu		4 at 3 ecu + 6 at 4 ecu = 36 ecu
31 January		5 at ?	5 at ? = ?

inventory until the unit's sale. In the example of Table 8.3, if specific costs were used, it would be necessary to see which five units were actually on hand. There are two problems with valuing using this assumption. First, many costs are overhead costs; that is, the costs are incurred for the processing of both all these units and perhaps other types of units as well, and they are therefore difficult to allocate to individual types of inventory, let alone to individual units. Second, profit can be manipulated by choosing which out of several similar units will be sold; if it were wished to defer some profit until next year, the most expensive units (probably the most recent ones) should be sold.

Average cost

This would be used if the company's business were regarded as a series of transactions that could not reasonably be separated. The physical flow is ignored, and the problems of allocating actual processing costs to individual units are avoided.

In the example of Table 8.3, the cost of the inventory used and the inventory remaining would both be 18 ecu (3.6 ecu per unit, i.e. 36 ecu ÷ 10 units). This weighted average cost method is common in some countries and can be claimed to provide an approximation to actual cost. With a computer-based accounting system, it is simple to use. In practice, the average for a period would be used rather than the average after each transaction.

First-in, first-out (FIFO)

FIFO is another method that could fulfil a 'fairest approximation' criterion. Here the assumption (which may have the merit of being somewhere near the truth) is that the goods that leave the firm are those that have been in inventory the longest.

Consequently, the inventory on hand is assumed to be the latest. Compared to average cost or LIFO (see below), this will lead, in times of rising prices, to:

- older, lower cost of sales expense;
- therefore, higher profit (which will raise taxation in some countries);
- more realistic (i.e. more current) balance sheet figures.

In the example in Table 8.3 the inventory used would be valued at 16 ecu (4 units at 3 ecu and 1 unit at 4 ecu), and the inventory remaining would be valued at 20 ecu (5 units at 4 ecu). The problem with the method is that, although there is an approximate matching of specific costs against specific revenues, there is not a matching of *current* costs against *current* revenues. This will be considered further when we consider adjustments necessary to allow for changing prices (Section 8.7).

Last-in, first-out (LIFO)

Using the LIFO flow assumption the example in Table 8.3 would lead to a charge against profit of 20 ecu (5 units at 4 ecu) and a closing stock of 16 ecu (1 unit at 4 ecu and 4 units at 3 ecu). So, the charge to profit is a better estimate of current costs, but the balance sheet holds an unrealistically low and out-of-date inventory figure. A balance sheet note of the current value would be a partial solution and provide an estimate of holding gains or losses.

Other problems are:

- when the inventory is physically reduced, absurd profit figures result from the use of very old material costs;
- if inventory values fall because of inefficient buying or deterioration, recognition will not be given to this because LIFO cost will probably still be below net realizable value;
- real gains from specific price rises in excess of general price rises are not reported.

Arguments in favour of using LIFO might be that physical usage of a particular inventory by a particular company corresponded to LIFO, or that a particular industry uses processes that rely on having a fixed amount of raw materials or work in progress in the pipeline. For example, an oil refinery might always have a number of tonnes of crude, which could only be sold or used up if the refinery were to cease production. If the refinery is to be treated as a going concern, the 'pipeline' inventory would be regarded as a fixed asset rather than a current asset. In this case the inventory charged against profit is that bought in the year. This creates an approximate matching of current costs and current revenues.

Standard cost

For the purposes of cost accounting, a business may have established a series of standard costs for its inventories at various levels of completion. These costs may be used for inventory valuation. Further reference to standard costs is left to books on cost accounting.

Retail inventory and gross profit margin

These methods are used to overcome the practical problems in large shops of counting and valuing great numbers of different items. Using these methods the inventory is counted on a periodic rather than a perpetual basis, and its value at selling prices is worked out. To find a value using any of the other methods discussed so far would be extremely difficult. Clearly, though, to value inventory at selling prices would be to take profit before sale. In order to avoid this, ratios of cost to price are worked out item by item or class by class; and these are applied to the inventories to reduce them to cost. Since current prices and current costs will be used, there will be a result similar to FIFO. This is called the *retail inventory method*.

An alternative method uses a gross profit margin, which is worked out using experience of prior years. Here, the valuation is even quicker, because the inventory cost is worked out by taking the goods bought *plus* opening inventory at cost, *less* the goods sold at selling price reduced to cost by application of the gross profit margin. So, no count is made. Consequently, this method should only be used as a check on other methods or when no other method is possible (e.g. due to a fire).

Effects of methods

Although the choice of inventory valuation method will not affect profits over the whole of the life of the company, it will certainly affect profits and asset value in any particular year. Therefore, choices, errors and manipulations related to inventory can have a great effect on the accounts.

For example, assuming that inventory prices are rising, then FIFO generally gives higher closing inventory and higher cost of sales (therefore lower profit) than LIFO. The simple numerical example of FIFO and LIFO above illustrates this. So, LIFO may be attractive to companies in those countries where LIFO is allowed for the calculation of profit for tax purposes.

It should be mentioned that it is important, for the comparability of profit figures from year to year, to be consistent in the method used. Consequently, any changes should be disclosed and quantified. This is clearly important for a proper reading of profit figures and balance sheets.

8.5 Fourth Directive and IASC rules

The following extracts from the relevant Articles of the Fourth Directive and IASC standards apply to inventories.

Article 43.1 (1) of the Fourth Directive requires that valuation methods should be disclosed:

1. In addition to the information required under other provisions of this Directive, the notes on the accounts must set out information in respect of the following matters at least:
   (1) the valuation methods applied to the various items in the annual accounts, and the methods employed in calculating the value adjustments.

Article 32 states in general that valuation should be based on the principle of purchase price or production cost. For current assets, Article 39 states:

1. (a) Current assets must be valued at purchase price or production cost, without prejudice to (b) and (c) below.
   (b) Value adjustments shall be made in respect of current assets with a view to showing them at the lower market value or, in particular circumstances, another lower value to be attributed to them at the balance sheet date.
   (c) The Member States may permit exceptional value adjustments where, on the basis of a reasonable commercial assessment, these are necessary if the valuation of these items is not to be modified in the near future because of fluctuations in value. The amount of these value adjustments must be disclosed separately in the profit and loss account or in the notes on the accounts.
   (d) Valuation at the lower value provided for in (b) and (c) may not be continued if the reasons for which the value adjustments were made have ceased to apply.
   (e) If current assets are the subject of exceptional value adjustments for taxation purposes alone, the amount of the adjustments and the reasons for making them must be disclosed in the notes on the accounts.
2. The definitions of purchase price and of production cost given in Article 35 (2) and (3) shall apply. The Member States may also apply Article 35 (4). Distribution costs may not be included in production costs.

Article 33 provides an option for member states to depart from the general valuation principle (historical cost valuation) by allowing valuation at current cost, subject to certain requirements. Chapter 5 contains a discussion of the Fourth Directive, and the text is given in the appendix to this book.

Article 40 of the Fourth Directive gives the basis for calculation of the purchase price as well as production cost:

1. The Member States may permit the purchase price or production cost of stocks of goods of the same category and all fungible items including investments to be calculated either on the basis of weighted average prices or by the 'first in, first out' (FIFO) method, the 'last in, first out' (LIFO) method, or some similar method.
2. Where the value shown in the balance sheet, following application of the methods of calculation specified in paragraph 1, differs materially, at the balance sheet date, from the value on the basis of the last known market value prior to the balance sheet date, the amount of that difference must be disclosed in total by category in the notes on the accounts.

IAS 2 'Valuation and Presentation of Inventories in the Context of the Historical Cost System' requires the use of the lower of cost and market valuation method, and allows the use of FIFO, LIFO and weighted average. The IASC Statement of Intent of July 1990 proposed to forbid the use of LIFO, but this was not acceptable to a sufficient majority of the IASC Board.

The Fourth Directive does not mention the difficulties raised by the accounting treatment of construction contracts, which in general terms means those contracts from customers for the construction of assets that extend over more than one accounting period. On the other hand, IAS 11 treats this problem specifically. It makes provision for two methods of accounting for results arising from this type of contract: the percentage of completion method and the completed contract method. In the former, a proportion of profit is taken as production proceeds; in the latter, profit recognition waits for completion. A numerical example of one version of the percentage of completion method is given in the appendix at the end of this chapter. The percentage of completion method will generally lead to earlier profits and higher current asset values than the completed contract method. Of course, as with many examples of the matching concept, it is necessary to make estimates (in this case of work done, etc.), so the percentage method is subject to manipulation.

Article 31.1 (c) (aa) of the Fourth Directive lays down that only profits made at the balance sheet date may be taken into account. Based on a restrictive interpretation of this text, some may argue that only the completed contract method is admissible from the point of view of the Fourth Directive. According to the other view, which is becoming dominant, the completed contract method could lead to the setting up of hidden reserves that would not comply with the objective of giving a true and fair view as required by Article 2.3 of the Fourth Directive (see Part II).

According to the Statement of Intent of 1990, the Board of IASC decided, in appropriate circumstances, to forbid the use of the completed contract method and to allow only the use of the percentage of completion method. IAS 11 (revised) sets out as a requirement for the percentage of completion method, that the outcome of the contract can be reliably estimated. The conditions are set out in paragraph 23:

23. In the case of a fixed price contract the outcome of a construction contract can be estimated reliably when all of the following conditions are satisfied:
    (a) total contract revenue can be measured reliably;
    (b) it is probable that the economic benefits associated with the contract will flow to the enterprise;
    (c) both the contract costs to complete the contract and the stage of contract completion at the balance sheet date can be measured reliably; and
    (d) the contract costs attributable to the contract can be clearly identified and measured reliably so that actual contract costs incurred can be compared with prior estimates.
24. In the case of a cost plus contract, the outcome of a construction contract can be estimated reliably when all of the following conditions are satisfied:
    (a) it is probable that the economic benefits associated with the contract will flow to the enterprise; and
    (b) the contract costs attributable to the contract, whether or not specifically reimbursable, can be clearly identified and measured reliably.

8.6 Practice

Under conventional accounting, the 'lower of cost and market' rule has been used for centuries. That is 'historical cost' is the usual basis of valuation unless there has been a *loss in value* since purchase. Such a loss in value can occur through obsolescence, physical deterioration, inefficient purchasing or a fall in the selling price of the goods to be manufactured. It is prudent accounting practice to recognize a loss in value as soon as it is discovered. So, profit is reduced immediately rather than at the point of sale. In some countries, 'market' is interpreted to mean net realizable value. In other, more conservative, countries, current replacement cost can be used if lower. In countries where accounting is heavily tax-influenced, there may be tax-allowed provisions relating to inventories, which reduce its recorded valuation.

The application of the 'lower of cost and market' rule should be carried out on an individual basis, in order to avoid the setting off of foreseeable losses against unrealized profits. Consider the example in Table 8.4. The individual comparison leads to a total inventory valuation of 720 ecu, whereas a total comparison would lead to 750 ecu (thus hiding the loss in value suffered by inventory B).

In inflationary times cost will nearly always be below net realizable value or replacement cost, and so in practice a very large majority of inventories will be valued at historical cost.

A problem with the 'lower of cost or net realizable value' rule is that it gives rise to inconsistency if, for example, opening inventories are valued at cost but closing inventories are valued at net realizable value. The profit figures will be distorted in consequence.

Based on a comparative survey of European practice, Table 8.5 shows the methods disclosed in company annual reports for the valuation of work-in-progress inventory. This shows the predominance of the 'lower of cost and market' basis, although it does not reveal nuances in the meaning of 'market'. Many of the companies reporting 'production cost' may also have been using the lower of cost and market, which led, in their cases, to cost.

Table 8.6 shows that the formula used to determine 'cost' is predominantly FIFO or weighted average, which gives similar results. LIFO is not allowed under most circumstances in several countries (e.g. in France and the United Kingdom), but is

Table 8.4 **Example of inventory valuation (ecu).**

	Cost	NRV	Lower by individual comparison
Inventory A	100	130	100
Inventory B	400	370	370
Inventory C	250	380	250
Total	750	880	720

Table 8.5 **Valuation basis of work-in-progress.**

Sample size	Bel 50	Den 32	Fra 40	Ger 49	Gre 30	Ire 38	Ita 30	Lux 12	Net 40	Spa 30	UK 50	Total 401
Evidence of work-in-progress	16	21	17	41	9	19	20	7	22	17	39	228
Valuation basis used for work-in-progress:[a]												
Purchase price	—	2	—	21	—	2	3	—	—	2	—	30
Production cost	7	15	16	31	1	6	10	1	13	6	1	107
Lower of cost or market price	7	7	14	26	8	14	7	6	7	5	38	139
Other	—	1	—	3	—	2	—	—	4	1	—	11
No disclosure of valuation basis for work-in-progress	2	—	1	1	—	2	1	—	1	5	—	13

[a] More than one answer possible.
Source: adapted from FEE, *European Survey of Published Accounts 1991*, Routledge, London 1991.

Table 8.6 **Cost formula[a] for work-in-progress**

Sample size	Bel 50	Den 32	Fra 40	Ger 49	Gre 30	Ire 38	Ita 30	Lux 12	Net 40	Spa 30	UK 50	Total 401
FIFO	2	5	2	—	2	4	2	1	2	1	8	29
Weighted average cost	3	—	5	6	1	—	5	1	1	5	1	28
LIFO	1	—	—	3	—	—	5	1	1	—	—	11
Latest purchase price	—	1	—	—	—	—	—	—	3	—	—	4
Specific identification	1	1	1	12	—	—	—	—	—	—	—	15
Other	2	1	2	—	3	1	3	1	6	—	—	19
Cost formula used not disclosed	8	13	7	21	3	14	5	4	11	11	31	128

[a] More than one answer possible.
Source: adapted from FEE, *European Survey of Published Accounts 1991*, Routledge, London, 1991.

allowed (and found), for example, in Germany, Italy and the Netherlands. Incidentally, it is the predominant method in the United States. This is because it is allowed for tax purposes there and, as noted earlier, tends to show lower profits than FIFO or weighted average.

Table 8.7 shows that, where there is evidence of long-term contracts, both completed contract and percentage-of-completion methods are used. The completed

Table 8.7 **Valuation basis of long-term contracts.**

Sample size	Bel 50	Den 32	Fra 40	Ger 49	Ire 38	Net 40	UK 50	Total 299
Evidence of long-term contracts	12	9	6	7	2	9	11	56
Valuation basis used for long-term contracts:								
Completed contract method	1	3	3	6	—	1	2	16
Percentage of completion method	4	5	2	—	1	5	7	24
Both	—	—	1	—	—	1	—	2
Other	1	—	—	—	—	1	—	2
Valuation basis not disclosed	6	1	—	1	1	1	2	12

Source: adapted from FEE, *European Survey of Published Accounts 1991*, Routledge, London, 1991.

contract method dominates in more prudent Germany, whereas the percentage method is normal in the Netherlands and the United Kingdom.

8.7 Current value accounting

Under systems of current value accounting, the valuation of inventory is usually based on replacement cost, because this will normally be the 'value to the business' or the 'deprival value' of the inventory. As an illustration of this, suppose that a business owns ten units of a common raw material. The business intends to maintain inventory at ten units. The units in inventory were bought earlier in the year for 10 ecu each. Their purchase was recorded on this basis, and they still have labels with '10 ecu cost' on them. At the year end, the cost of identical units has risen to 12 ecu. What is the recorded value of the units?

Under historical cost, specific costing can be used in this case. Assuming that net realizable value is higher and that no work has been done on the units, the valuation will clearly be 100 ecu. However, under current value accounting, recognition is made of the fact that, if the business were deprived of the inventory, it would buy another ten units at the current cost. Therefore the value to the business of the inventory is 120 ecu. Some discussion of current value accounting occurs in Chapters 2 and 6, but it is considered in detail in Chapter 11.

There will still be cases where inventory has lost value due to obsolescence or damage. Consequently, the net realizable value of inventory is to be used where it is lower than the replacement cost. So, the rule for the valuation of inventory under current value accounting becomes 'the lower of current replacement cost and net realizable value'. This is a more realistic estimate of the value of the inventory to the business as a going concern.

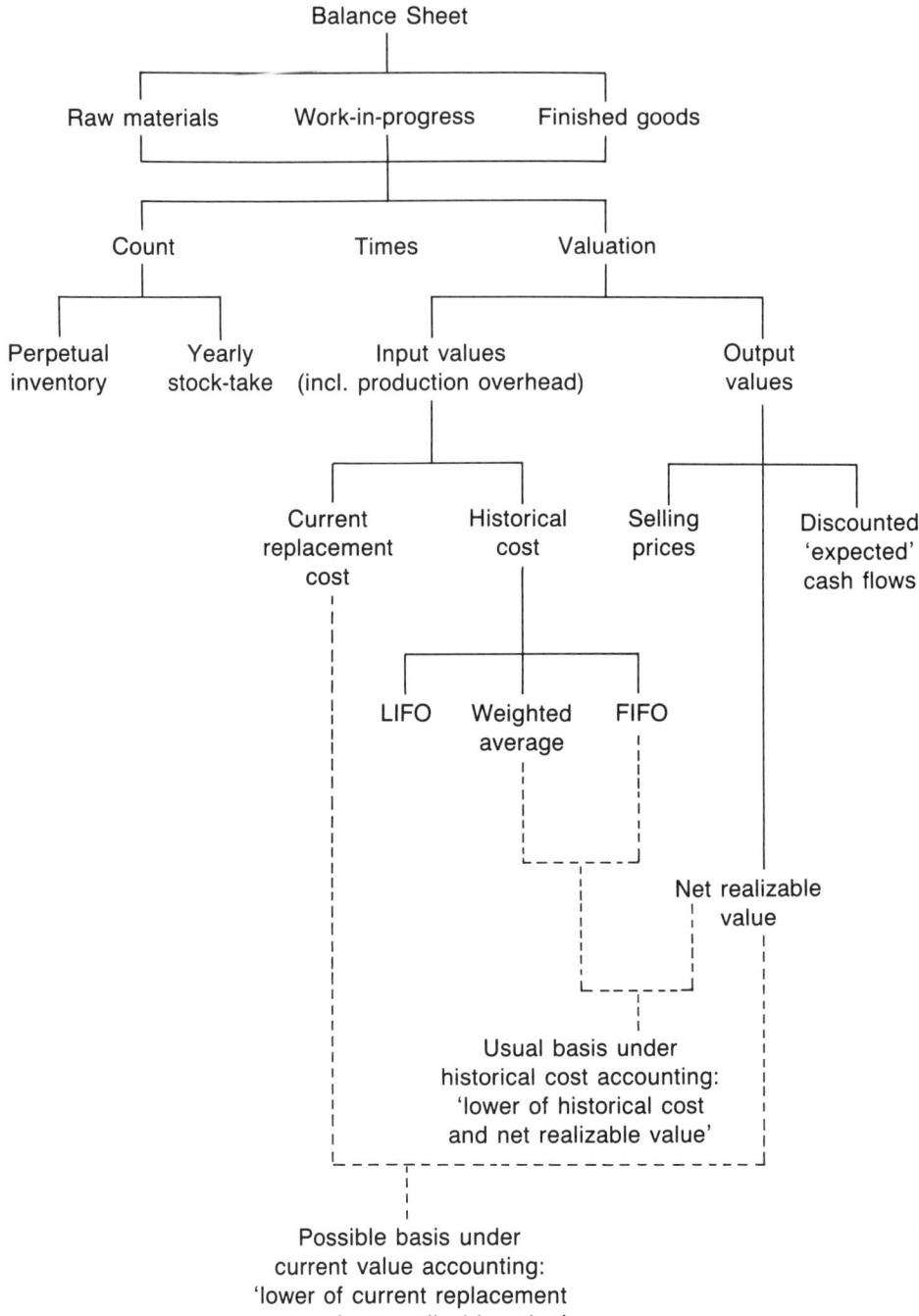

Figure 8.1 Inventory valuation.

> **SUMMARY**
>
> The valuation of inventory is important for profit measurement and for balance sheet valuations. There are some practical problems attached to counting the stock, but the important theoretical problems relate to the choice of a basis for valuation. There are several possible output and input values. Traditionally, inventory has been valued at the lower of historical cost and net realizable value. The historical cost is usually the lower, especially during inflation; therefore, it has been the normal basis. The alternative is useful for recognizing a loss in value.
>
> There are a number of difficulties with the use of historical cost. Which are the units left in stock? Which overheads should be included in cost? Should the comparison with the market value be universal or by item? Nevertheless, historical cost's advantages of prudence and objectivity have for many years outweighed these practical difficulties and the lack of realism of the results. Current value is also a possibility. The various methods are set out in Figure 8.1.
>
> Even where current value accounting is used, it is clear that profit is not taken until the stock is sold. There have been arguments about the fairness of this prudent approach. However, it clearly has strong advantages on grounds of objectivity. Nevertheless, when long-term contracts are being considered, the unfairness becomes particularly obvious and acute. This had led to acceptance in many countries of the idea of taking a proportion of expected profit at each year end.
>
> Practice with respect to cost formula and with respect to long-term contracts varies in Europe.

EXERCISES

8.1 'The production cost of inventory is always highly subjective and uncertain, because of the problem of overheads. Since the valuation of an inventory of manufactured items can never be reliable, accountants should concentrate on making it relevant.' Discuss.

8.2 V. O. Lynn commences business on 1 January buying and selling instruments. She sells two standard types, violas and cellos, and her transactions for the year are as follows (all prices are in ecu):

	Violas		Cellos	
	Buy	Sell	Buy	Sell
1 January	2 at 400		2 at 600	
31 March		1 at 600		
30 April	1 at 350		1 at 700	
30 June		1 at 600		1 at 1,000
31 July	2 at 300		1 at 800	
30 September		3 at 500		2 at 1,100
30 November	1 at 250		1 at 900	

You observe that the cost to V. O. Lynn of the instruments is changed on 1 April, 1 July and 1 October, and will not change again until 1 January following.

(a) Prepare a statement showing gross profit and closing inventory valuation, separately for each type of instrument, under each of the following assumptions:
  (i) FIFO;
  (ii) LIFO;
  (iii) weighted average (separately for each transaction);
  (iv) replacement cost.
(b) At a time of rising prices (i.e. using the cellos as an example), comment on the usefulness of each of the methods.

8.3 'The requirements of IAS 11 paragraph 43 (see Section 8.5) provide entirely adequate safeguards for the use of the percentage of completion method in long-term contracts. When these requirements are met, failure to use this method would lead to misleading financial statements.' Discuss.

Appendix: Construction contracts

This appendix reprints Appendix 3 of the UK accounting standard on inventory valuation (SSAP 9). This is done in order to provide a numerical example of the application of one version of the percentage of completion method of accounting for long-term contracts.

There is an interesting legal point, illustrated by the notes at the beginning of the appendix. According to the Fourth Directive, and therefore British law, inventories must be valued at the lower of cost and net realizable valve. However, if a percentage of profit were added to work-in-progress inventories, this would lead to valuation *above* cost. Therefore, legal counsel's opinion was that such amount should be shown under debtors not stocks (the latter is, of course, the British expression for inventories).

Long-term contracts: further consideration of financial statement presentation
1 The classification of an 'amount recoverable on contracts' within debtors is a somewhat unfamiliar concept which needs careful consideration.
2 The determination of the point at which ownership of completed work passes from the contractor to the customer is a complex matter of legal form and industry practice.
3 An 'amount recoverable on contracts' may not have the contractual status of a debtor in strict legal form. However, it is well established under the accruals concept of revenue and cost recognition that this should not preclude debtors and creditors from being recorded, where this is necessary to reflect the substance of a transaction.
4 An essential test for an 'amount recoverable on contracts' to be recorded as an asset is that it should be realisable. This applies equally whether the balance is classified as a debtor or as an element of work in progress.
5 An 'amount recoverable on contracts' represents an excess of the value of work carried out to date (which has been recorded as turnover) over cumulative payments on account. The amount and realisability of the balance therefore depend on the value of work carried out being ascertained appropriately. The balance arises as a derivative of this process of contract revenue recognition and is directly linked to turnover. In substance, it represents accrued revenue receivable and has the attributes of a debtor.
6 Accordingly, the standard concludes that 'amounts recoverable on contracts' should be classified as debtors, although separate disclosure is prescribed. Counsels' opinion obtained by the ASC confirms that 'amounts recoverable on contracts' should be classified under 'Debtors' and cannot be classified under 'Stocks'.
7 In determining the amounts at which long-term contracts should be included in the financial statements, contracting activity should be reviewed on an individual contract by contract basis. The following example illustrates the process of applying the principles set out in the standard to long-term contracts.

PROJECT 1

Profit and Loss Account – cumulative

Included in turnover	145
Included in cost of sales	(110)
Gross profit	35

Balance sheet
The amount to be included in debtors under 'amounts recoverable on contracts' is calculated as follows:

Cumulative turnover	145
LESS: Cumulative payments on account	(100)
Included in debtors	45

	Project Number					Balance Sheet Total	Profit & Loss Account
	1	2	3	4	5		
Recorded as turnover – being value of work done	145	520	380	200	55		1,300
Cumulative payments on account	(100)	(600)	(400)	(150)	(80)		
Classified as amounts recoverable on contracts	45			50		95DR	
Balance (excess) of payments on account		(80)	(20)		(25)		
Applied as an offset against long-term contract balances – see below		60	20		15		
Residue classified as payments on account		(20)	–		(10)	(30)CR	
Total costs incurred	110	510	450	250	100		
Transferred to cost of sales	(100)	(450)	(350)	(250)	(55)		(1,215)
	–	60	100	–	45		
Provision/accrual for foreseeable losses charged to cost of sales				(40)	(30)		(70)
		60	100		15		
Classified as provision/accrual for losses				(40)		(40)CR	
Balance (excess) of payments on account applied as offset against long-term contract balances		(60)	(20)		(15)		
Classified as long-term contract balances		–	80		–	80DR	
Gross profit or loss on long-term contracts	35	70	30	(90)	(30)		15

In this case, all the costs incurred to date relate to the contract activity recorded as turnover and are transferred to cost of sales, leaving a zero balance in stocks.

NB If the outcome of the contract could not be assessed with reasonable certainty, no profit would be recognised. If no loss is expected, it may be appropriate to show as turnover a proportion of the total contract value using a zero estimate of profit.

PROJECT 2

Profit and Loss Account – cumulative

Included in turnover	520
Included in cost of sales	(450)
Gross profit	70

Balance sheet
As cumulative payments on account are greater than turnover there is a credit balance, calculated as follows:

Cumulative turnover	520
LESS: Cumulative payments on account	(600)
Excess payments on account	(80)

This credit balance should firstly be offset against any debit balance on this contract included in stocks and then any residual amount should be classified under creditors as a payment received on account as follows:

Total cost incurred to date	510
LESS: Cumulative amounts recorded as cost of sales	(450)
	60
LESS: Excess payments on account (above)	(80)
Included in creditors	(20)

The amount to be included in stocks is zero and the credit balance of 20 is classified as a payment received on account and included in creditors.

The balance sheet note on stocks should disclose separately the net cost of 60 and the applicable payments on account of 60.

PROJECT 3

Profit and Loss Account – cumulative

Included in turnover	380
Included in cost of sales	(350)
Gross profit	30

Balance Sheet

As with Project 2, cumulative payments on account are greater than turnover and there is a credit balance calculated as follows:

Cumulative turnover	380
LESS: Cumulative payments on account	(400)
Excess payments on account	(20)

This credit balance should firstly be offset against any debit balance on this contract included in stocks and the residual amount, if any, should be classified under creditors as a payment received on account.

The amount to be included in stocks under long-term contract balances is calculated as follows:

Total costs incurred to date	450
LESS: Cumulative amounts recorded as cost of sales	(350)
	100
LESS: Excess payments on account (above)	(20)
Included in long-term contract balances	80

The balance sheet not on stocks should disclose separately the net cost of 100 and the applicable payments on account of 20.

PROJECT 4

Profit and Loss Account – cumulative

Included in turnover	200
Included in cost of sales	(290)
Gross loss	(90)

Balance Sheet

The amount to be included in debtors under 'amounts recoverable on contracts' is calculated as follows:

Cumulative turnover	200
LESS: Cumulative payments on account	(150)
Included in debtors	50

The amount to be included as a provision/accrual for foreseeable losses is calculated as follows:

Total costs incurred to date		250
LESS: Transferred to cost of sales	(250)	
Foreseeable losses on contract as a whole	(40)	
		(290)
Classified as provision/accrual for foreseeable losses		(40)

Note that the credit balance of 40 is not offset against the debit balance of 50 included in debtors.

PROJECT 5

Profit and Loss Account – cumulative

Included in turnover	55
Included in cost of sales	(85)
Gross loss	(30)

Balance Sheet

As cumulative payments on account are greater than turnover there is a credit balance, calculated as follows:

Cumulative turnover	55
LESS: Cumulative payments on account	(80)
Excess payments on account	(25)

The credit balance should firstly be deducted from long-term contract balances (after having deducted foreseeable losses) and the residual balance included in creditors under payments received on account as follows:

Total costs incurred to date		100
LESS: Transferred to cost of sales	(55)	
Foreseeable losses on contract as a whole	(30)	
		(85)
		15
LESS: Excess payments on account (above)		(25)
Included in creditors		(10)

The balance sheet note on stocks should disclose separately the net cost of 15 and the applicable payments on account of 15.

CHAPTER 9

Capital and liabilities

> **OBJECTIVES**
>
> - To clarify understanding, in both concept and terminology, of capital, reserves and types of liability
> - To explain the scope for different treatments and presentations, with corresponding implications for appraisal of the financial statements

9.1 Introduction

This brief chapter summarizes and highlights key points relating to capital and liabilities. Both matters are often largely ignored in accounting texts. Perhaps this is because the usual tendency is to concentrate on the definitions and valuation of assets, leaving capital and liabilities as balancing items in the balance sheet. However, in order to gain a full understanding of the workings and interrelationships of financial statements, it is important to think about capital and liabilities in their own right.

9.2 Definition and clarification

Various terms are in frequent use in this area, and unfortunately it cannot be assumed that each term will always be used with the same meaning. As already discussed in Chapter 3, the IASC framework defines a liability as:

> a present obligation of the enterprise arising from past events, the settlement of which is expected to result in an outflow from the enterprise of resources embodying economic benefits.

It defines equity (i.e. shareholders' funds) as:

the residual interest in the assets of the enterprise after deducting all its liabilities.

These definitions are consistent with the notion in Chapter 2 that capital is the balancing figure (i.e. the residual interest). In a company context, equity will be divided into its component parts of share capital and reserves. Reserves can therefore be defined in a roundabout way as: equity less share capital.

In practice, the crucial issue is the distinction between reserves and liabilities. 'Pure' liabilities, where a known amount remains unpaid, are clear, but estimated or uncertain liabilities cause considerable difficulty. Such liabilities, known as *provisions*, are covered by the Fourth Directive:

Article 20
1. Provisions for liabilities and charges are intended to cover losses or debts the nature of which is clearly defined and which at the date of the balance sheet are either likely to be incurred, or certain to be incurred but uncertain as to amount or as to the date on which they will arise.
2. The Member States may also authorize the creation of provisions intended to cover charges which have their origin in the financial year under review or in a previous financial year, the nature of which is clearly defined and which at the date of the balance sheet are either likely to be incurred, or certain to be incurred but uncertain as to amount or as to the date on which they will arise.
3. Provisions for liabilities and charges may not be used to adjust the values of assets.

Article 42
Provisions for liabilities and charges may not exceed in amount the sums which are necessary.

The comment in Article 42 is interesting. In a sense, it just states the obvious, but since provisions are by definition estimates, nobody can tell with any precision what 'the sums which are necessary' actually are. The estimates will need to be made in accordance with the general accounting principles, which in this context particularly implies prudence, but also that they must not lead to such a pessimistic overall picture so as to mislead, i.e. the 'true and fair view' must be maintained.

It must be remembered when considering current liabilities, as already noted in Chapter 2, that in some European countries proposed dividends will be removed from reserves and shown as current liabilities, whereas in other countries they will remain in reserves.

Contingent liabilities may arise when the event potentially causing the liability is itself uncertain. A law case which may be won or lost is a classic example. If the eventual liability is probable, contingent liabilities will usually be included in the balance sheet (and in the income statement as expenses). Of course, 'probable' is a highly subjective term and, again, the assessment must be done with adequate but not excessive prudence.

It is clear that in practice there is considerable scope in this area for flexibility and inconsistency of treatment, in two respects. First, the appraisal of any particular specific situation must to some extent be a matter affected by the individual personalities of the accountants and auditors. Second, and of particular importance for transnational appraisal and interpretation, national cultural and accounting norms may differ significantly as regards the degree of prudence required. Also, there are international differences with respect to the scope of provisions. There is agreement that next year's wages should not be provided for this year, but less agreement about next year's exchange rate fluctuations or planned redundancy payments. Excessive provisions will lead to secret reserves, as explained below.

Secret reserves are ownership claims on the business which are not recorded and not reported in the financial statements. Clearly this can only happen if the double entry for the unrecorded claim is not recorded either. The two classic ways of creating secret reserves are either to understate assets, or to overstate provisions. Given the definition of equity above (as the residual interest in the assets after deducting the liabilities), if the liabilities (including provisions) are artificially high, then the equity, and therefore reserves, are artificially low.

9.3 Some detailed distinctions

Types of share capital

All companies must have some ordinary shares. These are the residual equity in the business after all other more specific claims have been considered. In very simple terms ordinary shareholders come last in the queue of claimants on the business resources, and they are entitled to everything 'left over'. A wide variety of other types of share may also exist for any particular business. Non-voting shares are exactly what the name implies. Companies may issue different classes of ordinary share, e.g. 'A' and 'B' ordinary shares, where the precise rights of the different classes are defined by the company's constitution.

A more fundamental distinction exists with preference shares. These have preference over the ordinary shares as regards dividends, and usually also as regards the repayment of capital sums in the event of the company winding up. It must be remembered that a dividend is never receivable automatically as of right. Dividends are only receivable by shareholders of any type if both distributable profits are available in the company, and the directors of the company propose the payment or it is fixed as a percentage of profit, which is then approved by the company in general meeting. If only very limited scope for the payment of dividends exists, then the preference shareholders will come first in the queue for those limited dividends. Because preference shares are clearly safer than ordinary shares when things go badly, they can expect a lower return when things go well. Usually preference shares carry a known and fixed percentage entitlement to dividends (if dividends are available at all).

Preference shares may be cumulative, in which case any dividend 'entitlement' not declared in any particular year carries forward to the following year(s), and would need to be settled in the later year together with that year's preference entitlement, before the ordinary shareholders could expect any dividend at all. In many jurisdictions preference shares are no longer popular as, from an ordinary shareholder's perspective, it is usually beneficial from a tax point of view to raise loans rather than create further preference shares.

Some types of share, particularly preference shares, may be redeemable. This means that they may be paid off and cancelled under terms, and on or between dates, defined in the original offer document. Complicated provisions exist (which are outside the scope of this text) for ensuring that owners' equity as a whole is not reduced by this procedure to the detriment of creditors. The cancellation of ordinary shares in a similar way is permitted in most countries, but only under close legal restriction and supervision.

Types of reserve

Several types of reserve have been met in earlier chapters, and the position is summarized here. Broadly, reserves arise from three sources. First, revenue reserves arise from the trading activities of the company. Revenue reserves are realized, available for dividend, and the balance in the balance sheet consists of cumulative realized profits (net of losses) not yet distributed. Second, reserves arise connected with share transactions. The most common one is the share premium account. This occurs when shares are issued at a price greater than the nominal or par value. For example, if a 1 ecu share is issued for 3 ecu cash then the double entry will be:

Dr Bank	3 ecu	
Cr Share capital	1 ecu	
Cr Share premium	2 ecu	

Such reserves could be called capital reserves, and are not available for distribution as dividend.

The third type of reserve is the revaluation reserve. This represents the extra claims caused when assets are revalued. Depending on practice and legal restrictions, which vary widely in different countries (see Chapter 11), this reserve may be caused by *ad hoc* revaluation of certain assets, or may arise through a more rigorous and formal valuation policy. These reserves too, are generally regarded as not available for distribution, and under a historical cost-based legal system can never be available as long as the assets remain unsold. With fundamental changes in capital maintenance definitions (see Chapter 11), the position becomes more complicated.

Types of debenture

The crucial thing to remember about debentures is that they are a type of loan, and not a type of share. They carry rights to interest, which is an unavoidable business expense, and not to dividends which are an unenforceable appropriation of available profits. Debentures usually have detailed terms of issue specifying the terms of the loan. They are often secured, i.e. granted some priority rights over certain assets of the company in the event of any default by the company in the terms of interest or redemption payments. Such security may be over certain stated assets – a fixed charge – or may be over the continually changing assets of the business as a whole – a floating charge. Being lenders, the debenture holders have priority over shareholders of all types for repayment in the event of the company being wound up. In practice, because of the secured nature of many debentures, they often rank above most other creditors as well, a fact that current or potential suppliers should note carefully.

Hybrid securities

A whole industry has grown up in recent years creating various types of hybrid securities. Variations on the theme are almost infinite, but the principle usually is that the security is issued in one form with optional or guaranteed conversion at a later date into another form. For example, debentures may be issued with conversion rights into share capital at a predetermined price at some future date, or preference shares may be issued which provide for mandatory redemption by the issuer at a fixed or predeterminable future date. Such hybrid securities provide another example of the tension between substance and form which has been met so often in this book. It could be argued, to take the second example given above, that a preference share is a share until it is actually converted into something else. It could also be argued that a preference share with specified dividends and specified repayment rights at a specified date is, in substance, a loan, and should be shown as such throughout its existence.

Readers will be aware that attitudes to such arguments are likely to be very different between European countries. The variety of financial instruments thought of in recent years is immense, and leads to complexities well beyond our scope here. The IASC has recently addressed this issue in its proposed standard: 'Financial Instruments', issued in draft as E40 in 1991 and revised as E48 in 1993. This is firmly in the substance rather than the form camp, as the following extracts show from E40.

> The classification of a financial instrument, or its component parts, as between liabilities and equity should reflect the substance of the contractual arrangement on initial recognition. That classification should be consistent with the definitions of a financial liability and an equity instrument. (para. 38)
>
> A financial liability is any liability that is a contractual obligation:
>   (a) to deliver cash or another financial asset to another enterprise; or
>   (b) to exchange financial instruments with another enterprise under conditions that are potentially unfavourable.

Stockholders' equity and liabilities

Stockholders' Equity	
Capital Stock	2,330
Paid-In Capital	2,117
Retained Earnings	8,760
Unappropriated Profit	5,094
	18,301
Provisions	
Provisions for Old-Age Pensions and Similar Obligations	4,473
Other Provisions	1,312
	5,785
Liabilities	
Liabilities Payable to Affiliated Companies	8,636
Other Liabilities	653
	9,289
Prepaid Expenses	1
	33,376

Figure 9.1 Capital and liabilities. Daimler-Benz, 1992 (DM million).

> An equity instrument is any contract that evidences a residual interest in the assets of an enterprise after deducting all of its liabilities. (para. 4)

This is an area where care is needed when analyzing any particular given situation. Figures 9.1 and 9.2 show, as illustrations, the capital and liabilities sections of the balance sheets of Daimler-Benz (Germany) for 1992 and Total Oil (France) for 1991.

9.4 Implications for interpretation

This discussion has underlined the potential for uncertainty and therefore for different treatments regarding the credit side of the balance sheet in general, and of liabilities (and therefore of reserves) in particular. Much interest has been caused by the accounts of Daimler-Benz for 1992, which included the writing back into the accounts of some DM $4\frac{1}{2}$ billion of secret reserves. This was stated as being necessary to make the financial reports acceptable to the US authorities for subsequent quotation on the New York Stock Exchange. This should not necessarily be interpreted as implying or accepting that the accounts were previously 'wrong' by DM $4\frac{1}{2}$ billion, merely to illustrate the very real potential for the existence of inconsistent and misleading information.

Another specific interpretation point about reserves is the problem of untaxed reserves. In many countries companies are either required or allowed to transfer profits into certain designated reserves such that the profits so transferred are not

Shareholders' equity	28,098,104
Common stock	2,310,171
Paid-in surplus	8,771,452
Revaluation reserves	2,243,921
Legal reserve	193,858
Untaxed reserves	743,923
Other reserves:	
— General reserves	9,576,000
— Surplus arising on exchange of shares	14,335
Retained earnings	914,220
Income for the year	3,330,224
Other Equity	4,181,327
Perpetual subordinated notes redeemable in shares	4,181,327
Contingency reserves	2,217,900
Reserves for financial risks	31,900
Reserves for retirement benefits, pension plans and special termination plans	1,416,000
Reserves for specific industry risks	770,000
Debt	17,312,897
Loans	12,885,938
Convertible debentures	28,444
Other debentures	4,811,577
Other loans	7,952,799
Bank overdrafts	93,118
Liabilities	4,426,959
Accounts and notes payable – trade	2,910,749
Other payables	1,525,210
Other creditors and accrued liabilities	7,495
Translation adjustment	709,529
Total liabilities and shareholders' equity	52,527,252

Figure 9.2 Capital liabilities. Total Oil, 1991 (FF million).

subject to taxation in the year of the transfer. In some cases, the mechanism for this is to charge 'unreal' expenses. Usually, the profits will remain tax-free as long as they are retained in these designated reserves. It follows from this that if these profits are ever to be distributed to shareholders then they will no longer meet the conditions required for tax-free status. In one sense, perhaps, such untaxed reserves do all represent ownership claims as at the date of the balance sheet, but any attempt to settle these claims through dividends will cause the taxable proportion of the reserves to be paid to the government as taxation. In reality, therefore, such tax-free 'reserves' represent a mixture of true ownership claim, and deferred tax liability to the government. To treat tax-free reserves as entirely part of owners' equity may overstate the equity figure.

SUMMARY

This chapter has explored the concepts of equity, capital, reserves, liabilities, provisions and contingent liabilities. The broad distinction between equity and liabilities is clear, but each can be divided into complicated subsets, which are outlined. Further, the precise distinction of any specific real-life situation between equity and liabilities, particularly with hybrid securities, can be difficult to determine. The subjective nature of many liability decisions was noted, and its implication for reported owners equity, and therefore for interpretation of financial statements, underlined.

EXERCISES

9.1 'Owners' equity is the balancing item in a balance sheet. Therefore the job of the accountant is to get the assets figure right and the liabilities figure right. If this is achieved then the owners' equity figure must be right too.' Discuss.

9.2 'The distinction between a prudent approach to the quantification of provisions on the one hand, and the creation of secret reserves on the other, is incapable of objective definition, and will always be a matter for human attitude and whim.' Discuss.

9.3 'All credit balances which are included in a balance sheet are either capital and reserves, or liabilities actual or estimated.' Discuss.

CHAPTER 10

Accounting and taxation

> **OBJECTIVES**
>
> - To note the ways in which corporate taxation can vary internationally
> - To examine the tax base of corporate income taxation, e.g. the tax treatment of depreciation and interest expenses
> - To look at the main systems of corporate tax with respect to dividends
> - To explain the nature and practice of deferred tax

10.1 Introduction

There are several related purposes of studying taxation. First, corporate taxation obviously has some significant effects on net profit figures and other financial reporting matters. In particular, it has been shown earlier (e.g. in Chapters 4, 6 and 7) that in some continental countries the rules relating to corporate income taxation have a dominant effect on financial accounting measurement and valuation rules. For example, there is a strong influence of tax rules on depreciation charges in Germany; and if asset values are changed on a balance sheet, this generally affects tax liabilities in France. By contrast, neither of these two points is true for the United Kingdom.

Second, an understanding of corporate taxation in different countries is a necessary introduction to a study of business finance and management accounting. However, it is often poorly covered or omitted from books on these subjects. Hence there is a fairly detailed introduction here. Third, the taxation aspects of classification and harmonization are useful further illustrations of these processes, as described for financial reporting in Chapters 4 and 5.

Separate taxation for companies

In most countries, it has only been in this century that companies have begun to be treated differently from individuals for the purposes of taxation. However, the question whether a business is a separate entity from its owner or owners has a long history in the thought and practice of disciplines like accounting, company law and economics. Italian accountants had decided by the thirteenth century that they wished to separate the business from its owners, so that the latter could see more clearly how the former was doing. Consequently, as examined in Chapter 2, balance sheets of businesses show amounts called 'capital' that represent amounts contributed by the owners. During the nineteenth century, various laws were enacted in several European countries to the effect that companies have a legal existence independently from their owners, that these companies may sue and be sued in their own names, and that the owners are not liable for the debts of a company beyond their capital contributions. Economists have extended the separation of the owner from the business. When calculating the profit of the business to a sole trader, for example, economists might include as costs of the business the opportunity costs of the amounts the owner could have earned with his time, his property and his money if they had been invested outside his business instead.

As mentioned, it was not until this century that revenue law in most countries caught up with this separation and that companies began to be taxed in a different way from individuals. As is frequently the case with taxation, changes were associated with the need to finance warfare. In particular, the rearmament before the two World Wars imposed a heavy burden on government finances, which was partly supported by the revenue from taxes on companies.

This chapter is concerned with the taxation of corporate income, which is the major corporate tax in most countries. However, there are other taxes on corporations in Europe: on property, on share capital, on payroll, and so on. This is noted later.

Differences in taxes

The two fundamental types of difference between corporate income taxes might be called tax bases and tax systems. The international differences in corporate income tax bases (or definitions of taxable income) are very great. Although in all countries there is some relationship between accounting income and taxable income, in most continental countries the relationship is much closer than it is in the United Kingdom and the United States (see Chapter 4). Further, it has been pointed out throughout this book that the underlying measurement of accounting income itself varies substantially by country. These two points, which are of course linked, mean that similar companies in different countries may have vastly different taxable incomes.

The second basic type of difference lies in tax systems. Once taxable income has been determined, its interaction with a tax system can vary, in particular with respect to the treatment of dividends. Corporations may have both retained and distributed income for tax purposes. If business income is taxed only at the corporate level and only when it is earned, then different shareholders will not pay different rates of personal income tax. If income is taxed only on distribution, taxation may be postponed indefinitely. On the other hand, if income is taxed both when it is earned and when it is distributed, this creates 'economic double taxation' which could be said to be inequitable and inefficient (see Section 10.3).

These differences in tax bases and tax systems could lead to several important economic effects: for example, on dividend policies, investment plans and capital raising methods. Such matters are not dealt with extensively here. Neither are the important issues of transfer pricing and double taxation which, in practice, help to determine taxable profits and tax liabilities.

In some countries, e.g. Italy and Germany, there are regional as well as national corporate income taxes. Both these generally use a similar tax base, but the composite tax rate is, of course, higher.

Some other differences

The taxation of businesses is a very complex area, particularly when a business operates in more than one country. This chapter is only able to introduce some of the issues and therefore leaves out much of the detailed complexity.

One complication is that the legal types of businesses differ from country to country, as does the scope of particular business taxes. This chapter deals mainly with companies that can clearly be seen as separate from their owners for tax purposes.

Further international differences arise in the timing of the payment of taxes. For example, in some countries, corporate taxes are paid on a quarterly basis using estimates of taxable income for the year. In other countries, taxes are paid many months after the accounting year end, after the profit figures have been calculated and audited. In many continental countries taxes are not finally settled until a tax audit, which may be some years later.

Presentation

The tax expense is of sufficient importance that it is nearly always disclosed as a separate figure in a profit and loss account. It is generally shown after other expenses and before dividends, although the exact location varies. This, and the effect of tax on the interpretation of financial statements, is looked at again in Part IV.

Particularly in countries where there is a strong separation of accounting from tax, the location of figures above or below the tax line in a profit and loss account is not a reliable guide as to whether an item affects the actual tax bill.

10.2 Tax bases

The obvious way to classify corporate income taxation bases is by degrees of difference between accounting income and taxable income. As should be clear from Chapters 4, 6 and 7, the influence of taxation on accounting varies from the small in the United Kingdom to the dominant in Germany. Such is the importance of this difference for accounting that a simple classification of tax bases would look much like a simple classification of accounting systems (see Chapter 4). For example, a two-group classification in either case might put the United Kingdom, the United States and the Netherlands in one group, and France, Germany and Japan in the other.

In the former group, the requirement for financial accounting to present a 'fair' view to shareholders pre-dates and generally overrides taxation rules. Consequently many adjustments to accounting profit are necessary in order to arrive at the tax base: taxable income. In the other group, the needs of taxation have been dominant in the evolution of accounting and auditing. Consequently, the tax base corresponds closely with accounting profit. As discussed in many places in this book, several of these continental European countries have begun to decouple accounting from tax rules from the late 1980s.

Some of the differences in tax bases are discussed below; in a few cases this summarizes the coverage of topics elsewhere in the book.

Depreciation

Naturally, all the countries studied in detail in this book have tax authorities that take an interest in the amount of depreciation charged in the calculation of taxable income. This concern varies from fairly precise specification of the rates and methods to be used (as in most countries), to an interference only where charges are unreasonable (as in the Netherlands). As has been pointed out in earlier chapters, the vital difference for financial reporting is that tax depreciation must usually be kept the same as accounting depreciation in Franco-German countries, but not under Anglo-Dutch accounting. An interesting effect of this difference is that deferred taxation amounts are not large in Franco-German countries (see Section 10.4).

Examples of the specification of rates and methods for depreciation of fixed assets for tax purposes are shown below:

1. In the United Kingdom for 1993–4, machinery is depreciated at 25% on a reducing balance basis. There is a complete separation of this scheme of 'capital allowances' from the depreciation charged by companies against accounting profit. Unlike other countries, the United Kingdom does not give any depreciation tax allowance for most commercial buildings.

2. In the United States, there are depreciation ranges for different assets. Normally, fixed assets are written off for tax purposes using the 'modified accelerated cost recovery system'. The most common form of this involves three-, five- or seven-year classes. These are depreciated on the declining balance method, using twice the straight-line rate. Industrial buildings have a 31.5-year life on a straight-line basis.
3. In the Netherlands, depreciation is determined by individual companies. Straight-line depreciation may be used for any asset, and reducing balance for all assets except buildings. Companies may change from one method to another if there are good business reasons. A typical rate for plant is 12%.
4. In France, depreciation is allowed by tax law on a straight-line basis for nearly all assets at the following rates: industrial and commercial buildings 5%, office or residential buildings 4%, plant and fixtures 10–20%, vehicles 15–25%. It is possible to use a reducing balance basis for plant. The rates to be used are expressed as multiples of the straight-line rates depending on the asset's life. It is possible to change the basis. Accelerated depreciation is allowed for R&D, certain regions, anti-pollution and energy-saving assets.
5. In Germany and Japan, maximum tax depreciation rates are specified by tax law. Straight-line and reducing balance are available, except that straight-line is mandatory for buildings in Germany. The following rates apply in Germany: buildings 4%, plant 10%, office equipment 20%, office furniture 10%, vehicles 20–25%. It is possible to change methods only from reducing balance to straight-line. Accelerated allowances have been available for assets in certain areas and for certain assets.

Capital gains

The taxation of corporate capital gains varies substantially by country. In the United Kingdom, capital gains are added to taxable income. In the Netherlands, Germany, Japan and the United States, capital gains are also added to taxable income in full. In France, short-term capital gains (under 2 years) are fully taxed, but long-term capital gains are taxed at a reduced rate. Roll-over relief provisions also vary internationally.

Losses

Different treatment of losses can have important effects on taxable profits. These are illustrated in Table 10.1.

Table 10.1 Operating loss reliefs (years).

	Carry back	Carry forward
United Kingdom	1	No limit
United States	3	15
France	3	5
Germany	2	No limit
Netherlands	3	8
Japan	1	5

Dividends received

The degree to which the dividends received by a company must be included has an important effect on its taxable income. In the United Kingdom and Japan, domestic dividends are generally not taxed in the hands of a recipient company. In the United States, dividends from companies in the tax group are not taxed. However, 30% of dividends from other companies are taxed. In France, dividend income is fully taxed unless there is a holding of at least 10% or FF 150 million, in which case only 5% of dividend income is taxed; however, a group basis is available for such holdings. In Germany, dividends are fully taxable, except that an integrated structure for tax purposes can be used under certain conditions. In the Netherlands, a minimum 5% holding relieves dividends from tax.

Expenses

In the United Kingdom, United States and Netherlands, a number of expenses deducted in the calculation of profit may not be allowed in the calculation of taxable income. In France and Germany, what is deducted for financial accounting generally depends on what is allowed for tax purposes. Most countries are more generous than the United Kingdom in allowing expenses for taxation. For example, most of them allow entertainment expenses to be deducted. In the three other European countries mentioned there are also greater allowances for bad debts and various other provisions.

Other taxes

A very important complicating factor in determining overall tax burdens is the existence of other types of tax on companies and the degree of their deductibility for national corporate income tax purposes. In most countries there is some form of payroll tax or social security tax. In the United Kingdom there are local property 'rates'. In Germany there are regional income taxes, capital taxes and payroll taxes. In France there is a business licence tax. In Italy there is a regional corporation tax. In general, these taxes are deductible in the calculation of national corporation tax. However, because of these taxes, the total tax burden is much higher than might be thought at first sight in countries like Germany, where regional taxes are important.

Interest

Dividends paid are not tax-deductible in most systems, and of course nor are they considered to be expenses in the calculation of accounting profit. By contrast, interest payments are usually expenses for both accounting and tax purposes. Dividends are a share of post-tax profit paid to the owners of the company, whereas interest is a fixed payment which *must* be paid to outside lenders of money. Consequently, under most types of system, paying out 2,000 ecu in interest is less expensive for the company in post-tax terms than paying 2,000 ecu cash dividends, because the former payment reduces tax by 660 ecu (assuming, for example, a corporation tax rate of 33%). On the other hand, as shown below, 2,000 ecu of cash dividends would be worth more to an individual in an imputation system than 2,000 ecu of gross interest. This is because, although both incomes are taxed, the dividends receive a tax credit. The example shown in Figure 10.1 assumes a corporation tax rate of 33%, and a rate of withholding tax and tax credit like that illustrated in the following section.

	Dividend payment ecu	Interest payment ecu
Net profit before interest and tax	10,000	10,000
less Interest (1,400 net, 600 income tax withheld at source)	—	2,000
Net profit before tax	10,000	8,000
less Tax at 33%	3,300	2,640
Net profit after tax	6,700	5,360
Dividend (equivalent to 2,000)	1,400	—
Retained profit	5,300	5,360

Figure 10.1 Comparing the effect of payments of dividends and interest on the tax.

10.3 Tax systems

The preceding section has shown that the definition of taxable income varies greatly by country. The way in which taxable income is taxed depends upon the tax system. This also varies by country. Systems that have been used in the recent past in the countries studied in this book can be classified into three types, as examined below.

Classical systems

'Classical' systems are perhaps the easiest to explain. It is their alleged defects which other systems are designed to correct. Under a classical system, like most others, dividends paid are not deductible in the calculation of taxable income. Moreover, these dividends are fully taxable in the hands of the recipients. Interest payments, as in most systems, are usually tax deductible, though this is not an essential feature of classical systems. By 1993, the United States, the Netherlands and Luxembourg had been using classical systems for many years. The United Kingdom used such a system from 1965 to 1973. Belgium and Denmark had returned to classical systems in 1989 and 1991, respectively.

There are two main criticisms of classical systems; both rest upon what has been called the 'economic double taxation' of dividends whereby distributed income is taxed both to corporation tax and then to personal income tax. First, this double taxation is said to be inequitable when compared to the treatment of the distributed income of unincorporated businesses. In many countries, income of such businesses, whether physically distributed or not, bears no corporation tax but bears current income tax in the hands of the owners of the businesses. Such single taxation would not be so easy to arrange for corporations. This is because retained profit does exist, both in reality and for tax purposes, and so, if there were no separate corporation tax, taxation could be indefinitely postponed if companies delayed distribution. The alternative of taxing income only at the corporate level would mean that all individual recipients would have borne the same rate of tax. This would be unacceptable as part of an otherwise progressive income tax system. Thus, double taxation of the distributed income of corporations results from a desire by governments to ensure proper taxation of retained income.

The second case against economic double taxation is that it introduces a bias against the distribution of dividends. Since both total income and then distributed income are fully taxed, the larger the distribution, the larger is the total tax borne by a company and its shareholders. It might be thought that such an encouragement to retain profits would promote investment. However, more subtle economic thinking might suggest that profitable and efficient investment would be more likely to follow if companies distributed their profits and then shareholders allocated these funds through the new issue market to the most profitable companies. Unfortunately it is not proven that companies with a good earnings record will remain the most profitable.

The two cases against the economic double taxation of dividends have given rise to other systems of taxation that are designed to mitigate these effects of classical systems. Some of these systems are examined below, with a note on EC harmonization.

Imputation systems

A frequently used way of mitigating the effects of economic double taxation is to impute to the recipients of dividends some of the tax paid by a corporation on the income out of which the dividends are paid. Imputation systems are used in several EC countries and in Australia and Canada. Tables 10.2 and 10.3 illustrate the contrast between the United Kingdom's pre-1973 classical system and its imputation system in 1979–83. The rates of taxation are constantly changing, so it would not be especially useful to choose any particular country's actual rates at the time of writing.

Table 10.2 Classical and imputation systems (low pay-out).

		Classical £		Imputation £
Company				
income (say)		10,000		10,000
corporation tax (40%)		4,000	(52%)	5,200
distributable income		6,000		4,800
distribution (say) gross		2,000		
less income tax withheld at source (30%)	600			
net	1,400		cash	1,400
retained income		4,000		3,400
Shareholders (basic rate)				
dividend: cash received		1,400		1,400
income tax withheld at source		600		0
tax credit received ($\frac{3}{7}$)		0		600
gross dividend		2,000	'grossed up' dividend	2,000
income tax liability (30%)		600		600
less tax already withheld		600		0
less tax credit		0		600
tax due		0		0
Total tax	(4,000 + 600)	4,600		5,200

Table 10.3 Classical and imputation systems (high pay-out).

		Classical £		Imputation £
Company				
income (say)		10,000		10,000
corporation tax (40%)		4,000	(52%)	5,200
distributable income		6,000		4,800
distribution (say) gross		5,000		
less income tax withheld (30%)	1,500			
net	3,500		cash	3,500
retained income		1,000		1,300
Shareholders (basic rate)				
dividend: cash received		3,500		3,500
income tax withheld at source		1,500		0
tax credit received ($\frac{3}{7}$)		0		1,500
gross dividend		5,000	'grossed up' dividend	5,000
income tax liability (30%)		1,500		1,500
less tax already withheld		1,500		0
less tax credit		0		1,500
tax due		0		0
Total tax	(4,000 + 1,500)	5,500		5,200

In the United Kingdom there is a 'basic rate' of income tax, which is the marginal rate for a majority of taxpayers; it has been assumed for Tables 10.2 and 10.3 that this is 30%, that the classical corporate tax rate is 40%, and that the imputation rate is 52% as it was in the United Kingdom between 1973 and 1983. One would expect the tax rate to be higher under an imputation system than under a classical system, *ceteris paribus*, because the imputation system gives some tax credit back to the shareholders. The tax credit in the United Kingdom is linked to the basic rate of income tax for administrative simplicity. From 1979/80 to 1985/6, when the basic rate was 30%, the tax credit was 30/70 or 3/7. Under the pre-1973 system there was a withholding of standard rate income tax at source.

Let us look at the figures in Tables 10.2 and 10.3 in more detail. They assume that the taxable and accounting incomes are the same, and £10,000 in each case. Under the classical system shown on the left, corporation tax at 40% is borne, and then income tax at 30% is withheld at source. Thus, for basic rate taxpayers, there is no further income tax to pay. As the first column of Table 10.2 shows, the tax liability is £600 (i.e. 30% of the gross dividend of £2,000). The tax already withheld by the company and paid to the tax authorities is also £600. Thus, there is no net liability.

The imputation system is illustrated on the right of Table 10.2. Corporation tax of 52% is borne, and a tax credit of 3/7 the size of the dividend is given to shareholders. No further tax is deducted, so the dividend received by shareholders cannot sensibly be called 'net'. The tax liability is worked out on the cash dividend which is grossed up to include the tax credit. In this case, the example has been chosen to keep the 'grossed-up' (and post-tax) dividends the same for the two systems. Thus, the tax liability on the 'grossed-up' dividend of £2,000 is £600, but this may be settled with the tax credit of £600, leaving no net liability.

A comparison of Tables 10.2 and 10.3 shows that, for shareholders who pay only basic rate tax, the UK imputation system fully removes the double taxation of dividends. The total tax (£5,200 in the tables) under the imputation system does not

Table 10.4 **Classical and imputation systems (higher rate taxpayers).**

	Classical £		Imputation £
Low pay-out Company (as Table 10.2)			
Shareholders (50% marginal rate)			
dividend: cash received	1,400		1,400
income tax withheld at source	600		0
tax credit received ($\tfrac{3}{7}$)	0		600
gross dividend	2,000	'grossed up' dividend	2,000
income tax liability (50%)	1,000		1,000
less tax already withheld	600		0
less tax credit	0		600
tax due	400		400
Total tax (4,000 + 600 + 400)	5,000	(5,200 + 400)	5,600
High pay-out Company (as Table 10.3)			
Shareholders (50% marginal rate)			
dividend: cash received	3,500		3,500
income tax withheld at source	1,500		0
tax credit received ($\tfrac{3}{7}$)	0		1,500
gross dividend	5,000	'grossed up' dividend	5,000
income tax liability (50%)	2,500		2,500
less tax already withheld	1,500		0
less tax credit	0		1,500
tax due	1,000		1,000
Total tax (4,000 + 1,500 + 1,000)	6,500	(5,200 + 1,000)	6,200

alter as the level of dividends rises. However, the case is different when there are shareholders who pay a higher rate of personal income tax. Then there is still a double taxation and the bias against distribution remains. Table 10.4 illustrates this by showing that total taxation is higher when there is a larger pay-out, not only under the classical system but also under the imputation system. Examination of the top right-hand quarter of Table 10.4 shows that, where a taxpayer has a marginal rate of 50%, the £600 tax credit is insufficient to cover the liability on the £2,000 'grossed-up' dividend.

The position in the European Community with respect to these different systems is summarized in Table 10.5. As may be seen, most existing imputation systems involve partial imputation. That is, only part of the corporation tax paid by companies is imputed to shareholders (see column 5 of Table 10.5). The partial imputation systems of France, Belgium, Denmark and Ireland are broadly similar to that in the United Kingdom. However, only the UK and Irish systems base the

Table 10.5 EC corporation tax systems in 1991/92.

(1) Country	(2) System	(3) Corporation tax rate (%)[a]	(4) Tax credit as % of dividend	(5) Tax credit as % of underlying CT
Belgium	Classical[b] (Imputation 1963–89)	39	—	—
Denmark	Classical (Imputation 1977–91)	38	—	—
France	Imputation (1965+)	42	50	69.05
Germany	Imputation (1977+)	50 & 36[c]	56.25	100.00
Greece	Dividend deductible	46	—	—
Ireland	Imputation (1976+)	40	$33\frac{1}{3}$	50.00
Italy	Imputation (1977+)	48[d]	45.25	60.94
Luxembourg	Classical	44[e]	—	—
Netherlands	Classical[f]	35	—	—
Portugal	Imputation (1989+)	36	19.7	35.00
Spain	Imputation (1986+)	35	10	18.57
UK	Imputation (1973+)	33	$33\frac{1}{3}$	67.88

[a] Withholding taxes have been ignored throughout.
[b] The first BF 75,000 p.a. of dividends is not taxable.
[c] There is also a business tax of 5%.
[d] This includes a partially deductible local income tax of 16.2%.
[e] Including business and net worth taxes.
[f] The first Fl. 1000 p.a. of dividends are not taxable.
Source of columns 3 and 4: Section E of *The Taxation of Private Investment Income*, International Bureau of Fiscal Documentation, Amsterdam.

size of the tax credit on an income tax rate. Apart from the size of the tax credit, French imputation works in the same way as that in Table 10.5.

Unlike these systems, Table 10.5 shows that the German system involves full imputation. This removes the economic double taxation of dividends. It means that the eventual effect of the whole federal taxation system for distributed income is as though there were no separate corporation tax. However, as was mentioned in the last section, this is much too simple a picture to give an accurate impression of overall taxation, which includes other federal and local taxes. Note also in Table 10.5 that the German system has a higher rate for retained than for distributed profits.

Most continental European systems of taxation also contain 'withholding taxes' whereby some proportion of dividends is deducted at source. The presence of such a tax is not a differentiating feature for the classification of tax systems. Eventual tax burdens are not affected, since the withholding tax can be set against tax liabilities or reclaimed by most recipients of dividends. The main purpose of withholding taxes is to reduce evasion, particularly by holders of bearer shares and by foreign shareholders.

One further interesting feature of imputation systems is the way in which they ensure that tax credits are not granted to shareholders whose companies have not paid adequate corporation tax to cover the credits. In the United Kingdom, an advance corporation tax (ACT) equal to the size of tax credits is charged on all distributions. It is not generally an extra tax but merely an advance payment of the corporation tax bill. This helps the government's cash flow and also ensures that there is always revenue to cover the tax credits. This would otherwise have been a problem in the United Kingdom because of the possibility of large accounting profits, dividends and tax credits existing simultaneously with small taxable profits and corporation tax payments, due to generous capital allowances and other differences between accounting profit and taxable income.

There is also an ACT system in Ireland. In France, an extra tax called the *précompte* operates in those unusual cases where taxable income is too low to cover tax credits. A similar 'compensatory' tax exists in Germany.

It should be noted, in summary, that even a partial imputation system *can* totally remove double taxation and the bias against distribution in circumstances where the tax credit cancels the personal liability. Alternatively, the double taxation can be removed by fully imputing the corporation tax to shareholders. However, in this case, even if there is no double taxation because there is no effective liability to corporation tax, there could still be some bias against distribution if personal income tax is larger than the underlying corporation tax and if it operates only when dividends are paid.

Split-rate systems

A second way to reduce the effects of double taxation is to charge a lower rate of tax on distributed income than on retained income. The West German system up until the end of 1976 was a split-rate system with a 51% rate for retained income and a 15% rate for distributed income. The Portuguese system was also split-rate until 1989.

It is possible to reorganize a partial imputation system into a split-rate system with identical tax liabilities and therefore, presumably, identical economic effects. Therefore it could be said that, for the purposes of classification, split-rate systems and partial imputation systems are in the same category.

Other ways to mitigate double taxation of dividends

There are many other ways to reduce double taxation. In the United States, for example, the classical system was modified until 1987, in that the first $100 of dividends (plus interest) received by an individual each year was exempted from personal income tax. Such a system also operates in Belgium and the Netherlands. Alternatively, the 'primary dividend' system allows companies to deduct some proportion of dividends in the calculation of their taxable incomes. Such a system operates in Greece, where dividends are fully tax deductible, thus avoiding double taxation.

Harmonization

Although the EC Commission made various proposals to harmonize corporate taxation from the 1970s onwards, little progress has been made. A draft Directive of 1975 proposed the imputation system with a single tax rate between 45 and 55%. As Table 10.5 shows, this seems to have had little long-run effect in the European Community.

Particular criticisms of the Commission's efforts related to the lack of proposals to harmonize tax bases. In 1990, the Commission abandoned general harmonization in order to concentrate on those details that particularly affect cross-border activity.

10.4 Deferred tax theory

The area of deferred tax is one in which there are major differences in accounting. Deferred tax is *not* amounts of tax bills which the tax authorities have allowed the taxpayer to postpone. It is amounts of tax which, because of the accruals convention, accountants think relate to the current or previous accounting periods but which the tax system does not yet consider to be taxable. That is, deferred tax is caused by accounting for reversible timing differences between when expenses and revenues are included in the accounting calculations as opposed to when they are included in the tax calculations. The French expression, *impôt différé*, is probably clearer than the English expression.

A simple example of deferred tax would occur in the context of the revaluation of fixed assets. Suppose that a Dutch company revalues a holding of land in the balance sheet from fl 3m to fl 9m. Suppose, also, that the Dutch corporate tax rate on capital gains is 35%, but that the Dutch tax rules do not tax capital gains until disposal, which in this case is not intended by the company in the foreseeable future. No tax is payable as a result of revaluing, but it is possible to see how accountants might think that the potential liability to tax of fl 2.1m (i.e. fl 6m × 35%) relates to the period up to the balance sheet date. If so, they might account for the implicitly deferred tax in the balance sheet, as in Figure 10.2. Since, the revaluation is not realized, there will be no gain nor tax on the gain in the income statement.

In the United Kingdom, as will be examined further later, the accounting rules concentrate on whether tax is expected to be paid in the foreseeable future. In the above example, the tax will not be expected to be paid, particularly as in the United Kingdom gains can usually be 'rolled-over' into the purchase of a replacement asset. Consequently, UK companies would generally not account for the tax as in Figure 10.2, but would show a revaluation reserve of 6m.

In Germany, upward revaluation is not possible. In several other continental countries, revaluation is legal but would lead to current taxation (see Chapters 4 and 6). Consequently, in most continental countries, deferred tax would not arise in such a case.

The most frequently cited cause of substantial amounts of deferred tax in Anglo-Saxon countries is depreciation. Typically, depreciation is a large expense, and the tax rules can be substantially different from the accounting rules, as outlined in Section 10.2. Table 10.6 sets out a simple case, where there are 100% tax depreciation allowances in the year of purchase of plant and machinery; a 50% corporate income tax rate; the purchase for 10,000 ecu of a machine which is expected to last for five years; and a country where tax and accounting are separated. The existence of 100% tax depreciation is not fanciful. This applied for all plant and machinery in the United Kingdom from 1972 to 1984, to certain assets in West Berlin until the end of the 1980s, to capital investments in certain Greek islands, etc.

In Table 10.6, the accountants assume that the asset will have no residual value and will wear out evenly over time, irrespective of use. Consequently, for accounting purposes, they charge a depreciation expense of 2,000 ecu per year. By contrast, the tax authorities allow an expense of 10,000 ecu in the first year and, if the company takes this, no tax deductible expense after the first year. Consequently, there is a

Balance Sheet Adjustments

Fixed asset: +6	
	Revaluation reserve: +3.9
	Deferred tax: +2.1

Figure 10.2 Deferred tax on revaluation.

Table 10.6 **Depreciation and tax.**

Accounting records		Tax calculations		
Year	Depreciation	Year	Expense	Tax reduction
1	2,000	1	10,000	5,000
2	2,000	2	0	0
3	2,000	3	0	0
4	2,000	4	0	0
5	2,000	5	0	0

reduction in the tax bill of 5,000 ecu in year 1. This cash flow advantage is designed to be the incentive to invest.

Supposing that the company uses the new asset very inefficiently or does not use it at all in the first year. In this case, depreciation may still be charged because the asset is depreciating due to the passing of time. The net effect of the inefficient capital purchase on the post-tax accounting profit of year 1 is that the profit *increases* by 3,000 ecu (i.e. depreciation expense of 2,000 ecu, and tax reduction of 5,000 ecu). Of course, if the company uses the asset effectively, profit will increase by much more than this, as the company should at least be able to earn enough by using the asset to cover the depreciation on it.

The above strange effect on profit is caused by deliberately charging the depreciation expense slowly but taking the tax reduction immediately. In order to correct for this, it would be possible, for accounting purposes, to record the benefit of the tax reduction more slowly, over the life of the related asset. That is, as in Table 10.7, one could express the tax reduction for accounting purposes as 1,000 ecu per year, to fit with the depreciation expense. If this adjustment is made, it is called 'accounting for deferred tax'. In this example, it would be necessary, at the end of year 1, to increase the recorded tax expense by 4,000 ecu. The double entry would be:

Dr. Tax expense 4,000
Cr. Deferred tax 4,000

The deferred tax credit balance would generally be recorded as a liability. Each year, the above double entry would be reversed by 1,000 ecu, so that no balance would be left by the end of the asset's life. An alternative way of expressing the above calculation at the end of year 1 is that the deferred tax balance would be:

(tax depreciation − accounting depreciation) × tax rate
= (10,000 − 2,000) × 50% = 4,000

Table 10.7 **Depreciation and deferred tax.**

	Accounting records			Tax calculations	
Year	Depreciation	Tax expense reduction	Year	Expense	Tax reduction
1	2,000	1,000	1	10,000	5,000
2	2,000	1,000	2	0	0
3	2,000	1,000	3	0	0
4	2,000	1,000	4	0	0
5	2,000	1,000	5	0	0

Permanent and reversible differences

It should be noted that the above examples of capital gain and depreciation are 'reversible timing differences' between accounting numbers and tax numbers. That is, in both cases, the financial statements record the revenues or expenses at a different time from the tax calculations. In these two examples, this gives rise to deferred tax liabilities. There can also be examples of deferred tax assets, such as where losses have been made which may be used to reduce tax bills in the future. However, before recording these in financial statements, accountants need to be sure that they can be reclaimed against future tax payable.

There can also be examples of 'permanent differences', and these do not give rise to deferred tax. For example, in the United Kingdom, entertaining expenses are not allowed for tax purposes. This adjustment to accounting profit is permanent, so it leads to an increase in taxable income, without a subsequent decrease.

Figure 10.3 provides a numerical illustration of tax adjustments to accounting profit: the tax exempt income might be dividends from subsidiaries; the tax depreciation is typically larger than the accounting depreciation; and the general provisions for bad debts are not allowable in several countries. Assuming a corporate income tax rate of 33%, the accounting and tax calculations would be as follows:

Dr. Tax expense (490,000 × 33%)   161,700
Cr. Deferred tax (33,000 × 33%)   10,890
Cr. Tax payable (457,000 × 33%)   150,810

Theoretical problems

In the light of the discussions of Part I of this book, it is not entirely clear whether tax is an expense (and therefore potentially subject to allocation) as opposed to an

Facts: 1. Pre-tax accounting profit 500,000 ecu
2. Tax-exempt income included 10,000 ecu
3. Depreciation expense already charged 80,000 ecu
4. Tax depreciation to be claimed 120,000 ecu
5. Increase in general provisions for bad debts 7,000 ecu

Tax calculation:

Pre-tax accounting profit	500,000
Permanent difference:	
tax-exempt income	(10,000)
Accounting income subject to tax	490,000
Timing differences:	
excess of tax over book depreciation	(40,000)
increase in unallowable provisions	7,000
Taxable income	457,000

Figure 10.3 Tax adjustments.

appropriation of profit, or whether any deferred balance is a liability. The doubts about the latter become greater when a business has a continuing programme of investment in assets. In such a case, each year that the timing differences reverse, they will be replaced by new ones resulting from further purchases of assets. As a result, the 'deferred tax liability' may continually rise, especially in an expanding business or when prices are rising. In a sense, the balance then never has to be paid, so it might not be a liability. However, an overdraft may be expected to circulate continuously and to rise for the foreseeable future, but that does not mean that it is not a liability.

In the United Kingdom, for example, deferred tax balances were very large by the late 1970s. Directors of companies did not like the effect of accounting for deferred tax because it made post-tax earnings look lower and liabilities higher. As a result of the doubts above, the standard-setters were persuaded to remove the requirement to account fully for deferred tax, unless the 'liability' was expected to be settled in the foreseeable future. Consequently, there are three types of country with respect to deferred tax:

(a) countries where taxable income and accounting income are largely the same, so that deferred tax is relatively unimportant (e.g. Germany);
(b) countries where reversible timing differences are fully accounted for (e.g. the United States and the Netherlands);
(c) countries where reversible timing differences are partially accounted for (e.g. the United Kingdom).

Table 10.8 Disclosure of deferred taxation.

Sample size	Bel 50	Den 32	Fra 40	Ger 49	Gre 30	Ire 38	Ita 30	Lux 12	Net 40	Spa 30	UK 50	Total 401
Evidence of timing differences between accounting income and taxable income (deferred taxation)	2	28	34	29	—	31	11	3	32	17	49	236
Amount disclosed separately for deferred taxation:												
In balance sheet												
In provisions for liabilities and charges	—	19	—	1	—	11	10	—	16	—	2	59
In long-term liabilities	—	1	—	—	—	—	—	—	—	—	—	1
Other	—	1	1	2	—	—	—	—	—	—	—	4
In notes to the balance sheet:												
In current assets	—	—	—	2	—	—	—	—	—	—	—	2
In provisions for liabilities and charges	—	2	—	13	—	16	1	1	14	—	40	87
In long-term liabilities	—	—	—	7	—	2	—	—	—	2	2	2
Other	—	2	—	7	—	2	—	1	—	2	5	19
No disclosure of amount for deferred taxation	2	3	33	4	—	2	—	1	2	15	—	62

Source: adapted from FEE *European Survey of Published Accounts 1991*, Routledge, London, 1991.

Table 10.9 Causes of differences between accounting and taxable income.

	Bel	Den	Fra	Ger	Gre	Ire	Lux	Net	UK	Total
Sample size	50	32	40	49	30	38	12	40	50	341
Evidence of differences between accounting income and taxable income	30	28	34	31	16	31	3	32	48	253
Reasons for differences in the notes:[a]										
Loss carry forward	6	—	7	—	—	1	—	3	3	20
Investment facilities, grants	17	—	7	—	—	10	—	2	10	46
Results of affiliated undertakings abroad	8	—	2	—	—	—	1	1	2	14
Changes in deferred taxation	1	—	2	—	—	3	—	3	—	9
Under/overprovision in previous years	1	—	1	—	—	3	—	—	1	6
Revaluations to market value	1	—	—	—	—	—	—	3	1	5
Foreign taxation	2	—	1	—	—	1	—	—	—	4
Other	4	—	21	7	—	10	1	5	1	49
No disclosure of reasons	6	28	8	24	16	12	1	22	34	151

[a] More than one answer possible.
Source: adapted from FEE *European Survey of Published Accounts 1991*, Routledge, London, 1991.

Changes in tax rates

When corporate income tax rates change, should this affect the deferred tax balances that arose as a result of past transactions? Under the partial accounting method, since deferred tax balances are only recorded when they are expected to be settled in the foreseeable future, any change in tax rates is relevant because it will affect the size of the amount expected to be paid. Consequently, it seems logical to use the 'liability method', which raises or lowers the deferred tax balance as the tax rate rises or falls. For example, in the United Kingdom, SSAP 15 requires partial accounting and the liability method.

When fully accounting for deferred tax, the outstanding balances might be seen as deferred credits rather than as normal liabilities. Deferred tax accounting is carried out in order to correct the current year's income statement rather than to account for any liability. Consequently, the 'deferral method', which ignores subsequent tax rate changes, seems logical. This was the method used in the United States throughout the 1970s and 1980s. However, by the early 1990s, after a reduction in tax rates in the United States, the rules were changed (SFAS 109) to require full accounting for deferred tax but with the liability method. This concentrates on deferred tax assets and liabilities rather than on timing differences of income statement items.

10.5 Deferred tax practice

There are no rules requiring deferred tax accounting in the Fourth Directive, although it requires disclosure of deferred tax amounts. IAS 12 describes the various methods of deferred tax accounting. Proposals by the IASC to move towards the US approach were being considered in 1994.

In practice, as noted in the previous section, deferred tax is important in some countries but not in others. Table 10.8 shows that there are few disclosures relating to deferred tax in some countries (such as Belgium and France); frequent note disclosures in other countries (such as Germany and the United Kingdom); and frequent effects on the financial statements in others (such as Denmark and the Netherlands). The lack of effect of financial statements in the United Kingdom is caused by the use of partial accounting for deferred tax. Table 10.9 shows some disclosed causes of deferred tax.

SUMMARY

Corporate taxation is a major influence on some countries' financial accounting practices. Also, a knowledge of corporate taxation is important for international business finance. There is discussion here on differences in tax bases and in tax systems. Tax bases for corporate income tax differ in their treatment of depreciation, stockholding gains, capital gains, losses, dividends received, certain expenses and many other matters. The importance of taxes other than national corporate income taxation also varies.

Tax systems differ mainly in respect of their treatment of dividends. Classical systems treat corporations and their owners quite separately, giving rise to 'double taxation of dividends'. Other systems try to mitigate this for equity and efficiency reasons. For example, imputation systems give shareholders credit for some or all of the corporation tax underlying their dividends. Such systems are now predominant in the European Community and favoured by the Commission. Split-rate systems achieve a similar effect by taxing distributed income at a lower rate than retained income. Harmonization of systems was proposed by the Commission in a draft Directive, on which progress was slow.

Deferred taxation is a major accounting topic in those countries where there can be substantial differences between taxable income and accounting profit. Practice varies even within those countries.

EXERCISES

10.1 Outline and contrast the classical and imputation systems of corporate taxation.

10.2 (a) An asset attracting 100% tax depreciation allowance in the year of acquisition, costs DT Co. 80 ecu. It has an accepted life of 4 years, and nil expected scrap value. Depreciation is calculated on the straight-line basis. Taxation is payable at the rate of 50% on the taxable profit. Complete the following table. Assume that this example relates to a country where tax and accounting figures can be different.

	Year				
	1	2	3	4	Total
Accounting profit (after depreciation charge)	100	100	100	100	400
Accounting depreciation					
Tax allowance for depreciation					_____
Taxable profit					_____
Profit before tax					
Taxation (50% taxable profit)					_____
Profit after actual tax					======
Profit before tax					
Taxation charge if calculated on accounting profits					_____
Profit after accounting tax					======

Comment on the performance of DT Co. as indicated by the 'profit after actual tax' and 'profit after accounting tax' figures.

(b) Continue the above table to show appropriate deferred tax adjustments, and prepare the deferred tax account for the 4 years.

10.3 In addition to the information given in Exercise 10.2, DT Co. buys an asset in year 2 for 100, an asset in year 3 for 120, and two assets in year 4 for 100 and 120, respectively. All these assets also have an expected life of 4 years and nil expected scrap value. Complete the table using the new information and show the deferred tax account over the 4-year period. Comment upon the results.

10.4 The balance on the deferred tax account prepared in Exercise 10.3 seems to be continuously rising. Discuss the proposition that, since the liability is clearly not being paid, it need not have been provided in the first place.

CHAPTER 11

Accounting for price changes

> **OBJECTIVES**
>
> - To examine the meaning of 'inflation'
> - To uncover the effects of price changes on the interpretation of accounting information
> - To note that different European countries have different views about adjusting accounts
> - To investigate various theoretical and practical ways of adjustment for price changes in different countries

This chapter looks at some of the problems involved in adjusting accounting information for general and specific price changes. The chapter looks first at inflation, then at the reasons why inflation causes traditional profit figures to be unrealistic for some purposes and then at the problems that follow from this lack of realism. After that, there is an examination of the possible adjustments to correct accounts for general and specific price changes, and of actual accounting systems proposed in Europe and elsewhere to deal with the problems caused by changing prices.

11.1 The meaning and measurement of inflation

Inflation is a general increase in prices that causes a fall in the purchasing power of money. The causes of inflation are widely discussed and disputed, but they are not the province of this book. The average of prices faced by a particular consumer will change at a different rate from the average faced by another. Again, there will be a difference between price changes faced by consumers and those faced by producers. However, it is generally agreed that one useful and easily available general measure of inflation is an *index of retail prices*. As an example, the index for the average prices in the United Kingdom in the years 1968–77, with 1970 set at 100, is shown in Table 11.1. This period is chosen because it is the time in the second half of the twentieth century when inflation reached a peak in Europe, although there had been hyperinflation in Germany in the interwar years.

Such a series of indices as that in Table 11.1 can be used to estimate, for example, how much money would have been needed by the average consumer in 1977 to equal the value of £1,000 in 1973. The answer is about £2,065 (i.e. £1,000 × 254.4/123.2). Also, a measure of the rate of inflation can be calculated from these figures, as shown in Table 11.2. The United Kingdom had one of the highest European rates of inflation in that period. These high rates of inflation help to explain the large interest taken in some European countries during the 1970s in systems to adjust accounting for the effects of inflation. Amounts of inflation in the 1980s were generally lower. Those for EC countries in the late 1980s are shown in Table 11.3.

Indices of retail prices are produced on a monthly basis by governments in most European countries. There are many technical problems relating to the choice of items involved, their weighting and delays in the collection of information. For the input costs and output prices of a particular business, such a general index is not likely to be very informative. The costs of different raw materials and capital equipment may move up (and down) at very different rates. Therefore, some governments also produce fairly specific *wholesale price indices* that cover various raw materials and intermediate outputs. In addition some governments (e.g. the French and the British) produce specific price indices covering capital equipment, other purchases and stocks. Some companies keep their own very specific price indices, and of course actual current costs can be discovered from invoices or price lists.

Table 11.1 UK index of retail prices, 1968–77.

Year	Index
1968	89.2
1969	94.0
1970	100.0
1971	109.4
1972	114.8
1973	123.2
1974	152.0
1975	188.7
1976	219.6
1977	254.4

Sources: Central Statistical Office, *Economic Trends*, No. 3, HMSO, London, 1977, p. 96; and Central Statistical Office *Monthly Digest of Statistics*, HMSO, London, 1978 May, p. 157.

Table 11.2 **Increase in yearly average of the UK general index of retail prices, 1968–77.**

Year	% change in index
1968–9	5.4
1969–70	6.4
1970–1	9.4
1971–2	4.9
1972–3	7.3
1973–4	23.4
1974–5	24.1
1975–6	16.4
1976–7	15.8

Source: Calculated from Table 11.1

Table 11.3 **Inflation in the European Community, 1984–89.**

	Annual Inflation
Belgium	2.4
Denmark	4.3
France	3.5
Germany (West)	1.3
Greece	18.1
Ireland	3.7
Italy	7.1
Luxembourg	1.8
Netherlands	0.7
Portugal	15.6
Spain	6.9
United Kingdom	5.3

Source: *Vital World Statistics*, The Economist, London, 1990.

It is obvious that specific price information is relevant to the planning and budgeting of a business. How to take account of it in the reporting of past financial results is not so clear.

11.2 Effects of price changes on accounting

The effects of price changes are at their clearest when considering the valuation of assets in a conventional balance sheet. For example, freehold properties may be recorded and added together at a variety of values, including historical cost and subsequent valuations. Similar properties may be recorded and added together at very different values because they were bought at different times. For those users of a balance sheet who are expecting to gain information about the value of a business, such a balance sheet may be very misleading. Proposed solutions for this problem will be examined later.

The effects on profit measurement are more complicated. Normally, three main deficiencies are identified. In each case the problem concerns *matching* – one of the conventions introduced in Chapter 3 as an important rule in the calculation of profit by the comparison of revenue with expenses. The point here is that, unless adjustments are made to correct for changing prices, some expenses based on *past* costs will be matched against revenues based on *current* sales prices.

The first of the three deficiencies concerns depreciation charges, which may be in some sense inadequate because they are based on past costs (i.e. the historical cost of fixed assets). This has been mentioned in Chapter 7 on depreciation. For example, one year's usage of a machine with no scrap value and a five-year life may more realistically be said to incur a charge of $\frac{1}{5}$ of the replacement cost of the asset rather than $\frac{1}{5}$ of its historical cost. This would suggest a *depreciation adjustment* to historical cost profit, since the latter only allows for the historical cost of fixed assets used up.

Second, it has been mentioned in Chapter 8 that the value of stocks may reasonably be considered to be their replacement cost, because this is what the business would have to pay if it did not already own the stocks or if it were deprived of them. Similarly, the using up of stocks can be said to involve an expense that is equal to their replacement cost rather than their historical cost. This would suggest a *cost of sales adjustment* to historical cost profit, since the latter only allows for the historical cost of stocks used.

The third deficiency concerns gains and losses on monetary items. A company that borrows money long term in inflationary periods is making a gain, in the sense that the money eventually paid back will be worth less in real terms. The same factor affects those short-term assets and liabilities that are fixed in money terms. If there is inflation, a 'gain' will be made on holding overdrafts and creditors, and a 'loss' will result from holding debtors and cash. Deciding upon the correct treatment of these long-term and short-term monetary items has given rise to the most controversy of the three deficiencies discussed here.

It is generally agreed that, if profit is used to measure the economic performance of a company, historical cost profit is greatly overstated due to the lack of depreciation and cost of sales adjustments. Unless this net overstatement of profit is recognized, the usefulness of accounting data for decision-making will be seriously impaired. For example, decisions about what dividends to pay or what pay rises can be afforded may be seriously in error. Even if the company understands the problem, shareholders and employees may not, and may press for payments based on historical cost results.

There is a similar problem with tax on the profits of businesses. As taxation is levied on taxable profit, which is based on overstated historical cost accounting profit, the effective rate of tax on a more realistic measure of profit will surely be very high. However, as shown in Chapter 10, there are substantial adjustments involved in the calculation of taxable profit in some countries. For example, from the early 1970s to the mid-1980s in the United Kingdom, two of these adjustments corrected the taxation system for inflation: high first-year capital allowances and stock (inventory) appreciation relief. The former allowed the full cost of plant and machinery to be deducted in the calculation of taxable profit in the first year, when the replacement cost *was* the historical cost. The latter relief approximated to an adjustment for the cost of sales. In France and Italy, adjustments have been made to the accounting rules in order to adjust taxation for this inventory relief: in France there have been provisions for *hausse des prix*, in Italy the use of LIFO has a somewhat similar effect.

Problems, which are perhaps even more serious, concern the effects on the decision-making of management. In decisions about prices, types of production, the assessment of the performance of managers, and so on, accounting information will be used. Correct decisions require relevant information, which includes adjustments for the effects of inflation.

11.3 European disagreement

Although the problems outlined in the last section are clear, there has been opposition from some countries to any adjustments to financial reporting designed to correct for price changes. The most obvious opposition to departures from historical cost has come from Germany, which suffered more than any other European country from hyperinflation before the Second World War. The German view is that accounting should not be adjusted away from reliable factual numbers. The purpose of accounting is connected to the distribution of profits, the protection of creditors and the calculation of taxes. These, it is claimed, will all be jeopardized by such tinkering.

There was German opposition to inclusion in the Fourth Directive of optional departures from historical cost. These options were examined in Chapter 6. They have not been permitted in Germany.

In many other European countries, either the accountancy profession or the government has made moves to adjust accounting for inflation, and most countries have taken some of the optional provisions in the Fourth Directive to enable revaluations (as discussed in Chapter 6). Full systems of inflation accounting have only been seriously proposed in Europe in countries where the government takes a hands-off approach to accounting and where tax numbers can be disconnected from accounting numbers. This is because price adjustment can be so complex and can have such large effects on accounting that full-scale, continuous use of it seems inappropriate as a legal requirement for all companies. Consequently, it is at present only in countries such as the United Kingdom and the Netherlands that the systems discussed in the next section could work.

11.4 General or specific adjustment

The major divide between different systems of accounting for price changes is that between those systems which adjust primarily for the changes in prices of the specific assets owned by the business, and those which adjust for a general price movement, inflation. The latter can be called *current purchasing power* (CPP) *accounting* systems. Those current value systems which do not include an adjustment for general price changes have been said by some not to be systems of *inflation* accounting at all because they do not take account of the falling value of money. The type of adjustments for depreciation and cost of sales depends upon which system is being used.

The underlying difference between the two systems concerns the concept of *capital maintenance*. In Chapter 2 of this book it has been mentioned that one way of measuring profit for a year is to compare the net worth of a business at the beginning of the year with that at its end. Any increase will be the profit, assuming that no capital has been introduced or withdrawn. That is, profit is any excess left over after maintaining the capital of the business.

When there are specific and general price changes, the concept of capital maintenance involves several possible results. Consider a simple business which buys one property for 10,000 ecu with cash introduced by the owner. It may be represented as in Figure 11.1. After several years the business sells the property for 15,000 ecu. In the meantime the general price index has risen from 100 to 130, and the specific property index has risen from 100 to 145. The business intends to buy a very similar replacement for 14,000 ecu in a more convenient location. What profit does the business make on the sale of the property? The answer depends upon which concept of capital maintenance is being used.

The historical cost (HC) concept is that the original nominal money capital should be maintained. Immediately after the original building has been sold, the balance sheet will appear as shown in Figure 11.2, showing a profit of 5,000 ecu, which is

Balance sheet

Property	10,000	Capital	10,000
	10,000		10,000

Figure 11.1 Cash of 10,000 ecu is introduced and used to buy property.

HC balance sheet

		Capital	10,000
Cash	15,000	Profit	5,000
	15,000		15,000

Figure 11.2 Balance sheet after sale of the property based on historical cost.

the current sales revenue *less* the original historical cost. (It has been assumed for the moment that the property has been sold, since this avoids the problem of unrealized profit.)

An alternative concept is that the business should maintain the purchasing power of the original capital and treat any excess over this as profit. In this case, to maintain the real value of the capital to the owners will require 13,000 ecu (i.e. 10,000 ecu × 130/100). This will lead to a profit of 2,000 ecu, as shown in the restated balance sheet (Figure 11.3).

A further possibility is to hold that the business only makes profit after it has maintained its physical capital intact. This is a current value (CV) concept. It need not mean that the exact original assets are maintained, but it does mean that there is the same productive potential. Since the capital figure in this case is represented by the single property, it can be said that to maintain the physical capital will require a figure of 14,500 ecu (i.e. 10,000 ecu × 145/100). This will lead to a profit of 500 ecu (see Figure 11.4). The 'specific adjustment' to capital may be called a *capital maintenance reserve*.

However, it should be noted that the specific property price index is only used as a proxy for more detailed information about the actual replacement cost (RC) of the business's asset. In this case the business has decided that it can maintain its productive potential by buying a replacement costing 14,000 ecu. When this transaction is completed, it is very clear that the physical capital has been maintained and that the profit on a current value basis should be regarded as 1,000 ecu. An alternative way of looking at this is that current 'expense' (replacement cost) has been compared to current sales revenue (Figure 11.5).

CPP balance sheet

		Original capital	10,000
		Purchasing power adjustment	3,000
		CPP capital	13,000
Cash	15,000	Profit	2,000
	15,000		15,000

Figure 11.3 Taking the general price index into account.

CV balance sheet

		Original capital	10,000
		Specific adjustment	4,500
		Current value capital	14,500
Cash	15,000	Profit	500
	15,000		15,000

Figure 11.4 Profit after physical capital is maintained.

CV balance sheet

Property	14,000	Original capital	10,000
		Specific adjustment	4,000
		Current value capital	14,000
Cash	1,000	Profit	1,000
	15,000		15,000

Figure 11.5 Actual current value.

These various possibilities are summarized in Table 11.4. There are arguments in favour of each of them. The historical cost concept is simple to use and avoids the need for subjective estimates. Also, for the purposes of strict accountability, there is an advantage in the sense that the accounting system deals only with actual amounts of money received or spent. This makes it easily verifiable.

From the point of view of the owners it may be said that the effect of inflation on the spending power of their capital is more relevant than the specific price changes of the business's assets. If this were the case, a current purchasing power system would be preferred. However, it is more usual in accounting to use the *entity convention* whereby the business is viewed as being quite separate from the shareholders. It is also a fundamental accounting concept that the business is usually assumed to be a going concern. Therefore, it does not intend to return to the owners

Table 11.4 Capital maintenance concepts.

Concept	Capital to be maintained	Profit
Historical cost	Historical cost capital	5,000
Current purchasing power	Capital adjusted by general index	2,000
Current value (approx.)	Capital adjusted by specific index	500
Current value (actual)	Capital adjusted by specific RC	1,000

the assets that represent the capital. Normally (including this case), the business will intend to replace the original property with another of similar productive potential. Since the assets are not to be returned to the owners but to be replaced by similar assets, their specific current value is surely of greater relevance than their general purchasing power.

If this argument is followed, it will lead to the adoption of a current value approach. The use of the specific replacement cost is clearly more accurate than a specific index. However, obtaining the former information before the asset is sold may often be too difficult or too expensive to be practical.

Critics of current value systems have pointed out that, although there are obvious advantages of such systems irrespective of any general movement in prices, they do not take account of *inflation* as previously defined in terms of a general decline in the purchasing power of money. In order to meet this criticism it is possible to combine adjustments for both general and specific price changes. The original capital of the owners can be adjusted for inflation by using a general index. However, the need for the going concern to take account of specific price changes can also be recognized. This is done by ensuring that any part of current purchasing power 'profit' that relates to the specific increase in the value of assets is treated as an undistributable holding gain. Returning to the earlier example, the balance sheet will thus appear as shown in Figure 11.6.

Such a system may be considered to be too complex for many users of accounts. However, it has the obvious advantage of adjusting the assets for specific price changes and the capital for changes in purchasing power.

Once an approach to capital maintenance has been chosen, the detailed problems of adjusting the accounting system for price changes can be looked at. In practice, balance sheets and profit and loss accounts are required yearly without the above simplifying assumption that the property has been sold. Therefore, the assets as well as the capital must be adjusted for specific or general price changes. The adjustments to profit follow from this. For example, the type of adjustment for depreciation will depend upon whether a fixed asset is restated using a general or a specific index. If a current value approach is adopted, a fixed asset will be restated

Balance sheet

Property	14,000	Original capital	10,000
		Purchasing power adjustment	3,000
Cash	1,000	CPP capital	13,000
		Undistributable reserve	1,000
			14,000
		Distributable profit	1,000
	15,000		15,000

Figure 11.6 Treating the 'profit' on property as an undistributable gain.

using a specific index, and depreciation for a year will be based on this restated amount. This is discussed in the next sections, where actual proposals for new systems of accounting to replace or supplement historical cost are examined.

11.5 General price-level adjusted systems

General price-level adjusted (GPLA) accounting systems were being discussed as long ago as the 1930s, particularly in Germany, the Netherlands and the United States. In the early 1970s, when interest in inflation accounting was very strong due to the high levels of inflation mentioned earlier, many accountancy bodies in the English-speaking world investigated such systems. In 1974 a provisional Standard (PSSAP 7) on this was issued by the UK accountancy bodies. In the United Kingdom, it was called current purchasing power (CPP) accounting, but it did not become standard practice because of the intervention of the government-sponsored Sandilands Committee in favour of current cost accounting (see Section 11.7). However, about 150 UK companies produced supplementary CPP information in their annual accounts. The place to look for more consistent and general use of GPLA systems is South America.

GPLA systems are based on historical cost accounts adjusted with general price index numbers. The basic task is to translate money of different periods into current money of uniform purchasing power. Current items in the balance sheet are already in end-of-year money, but fixed assets need to be analyzed by age and adjusted accordingly, using the general price index.

The profit and loss account adjustments are the three discussed earlier: depreciation, cost of sales and monetary items. In each case the general price index is used, so that all figures are adjusted for *inflation* rather than for specific price changes.

The work involved in producing GPLA accounts need not be prohibitive. There are fewer difficulties than those involved with the specific adjustments of CV systems, and GPLA accounts remain fairly objective. However, the major reason for the failure of GPLA accounting to be adopted in the English-speaking world is the serious doubt about whether the information that it provides is particularly useful. Criticisms have been made about the difficulty of comprehending accounts not produced in 'physical money' terms but in constantly changing units, about the lack of relevance of adjusting fixed assets, depreciation and stocks by a general index and about the inclusion of monetary gains in published profit figures.

11.6 Current value accounting

The CV of an asset can be considered to be based on one of the three concepts briefly introduced in Chapter 6: *economic value* (EV), *net realizable value* (NRV) and *current replacement cost* (CRC). It would be possible to establish complete accounting systems based on each of these concepts or, alternatively, to combine them in such a system as current cost accounting (see Section 11.7).

Economic value

A current value accounting system based on economic values would have a strong theoretical basis, because the real value of an asset depends upon the discounted future net flows of money from it. However, there are serious practical problems in estimating such future flows and establishing suitable discount rates. The resulting costs would be very high. Also, the attendant subjectivity would make an auditor's job very difficult and reduce the reliability of accounting information. In addition, if the individual assets and liabilities of a business were all to be separately valued using an economic value basis, there would be the theoretical problem that cash flows result from assets working in combination. The estimation of the flows resulting from one asset alone is perhaps not a sensible task.

For these reasons no country has seriously considered proposing a system of accounting based mainly on economic values. Nevertheless, EV has been included as a basis to be used in exceptional circumstances within systems like current cost accounting.

Net realizable value

Another possibility is to have a current value system based on net realizable values. An example of such a system is 'continuously contemporary accounting' (CoCoA), proposed by the Australian academic, R. J. Chambers (1975). Under such a system, assets are adjusted to NRV, and depreciation is measured as the fall in the NRV of a fixed asset over an accounting period.

This approach may well provide useful information for management when making decisions about the future of assets, for creditors and for banks. However, it is fairly complex and difficult to use. For example, it is not possible to rely on the use of index numbers in the calculation of second-hand values of many fixed assets or partially completed stocks. Therefore, individual values must be calculated. Also, major criticisms concern the subjectivity involved and the fact that most businesses have no intention of selling most of their fixed assets in the near future, which casts doubt on the relevance of NRVs. However, as an exceptional basis, NRV is included in the proposals for current cost accounting examined in the next section.

Current replacement cost

A third basis for a current value system is current replacement cost. Here the values of fixed assets are their depreciated CRCs. The gross CRC may be determined by valuers, by suppliers' catalogues or by age-analysis of fixed assets followed by the application of specific indices. Suppose that a company buys a machine for 10,000 ecu on 1 January 1990. The machine is expected to have a useful life of five years and no scrap value. It is to be depreciated at 20% per year on a straight-line basis. After three years on 31 December 1992, a CRC balance sheet is drawn up. The specific index has risen over the three years from 100 to 140. Therefore the gross CRC, in the absence of more exact information, will be 14,000 ecu (i.e. 10,000 ecu × 140/100). The net CRC will be 5,600 ecu (i.e. 14,000 ecu *less* 60% cumulative depreciation of 8,400 ecu). The value of stocks will also be based on their CRC, although this may be difficult to determine in the case of partially worked or finished goods.

One of the problems with CRC for any asset is the difficulty that there may be in finding the cost of an identical replacement. This is particularly obvious in the case of obsolete fixed assets. It is necessary to establish the concept of the 'modern equivalent asset', the current cost of which is adjusted for any improvements that it embodies compared with the asset that it replaces. When the CRCs have been established, the excesses over historical costs are reflected in an asset revaluation reserve.

As far as the profit and loss account is concerned, there are two important adjustments. Depreciation is based on the current cost of fixed assets. It is generally proposed for simplicity that the end-of-year rather than the average-for-the-year CRC of a fixed asset be used. The second adjustment would be to eliminate the stock-holding gains from profit by increasing the value of stocks used by a cost-of-sales adjustment. This would be done by using a company's detailed records or a set of specific indices. It is generally thought that these holding gains should not be regarded as distributable because they are part of maintaining capital. An adjustment for gains and losses on monetary items is not usually included in CRC systems, which concentrate on specific price changes of physical resources.

The Netherlands has been the leader in replacement cost theory and practice. Professor Limperg developed an extensive theory, based in microeconomics, which has been influential in the teaching of accounting. Many companies, notably including Philips, have used replacement cost accounting (or elements of it) at various times since the 1950s. Nevertheless, there have been no direct requirements for departures from historical cost, and this has always been only minority practice.

CRC is the main basis involved in those current value systems which have been seriously considered or partially introduced in many English-speaking countries. The advantages and disadvantages of CRC will be mentioned in the next section.

11.7 Current cost accounting

The countries in Europe that have come closest to a generalized system based on replacement cost accounting are the United Kingdom and Ireland. Their system of the early 1980s will now be outlined. During the period in which the UK accountancy profession was considering a supplementary CPP system, the government became sufficiently concerned about inflation accounting to appoint its own committee of inquiry, the Sandilands Committee, which reported in 1975. It suggested that if 'company accounts are to show more adequately than at present the effect of changes in prices, it is accounting practices that must be changed, not the unit of measurement in which accounts are expressed' (Sandilands Committee, 1975, para. 415). The recommendation was that, instead of the supplementary CPP accounts provisionally proposed by the profession, historical cost accounts should be completely replaced for all companies by a system of current cost accounting (CCA). This would involve the continued use of money as the unit of measurement, the expression of assets and liabilities in the balance sheet at a current valuation, and the measurement of profit after allowing for the 'value to the business' of resources consumed.

One of the fundamental proposals in CCA is that assets be shown at their 'value to the business', which means 'the maximum amount of the loss that would be suffered by the company if it were deprived of the assets concerned' (ED 18, para. 183). This deprival value concept had been advanced in the United States as early as the 1930s for property valuation. Depending on the circumstances, the deprival value will be either the CRC, the NRV or the EV of the asset.

Suppose that a business intends eventually to replace a particular machine with an identical new asset. The deprival value of the machine will be the maximum amount that would be lost if the machine were stolen, blew up or disappeared in some other way. In this case, the business would buy a replacement, so that the deprival value will be the depreciated CRC. This is the normal case, in which the EV of the machine is greater than the CRC, and the NRV is smaller than the CRC (i.e. EV > CRC > NRV). Thus, it would be sensible to replace it and not sensible to sell it. The deprival value is not as high as the EV; this is because the EV would not be lost, because the asset would be replaced.

On the other hand, if the business is about to sell the asset because CRC > NRV > EV, the deprival value will be what will be gained from the sale (i.e. the NRV). If the business intends to continue using the asset but not to replace it because CRC > EV > NRV, the deprival value of the asset will be the loss of future revenues from it (i.e. the EV).

Logically, there are six possibilities of arrangement for these three current values, but the above three are the most likely to occur, and that which leads to CRC should apply to the great majority of fixed assets. These possibilities can be arranged in diagrammatic form, as in Figure 11.7.

The profit and loss account would contain current cost figures for cost-of-sales and depreciation charges. There would be no adjustment for monetary items. Estimates of the effects of CCA on profit figures in the United Kingdom suggested that there would be a fall of over 50% on average across all industries in a year of high inflation such as 1975. CPP would produce no fall on average, although there would be large sectoral differences.

The advantages of a system of current cost accounting compared with historical cost accounting are said to be that it provides a balance sheet that gives a much

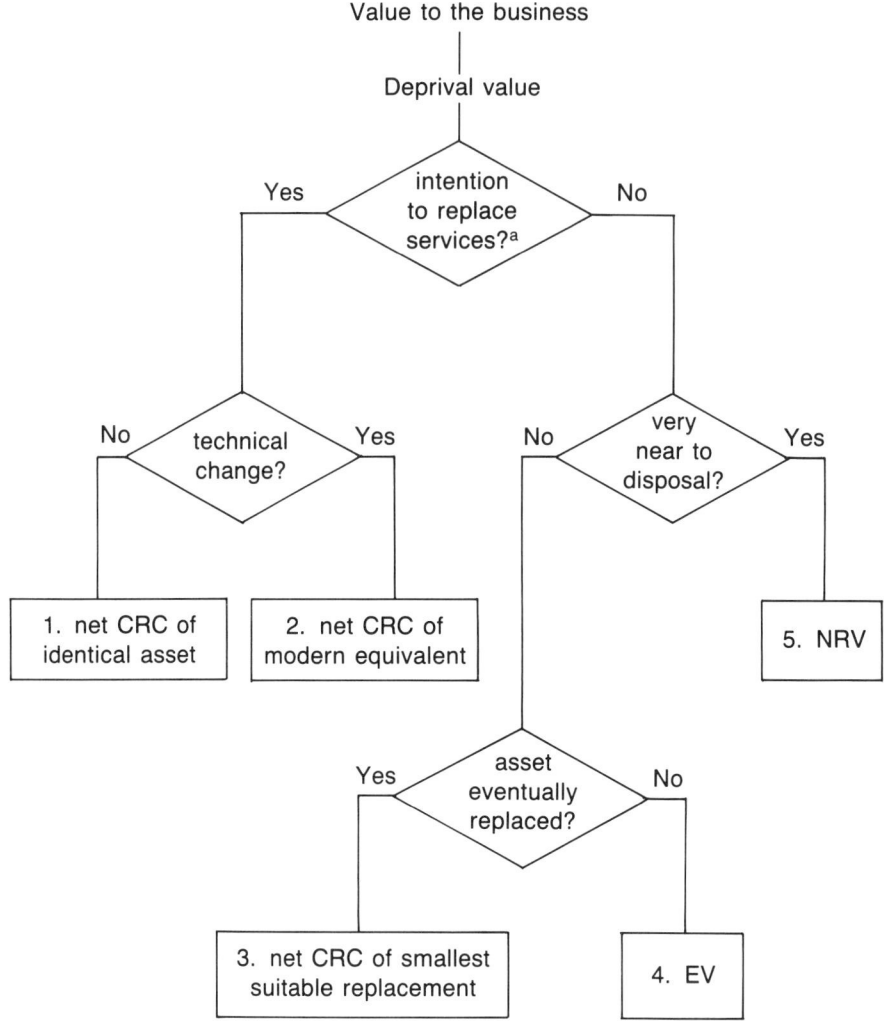

Figure 11.7 Valuation of plant under CCA (CRC = current replacement cost; NRV = net realizable value; EV = economic value (future earnings potential)).
[a] This diamond represents the decision whether to replace the services of the asset fairly exactly. 'Yes' will be the usual answer.

better indication of the value of individual assets and a whole business, and that CCA profit figures can reasonably be used as measures of distributable profit and business performance and for decisions about prices and output. CCA was implemented on an experimental and voluntary basis by many large UK companies in the late 1970s. However, opposition from the bulk of practising accountants and from many companies was strong. Vociferous objections were raised concerning:

- the great complexity of the system and the consequent cost;
- the impracticability of the EV basis required for some fixed assets and the expense of finding CRC for stocks;
- the 'enormous' burden and doubtful value of CCA for small companies;
- the 'disastrous' effects on profit figures; and
- the planned disappearance of familiar historical cost accounting.

This opposition led to a call for a vote by the membership of the Institute of Chartered Accountants in England and Wales (ICAEW), which was held in July 1977 and showed a majority against the compulsory replacement of historical cost accounting by current cost accounting.

After this, several further UK documents were produced leading to a standard (SSAP 16) in 1980. This required supplementary CCA financial statements from all large and listed companies. However, by the mid-1980s there was increasing non-compliance with this standard as inflation fell. The standard ceased to be mandatory and was eventually formally withdrawn in 1988.

11.8 Partial adjustments

There have been a number of attempts to make relatively simple adjustments to historical cost accounting. This section will examine five of them.

Ad hoc government-controlled revaluations

In France, Spain, Italy and Greece revaluations of fixed assets and inventories have occurred several times in the last decades. Some examples are briefly noted here.

1. *France*. A revaluation of fixed assets and inventories was required, for companies with traded securities, in balance sheets at 31 December 1978. This used specific indices as published by the government for 31 December 1976 prices. The revaluation was tax exempt, and subsequent depreciation charges were adjusted back to historical cost in order to avoid changing the tax calculations.
2. *Spain*. A revaluation was carried out in 1983. This was tax exempt but had a subsequent beneficial tax effect in that it increased depreciation charges for the calculation of taxable income. Thus it aided the liquidity of Spanish companies in an inflationary period.
3. *Italy*. Revaluations were required for certain companies in 1983, 1991 and other years. These have some tax effects.

Ad libidum revaluations

In the United Kingdom, Ireland, Denmark and the Netherlands, fixed assets can be revalued, largely at the discretion of the directors of companies. A few Dutch companies use full systems of current value accounting, but generally revaluation in these countries involves only some companies, a selection of assets (particularly land and buildings), and is not necessarily performed annually. These revaluations are mostly a rather messy partial attempt to update accounts for price changes.

Special reserves

One suggestion that would provide information for the users of accounts without altering published profit calculations is that amounts should be appropriated to inflation reserves to reflect either general or specific price changes. As early as 1952 it was proposed that companies should consider 'setting amounts aside from profits to reserve in recognition of the effects that changes in the purchasing power of money have had upon the affairs of the business, particularly their effect on the amount of profit which, as a matter of policy, can be prudently regarded as available for distribution' (ICAEW, 1952). Little notice was taken of this suggestion in the United Kingdom or anywhere else.

Reserves for specific price changes of fixed assets have also been operated by some companies. These may be called *replacement reserves*. The criticism of both general and specific reserves is that they do not affect the calculation of profit and therefore still allow a misleading impression of the operating performance of a company. However, such efforts are better than nothing or than the general and imprecise tendency of companies to avoid distributing more than a certain proportion of their profits in order to allow for the effects of inflation.

LIFO inventory valuation

The last-in, first-out (LIFO) method of inventory valuation has been discussed in Chapter 8. It is a method that matches the most recent purchases against current sales and thus charges an approximately current cost for inventory used. A disadvantage is that the oldest purchases are deemed to remain in inventory, which leads to an unrealistically low balance sheet figure. Also, if inventory levels are reduced, some very old costs will enter the cost-of-sales calculation.

Nevertheless, the use of LIFO does approximately adjust the cost-of-sales figure for specific price changes, particularly if purchases are frequent. Thus, it reduces profit figures during inflationary periods. It is now used by a majority of corporations in Italy and in the United States, mainly because it is allowed for tax purposes as a form of stock appreciation relief. In most European countries it is not allowed for tax purposes, and it is not allowed by law or accounting standard.

Replacement cost depreciation

The suggestion that depreciation charges should be based on the replacement costs of fixed assets has been put into practice by some Dutch companies and forms a part of systems of *current value* (CV) accounting. However, as an individual partial adjustment for price changes it has had little practical application.

SUMMARY

Inflation ran at a very high level in much of Europe in mid-1970s, thus encouraging attempts to adjust historical cost accounting for general or specific price changes. Indices for both are available in many countries. The effects of price changes cause deficiencies in historical cost balance sheets and profit calculations. The effects on profit are more complex and may involve adjustments for depreciation, for cost of sales and for gains and losses on monetary items. Unless adjustments are made, users of accounts may be seriously misled about the value of a business and about what may be suitable levels of dividends, wages or prices. However, some countries oppose any departure from historical cost.

Adjusted systems of accounting fall into two groups: those which adjust for general price changes and those which adjust for specific price changes. The underlying difference concerns the concept of capital maintenance. General adjustment aims to maintain the inflation-adjusted value of the owners' capital. Specific adjustment aims to maintain the productive capacity of the business. The choice determines how assets are to be restated, and in each case profit is what remains after the appropriate measure of capital has been maintained. It is possible to combine the two approaches, so that both inflation and specific price changes are taken into account.

A full supplementary system of current purchasing power accounting was provisionally proposed in the United Kingdom in 1974. It was adopted by several companies in the following two years. However, a government-sponsored report recommended a system of current cost accounting based on adjustments for specific price changes.

Current value systems could be based purely on economic values, on net realizable values or on current replacement costs. Current cost accounting is a system that uses all three bases, although mainly current replacement cost. In the United Kingdom and Ireland current cost accounting was proposed by the accountancy bodies. However, this was rejected by a majority of practising accountants as being too complex, subjective and expensive for a compulsory system for all companies. In 1980, requirements were issued about supplementary CCA accounts, but these soon fell into disuse. In the Netherlands, some companies have used full or partial current value systems.

In the absence of a standard method of adjusting accounts for changing prices, a number of partial adjustments were experimented with in Europe. These include government-controlled or *ad lib* revaluations, the creation of special reserves, the use of LIFO for calculating the cost of sales and the calculation of depreciation using replacement costs.

References

R. J. Chambers, (1975), *Accounting for Inflation*, University of Sydney Press, Sydney.
Institute of Chartered Accountants of England and Wales (ICAEW) (1952), *Accounting in Relation to Changes in the Purchasing Power of Money*, N.15, ICAEW, London, para. 31.
Sandilands Committee (1975), *Inflation Accounting* HMSO, London.

EXERCISES

11.1 P is a computer dealer. From the information below, compute:

(a) the income statements and closing balance sheets for each of the years 19X0 and 19X1 under historical cost principles;
(b) the income statements and closing balance sheets for each of the years 19X0 and 19X1 under current replacement cost principles;
(c) comment briefly on the significance of the results.

All figures are in ecu.

		'Wealth'	
Date	*Event relating to trading in computers*	*Computers*	*Cash balance*
1/1/X0	Set up business with 10,000 in the bank		10,000
2/1/X0	Buy six computers for 1,000 each	6	4,000
1/5/X0	Sell two for 1,500 each (RC = 1,100)	4	7,000
1/9/X0	Buy two computers for 1,200 each	6	4,600
1/10/X0	Pay annual rent of 600	6	4,000
31/12/X0	Financial year end. Pay tax of 200	6	3,800
3/3/X1	Sell two computers for 1,800 each		
	(RC = 1,300 each)	4	7,400
1/10/X1	Pay annual rent 700	4	6,700
1/11/X1	Buy two computers for 1,400 each	6	3,900
31/12/X1	Financial year end. Pay tax of 450	6	3,450

11.2 Duck Co. was formed on 1 January 19X0 with 10,000 issued 1 ecu ordinary shares. The same day it obtained a 12% loan of 8,000 ecu and bought fixed assets for 9,000 ecu.

During 19X0, purchases and sales of widgets were as given in the table below.

	Purchases		Sales	
3 January	100 at 80	8,000		
1 February			60 at 120	7,200
1 April	110 at 75	8,250		
1 May			90 at 120	10,800
1 July	100 at 85	8,500		
1 August			130 at 120	15,600
1 October	120 at 90	10,800		
1 November			110 at 130	14,300

You are also told that:

(i) Purchases and sales were all paid for in cash.
(ii) The loan interest was paid early in 19X1.
(iii) The buying price of widgets changed on 1 March, 1 June, 1 September and on 1 December (when it was 100).
(iv) The fixed assets are to be depreciated at 10% per annum. At 31 December 19X0, their buying price was 12,600 ecu.
(v) General expenses during the year were 13,200 ecu.

(a) Prepare a balance sheet as at 31 December, 19X0 together with an income statement for the year to 31 December 19X0, on replacement cost lines.
(b) What are holding gains? In what circumstances are they distributable?

11.3 A company commences business with capital in cash of 15,000 ecu. It buys a fixed asset for 10,000 ecu. The following information is available:

	Year 1	Year 2
	ecu	ecu
NRV of fixed asset	6,000	4,000
Sales	20,000	25,000
Cost of sales	11,000	12,000
Closing stocks: cost	2,000	3,000
NRV	2,500	3,800

Prepare net realizable value (current exit value) income statements and balance sheets for each of the two years.

11.4 Six people, A to F, own six assets, U to Z, respectively. The various monetary evaluations (in ecu) of each asset by its owner are shown in the following table:

Person	Asset	HC	RC	NRV	EV
A	U	1	2	3	4
B	V	5	6	8	7
C	W	9	12	10	11
D	X	16	15	14	13
E	Y	17	19	20	18
F	Z	23	22	21	24

All six people signed a contract with an insurance agent, under which they shall be reimbursed, in the event of loss of their assets, by 'the amount of money a rationally acting person will actually have lost as a result of losing the asset'.

Put yourself in the position of the rationally acting person, decide what action you would take in each circumstance, and then calculate the net effect on your monetary position. (Figure 11.7 in the text should help.)

11.5 From the following historical cost accounts of P Co., prepare a set of CPP accounts for the year ended 31.12.X8.

	31.12.X7 000 ecu		31.12.X8 000 ecu	
Fixed assets				
Cost (purchased 1.1.X5)		500		500
less depreciation		300		400
		200		100
Current assets				
Inventory (purchased 31 October)	100		150	
Debtors	200		300	
Bank	150		350	
	450		800	
less *Current liabilities*				
Creditors	300		400	
		150		400
		350		500
Share capital		100		100
Reserves		250		400
		350		500

Income statement for the year ended 31 December year X8:

		000 ecu
Sales		1,850
Cost of goods sold:		
opening inventory	100	
purchases	1,350	
	1,450	
less closing inventory	150	
		1,300
		550
Gross profit		
Expenses	300	
Depreciation	100	
		400
Net profit		150

The movement on the retail price index has been as follows:

1 January year X5	180
1 January year X7	200
Average for year X7	210
31 October year X7	215
31 December year X7	220
Average for year X8	230
31 October year X8	235
31 December year X8	240

Assume all sales, purchases and expenses accrue evenly throughout the year.

11.6 Explain and demonstrate how replacement cost accounting affects reported profit compared with historical cost.

11.7 Is replacement cost more or less prudent than historical cost?

11.8 Discuss the proposition that businesses should be required to publish their income statement on replacement cost lines and their balance sheet on net realizable value lines.

11.9 What do CPP adjustments do, and how do they do it?

11.10 Are general indices more or less useful in financial reporting than specific price changes?

CHAPTER 12

Group accounting

OBJECTIVES

- To consider the concepts of control, dominance and significant influence
- To explain and illustrate the various methods of presenting a combined report on a group of linked entities, including:

  the parent company approach with and without the use of fair values
  proportional consolidation
  the equity method
  merger (pooling of interest) accounting

- To outline the EC and IAS pronouncements in the area
- To note the variety in practice, and to consider the implications of this

---

12.1 Background

The production of consolidated financial statements (group accounts) is done on the basis that a group of enterprises is a single accounting entity. It is usual to distinguish three concepts of what is and what is not an 'accounting entity' for this purpose; the parent company concept, the entity concept and the proprietary concept.

The parent company concept assumes that a group contains a parent company and a number of dependent or subsidiary companies. This concept is based on legal control, generally resulting from majority shareholdings and voting rights. However, legal control can also be attained (where company legislation permits, as it does in Germany, for example) by the use of control contracts whereby one company is placed under the legal domination of another. The parent company concept sees the group from the point of view of the parent company's shareholders.

A possible alternative is the 'entity' concept of a group, based on economic control. This emphasizes the economic unity of all enterprises in the group and gives equal importance to all shareholders, whether the parent company or minority interests. This way of looking at a group is, it can be argued, more appropriate for such users as employees and managers.

Neither the parent company nor the entity concept, however, copes satisfactorily with enterprises that belong to more than one group or only partially to a group. In these cases there is neither legal dominance nor economic control. These situations are, however, covered by the 'proprietary' concept which emphasizes not legal control or economic unity, but ownership or proprietorship.

12.2 Control

It is crucial to establish when a parent/subsidiary relationship actually exists. The major influences in this area are the EC Seventh Directive and a series of IASs. The Seventh Directive was adopted in 1983. National laws of EC countries implementing the Directive were required to be enacted by 1988 and their provisions were to apply by 1990. Many countries failed to meet these deadlines, and the final country, Italy, was not required to produce consolidated financial reports under the Directive until 1994 year-ends. The IASC, as already outlined in Section 5.5, has produced and is amending a number of statements.

The Directive (Article 1) requires consolidation when there is any one of the following circumstances:

(a) a majority of the share voting rights;
(b) a shareholding plus a right to appoint or remove a majority of the directors;
(c) a dominant influence pursuant to a control contract (whether or not the parent is a shareholder);
(d) a shareholding plus a majority of the voting rights with the agreement of other shareholders.

Additionally EC member states *may* require consolidation where there is:

(e) a participating interest plus an actual dominant influence or unified management.

IAS 27, says the following (para. 6):

Control... is the power to govern the financial and operating policies of an enterprise so as to obtain benefits from its activities.

Control is presumed to exist when the parent owns, directly or indirectly through subsidiaries, more than one half of the voting power of an enterprise unless, in exceptional circumstances, it can be clearly demonstrated that such ownership does not constitute control. Control also exists even when the parent owns one half or less of the voting power of an enterprise when there is:

(a) power over more than one half of the voting rights by virtue of an agreement with other investors;

(b) power to govern the financial and operating policies of the enterprise under a statute or an agreement;
(c) power to appoint or remove the majority of the members of the board of directors or equivalent governing body; or
(d) power to cast the majority of votes at meetings of the board of directors or equivalent governing body.

A subsidiary should be excluded from consolidation when:

(a) control is intended to be temporary because the subsidiary is acquired and held exclusively with a view to its subsequent disposal in the near future; or
(b) it operates under severe long-term restrictions which significantly impair its ability to transfer funds to the parent.

Such subsidiaries are accounted for as if they are investments.

These exclusion provisions are similar to those in the Seventh Directive (Articles 13 and 14). In addition the Directive requires the exclusion from consolidation of any subsidiary whose activities are 'so different' that inclusion would lead to the consolidated accounts not giving a true and fair view.

Clearly the issue of defining control in a practical situation is important. It is also often extremely difficult. Consider the following three situations:

1. H owns 75% of the voting shares of S which in turn owns 40% of the voting shares of S1. H also owns directly 15% of the voting shares of S1.
2. H owns 100% of the voting shares of S which in turns owns 30% of S1. H also owns 75% of S2 which in turn owns 25% of S1.
3. H owns 60% of the voting shares of S which in turn owns 20% of the voting shares of S1. H also owns directly 20% of the voting shares of S1.

The relationships are easier to see if a diagram is drawn.

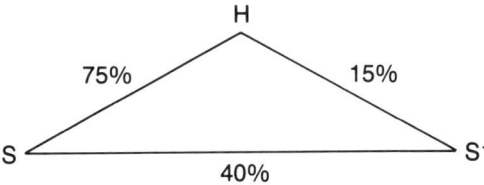

1. S is a subsidiary of H (75% ownership); S1 is not a subsidiary of S (assuming no dominant influence). H directly owns:

$$75\% \times 40\% \text{ of S1} + 15\% \text{ of S1}$$
$$= 30\% + 15\%$$
$$= 45\%$$

which might seem to imply no subsidiary relationship. However, H *controls* S and thus controls 40% of S1 plus 15%. Therefore S1 *is* a subsidiary of H.

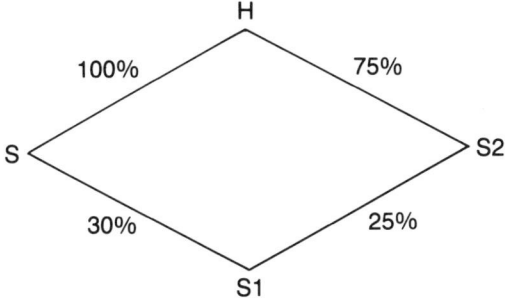

2. S and S2 are subsidiaries of H. H directly owns:

$$100\% \times 30\% + 75\% \times 25\% \text{ of S1}$$
$$= 30\% + 18.75\%$$
$$= 48.75\% \text{ only}$$

However, H *controls* 30% + 25% = 55% of S1. Thus S1 is subsidiary of H.

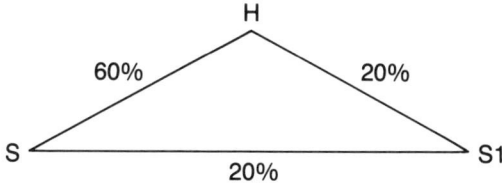

3. S is a subsidiary of H.

    H owns   60% × 20% + 20% of S1 = 32% of S1
    H controls 20% + 20% of S1 = 40%

Thus S1 is *not* a subsidiary of H (assuming no dominant influence).

This last point concerning dominant influence is an important and problematic one. It must inevitably be a subjective matter to be settled on a case-by-case basis. Those countries which tend to adopt a 'substance over form' approach in national legislation or the interpretation of it are more likely to allow or require such practical considerations to overrule the formal legal structure.

12.3 The parent company approach

This approach follows the assumption that the group accounts are being prepared to be primarily of use to the shareholders of the controlling parent company. The combined accounts incorporate the results and resources *controlled* by the parent.

The proportion of these results and resources which is not actually owned by the parent (the minority interests) are then shown:

(a) in the income statement as a reduction in net profits to arrive at earnings attributable to the shareholders of the parent company,
(b) in the balance sheet separately from shareholders' funds and liabilities.

The minority interests shown as (b) represent a claim on the group resources by those *outside* the main ownership interest, which is the interest of the owners of the parent. Consider the situation shown in Figure 12.1, in which Big Co. acquired the whole of the issued ordinary share capital of Little Co. at a price of 1.5 ecu per share for cash as at 30 June, at which date their respective balance sheets were as shown.

As at this date, the estimated fair values[1] of Little Co. assets were:

Land and buildings	30,000
Plant	22,000
Sundry other assets	15,000
Total	67,000

Think first about the accounts of Big Co. (the 'holding' company) in isolation. If these accounts were sent to the shareholders of Big, how useful would this information be? In Big's balance sheet the shareholding in Little will simply appear as an investment at historical cost. However, as with any other asset in a balance sheet, the use of historical cost would not normally give the shareholders of Big Co. any indication of the value of the subsidiary or of the underlying assets. In Big's

	Big Co. (ecu)	Little Co. (ecu)
Land and buildings	100,000	25,000
Plant	40,000	20,000
Investment in Little Co.	75,000	—
Sundry other assets	20,000	15,000
	235,000	60,000
1 ecu ordinary shares	150,000	50,000
Reserves	85,000	10,000
	235,000	60,000

Figure 12.1 Balance sheets for Big Co. and Little Co.

---

[1] Fair value is the price at which an asset could be purchased, or a liability settled, in an arm's length transaction between knowledgeable willing parties, i.e. it is the open market price between two properly independent parties. This contrasts with the figures in Little's own balance sheet which may be historical cost.

income statement, the only reference to the subsidiary would be 'dividends received from Little' (assuming there were any) and, of course, this would give no indication of the subsidiary's profitability.

As far as the group is concerned, the holding company's accounts give no meaningful information about the whole group's activities.

In order to highlight one issue at a time, the example in Figure 12.1 has no minority interest, as the subsidiary is wholly owned. The basic process of consolidation takes the balance sheet of Big Co. as the starting point. In order to show the group as a single entity, the 'Investment in Little' must be removed and replaced by the resources in Little which it represents and the remaining difference shown as 'Goodwill on Consolidation'. This procedure means that the resulting group balance sheet shows no 'Investment in Little', which is logical because a group cannot own an investment in itself.

The above procedure leaves a crucial question unresolved, as two alternative values are available for the resources in Little Co., first, the figures taken from the company's own accounting records as shown in its balance sheet, and second the 'fair values'. It is obviously technically possible to use either set of figures, under the parent company method, as the goodwill on consolidation is simply the balancing number. The consolidated balance sheet using book values is shown in Figure 12.2, and using fair values in Figure 12.3.

As with any consolidation, only the holding company's share capital is shown as the capital of the group. The subsidiary's own share capital reflects internal financing within the group, and is simply a reflection of the investment in the subsidiary as shown in the assets of the holding company's individual balance sheet. In essence, these two items are 'netted off' as part of the 'goodwill on consolidation' calculation.

The figure called 'goodwill on consolidation' can be thought of in a number of ways. The easiest way, of course, is to think of it simply as a number, as a difference created by the bookkeeping; but note how it has been calculated. It is what Big Co.

	ecu	
Goodwill on consolidation	15,000	(75,000 – 60,000)
Land and buildings	125,000	(100,000 + 25,000)
Plant	60,000	(40,000 + 20,000)
Sundry other assets	35,000	(20,000 + 15,000)
	235,000	
Ordinary share capital	150,000	
Reserves	85,000	
	235,000	

Figure 12.2 Big and Little consolidated balance sheets (book values).

	ecu	
Goodwill on consolidation	8,000	(75,000 − 67,000)
Land and buildings	130,000	(100,000 + 30,000)
Plant	62,000	(40,000 + 22,000)
Sundry other assets	35,000	(20,000 + 15,000)
	235,000	
Ordinary share capital	150,000	
Reserves	85,000	
	235,000	

Figure 12.3 Big and Little consolidated balance sheet (fair values).

paid, less what it bought. Big Co. bought 100% of the ownership interest in Little Co., paying 75,000 ecu for a collection of resources which, under either the book value or the fair value figures, appear to be worth less than 75,000.

Why did Big pay 75,000 ecu? There are only two possible reasons:

(a) the directors of Big are stupid or interested in expansion at any cost;
(b) the directors of Big believe the purchase to be worth at least 75,000 ecu.

Ignoring the first possibility, it follows that:

(a) the goodwill on consolidation balance results from a transaction,
(b) H acquired something labelled goodwill on consolidation which it possesses or controls,
(c) H believes that this goodwill on consolidation will lead to benefits in the future.

Consider now the following definition (seen in earlier chapters):

> An asset is a resource controlled by the enterprise as a result of past events and from which future economic events are expected to flow to the enterprise (IASC, 'Framework for the Preparation and Presentation of Financial Statements', para. 49(a)).

Such an item should be incorporated in the balance sheet if:

> (a) it is probable that any future economic benefit associated with the item will flow to or from the enterprise; and
> (b) the item has a cost or value that can be measured with reliability (IASC Framework, para. 83).

In the light of these definitions, it seems that the goodwill on consolidation can normally be properly regarded as an asset. It is not just a balancing number; it has logical and economic meaning.

The argument that this difference on consolidation is an asset has never been universally accepted, however. It can be argued that for something to be 'a resource'

GROUP ACCOUNTING

it must be capable of being severed from its existing situation and transferred elsewhere, in other words it must be separable. This goodwill on consolidation does not meet that criterion. Little Co. with its goodwill on consolidation could presumably be sold by Big Co. to another party, but the goodwill on consolidation cannot be sold in isolation. The whole question of goodwill on consolidation is discussed in more detail in Section 12.9 below.

Comparing the two balance sheets of Figures 12.2 and 12.3, only the assets side is different in this simple example:

	Book value	Fair value
	ecu	ecu
Goodwill on consolidation	15,000	8,000
Land and buildings	125,000	130,000
Plant	60,000	62,000
Sundry other assets	35,000	35,000
	235,000	235,000

Since the total is the same, does it matter? The answer is that it does, because the individual items will be treated in different ways as regards the method and extent to which they will be charged as expenses. Plant depreciation expense will be higher under the fair value method than under the book value method, for example, and of course the goodwill on consolidation comes out at a completely different figure.

It is not difficult to produce arguments in favour of both book value and fair value methods. For example:

1. The acquired company usually still exists, and still operates. There has therefore been no break, no true transaction as regards the individual identifiable assets and liabilities, and so there is no reason to alter the book value.
2. Little Co. has just been acquired and is now part of the 'empire' of the shareholders of Big. They now control the identifiable assets and liabilities of Little, and can be assumed to have just bought those assets and liabilities at the price (cost) currently ruling, i.e. the fair value.

The fair value method obviously introduces more up-to-date economic information and it is the estimate of 'cost' of the group's new assets – powerful arguments. Remember though, that the assets of Big are still not at fair value, only the assets of Little, so the 'fair value basis' balance sheet is only a bit at fair value, and the figures in it relate to different dates and circumstances.

12.4 Minority interests

The following example in Figures 12.4 and 12.5 introduces two additional complications within the parent company or acquisition method. The consolidation relates to a date some time after acquisition, and less than 100% of the subsidiary

	H Co (ecu)	S Co (ecu)
Plant and machinery	60,000	5,000
Investment in S Co.	9,600	—
Sundry current assets	35,000	6,000
	104,600	11,000
1 ecu ordinary shares	40,000	8,000
Reserves	64,600	3,000
	104,600	11,000

Figure 12.4 Balance sheets of H and S at 31 December year 2.

	ecu	
Goodwill on acquisition (Note 1)	1,600	
Plant and machinery	65,000	
Sundry current assets	41,000	
	107,600	
1 ecu ordinary shares	40,000	
Group reserves (Note 2)	65,400	
Minority interests (Note 3)	2,200	
	107,600	

Notes

1. Cost of investment in S Co.		9,600
less 80% of net assets of S Co. (= shareholder's funds) at 31 December year 1		
80% × (8,000 + 2,000)		8,000
		1,600
2. Reserves of H Co. at 31 December year 2	64,000	
Reserves of S Co. accruing to group since date of acquisition	800	
(3,000 − 2,000) × 80%		65,400
3. Share capital at 31 December year 2 of S Co. relating to minorities (20% × 8,000)		1,600
Reserves at 31 December year of S Co. relating to minorities (20% × 3,000)		600
		2,200

Figure 12.5 Consolidated balance sheet of H and S at 31 December year 2.

is bought by the holding company. This latter point leaves a *minority* set of shareholders in the subsidiary who are not part of the group. Since 100% of the assets of S (all of which are *controlled* by H) are being brought in, it is necessary to account for the minority's 20% claim. From the point of view of the shareholders of H, and therefore from the point of view of the consolidated accounts, the minority interest is not part of the ownership interest.

Consider the situation where H Co. purchased 80% of the 8,000 equity shares of S Co. for cash at 31 December year 1 at a price of 1.5 ecu per share, when the balance on S Co.'s reserves stood at 2,000 ecu. The purchase price is 9,600 ecu (i.e. 80% × 1.5 ecu × 8,000 shares).

The consolidation is illustrated at 31 December year 2, at which point the individual balance sheets of the two companies are as shown in Figure 12.4. The consolidated balance sheet as at 31 December year 2 would be as shown in Figure 12.5.

12.5 Proportional consolidation

Consider two companies, H Co. and S Co. H Co. acquired 50% of the equity share capital of S Co. for cash at 31 December at a price of 1.5 ecu per share, and their respective balance sheets as at 31 December were as shown in Figure 12.6. Suppose that another company owns the other half of S's shares and that S is therefore a jointly controlled 'joint venture'.

One way of dealing with this in the group accounts is by proportional consolidation. Using this method we simply add together the various components of each company's balance sheet (assets and liabilities) on the basis of H Co.'s proportionate interest in S Co. in order to arrive at the 'group' picture.

	H Co. (ecu)	S Co. (ecu)
Plant and machinery	50,000	4,000
Investment in S Co.		
(i.e. 8,000 shares × 50% × 1.50)	6,000	—
Sundry current assets	28,600	6,000
	84,600	10,000
1 ecu Ordinary shares	40,000	8,000
Reserves	44,600	2,000
	84,600	10,000

Figure 12.6 Balance sheets of H Co. and S Co.

	ecu	
Goodwill on consolidation	1,000	(6,000 − 50% × (8,000 + 2,000))
Plant and machinery	52,000	(50,000 + 50% × 4,000)
Sundry current assets	31,600	(28,600 + 50% × 6,000)
	84,600	
Ordinary share capital	40,000	
Reserves	44,600	
	84,600	

Figure 12.7 Proportional consolidation of H and S.

The effect of this is to remove the 'Investment in S Co.' from H's balance sheet and replace it with the proportion of all the individual items which it represents. The results are shown in Figure 12.7. For simplicity, any subsidiaries of H are left out of the group accounts.

Proportional consolidation is optional in the Seventh Directive for the treatment of joint ventures in group accounts and is used in practice in several European countries. For example, in France it is compulsory, and in the Netherlands and Germany it is common. In the United Kingdom, it is prohibited, except for holdings in joint ventures that are not themselves companies.

12.6 Investments in other non-controlled companies

Other major points can be summarized here by quoting directly from IAS 28 (para. 2):

> An *associate* is an enterprise in which the investor has significant influence and which is neither a subsidiary nor a joint venture of the investor.
>
> *Significant influence* is the power to participate in the financial and operating policy decisions of the investee but is not control over those policies.

IAS 28 is consistent with the Seventh Directive, which says in Article 33:

> Where an undertaking included in a consolidation exercises a significant influence over the operating and financial policy of an undertaking not included in the consolidation (an associated undertaking) in which it holds a participating interest, ... that participating interest shall be shown in the consolidated balance sheet as a separate item with an appropriate heading. An undertaking shall be presumed to exercise a significant influence over another undertaking where it has 20% or more of the shareholders' or members' voting rights in that undertaking.

In individual company accounts in most countries, investments in subsidiaries, joint ventures or associates are shown using the cost method. Under this the shares purchased are shown at cost (subject to any reduction for diminution in value under the prudence principle). If a dividend is received then it is shown as income. If no dividend is received then no income is shown (even if the company in which some shares are owned itself has a very high income).

The equity method, on the other hand, is generally used in group accounts to account for associates, IAS 28 (para. 2) says:

> The *equity method* is a method of accounting whereby the investment is initially recorded at cost and adjusted thereafter for the post acquisition change in the investor's share of net assets of the investee. The income statement reflects the investor's share of the results of operations of the investee.

An illustration of equity accounting

X acquired 600 ordinary shares in Y (i.e. 30% of the company) at a price of 1.50 ecu per share on 31 December 19X1, at which point the profit and loss reserve of Y had a credit balance of 800 ecu. Thus, the investment in the associate was 900 ecu (600 × 1.5). The respective balance sheets of X and Y as at 31 December 19X2 are shown in Figure 12.8.

X also has a subsidiary company, Z, and it is proposed to prepare consolidated accounts for the X Co. group for the year ended 31 December 19X2. First one could draft the initial consolidated balance sheet of the group as at that date before inclusion of the results of the subsidiary Z, but inclusive of the associate's figures. The effects of the equity method are shown in Figure 12.9. There is an assumption that no dividends are paid by the associate.

This illustration quite clearly demonstrates the effect of equity accounting for the results of an associate in a group's balance sheet. This method is often known as a one-line consolidation. The simple effect is that the assets (Investment in Y) and claims (Reserves) have both been increased by 660 ecu. In a sense the equity method

	X	Y
Fixed assets	15,000	3,200
Investment in Y	900	—
Net current assets	1,000	1,800
	16,900	5,000
Share capital	8,000	2,000
Reserves	8,900	3,000
	16,900	5,000

Figure 12.8 Balance sheets of X and Y.

		Note
Fixed assets	15,000	1
Investment in Y Co.	1,560	2
Net current assets	1,000	1
	17,560	
Share capital	8,000	1
Reserves	9,560	3
	17,560	

Notes
1. Assets and share capital of X only, since Y is an associated company and will therefore be shown in the group balance sheet as an investment.
2. Cost   900
   + share of post-acquisition profit
   = 30% × 2,200 (i.e. 3,000 − 800)   660
       1,560
3. Reserves of X   8,900
   + group's share of post-acquisition
   reserves of Y (30% × 2,200)   600
       9,560

Figure 12.9 Initial equity accounting of Y.

is a proportional consolidation. The difference is that the proportion is added as one figure to the Investment, not as separate figures to the individual asset (and liability) accounts.

If, in the Figure 12.9 example, dividends had been paid by the associate out of profits made since 31 December 19X1, the effect would have been to increase the reserves of X by 30% of the dividends, and to reduce X's *share* of the 'post-acquisition' reserves of Y by the same amount, thus leaving the combined reserves figure at 9,560 ecu. However, since cash has moved into the group, the group cash figure rises by the size of the dividend received, and the 'Investment in Y' falls by the same amount.

Remember that there are a variety of distinctions to be made here. An investment without 'significant influence' is accounted for under the cost method. An investment with 'significant influence' is accounted for under the equity method. An investment with '*dominant* influence' is accounted for under the parent company method. A jointly controlled investment might be accounted for by proportional consolidation. These distinctions, in a real business situation, will often contain elements of uncertainty. The 20% threshold for 'significant influence' is obviously arbitrary. The choices made will lead to completely different accounting treatments and therefore to completely different consolidated financial numbers.

12.7 Intercompany transactions

It is extremely likely that companies within a group will trade with each other and lend to each other. Remembering that H and S (holding and subsidiary companies) are separate legal entities, if H sells goods to S at above their cost, then H has made a profit. If S has not yet sold the goods to outsiders, then the total group has made no profit or loss, as the group, considered as an economic entity, has not done anything. In preparing consolidated accounts, therefore, the positions and results of H and S cannot simply be added together. These sales and profits 'made' by H must be removed from the consolidated results so as to leave only those profits that have been 'made' by the group as a whole by selling to outsiders. Intercompany loans between companies within the group structure must be similarly cancelled out, so as to present a picture of loans made by or to the group considered as a single economic entity.

If, for example, H owns 75% of S then it could be argued that 25% of the profits have really been 'made' by the group, as 25% of the sale from H to S related to the minority interest which is obviously not part of the group. This logic leads to the conclusion that only 75% of the profit made between H and S would need to be removed on the consolidation. The Seventh Directive allows this. However, this practice is usually felt to be imprudent, especially as H controls S and therefore controls the sale. General practice is to remove 100% of such intercompany profits. This is also arithmetically easier for complex groups.

12.8 Merger (pooling of interest) accounting

Everything that has been said and discussed so far is based on the concept of a take-over situation or at least of an acquisition. However, it is possible for two enterprises to come together by agreement and on a more or less equal basis. In accounting terms this is referred to as merger, pooling of interests or uniting of interests, in which two or more companies merge their previously separate businesses into one integrated unit and in which the combined new ownership's interests mirror the relative interests of the original entities. It should be noted that in several countries, e.g. the United Kingdom and the United States, these 'mergers' are usually achieved legally by a take-over. In other countries, a 'legal merger' (*fusion* in French or *fusione* in Italian) may occur.

Merger accounting is allowed under the Seventh Directive (Articles 19 and 20), and under IAS 22. The method assumes no purchase, and therefore there is no goodwill and no fair value exercise. The method is rare or non-existent in most European countries except that it is occasionally seen in the United Kingdom.

12.9 Treatment of goodwill on consolidation

The preparation of consolidated accounts under the parent company method will virtually always lead to a difference, i.e. to goodwill on consolidation. Once it is there, the question obviously arises as to what to do with it. A variety of ideas have been thought of over the years, including:

(a) leave it in the balance sheet, unless it has demonstrably become worthless;
(b) write it off slowly to the income statement;
(c) write it off all at once to the income statement;
(d) write it off all at once directly to reserves (i.e. with no reduction of earnings).

Methods (b) and (d) have generally been the practice in Europe over recent years. The EC Directives say the following about goodwill (Article 30, Seventh Directive):

> 1. A separate item as defined in Article 19(1)(c) which corresponds to a positive consolidation difference shall be dealt with in accordance with the rules laid down in [the Fourth] Directive for the item 'goodwill'.
> 2. A Member State may permit a positive consolidation difference to be immediately and clearly deducted from reserves.

The rules from the Fourth Directive, are as follows. Articles 34.1 (a) and 37.2 state the maximum amortization period for goodwill.

> Where national law authorizes the inclusion of formation expenses under 'Assets', they must be written off within a maximum period of five years. (Article 34.1 (a))

> Article 34(1)(a) shall apply to goodwill. The Member States may, however, permit companies to write goodwill off systematically over a limited period exceeding five years provided that this period does not exceed the useful economic life of the asset and is disclosed in the notes on the accounts together with the supporting reasons therefor. (Article 37.2)

> IAS 22 (revised in 1993) states as follows:

> 46. Goodwill should be amortised by recognising it as an expense over its useful life. In amortizing goodwill, the straight-line basis should be used unless another amortisation method is more appropriate in the circumstances. The amortization period should not exceed five years unless a longer period, not exceeding twenty years from the date of acquisition can be justified.

European practice for certain countries might be summarized as follows:

1. *France*. Generally goodwill is capitalized. It is amortized over periods varying typically between 10 years and 40 years.
2. *Germany*. Goodwill is written off immediately against reserves by some companies, but others capitalize and amortize over 5, 15 or more years.
3. *Spain*. From 1991, goodwill is capitalized and amortized over 5 years.
4. *United Kingdom*. Goodwill is generally written off immediately against reserves.

GROUP ACCOUNTING

Table 12.1 Valuation basis used for income effect for goodwill on consolidation.

Sample size	Bel 50	Den 32	Fra 40	Ger 49	Gre 30	Ire 38	Lux 12	Net 40	UK 50	Total 341
Evidence of goodwill on consolidation	—	15	21	35	—	17	—	6	33	127
Valuation basis used:										
Amortization of amount capitalized:										
Period disclosed	—	3	15	15	—	2	—	—	3	38
Basis not specified	—	—	2	3	—	—	—	—	—	5
Whole cost expensed to income in year in which it incurred	—	—	—	1	—	—	—	—	—	1
No disclosure of valuation basis	—	—	3	3	—	—	—	2	—	8
No income effect (all amounts capitalized, no amortization)	—	—	1	—	—	1	—	—	—	2
No income effect (all amounts taken to reserves on acquisition)	—	12	—	13	—	14	—	4	30	73

Source: adapted from FEE, *European Survey of Published Accounts 1991*, Routledge, London, 1991.

The 1991 FEE survey results regarding goodwill on consolidation are interesting (see Table 12.1). The position is summarized by John Flower in his review of the survey in the *European Accounting Review* (May 1992) as follows:

> In 57 per cent of the surveyed cases that involved goodwill, it was written off directly against reserves. The distribution among countries is revealing: in four countries, France, Finland, Sweden and Norway, there was not a single case; in four countries, Denmark, Ireland, the Netherlands and the UK, it was the prevalent practice; three countries were in the middle: Germany 37 per cent, Spain 25 per cent, Switzerland 42 per cent. There was no information on Belgium, Greece, Italy and Luxembourg. Notwithstanding reservations about the nature of the sample, one can conclude that this point is a major source of differences between countries.

The differences of course have major effects on the size of net assets, and rapid amortization has major effects on the earnings calculation.

12.10 Flexibility in consolidated accounts

As readers will by now be aware, there are many restrictions on the preparation of national published accounts. So, if accounting rules in two EC countries are largely determined by fiscal requirements and the two countries have different fiscal systems, accounting harmonization seems impossible.

A way round this is to leave the accounts of *individual* companies to national tax-related regulation, but to allow greater flexibility in the published consolidated accounts. It is the *consolidated* accounts which are most useful for companies with shares quoted on stock exchanges, and it is therefore the consolidated accounts which provide the key information – for the effective operation of a supranational 'single market'. Flexibility in the sense of release from the constraints of tight local control, fiscal or otherwise, can allow greater harmonization unfettered by national constraints, but encouraged by the practical workings of international financial markets. The EC Seventh Directive specifically allows for group accounts to depart from the rules used in parent company accounts. In France, for example, the rules for group accounts are much more flexible than those for individual accounts.

The second aspect of flexibility however is more negative. Choice and flexibility lead to great difficulty in interpreting financial statements. Detailed study of interpretation is left to Part IV. However, to illustrate the point, consider the four balance sheets in Figure 12.10. Column 1 is the Big and Little book value method balance sheet from Figure 12.2. Column 2 is the Big and Little fair value method balance sheet from Figure 12.3. Columns 3 and 4 are the column 1 and 2 balance sheets as they would appear if goodwill on consolidation were immediately written off against reserves. These represent four very different ways of presenting the identical economic reality, and it is the economic reality that is the target for understanding when financial statements are read and interpreted.

	1	2	3	4
Goodwill on consolidation	15	8	0	0
Land and buildings	125	130	125	130
Plant	60	62	60	62
Sundry other assets	35	35	35	35
	235	235	220	227
Ordinary share capital	150	150	150	150
Reserves	85	85	70	77
	235	235	220	227

Figure 12.10 Big Co. and Little Co. Four different balance sheets (000 ecu).

SUMMARY

This chapter has explored the issues involved in the preparation of group (consolidated) accounts at some length. Fair value and book value methods were illustrated, and considered in the context of EC and IAS pronouncements. Investments involving significant but not dominant influence were discussed, and the equity method illustrated. The broad intention behind current practice is to reflect the economic resources under the control of the group management. As shown, however, this practice is based on assumptions that are sometimes arbitrary or debatable.

Tho alternative, pooling of interest methodology was investigated, and its assumptions and implications noted and contrasted, and compared with the parent method philosophy. Finally, the chapter explored the alternative treatments of goodwill on consolidation and the considerable variety in current practice; the significance of the large degree of choice and flexibility still existing across Europe in the whole consolidation area was underlined.

EXERCISES

12.1 Explain the concepts of:

subsidiary
joint venture
associate
investment in shares

Outline and discuss the usual approach to the accounting treatment in each case.

12.2 A Co. owns 75% of the shares in B Co. bought when the reserves of B were 200,000 ecu. The individual balance sheets of A and B as at 30.6.X2 are given below. During the year B has sold goods to A at a profit margin of 25% on cost. 50,000 ecu of these goods lie in A's closing stock as at 30.6.X2. Also B owes C, an outside supplier, 2,000 ecu and C owes A 5,000 ecu as at 30.6.X2. Prepare the consolidated balance sheet as at 30.2.X2.

Individual balance sheets 30.6.X2

	A 000s ecu	B 000s ecu
Assets		
Land and plant	1,000	200
Investment in B	275	—
Inventory	600	400
Debtors	200	40
	2,075	640
Liabilities		
Creditors	30	16
	2,045	624
Represented by:		
Ordinary 1 ecu shares	1,000	100
Reserves	1,045	524
	2,045	624

12.3 The balance sheets of A and B on 30 June 19X4 were as follows:

		A 000s ecu		B 000s ecu
Land and buildings	108		64	
less Depreciation	20	88	32	32
Plant and machinery	65		43	
less Depreciation	25	40	29	14
		128		46
Shares in B		35		—
Current assets				
Inventory	25		27	
Debtors	48		21	
Bank	22		6	
	95		54	

Creditors < 1 year				
Creditors	112	(17)	34	20
		146		66
Represented by				
Ordinary 1 ecu share		100		50
Capital reserves		10		—
Revenue reserves		36		16
		146		66

(a) A acquired 37,500 shares in B in 19X0 when there had been a debit balance on the revenue reserve of 3,000 ecu.
(b) During the year ended 30 June 19X4, A purchased a machine from B for 5,000 ecu which had yielded a profit on selling price of 30% to that company. Depreciation on the machine had been charged in the accounts at 20% on cost.
(c) B purchases goods from A, providing A with a gross profit on invoice price of $33\frac{1}{3}$%. On 30 June 19X4 the inventory of B still included an amount of 8,000 ecu being goods purchased from A for 9,000 ecu.

Prepare the consolidated balance sheet of A and its subsidiary as at 30 June 19X4.

12.4 Two companies, A and M have balance sheets as at 30 June 19XX as shown:

	A (ecu)	M (ecu)
Plant and machinery	6,000	7,000
Net current assets	5,000	2,000
	11,000	9,000
Issued ordinary shares (1 ecu)	9,000	6,000
Reserves	2,000	3,000
	11,000	9,000

A acquired the whole of the share capital of M on the basis of a one-for-one share exchange as at the above date, at which point the market values of their respective share were:

A   4 ecu
M   4 ecu

The fair values of M's tangible assets as at 30 June 19XX were:

Plant and machinery   8,000 ecu
Net current assets   2,500 ecu

Prepare consolidated balance sheets under both the acquisition and merger methods. Comment on the major differences which emerge.

12.5 (a) How would you define goodwill?
 (b) Three possible accounting treatments of goodwill are:

 (i) retain goodwill as an asset to be amortized over its estimated useful life;
 (ii) retain goodwill as an asset indefinitely;
 (iii) write off goodwill to reserves at the time of acquisition.

Discuss briefly the principles underlying each of these three approaches. Indicate your preferences.

CHAPTER 13

Foreign currency translation

OBJECTIVES

- To separate out the various issues involved in currency translation
- To examine basic accounting transactions in foreign currencies
- To outline and illustrate the two major methods of translating foreign financial statements
- To note the sparseness of rules on this subject internationally
- To survey the practices in several European countries

13.1 Issues and terms

Several linked issues need to be discussed under the heading of currency translation. First, a note on technical terms is necessary.

1. *Conversion* is the process of changing one nation's currency into another's, as typically conducted in a bank or a *bureau de change*.
2. *Transactions translation* is the accounting activity whereby transactions in foreign currency are re-expressed in the currency of the enterprise's accounting records or financial statements; for example, sales to foreign customers or loans from foreign banks.
3. *Translation of financial statements* is the accounting activity whereby financial statements are re-expressed in another currency, typically the translation of a foreign subsidiary's statements for the purpose of preparing group accounts.

This chapter does not deal with point 1 above. It only deals with point 3 for the main purpose of group accounting. For other purposes, e.g. assessment of an overseas company by an analyst, the users of foreign financial statements can choose their own methods of translation, usually the exchange rates ruling on the balance sheet date.

Language can be a problem here. For example, accounting terms are sometimes not easily translated:

English terms	French terms
Conversion	*Change*
Translation	*Conversion*

Consequently, an inexpert translator may mislead the readers of an annual report which has been translated from one language to another.

13.2 Transactions

This section deals with the problems of a company that has no subsidiaries or parent but engages in certain foreign activities. Business is increasingly international, and whenever an enterprise has any dealings abroad, it will be involved in foreign currencies. Since it must keep its accounting records and prepare accounting reports in its own 'home' currency, figures expressed in foreign money units need to be re-expressed in home units. If foreign currency exchange rates remain absolutely constant, i.e. if the value of one currency in terms of the other does not change, then no difficulties arise. However, this is not the case, as exchange rates can and do fluctuate considerably over relatively short periods.

The easiest situation is where an overseas transaction is completed within an accounting period. Consider, for example, a Ruritanian company that keeps its accounts in the local currency, R, but sells goods to a Swiss company in May 19X9 for SF 750,000. Payment is received in August 19X9. Assuming a December 31 year end, in May the company will record a debtor in its records of the Ruritanian equivalent of SF 750,000 at the exchange rate in May 19X9 of 1R = 3.5544 SF, i.e. it will be recorded at R211,006. When payment is received in August the exchange rate has moved to 3.7081 so that the actual amount received is R202,260. The loss on exchange of R211,006 – R202,260 = R8,746 should be reported in the income statement. So the formal double entry in May will be:

Debit	Debtors	211,006	
Credit	Sales		211,006

and in August:

Debit	Bank	202,260	
Debit	Loss on exchange	8,746	
Credit	Debtors		211,006

Any profit on exchange would similarly be credited to the income statement.

Similarly if, in May 19X9, the Ruritanian company bought a fixed asset, such as a machine, for SF 750,000, this would be translated and recorded into its accounts as a debit to machine account for R211,006. The subsequent exchange rate change would not affect the recorded amount for the machine, but any gain or loss on settlement would be charged to the income statement.

However, suppose that a sale or purchase transaction is not completed by the accounting year end, in the sense that a debtor or creditor is still outstanding. In this case, the debtor or creditor needs to be translated into the home currency so that it can be shown in the balance sheet, and a gain or loss might be thought to arise. For example, a Ruritanian company bought a machine from a Belgian company in November 19X8 for BF 11m when the exchange rate was 1R = BF 62.09. At the accounting year end of 31 December 19X8, the payment for the machine had not been made. The machine would be recorded at R177,162, using the November rate. However, the creditor in the closing balance sheet would be recorded at the 31 December rate of 1R = BF 61.29, i e. at R179,475. This would mean that a loss on exchange of R2,313 is recognized in the income statement of 19X8. If the exchange rate continues to move in the same direction until the transaction is settled in January 19X9, then a further loss will be recognized; this time in the 19X9 income statement.

Controversy arises on the accounting treatment in cases like the above but where exchange rates move such that a *gain* might be recognized at the 31 December 19X8 year end. Many European countries (basically those on the left of the chart in Chapter 4, e.g. the United Kingdom and the Netherlands, but also Spain) believe that fairness demands that unsettled gains should be recognized as well as unsettled losses. They can even be called 'realized' in the same way as are profits on credit sales where the customer has not yet paid. Other European countries (basically those on the right of the chart in Chapter 4, e.g. Germany or Sweden) believe that such a treatment is imprudent, and that gains should be recognized on settlement only.

In Germany, for example, it is normal to translate foreign currency debtors or creditors at the worse of the year end or transaction rates. This recognizes losses but not gains. It also, on average, records lower debtors and higher creditors than would be recorded in the United Kingdom. For example, Daimler-Benz' annual reports note:

Currency translation
Foreign currency receivables are translated in the individual financial statements at the bid price on the day they are recorded or at the spot rate on the balance sheet date if lower. Foreign currency payables are translated at the asked price on the day they are recorded or the spot rate on the balance sheet date if higher.

In France year-end rates are used, but gains are stored in the balance sheet as deferred credits until they are settled. A further complication with France, as mentioned in Section 12.10, is that French group accounts can use the less cautious Anglo-American style of recognizing both gains and losses. For example, Total Oil's annual reports note:

Monetary transactions
Monetary assets and liabilities denominated in foreign currencies in the balance sheets of consolidated companies are translated at the exchange rates prevailing at the end of the period. The resulting gains or losses are recorded in 'Other income (expense)' in the consolidated statement of income. However, where foreign currency loans are

specifically contracted to protect a net investment in a foreign consolidated subsidiary or equity investee from the effect of exchange rates fluctuations, translation differences arising on these loans and investments are offset.

The 'However' in the above extract points out that there are many complications in this area, which this introductory chapter will not delve into. In general, though, where hedging or forward buying of currencies are practised, this reduces the recognition of gains and losses.

The discussion so far has concerned transactions which are settled or are soon to be settled. Similar issues arise when there are long-term foreign currency items, such as a ten-year foreign currency loan. Suppose that a UK company borrowed $10,000 from a US bank in London from 1984 to 1994. At each year end, the loan must be shown in pounds sterling in the company's balance sheet. In most countries (though not in Germany, see above), the year-end rate would be used. So the following year-ends and translations (approximately) would have occurred:

31.12.84	$10,000 at £1 = $1 :	£10,000
31.12.85	$10,000 at £1 = $1.5:	£6,667
	Gain in 1985	£3,333

Because the pound strengthened against the dollar during 1985, a gain is implied. Some countries (such as the Netherlands and the United Kingdom) would recognize the gain in the 1985 income statement. Others (such as France) would defer it. The same caveats about French group accounts, hedging, etc., apply, as above.

It seems unreasonable to say that the £3,333 gain is 'realized' in 1985, as it will not be settled until 1994. In the case of the United Kingdom, the accounting standard (SSAP 20) admits this and suggests that prudence needs to be overridden in order to obey the Fourth Directive's demand for matching and a true and fair view.

13.3 Translation of financial statements

This section concerns the translation of a foreign subsidiary's financial statements into the currency of the parent for the purposes of preparing consolidated accounts. At first sight there may seem to be little difficulty. Why not translate the financial statements at the balance sheet date rate of exchange? Indeed, this is the method generally used around the world for foreign currency balance sheets.

A minor complication arises for the income statement which is clearly not a statement *at* a point in time but *for* a period. Consequently, it is common to use the average rate for the year, perhaps calculating a weighted average where transactions are not evenly spread throughout the year. For example, the rules in Spain and the United States require this, whereas either the year-end rate or the average rate is allowed in the United Kingdom. Gains and losses arise because of using different rates from one year to the next or in one of the two financial statements compared with the other. It is normal to take such gains and losses to reserves in the group balance sheet.

This procedure is called the current rate method (United States) or closing rate method (United Kingdom). Most European companies are either required to use this or choose to do so, as in the case of the French company Total Oil for example:

> **Translation of financial statements denominated in foreign currencies**:
> The balance sheets of consolidated subsidiaries or equity investees are translated into French francs on the basis of exchange rates at the end of the period. Foreign exchange differences resulting from such translation are recorded as follows:
>
> - for the Company's share, as 'Cumulative translation adjustment' in the shareholders' equity,
> - for the minority share, as 'Minority interest'.
>
> Income statement items are translated as follows:
>
> - net income, depreciation, depletion and amortization expenses and valuation allowances are translated at exchange rates prevailing at the end of the period,
> - other income statement items are translated at the average exchange rates in effect during the period.

However, in certain countries at certain times, other methods have been used, most notably the 'temporal method', which uses historical rates of exchange for certain items. This method was required in the United States under SFAS 8, between 1975 and 1981, and is still in use by a number of countries in cases where the subsidiary is regarded as an integral part of the parent's business rather than as an independently operating entity. It is the method chosen by some German multinationals, e.g. by Daimler-Benz (until 1993):

> The accounts of all foreign companies are translated to D-marks on the basis of historical exchange rates for non-current assets, and at year-end exchange rates for current assets, liabilities and unappropriated profit. Stockholders' equity in D-marks is the remaining difference between translated assets less translated liabilities and unappropriated profit. The difference resulting from the translation of balance sheet items is recorded in consolidated retained earnings.
>
> Expense and income items are essentially translated at average annual exchange rates. To the extent that they relate to fixed assets (fixed asset depreciation, profit or loss from disposal of fixed assets), they are translated at historical costs. Net income, additions to retained earnings, and the unappropriated profit are translated at year-end rates. The difference resulting from the translation of annual net income, between annual average rates and the exchange rates at the balance sheet date, is reflected in other operating expenses.

This extract illustrates the use of historical rates for fixed assets and depreciation on them, because these items are valued at historical cost. The result of using an historical exchange rate with a foreign historical cost is a translated amount which seems to represent a historical cost in the parent's currency. There seems a certain logic to this.

262   ISSUES IN FINANCIAL REPORTING

Another feature of some versions of the temporal method, but not that illustrated by Daimler-Benz, is the recording of gains and losses in the profit and loss account not the balance sheet. It would take a more detailed text than this to explore all these issues. However, it must already be clear that very different group accounts will result depending on whether the closing rate or the temporal method is used.

13.4 A numerical illustration

The closing rate and temporal methods are illustrated below for a French parent with a subsidiary in a foreign country where the currency is T. Suppose that Home SA established a 100% owned subsidiary Away Ltd, on 1 January 19X1 by subscribing FF25,000 of shares in cash when the exchange rate was 12 T to the FF. Away Ltd raised a long-term loan of 100,000 T locally on 1 January 19X1 and immediately purchased equipment costing 350,000 T, which was expected to last ten years with no residual value. It was to be depreciated under the straight-line method.

Table 13.1 shows the accounts of Away Ltd for 19X1, during which the relevant exchange rates were:

	T to FF
1 January	12
Average for year	11
Average for period in which closing stock acquired	10.5
31 December	10

The T column shows the original balance sheet in the foreign currency. The FF (closing) column shows the translation using a version of the closing rate method which uses the year-end rate for the income statement. Note that, under any method, the share capital is translated at the historical rate. The exchange difference could be worked out in detail, but is also the balancing figure in shareholders' funds. The 'FF (temporal)' column shows the translation using the temporal method, involving the historical rate for certain items. The profits figure in the balance sheet comes from the income statement. The exchange loss could be worked out in detail but, again, is also the balancing figure. Under certain versions of the temporal method, the 651 FF exchange loss would be recorded in the income statement, but otherwise the exchange differences will be taken to reserves.

Implications

By the time that the subsidiary's translated accounts from Table 13.1 are consolidated into the group accounts, the translation method chosen may have a major effect on the financial statements and the interpretation of them. The

Table 13.1 **Away's financial statements.**

Income statement for 19X1	T	FF (closing)	FF (temporal)
Sales	450,000	45,000	40,909[a]
Less Cost of sales	(360,000)	36,000	32,727
Gross Profit	90,000	9,000	8,182
Less Depreciation	(35,000)	(3,500)	(2,917)[b]
Other expenses	(15,000)	(1,500)	(1,364)[a]
Net profit	40,000	4,000	3,901

Balance sheet as at 31 December 19X1			
Equipment at cost	350,000	35,000	29,167[b]
Less Depreciation	(35,000)	(3,500)	(2,917)[b]
	315,000	31,500	26,250
Inventory at cost	105,000	10,500	10,000[c]
Net monetary current assets	20,000	2,000	2,000[d]
Less Long-term loan	(100,000)	(10,000)	(10,000)[d]
	340,000	34,000	28,250
Share capital	300,000	25,000[b]	25,000[b]
Retained profits	40,000	4,000	3,901
Exchange differences	—	5,000	(651)
	340,000	34,000	28,250

Note on exchange rate used:
[a] 11T to FF
[b] 12T to FF
[c] 10.5T to FF
[d] 10T to FF

exchange rate movements in Table 13.1 are fairly small, but still group profit would be affected by inclusion of the different figures:

	closing rate profit	FF	4,000
	temporal method profit	FF	3,901
	– translation loss	FF	(651)
		FF	3,250

This assumes a version of the temporal method where translation gains or loss are taken to the group income statement. The difference between the closing rate and temporal method could have a major effect on group earnings.

The apparent level of group gearing (see more details in Part IV) will be affected. One measure of gearing is made by a comparison of long-term debt with shareholders' funds. In this case, the subsidiary's figures (which will then affect the group accounts) show:

$$\text{closing rate gearing} = \frac{10,000}{34,000} = 29.4\%$$

$$\text{temporal gearing} = \frac{10,000}{28,250} = 35.4\%$$

So, in this case, the temporal method will lead to the presentation of higher gearing figures, which would generally be perceived as worse.

13.5 Some rules

The EC Directives do not directly address the matter of translation, except to require the disclosure of a company's accounting policy on the matter. Consequently, most national laws are also silent on the subject of the translation of foreign subsidiaries. The IASC examines the issue in IAS 21 (revised 1993), which sets out the practice as described above for transactions, requiring the recognition of unsettled gains. IAS 21 generally requires the current rate method for the translation of subsidiaries, with average rates for the profit and loss account. Nevertheless, the temporal method is to be used in certain circumstances, as previously noted.

Some EC member states have accounting standards on this subject (e.g. the Netherlands and the United Kingdom) and Spain has some legal requirements (introduced in a 1989 law). In all these cases, the current/closing rate is the general method proposed.

13.6 Practice

The FEE *European Survey of Published Accounts* 1991 shows a predominance of the closing rate method for balance sheet translation (see Table 13.2). For the profit and loss account, the picture is more varied (see Table 13.3). For example, the average rate seems more common in Germany and the United Kingdom, whereas the closing rate is more common in Denmark and France.

SUMMARY

There are several topic areas that might be considered under the heading of foreign currency translation, and there are some linguistic difficulties in making it internationally clear what topic one is discussing. This chapter deals with foreign currency transactions of individual companies and then with the translation of the financial statements of foreign subsidiaries.

Transactions are generally translated at the rate of exchange ruling on the

Table 13.2 Basis for translation of balance sheets for consolidated accounts.

	Den	Fra	Ger	Ire	Net	Nor	Swe	Swi	UK	Total
Sample size	32	22	49	38	40	10	9	11	50	261
Evidence of foreign operations	21	18	36	22	28	5	6	10	36	182
Translation of entire balance sheet at:										
Closing rate	19	14	19	18	26	4	5	8	33	146
Historical rate	2	—	2	—	1	—	—	—	3	8
Temporal method	—	—	9	1	—	—	—	1	—	11
Other	—	3	—	1	—	—	1	1	—	6
Different bases for individual items	—	1	3	—	—	—	—	—	—	4
No disclosure of translation basis	—	—	3	2	2	1	—	—	—	8

Source: adapted from FEE *European Survey of Published Accounts 1991*, Routledge, London, 1991.

Table 13.3 Basis for translation of income statements for consolidated accounts.

Sample size	Den 32	Fra 22	Ger 49	Ire 38	Net 40	Nor 10	Swe 9	Swi 11	UK 50	Total 261
Evidence of foreign operations	21	18	36	22	28	5	6	10	36	182
All profit and loss items translated at:										
Closing rate	15	9	11	6	10	—	1	1	11	64
Historical rate	1	—	1	—	2	—	—	1	5	10
Temporal method	1	—	—	—	—	—	—	1	—	2
Forward rate	—	—	—	—	—	—	—	—	—	—
Average rate	3	5	21	13	9	4	5	7	18	85
Other	1	3	—	—	2	—	—	—	—	6
All profit and loss items except for non-monetary items translated at:										
Historical spot rate	—	—	—	—	—	—	—	—	1	1
Average rate	—	1	—	—	—	—	—	—	—	1
No disclosure of translation basis	—	—	3	3	5	1	—	—	1	13

Source: adapted from FEE *European Survey of Published Accounts 1991*, Routledge, London, 1991.

date of the transaction, so asset purchases are generally frozen into home currency at the date of purchase. Outstanding debtors and creditors are translated in most countries at current rates, but in some countries at the worse of transaction and current rates, thereby not recognizing translation gains until settlement. In some countries where current rates are used, resulting gains are thereby recognized but postponed.

For translation of foreign subsidiaries' financial statements, the current/closing rate is the most popular internationally. Both average rates and closing rates are common for the income statement. In general, gains and losses that result from this process are taken to reserves. Nevertheless, the use of historical rates for certain items is not unknown, and this can have a large effect on group financial statements. Many countries have no rules in this area because full-scale consolidation is recent in some of them, because the topic was not covered by the EC Seventh Directive, and because group accounts are not relevant for tax purposes.

EXERCISES

13.1 A loan is made to a company of $20,000, which is equal to 10,000 ecu in year 1. The loan is denominated in dollars. At the end of year 1 the loan is translated as 9,500 ecu, at the end of year 2 as 10,500 ecu and during year 3 it is repaid, the proceeds being converted to 10,600 ecu. The company keeps accounts in ecu.

(a) Show the accounting entries for each year.
(b) State how you would deal with the gains or losses on exchange for each year, at that time.
(c) Justify your answers.

13.2 Home (an American company) has a wholly owned subsidiary, S, which it acquired on 1.1.X0. The balance sheets of S as at 1.1.X0 and 31.12.X0 are as follows in FC units:

		1.1.X0		31.12.X0	
		FC units		FC units	
Fixed assets			450		330
Inventory	240		360		
Debtors	120		240		
	360		600		
Creditors	210	150	240	360	
		600		690	
Ordinary share capital		600		600	
Retained profits		—		90	
		600		690	

The income statement account for the year 31.12.X0 is:

Sales		1,500
Cost of sales (240 + 1,200 − 360)	1,080	
Depreciation	120	1,200
Net profit		300
Taxation		150
		150
Proposed dividend		60
Retained profit		90

Translate the accounts of S using both the closing rate method and temporal method given:

```
1 January 19X0, $1   = 3FC
30 June 19X0, $1     = 2.5FC
31 December 19X0, $1 = 2FC
```

13.3 'The variety of possible methods of foreign currency translation, and the different ways of treating gains arising, show that adequate harmonization for international comparison purposes is a long way away.' Discuss.

PART IV

Analysis of financial statements

CHAPTERS	
14 Profitability analysis	271
15 Liquidity analysis	290
16 Valuation and analysis	310
17 International analysis	324

CHAPTER 14

Profitability analysis

> **OBJECTIVES**
>
> - To outline the strengths and weaknesses of comparisons and ratio analysis
> - To examine how to analyze, compare and appraise the earnings of business organizations
> - To examine how to analyze, compare and appraise the profitability of business organizations, by relating earnings to measures of resources used by the organization

14.1 Introduction

Now that many of the major problem areas of financial reporting have been considered, it is time to investigate in detail how to *use* financial statements. An essential part of the analysis of financial statements is to be fully aware of their weaknesses. Some of these are inherent in the tools of analysis used, but most of the important ones arise from the content and characteristics of the original data as prepared or published. That is why the conventions, practices and problems of accounting covered in the earlier parts of this book have to be thoroughly understood before effective financial analysis can be achieved.

The first two chapters of Part IV cover the key techniques of financial statement analysis and interpretation. The third looks rather more briefly at the valuation of businesses and at unrecorded assets, and the fourth discusses the extra difficulties arising from comparison and analysis across national boundaries and across different accounting cultures. Finally, at the end of Chapter 17, there are some exercises in a European and multinational context. These are designed to show the application, and the limitations, of financial statement analysis.

14.2 Ratios and percentages

A number, in isolation, is not a very helpful piece of information. For example, 'sales last year were 20 million Australian dollars'; what information does this give? Without knowledge of the exchange rate between the home currency and Australian dollars, no comparison with home sales is possible. Without knowledge of the size of the Australian market for the products concerned, and without knowledge of the structure of that market in terms of size and number of competitors, no comparison with the general situation in Australia is possible. And without knowledge of sales figures for earlier years, and of the assets available and the expenses consumed to create those sales, no appraisal of progress, effectiveness or efficiency is possible.

Comparison is the key. A ratio is potentially a very powerful tool, but is also a very simple one. A ratio is one number divided by another. If the total Australian market for the product is 400 million Australian dollars, then the ratio of sales by the company mentioned above to its total home market is 20:400 (or 1:20 or 5%).

In many instances, perhaps only because of habit and experience, a percentage seems most helpful and easy to understand. One simple but effective application of this technique is the idea of *common size statements*. This involves reduction of the monetary figures in financial statements to percentages of relevant totals.

A common size income statement is usually prepared by expressing each item as a percentage of total sales. If this technique is applied to the income statements of two different businesses then two benefits emerge. First, any size differences are controlled for, and the internal relationships can be compared on equal terms. Second, the internal relationships themselves are clarified and highlighted in a manner convenient to the eye and the mind. An example is shown later in Section 14.3. A similar technique can be used for balance sheets. Each item will be expressed as a percentage either of total assets or of total fixed assets plus net current assets, depending on the balance sheet structure preferred.

For effective comparison in practice, a number of years' results need to be taken, preferably five or more. Note, however, that the more years that are considered, the greater the risk of changes in the accounting policies used over the period. Such changes will distort any trend considerations. They should be looked for and eliminated as far as possible, if necessary on a subjective basis.

14.3 Profit ratios

Tables 14.1 and 14.2 give the summarized financial statements for a retail company, Bread Co., for two successive years. These will be used as a basis of calculation and illustration throughout Chapters 14 and 15. The income statement will be explored first, beginning with ratios constructed entirely from within the income statement itself.

Table 14.1 Bread Co. income statements (all figures in 000 ecu).

	Year ended 31 Dec 19X1		Year ended 31 Dec 19X2	
Sales		150		250
Opening inventory	8		12	
Purchases	104		180	
	112		192	
Closing inventory	12		16	
Cost of sales		100		176
Gross profit		50		74
Wages and salaries	20		26	
Depreciation	4		8	
Debenture interest	—		2	
Other expenses	14		16	
		38		52
Net profit before tax		12		22
Taxation		4		10
Net profit after tax		8		12
Proposed dividends		4		6
Retained profit for the year		4		6

Table 14.2 Bread Co. balance sheet (all figures in 000 ecu).

	At 31 Dec 19X1		At 31 Dec 19X2	
Fixed assets		72		110
Current assets				
Inventory	12		16	
Debtors	18		40	
Bank	10		4	
	40		60	
Creditors less than one year				
Creditors	10		28	
Taxation	4		10	
Proposed dividends	4		6	
	18		44	
Net current assets		22		16
Creditors greater than one year				
10% debentures		—		20
		94		106
Financed by				
Ordinary share capital		70		76
Retained profits		24		30
		94		106

Gross profit margin

The gross profit is the difference between the sales price and the cost of the goods sold. The gross profit margin is an indication of the extra inflow from an extra unit of sales. The formula is:

$$\text{Gross profit margin} = \frac{\text{gross profit}}{\text{sales}} \times 100$$

For Bread Co. the figures (from Table 14.1) are:

$$19X1: \frac{50}{150} = 33.3\%$$

$$19X2: \frac{74}{250} = 29.6\%$$

An alternative way to consider this aspect is to relate the gross profit to the cost of sales figure, thus giving the mark-up as a percentage of cost. This might well be the way the business manager arrived at the selling price in the first place. The figures for mark-up would be:

$$19X1: \frac{50}{100} = 50\%$$

$$19X2: \frac{74}{176} = 42\%$$

For Bread Co. the gross profit margin has fallen since the previous year. Some of the possible reasons for this are obvious. The selling price may have been deliberately lowered, or the cost of sales may have increased but a decision made not to increase selling prices correspondingly. The mix of sales may have altered, with an increase in the relative volume of low-margin goods. There may be other less visible reasons, however. For example, note how the cost of sales and therefore gross profit figures are directly affected by the inventory figures. The fall in gross profit margin, if unexpected, could suggest an error in the calculation of one of the inventory figures, or that goods are being stolen from the business in 19X2.

The calculations for a manufacturing business would be more complicated because cost of sales will include a variety of separate items including direct labour and materials, production overheads and possibly some arbitrary proportion of some of the more general overheads as well. Full information enabling a proper split of the results between gross profit and net profit may be absent, and if it is available it is likely to be based on arguable assumptions covering cost behaviour and cost allocation.

An additional practical problem is that many companies use the alternative format for the income statement allowed in the Fourth Directive. This does not reveal cost of sales and gross profit, but merely adds an increase in inventory to sales, and then deducts all expenses including raw materials or finished products obtained from outside. Sometimes reasonable assumptions can be made to produce a useful approximation to gross profit, but sometimes such assumptions will be based on so much guesswork as to be self-defeating.

Net profit margin

The net profit is the difference between the sales or turnover, and all the expenses. The net profit margin therefore shows the net benefit to the business per unit of sales. The formula is:

$$\text{Net profit margin} = \frac{\text{net profit before tax}}{\text{sales}} \times 100$$

For Bread Co. the figures are:

$$19X1: \frac{12}{150} = 8.0\%$$

$$19X2: \frac{22}{250} = 8.8\%$$

This shows that the efficiency which Bread Co. shows in turning sales into profit generation has slightly increased in 19X2. The issue of whether to use profit figures before or after tax is considered in Section 14.5.

The net profit margin will be affected by two major considerations, namely, the gross profit margin and the significance of the expenses. It may be useful, therefore, to compute an expenses to sales ratio as well.

Expenses to sales

This explains the movement between gross and net profit margins. The formula for the expenses to sales ratio is:

$$\frac{\text{expenses}}{\text{sales}} \times 100$$

For Bread Co. the figures are:

$$19X1: \frac{38}{150} = 25.3\%$$

$$19X2: \frac{52}{250} = 20.8\%$$

Bread Co. has successfully managed to increase sales quite substantially in 19X2 without a corresponding pro rata increase in the expenses of running the business operation. It is interesting to put together the ratios that have been calculated so far.

	19X1	19X2
Gross profit margin %	33.3	29.6
Expenses to sales %	25.3	20.8
Net profit margin %	8.0	8.8

The reduction in gross profit margin in 19X2 has been more than compensated for by the reduction in the relative size of the expenses, leading to the slight improvement in the net profit margin.

These figures go part way towards the preparation of common size income statements. These are shown complete in Table 14.3, and give more detail of the way in which the success in controlling total expenses has been achieved.

It should be noted that ratio preparation is a pragmatic business. It is, of course, possible to calculate a ratio that is 'wrong' in the sense of being defined or calculated in an illogical manner. Once that hurdle has been overcome, it is misleading to think of a limited list of 'right' ratios. For example, in the above discussion the debenture interest has been treated as just another expense. However, depending on the purpose of the analysis, it may be more helpful to view the debenture interest as different and separate from the other expenses, on the grounds that it is concerned with the financing rather than the operation of the business activities. This leads to the idea of calculating a net *operating* profit to sales percentage, i.e. taking the profit *before* deduction of the debenture interest.

For Bread Co.

$$\text{Net operating margin} = \frac{\text{net operating profit}}{\text{sales}} \times 100$$

$$\text{for 19X1: } \frac{12}{150} = 8.0\%$$

$$\text{for 19X2: } \frac{24}{250} = 9.6\%$$

Is net operating margin a more useful ratio than net margin? The question may not be a sensible one. They are not mutually exclusive alternatives. They are both providing useful insights into the situation and progress of the business.

14.4 Profitability ratios

It is not sufficient to analyze the income statement and the profit position in isolation. Business operation requires the use of scarce resources which are not cost-free and which need to be used as efficiently as possible. It is essential to analyze the results of the business operations in relation to the resources being used by the business and controlled by the management of the business. This leads to a variety of relationships and ratios that need to be explored.

Table 14.3 **Bread Co. common size income statements (all figures are percentages of sales).**

	Year ended 31 Dec 19X1		Year ended 31 Dec 19X2	
Sales		100		100
Cost of sales		66.7		70.4
Gross profit		33.3		29.6
Wages and salaries	13.3		10.4	
Depreciation	2.7		3.2	
Debenture interest	—		0.8	
Other expenses	9.3		6.4	
		25.3		20.8
Net profit before tax		8.0		8.8

Asset turnover ratios

One approach to exploring the relationship between returns and resources is to consider some or all of the assets as recorded in the balance sheet. Possibilities include considering total assets, net assets (i.e. fixed assets plus net current assets) or fixed assets alone. These could be related with, for example, turnover, gross profit, net profit or net operating profit.

Table 14.4 shows six such ratios calculated for Bread for 19X1 and 19X2. Care has to be taken in applying ratios like this, as there are many influences on the asset figures used which are arbitrary and not logically related to business efficiency. Total assets is a particularly flexible concept. A business that buys additional inventory without paying for it, just before the balance sheet date, will show an increase in total assets, but not an increase in net assets, and it is surely the net asset picture which better reflects the economic reality here. The figures used for fixed assets (which are incorporated into both the other asset figures as well) are notoriously susceptible to changes in depreciation, valuation or asset replacement policies. Nevertheless useful indications of trend can often be discovered from ratios like these, provided that the weaknesses and peculiarities behind the figures in each particular business are explored and understood.

Looking at Table 14.4 it can be suggested that the efficiency of usage of net assets has increased significantly from, 19X1 to 19X2, as turnover to net assets and net profit to net assets have both risen sharply. The other four ratios presented have increased a little. It should also be noticed, however, that net assets itself has not increased much, whereas fixed assets and total assets have both increased very substantially. The net assets, unlike either of the other two asset definitions, have been held down by a sharp increase in current liabilities.

Table 14.4 **Bread Co. – some asset turnover ratios.**

	19X1	19X2
$\dfrac{\text{turnover}}{\text{fixed assets}}$	$\dfrac{150}{72} = 2.1$	$\dfrac{250}{110} = 2.3$
$\dfrac{\text{turnover}}{\text{net assets}}$	$\dfrac{150}{94} = 1.6$	$\dfrac{250}{106} = 2.4$
$\dfrac{\text{turnover}}{\text{total assets}}$	$\dfrac{150}{112} = 1.3$	$\dfrac{250}{170} = 1.5$
$\dfrac{\text{net profit}}{\text{fixed assets}}$	$\dfrac{12}{72} = 0.17$	$\dfrac{22}{110} = 0.20$
$\dfrac{\text{net profit}}{\text{net assets}}$	$\dfrac{12}{94} = 0.13$	$\dfrac{22}{106} = 0.21$
$\dfrac{\text{net profit}}{\text{total assets}}$	$\dfrac{12}{112} = 0.11$	$\dfrac{22}{170} = 0.13$

Non-financial resource ratios

It is important to remember that much useful information about business activities is non-financial. This not only applies to some of the important outputs, such as chemical or noise pollution, but also to some of the inputs. Concentration on non-financial data may be especially useful in relation to a resource input which is particularly scarce or expensive. Turnover per employee is a good example of this type of ratio, where turnover could be expressed in money terms or in non-financial terms such as the number of units produced each year, per employee. Another example is output or turnover per square metre of factory space.

Whether non-financial ratios like these are useful will depend on the particular situation and available information. However, they may permit useful comparisons of different organizational structures and different trends of development.

14.5 Finance ratios

A further approach to investigating the relationship between returns generated by a business and the resources employed to create the returns is to consider the sources of finance on the other side of the balance sheet. This is probably the most interesting, because it enables financial statement analysts to focus on various subsets of the total finance being provided, and to consider the return generated *for* that particular subset and its providers.

Return on owners' equity (ROOE)

This ratio relates the return made by the business *for* the shareholders with the finance made available to the business *by* the shareholders. It can be calculated either before tax deductions or after tax deductions, and it may well be useful to do both. If the issue to be explored is the return potentially available for distribution to the shareholders, then obviously the after-tax position has to be taken. On the other hand, if an investigation of the efficiency of management in organizing the economic operation of the business is required, or comparison of ROOE with rates of return on other sources of finance, then the deduction of tax figures is an artificial distortion. In such cases before-tax returns may be more useful.

The formula for return on owners' equity is:

$$\frac{\text{net profit}}{\text{share capital and reserves}}$$

For Bread Co. the ROOE figures are:

before tax

$$19X1: \frac{12}{94} = 12.8\%$$

$$19X2: \frac{22}{106} = 20.8\%$$

after tax

$$19X1: \frac{8}{94} = 8.5\%$$

$$19X2: \frac{12}{106} = 11.3\%$$

The increase in ROOE before tax is large, but is partly reduced by a larger than proportional tax charge.

Return on capital employed (ROCE)

In terms of assessing the efficient usage of the resources provided to the business, this is probably the most important single ratio of all. The capital employed is defined as the owners' equity plus the long-term borrowings of the business. It seeks to embrace all the long-term finance made available to the business. The ratio therefore investigates the efficiency of the business as a whole, not from the point of any particular subset such as the owners. Notice that the ROOE compared the return made for the share capital and reserves with the amount of that share capital and reserves. In the case of the ROCE, the target is to compare:

(a) the return made for the total of the share capital, the reserves and the long-term borrowings with
(b) the amount of that total.

In contrast to the ROOE, the denominator of the ROCE ratio is larger by the amount of the borrowings. It therefore follows that the numerator of the ROCE needs to be larger than the numerator of the ROOE by the amount of the return which relates to those borrowings, i.e. *interest*. This interest, being an expense of the business, has been deducted in arriving at net profit. So, in order to arrive at the correct 'return' figure relevant to the ROCE calculation, the interest concerned must be added back to the net profit figure.

The formula for return on capital employed is:

$$\frac{\text{net profit plus interest on long-term borrowings}}{\text{owners' equity plus long-term borrowings}}$$

Profit before tax is used because interest figures are given gross of any tax effect, and to take after-tax profit and then adjust for interest net of tax would require subjective adjustments to the tax charge.

For Bread Co. the ROCE figures are:

$$19X1: \frac{12}{94} = 12.8\%$$

$$19X2: \frac{22 + 2}{106 + 20} = \frac{24}{126} = 19.0\%$$

It is instructive to compare the ROOE and ROCE calculations (taking ROOE before tax to ensure consistency with ROCE):

	19X1	19X2
ROOE	12.8%	20.8%
ROCE	12.8%	19.0%

In 19X1 the figures are of course identical, because there were no long-term borrowings. In 19X2 the return made by the business as a whole, considering all the long-term finance, was 19.0%, yet the return to the shareholders at 20.8% was more than this. The shareholders have managed to construct a company structure where they have attributed to them more than their simple proportion of the ROCE. The reason for this should be clear: the providers of the remainder of the capital employed have accepted a fixed return which is *less* than their simple proportion of the ROCE would be: ROCE is 19.0%, interest on debentures is 10.0%. Therefore for that part of capital employed represented by the debentures, the difference of $19.0 - 10.0 = 9.0\%$ is available for the owners, in addition to the 19.0% that has been earned for them on their own proportion of the capital employed.

The relationship between owners' equity and long-term borrowings is known as gearing or leverage. There are two common ways of calculating a gearing ratio:

(a) compare the debt, or long-term borrowings, with the owners' equity, and
(b) compare the debt with the capital employed (i.e. owners' equity plus debt).

Formulae for the two gearing ratios are:

(a) $\text{Gearing} = \dfrac{\text{debt}}{\text{share capital plus reserves}}$

or

(b) $\text{Gearing} = \dfrac{\text{debt}}{\text{share capital plus reserves plus debt}}$

For Bread Co. the figures are:

(a) 19X1: 0

19X2: $\dfrac{20}{106} = 18.9\%$

(b) 19X1: 0

19X2: $\dfrac{20}{126} = 15.9\%$

With the figures that are emerging here, it seems to be in the interests of the shareholders to maximize the proportion of the total capital employed which is financed by debt rather than by themselves. For example, if the capital employed of 126 consisted of capital plus reserves of 66 and debentures (with 10% interest) of 60, then the ratios for 19X2 would be as follows:

$$\text{ROCE} \;\; \dfrac{24}{126} = 19.0\%$$

$$\text{ROOE} \;\; \dfrac{24 - 6}{66} = 27.3\%$$

There are limits to the feasibility of this process, however. It is more risky to lend to a business which already has significant debt, and therefore increasing interest rates would be needed to attract such lending – if indeed it could be attracted at all. Consider what happens to a highly geared structure when operating profits fall.

Suppose that Bread Co. does alter its capital structure to give owners' equity of 66 and 10% debentures of 60, but then in 19X3 the level of operating profit falls back to that of 19X2, i.e. 12. This would lead to 19X3 ratios as follows:

$$\text{ROCE } \frac{12}{126} = 9.5\%$$

$$\text{ROOE } \frac{12-6}{66} = 9.1\%$$

Now the gearing is working in the other direction, to magnify the fall suffered by the shareholders rather than to magnify the rise. It should be remembered also that a company that cannot afford to pay dividends does not have to pay them. However, a company that cannot afford to pay interest still has legally to pay it. This can be the road to disaster.

Further analysis of ROCE and ROOE

Bread Co. is a grossly simplified situation, and in practice life is much more complicated. The text and case studies of this book are not designed to cover all possible complications that might be met, but to enable the diligent reader to work out how to deal with them. To begin this process, two complications are mentioned at this stage.

What is long-term borrowing?

It can reasonably be deduced that, if a liability is defined in published financial statements as long-term or non-current borrowing, then it is indeed long-term or non-current borrowing. However, if a liability is defined as 'falling due within one year' or some similar phrase, the reality behind the picture may not be so clear-cut. For example, consider the following amounts falling due within one year.

	19X4	19X5
Bank loans	18	19
Bank overdrafts	5	4
Bills payable	20	10
Trade creditors	50	55
Taxation	32	34
Dividends	20	25
Sundry creditors and accruals	18	20
	163	167

Does it look as though all of these items are genuine short-term liabilities arising from the trading and operating cycle? Or do some of them seem likely to be a continuing source of finance which happens to be legally constructed so as to be finite (but renewable) within one year? These are subjective questions, but it seems likely that the bank loans and overdrafts, and possibly also the bills payable, are being used to finance the activities of the business, rather than being an integral part of those activities.

If that view is taken, then these items should be included as long-term borrowing for the purposes of calculating capital employed. Further, the interest on those 'current' liabilities must also be added back to net profit (or not deducted from operating profit) in arriving at the correct return figure for the ROCE ratio. This may involve a very careful analysis and division of the interest payable amount between the various loans to which it relates.

Different classes of owners

The above discussions also assume that all shareholders are equal and identical. However, there may be several classes, and each class will then have its own viewpoint on the performance of the business. For example, suppose now that the share capital of Bread Co. includes 10,000 1 ecu preference shares, each bearing a fixed 10% dividend entitlement, the ordinary share capital then being 60,000 and 66,000 at 31 Dec 19X1 and 31 Dec 19X2 respectively. The ROOE (and ROCE) will be the same as previously shown (pp. 279 and 280). ROOE, taking before-tax figures to ease comparison, was:

$$19X1: \frac{12}{94} = 12.8\%$$

$$19X2: \frac{22}{106} = 20.8\%$$

However, it is also possible to calculate the ordinary owners' return (ROOOE). For this, the preference share capital must be deducted from the denominator, and the preference shareholders' dividend return must be deducted from the numerator.

$$\text{ROOOE in } 19X1: \frac{12-1}{94-10} = \frac{11}{84} = 13.1\%$$

$$19X2: \frac{22-1}{106-10} = \frac{21}{96} = 21.9\%$$

This leads to a complete table as follows:

	19X1	19X2
ROCE (all capital employed)	12.8%	19.0%
ROOE (all shareholders' equity)	12.8%	20.8%
ROOOE (all ordinary owners' equity)	13.1%	21.9%

The effect on the ordinary shareholders of adding a tranche of preference shareholders with a lower dividend, is similar to the effect on all shareholders together of adding a tranche of debentures with a lower interest rate.

14.6 Investment ratios

The profitability and finance ratios discussed above investigate various relationships within the accounts. Investment ratios consider items in and outside the accounts from the outside equity investor's perspective. The connection between an investor and the business is obviously through the medium of a share, and most investment ratios relate shares to some aspect of the financial statements.

Book value per share

The book value of an ordinary share is the value attributable to each ordinary share if the assets and liabilities of the company were sold or settled at the figures shown in the published balance sheet (i.e. at the 'value in the books'). The book value of an ordinary share is therefore the ordinary shareholders' equity divided by the number of issued ordinary shares. Since most figures in the balance sheet are not designed to show the value of the item in any market-orientated sense of value, this ratio, at least in isolation, is not particularly useful.

Market value per share

For a publicly quoted company this is easily obtainable from reports of stock exchange transactions. For a private company, it is probably impossible to obtain except by guesswork because there is no regular market in its shares. If there is no market, there can be no market prices and no market value.

Earnings

A number of ratios focus on the crucial figure of earnings, i.e. on the profits of the year available for the ordinary shareholders. Before investigating these ratios in detail, it is important to consider the concept of earnings itself more carefully.

Perhaps the best way to highlight the issues is to ask why the earnings figure is of interest. In essence there are two possible answers:

(a) the analyst or shareholder may want to know what has happened to the business which affects the owners;
(b) the analyst or shareholder may want to know what the recent past suggests is most likely to happen to the business in the future.

Answer (a) looks to what is known as the all-inclusive concept of earnings. IAS 8, 'Unusual and Prior Period Items and Charges in Accounting Policies', issued by the IASC and operative from 1 January 1979 puts this as follows:

> Under *the all-inclusive concept*, transactions causing a net increase or decrease in shareholders' interests during the period, other than dividends and other transactions between the enterprise and its shareholders, are included in the net income for the period. Non-recurring items, including unusual items arising in the current period, prior period items, or adjustments related to changes in accounting policies, are included in net income but there may be separate disclosure of the individual amounts.

Answer (b) looks to the current operating performance concept which attempts to exclude unusual items. Again, to quote IAS 8:

> Under *the current operating performance concept*, non-recurring items are excluded from reported net income. The items are shown after the determination of net income or as adjustments to retained earnings. Some consider that this approach facilitates comparisons between the current and prior periods because only items related to the recurring operations of the enterprise are included in the income statement. However, there is a danger that the importance of items excluded from the reported net income may not be clearly recognised by users of the financial statements.

In either case, there is acceptance that full disclosure of unusual items is necessary. This disclosure enables the analyst to make such adjustments as seem necessary for the particular situation under investigation. However, if different formats appear from different companies or different countries but with additional disclosure, this is only effective if the analyst understands the significance of the disclosure and is able to make the sensible adjustments consistent with the underlying purposes of the analysis. The exact characteristics of the appropriate answer depend on the exact definition of the question!

The general approach to practical presentation is well summarized in IAS 8:

> Items described in some countries as extraordinary or special items are included within the term 'unusual item' as used in this Statement. In those countries the terms extraordinary or special items have a defined meaning and a requirement normally exists for the incorporation of a sub-total within the income statement described as 'income before extraordinary (or special) items'. This Statement does not set forth the specific format of the income statement. Instead it places emphasis on the separate disclosure of unusual items with an explanation of their nature.
>
> The gains or losses that may require separate disclosure as unusual items are not determined solely by the nature of the event or transaction but by the nature of the event or transaction in relation to the business ordinarily carried on by the enterprise. For example, in an enterprise which regularly trades in properties, the gains or losses arising on the sale of property would not be an unusual item.

The last point should be well noted: what is not ordinary depends on what *is* ordinary, and what is ordinary to any particular business may be a unique consideration for that business. Second, notice the explicit lack of any attempt to specify a particular format. Within the European Community there is a requirement to show extraordinary items separately under the formats, and abnormal but 'ordinary' items (e.g. the write-off of a very large receivable from a regular trade customer) will usually be listed in the notes to the accounts. It should certainly not be assumed that the practical definitions and interpretations of the terms and concepts are identical across European businesses. Each individual case will need consideration on its own merits.

'Earnings' is generally defined as the net profit after tax and extraordinary (or unusual) items as discussed above. This is fortunate because the international variability in the meaning of 'extraordinary' is great, despite a basic definition in the EC Fourth Directive, 'Income and charges that arise otherwise than in the course of the company's ordinary activities must be shown under "Extraordinary income and extraordinary charges"'. In France and Spain, the concept is similar to non-trading or non-recurring. In the UK, 'extraordinary' is very narrowly defined and intended to be rare. IAS 8 was being revised in 1993, and the IASC also agreed a draft statement of Principles on Earnings per share in that year.

Earnings per share (e.p.s.)

As well as the very real difficulty of deciding on exactly what to include in earnings for the purpose of e.p.s. calculations, there may be two problems with the denominator, the number of shares where there are:

(a) changes in the equity share capital during the financial year under consideration,
(b) securities in existence, at the end of the period under consideration, with no current claim on equity earnings, but which will give rise to such a claim in the future.

Broadly speaking, the first problem is dealt with by averaging calculations designed to give a reasonable indication of the position as related to the year as a whole. The details can become complicated, but will have been dealt with in the figure as included in published financial statements. The second problem is dealt with by calculating e.p.s. twice on the assumptions that:

(a) the earnings are related to the number of shares actually in issue at the balance sheet date (the basic e.p.s.),
(b) the earnings are related to the number of shares which would be in issue if all the convertible securities concerned were to be converted into shares (the diluted e.p.s.).

EXAMPLE 14.1

		(all figures in 000 ecu)
Profit before taxation, year to 31 December 19X6		1,000
Taxation		300
		700
Preference dividend	50	
Ordinary dividend	100	150
Retained profit for the year		550

The number of ordinary shares in issue is 2 million. In addition, there exists convertible loan stock of 500,000 ecu bearing interest at 10%. This may be converted into ordinary shares between 19X8 and 19X9 at the rate of one ordinary share for every 2 ecu of loan stock. Assume that the corporate income tax rate is 50%.

The basic e.p.s. will be:

$$\frac{\text{profit after tax, less preference dividends}}{\text{number of ordinary shares}}$$

$$= \frac{700{,}000 - 50{,}000}{2 \text{ million}} = \frac{650{,}000}{2{,}000{,}000}$$

$$= 0.325 \text{ ecu per share.}$$

To calculate the diluted e.p.s, there are two effects to consider:

1. The share capital would increase by 250,000 shares (1 share for every 2 ecu of the 500,000 ecu loans).
2. The 'earnings' would increase by the amount of interest on the loan which would no longer be payable, less the extra tax payable as a result of the removal of the interest expense. The interest at 10% on 500,000 ecu is 50,000 ecu, but the extra tax on this profit increase would be 50% of 50,000, i.e. 25,000 ecu. Earnings will therefore increase by $50{,}000 - 25{,}000 = 25{,}000$ ecu.

The diluted e.p.s. will be (after removing 000 from all figures):

$$\frac{(700 + 25) - 50}{2{,}250} = \frac{675}{2{,}250}$$

$$= 0.30 \text{ ecu per share}$$

This latter figure will be the better indication of what a potential investor would be obtaining in the long run, on the assumptions that:

(a) the current earnings figure is a meaningful figure as regards future trends;
(b) those others who have *already been given* rights to convert into newly created additional ordinary shares do so.

These assumptions, while clearly no more than assumptions, do probably allow useful indications of the relative strengths of different investment opportunities to be prepared.

Dividend cover

The dividend cover is the number of times that a company can pay the intended dividend out of the available profits of the current year. As before, alternative possibilities exist as to the inclusion or exclusion of unusual items in the calculation of the derived earnings figure. The formula for dividend cover is:

$$\frac{\text{earnings}}{\text{total dividends on ordinary shares}}$$

The higher the ratio, the greater the coverage, or safety margin, of earnings over dividends.

Dividend yield

The formula for dividend yield is:

$$\frac{\text{dividend per share}}{\text{market price per share}}$$

The ratio indicates the rate of return in terms of profit distribution if an investor buys one share at the current market price. It can be compared with the ruling level of interest rates on investments, but of course it ignores those additional undistributed profits which are nevertheless attributable to the shareholders (i.e. the rest of earnings). These retained profits will theoretically help the expansion of the business and thus lead to increased future dividend rates, and to eventual capital gains for the investor through a rising share price.

Price/earnings (P/E) ratio

The formula for the P/E ratio is:

$$\frac{\text{market price of one share}}{\text{e.p.s.}}$$

The P/E ratio can be said to represent the number of years' earnings it is necessary to pay in order to acquire a share. It is potentially a highly volatile ratio which will be affected both by changes in earnings per share (or in its definition), and by movements in the share price as quoted on a stock exchange.

P/E is widely regarded as important, and in some countries is published daily, for large quoted companies, in the financial pages of many newspapers. In practical terms, the P/E ratio represents the market's view of the strength or risk of the company, and of its expected further growth. A high P/E indicates that the market has a high opinion of the future prospects of the company. If Company A has a P/E of 10, and Company B has a P/E of 12, then the 'market' is willing to pay 12 times earnings to acquire a share in B, but only 10 times earnings to acquire a share in A. This must mean that future improvements in the performance of B are expected to be greater (or more likely) than in the case with A.

SUMMARY

This chapter has explored techniques for investigating the earnings structure, the profitability, and investment potential of business organizations. First, methods of analyzing relationships within the income statement were considered, and second, the interconnection between income statement and balance sheet was explored. Gearing is seen to be an important consideration which can significantly affect the return attributable to investors as compared with the return created by the business as a whole. Interpretation and analysis is very much an integrative and cumulative activity and the whole area of liquidity appraisal remains to be explored in the next chapter. Exercises and case studies are deferred until the end of Chapter 15.

CHAPTER 15

Liquidity analysis

> **OBJECTIVES**
>
> - To analyze, compare and appraise the liquidity of business organizations
> - To analyze and interpret statements of cash and funds flow
> - To integrate profitability and liquidity analysis into an overall appraisal and comparison of business position and performance

15.1 Introduction

This chapter begins by exploring a number of ratios related to the liquidity and fund management position of a business. Statements of cash or funds flow are a useful adjunct to liquidity analysis, and a number of the different possible formats are considered. However, in many ways the division of ratios and of analysis between profitability considerations and liquidity considerations is an artificial one, and the chapter concludes with some exercises and case studies which begin to develop an overall view.

15.2 Liquidity ratios

A number of ratios can be calculated which compare short-term assets with current liabilities. Each ratio takes a different interpretation of just how short-term the assets or liabilities should be. The shorter the term considered, the more prudent, pessimistic or safe is the approach adopted. Each ratio in this section shows the extent to which the particular definition of short-term assets chosen would allow (if the assets concerned turn into cash at their balance sheet value) the repayment of the current liabilities in existence at that date.

Three such ratios are given here, and calculated for Bread Co. from the figures in Table 14.2 of the previous chapter:

1. Cash ratio $= \dfrac{\text{cash plus marketable securities}}{\text{current liabilities}}$

   For Bread Co.

   $$19\text{X}1 \quad \frac{10}{18} = 0.55:1$$

   $$19\text{X}2 \quad \frac{4}{44} = 0.09:1$$

2. Acid test (or quick assets) ratio $= \dfrac{\text{current assets less inventory}}{\text{current liabilities}}$

   For Bread Co.

   $$19\text{X}1 \quad \frac{28}{18} = 1.6:1$$

   $$19\text{X}2 \quad \frac{44}{44} = 1.0:1$$

3. Current ratio $= \dfrac{\text{current assets}}{\text{current liabilities}}$

   For Bread Co.

   $$19\text{X}1 \quad \frac{40}{18} = 2.2:1$$

   $$19\text{X}2 \quad \frac{60}{44} = 1.4:1$$

It is important to remember that all three of these ratios take a completely static view of the situation. They assume that the relevant assets as defined are all that will be or will become available to settle the current liabilities, and they assume that the assets as defined will provide the cash amounts as recorded in the balance sheet (even though inventory is normally recorded at cost, i.e. below selling price). So, for example, the quick ratio assumes that all the debtors stated will pay, but excludes any cash sales from inventory.

The safety or acceptability of any particular ratio figure for any particular business will be very much related to the everyday operations of the business. Each industry will have a typical operational and financial structure, and calculated ratios should be compared with competitor or general industry figures, or with past trends, to enable any meaningful comparisons to be drawn.

15.3 Interest cover

Long-term liquidity is connected to gearing, as examined in Chapter 14. The balance sheet perspective discussed there can be supplemented by considering the interest cover, in the same way as dividend cover was investigated in Section 14.5.

The interest cover is the number of times a business could pay the necessary interest charges out of the available operating profits of the current year. The formula for interest cover is:

$$\frac{\text{net profit before interest and tax}}{\text{interest charges}}$$

For Bread Co the figures will be:

$$19X1 \quad \frac{12}{0} \text{ i.e. infinite}$$

$$19X2 \quad \frac{22 + 2}{2} = 12 \text{ times}$$

15.4 Fund management ratios

Considerable insight into the cash and liquidity implications of the day-to-day operations of a business can be gained by examining the constituent elements of working capital, i.e. inventory, debtors and creditors. In each case the amount of the item is compared with the flow related to it. Frequently the amount is taken from the closing balance sheet, but a more theoretically valid ratio is obtained by using the average amount of each item in existence over the trading cycle. A simple average of opening and closing balance sheet figures may well be a better approximation to the true average than simply taking the closing balance sheet figure.

These ratios can be expressed in a number of ways, but probably the most easily understandable is to express the answer in days rather than as a pure mathematical ratio.

Debtors' turnover ratio

This ratio compares trade debtors with sales (turnover). To calculate the average debtor collection period in days, the formula is:

$$\frac{\text{trade debtors}}{\text{sales}} \times 365$$

Arguably cash sales should be excluded from the denominator, but the information is unlikely to be available to an outside analyst. If necessary, because of lack of information, total debtors will have to be used instead of trade debtors.

Creditors' turnover ratio

A similar ratio can be calculated for creditors. To calculate the average creditor payment period it is theoretically necessary to relate trade creditors with annual purchases. Frequently the purchases figure is not available and then cost of sales will have to be used as a surrogate. In some income statement formats, cost of sales is not shown either, so sales has to be used. Where cost of sales is available, the formula becomes:

$$\frac{\text{trade creditors}}{\text{cost of sales}} \times 365$$

Inventory turnover ratio

The inventory turnover ratio indicates the time inventory remains in the business between purchase and sale, on the average. Since inventory is evaluated at cost, it should be compared with cost of sales (which is obviously at cost) rather than with sales (which are at selling price). Again, this assumes that the data are available.

The formula is:

$$\frac{\text{inventory}}{\text{cost of sales}}$$

For Bread Co. these three ratios can be calculated as shown in Table 15.1.

Trends can be explored between 19X1 and 19X2 showing, for example, that customers seem to be taking longer to pay in 19X2. The ratios can also be related together. In 19X1, if purchases were made on day 1 then they were paid for (on

Table 15.1 **Calculation of fund management ratios.**

Ratio	19X1	19X2
Debtors' turnover	$\frac{18}{150} \times 365$	$\frac{40}{250} \times 365$
	= 44 days	= 58 days
Creditors' turnover	$\frac{10}{100} \times 365$	$\frac{28}{176} \times 365$
	= 36.5 days	= 58 days
Inventory turnover	$\frac{\frac{8+12}{2}}{100} \times 365$	$\frac{\frac{12+16}{2}}{176} \times 365$
	= 36.5 days	= 29 days

average, of course) some 36 days later. Those purchases remained in store (or process) for some 36 days, were then sold, and the sales were actually paid for some 44 days after the sale. The outward cash flow therefore occurs on day 36, but the inward cash flow not until day 80. Useful information!

15.5 Cash and funds flow statements

To emphasize the importance of such statements, consider the following two summarized statements about Bread Co. in 19X2:

1. Summarized income statement (from Table 14.1)

Sales	250
less cost of sales	176
	74
less other expenses	44
	30
less depreciation	8
	22
less taxation provided	10
	12
less dividend proposed	6
retained profit	6

2. Summarized statement of cash flow

Receipts from sales	228
less payments for goods for resale	162
	66
less payments for other expenses	44
	22
less capital expenditure	46
	(24)
less taxation paid	4
	(28)
less dividend paid	4
borrowing, cash decrease, share issue	(32)

The first, the income statement, shows a successful year and positive results, based, quite logically and sensibly, on the going concern and matching conventions. The second is a summary of cash flows (explained in more detail later). This shows a reduction in the cash resources of the business even without the payment of the dividend, then made worse by the dividend itself. In any one year such a reduction may be sensible, even desirable as a means of maximizing long-run returns; but, of course, in the long run such reductions cannot be allowed to continue, and an analyst or potential investor would need to monitor the cash situation and prospects very carefully.

The general point is that a report on the cash or liquid funds provides useful and important information, different in focus and information content from the income statement.

Formal requirements

Given the obvious significance of the additional cash-directed focus of these statements, the legal position is very surprising. There is no mention at all in the Fourth (or Seventh) EC Directive of the possibility of statements showing cash or funds movements. Nor is there any requirement in most national companies legislation, either in Europe (except in Spain) or elsewhere. The recommendations or specifications of such statements are contained in some countries in accounting standards, and in the listing requirements of various stock exchanges.

It is not surprising that this lack of formal control, or of attempted harmonization, has led to a considerable diversity in presentation. Financial statement analysis requires the ability to appraise and interpret the statements whatever their precise format or contents. The scope for flexibility is well illustrated by quoting the *complete* requirements of IAS 7, entitled 'Statement of Changes in Financial Position', effective for reporting periods beginning on 1 January 1979 to 31 December 1993 inclusive.

> A statement of changes in financial position should be included as an integral part of the financial statements. The statement of changes in financial position should be presented for each period for which the income statement is presented.
>
> Funds provided from or used in the operations of an enterprise should be presented in the statement of changes in financial position separately from other sources or uses of funds. Unusual items which are not part of the ordinary activities of the enterprise should be separately disclosed in the statement.
>
> Each enterprise or group of enterprises should adopt the form of presentation for the statement of changes in financial position which is most informative in the circumstances.

IAS 7 has been revised, under the title of 'Cash Flow Statements', to give rather more specification. IAS 7 (revised) became operative for reporting periods beginning on or after 1 January 1994. The change is briefly discussed below.

Traditional funds flow statements

Historically, the practice of presenting funds flow statements grew up in an era when wide information disclosure was even less fashionable than it is now. The format of such statements was therefore explicitly designed to present existing information with a new and different focus, but without actually disclosing any new information. In other words, all the figures in such traditional funds flow statements came from, or could be derived directly from, the figures included in the published income statement, balance sheets and the notes thereto.

A typical funds flow statement consists of four sections (as illustrated in Table 15.2):

(a) funds derived from operations;
(b) funds derived from external sources;
(c) application of funds to outside parties;
(d) changes in working capital items (current assets and liabilities), including the movement in liquid funds, probably, but not necessarily, defined as cash and bank balances.

Table 15.2 **Funds flow statement (000s ecus).**

Net source of funds		
(a) *Internal sources*		
profit before taxation		2,978
adjustment for items not involving the movement of funds – depreciation		+272
		3,250
(b) *External sources*		
disposal proceeds of fixed assets		+890
		4,140
(c) *Applications*		
dividends paid	1,296	
tax paid	1,298	
expenditure on fixed assets	1,352	
		3,946
net source of funds		194
(d) *Movements in working capital*		
increase in inventory and work-in-progress		5,663
increase in debtors		14
increase in creditors		(182)
		5,495
less movement in liquid funds – increase in overdraft		5,301
		194

It is perhaps worth standing back a little and thinking about what is going on here. The accounting process is based on transactions, and the vast majority of data enter the recording system because of monetary purchases and sales. However, these monetary transactions, reflected by money receipts and payments, are then adjusted for accruals, prepayments, depreciation, provisions and so on, all supported by the matching and other conventions, to arrive at the published income statement.

The funds flow statement of the type shown in Table 15.2 takes this income statement and attempts to turn the focus *back* from the matching-based income statement towards the money movement focus, but only goes as far as it is able to go without revealing any new data. This is a complicated (and arguably uninteresting) procedure, but it helps to explain what is going on. Starting with the profit before taxation, it is necessary to remove from this figure any adjustments made which obviously have no effect on the money or liquidity position in the year. The most obvious one is depreciation.

If a fixed asset is bought in the year then the payment represents an application of funds. If a fixed asset is sold in the year then the receipt obviously represents a direct source of funds. These two possibilities illustrate all the money movements involved. Depreciation is merely the allocation of the cost over different accounting periods, involves no money flows, and so must be removed. Depreciation has been deducted in arriving at the profit before taxation figure. It is this deduction which must now be removed. The deduction must be added back to the net profit figure. This logic is also applied to any other relevant items.

Sections (b) and (c) are straightforward, but (d) may require some explanation. The thinking here is that money has been *applied* in increasing the inventory and work-in-progress, money has been *applied* in increasing the debtors (if a business is owed more, then it has so far received less), and the increase in creditors represents a *source* of money to the business (if a business owes more, then it has so far paid less, so its current remaining money balance will be more). The resulting net application from working capital movements, of 5,495, is made possible by two reasons. First, there was an increase in bank borrowings of 5,301, and second, there was a small surplus of net sources from Sections (a) to (c) of the statement.

The statement in Table 15.2 could, of course, be rearranged in many ways. Comprehension is perhaps improved if (d) is altered to arrive at the cash changes as shown in Table 15.3.

A worked example

From the financial statements of Bread Co. shown in Tables 14.1 and 14.2 prepare a summarized funds flow statement in accordance with the format of Table 15.2. The solution is shown in Table 15.4. The adventurous reader may like to try the calculations first.

The table shows that debtors and creditors have both increased sharply, the effects largely cancelling out, and large investments in new fixed assets have been financed

Table 15.3 **Cash focus of funds flow statement.**

net sources brought forward	194
increase in working capital (detailed)	5,495
net total applications	5,301
financed by increase in bank borrowings	5,301

Table 15.4 **Funds flow statement for Bread Co. year 19X2 (000 ecu).**

Sources of funds		
net profit before tax	22	
add back depreciation, not involving the movement of funds	8	
funds generated from operations		30
issue of share capital	6	
issue of debentures	20	
funds generated from external sources		26
		56
Applications		
purchase of fixed assets	46	
payment of taxation (as provided in 19X1)	4	
payment of dividends (as provided in 19X1)	4	
external applications		54
		2
Movements in working capital		
increase in inventory	4	
increase in debtors	22	
	26	
increase in creditors	18	
net application to working capital		8
fall in bank balance		6
		2

partly by internal cash generation, $30 - 4 - 4 = 22$ (funds from operations less tax and dividends paid), and partly by a new loan of 20 through issuing debentures. It is perhaps worth noting that the cash outflows expected in 19X3 for tax and dividends are higher, at 10 and 6 respectively, than those for 19X2. Are there any danger signs here for future years?

The cash flow statement alternative

The funds flow statement is complex and not particularly easy to interpret. Perhaps more importantly, it is not a very good indicator of that which it purports to indicate, namely, the cash or short-term liquidity position of the business in flow rather than in static terms. If a true analysis of cash flows is required, then the most obvious way to achieve it is by analyzing the cash flows themselves directly. Sensible subheadings might include:

Cash received from customers
Cash paid to suppliers
Cash paid to employees
Cash paid for services
Net cash inflow from operating activities (continued on next page)

Cash flows from operating activities		
Cash receipts from customers	30,150	
Cash paid to suppliers and employees	(27,600)	
Cash generated from operations	2,550	
Interest paid	(270)	
Income taxes paid	(900)	
Cash flow before extraordinary item	1,380	
Proceeds from earthquake disaster settlement	180	
Net cash from operating activities		1,560
Cash flows from investing activities		
Acquisition of subsidiary X, net of cash acquired	(550)	
Purchase of property, plant and equipment	(350)	
Proceeds from sale of equipment	20	
Interest received	200	
Dividends received	200	
Net cash used in investing activities		(480)
Cash flows from financing activities		
Proceeds from issuance of share capital	250	
Proceeds from long-term borrowings	250	
Payment of finance lease liabilities	(90)	
Dividends paid[a]	(1,200)	
Net cash used in financing activities		(790)
Net increase in cash and cash equivalents		290
Cash and cash equivalents at beginning of period		120
Cash and cash equivalent at end of period		410

[a] This could also be shown as an operating cash flow.

Figure 15.1 Direct method cash flow statement.

Interest and dividends received
Interest and dividends paid
Taxation paid
Investing activities
Financing activities
Change in cash

The summarized statement of cash flows for Bread Co. given early in Section 15.5 was in exactly this form, although the example is much simplified.

This purer statement, of cash flow rather than funds flow, is the direction taken by IAS 7 (revised). This encourages enterprises to prepare a statement in accordance with the illustration shown in Figure 15.1 (taken from IAS 7 (revised)). This uses the 'direct method', showing an analysis of the cash flows relating to operating activities. However, it also allows the breakdown of 'net cash from operating activities' to be shown by the 'indirect method', i.e. as a reconciliation from net profit as illustrated in Figure 15.2 (again taken from IAS 7 (revised)). Figure 15.2 is related closely to the funds flow methodology of the original IAS 7, and is arguably considerably less revealing and useful.

One further complication of IAS 7 (revised) is that it refers to cash and cash equivalents, and effectively treats them as synonymous. It defines these terms as follows:

Cash comprises cash on hand and demand deposits.
Cash equivalents are short-term, highly liquid investments that are readily convertible to known amounts of cash and that are subject to an insignificant risk of changes in value.
Cash flows are inflows and outflows of cash and cash equivalents.

Cash flows from operating activities		
Net profit before taxation, and extraordinary item	3,350	
Adjustments for:		
Depreciation	450	
Foreign exchange loss	40	
Investment income	(500)	
Interest expense	400	
Operating profit before working capital changes	3,740	
Increase in trade and other receivables	(500)	
Decrease in inventories	1,050	
Decrease in trade payables	(1,740)	
Cash generated from operations	2,550	
Interest paid	(270)	
Income taxes paid	(900)	
Cash flow before extraordinary item	1,380	
Proceeds from earthquake disaster settlement	180	
Net cash from operating activities		1,560

Figure 15.2 Indirect method.

Clearly the possibility exists of uncertainty as to which investments are 'cash equivalents' and which are not.

It is difficult to predict the effect of the revision of IAS 7 over the next few years. The lack of legal requirement and specification, the variability of cash and funds definitions, and the highly variable degree of influence of IASs in different European countries all conspire to suggest a chronic lack of detailed harmonization in this area between European countries.

Conclusions on cash and funds flow statements

The key conclusion is that the format and content of such statements will be extremely variable, and so analysis and comparison is not likely to be easy. Some exercises and case studies in the interpretation of such statements follow. They have been deliberately designed to be as variable as possible, to give practice at the flexibility and adaptability necessary.

The path of development and possible harmonization over the next few years is far from clear. To illustrate one possible direction of change, we present as Tables 15.5, 15.6 and 15.7 the published statements of a UK company for 1991 under the funds flow basis, and for 1992 under the cash flow basis complete with voluntary disclosure of the direct operating cash flows. The 1992 statement also shows the 1991 figures recalculated on to a comparative basis to the 1992 figures, so the effects and differences can be thoroughly explored. Think which format you find most helpful, and why. However, it is by no means obvious that changes in the cash flow direction will appear in all countries.

SUMMARY

This chapter has extended the analysis begun in Chapter 14 to cash, liquidity and fund analysis, involving both ratio considerations and cash/funds flow statements. Various liquidity and fund management ratios were suggested, and the importance of establishing an overall picture demonstrated. Cash and funds flow statements were introduced as a means of highlighting the liquidity rather than the profit movements of business operations. The lack of consistency of presentation in this area was noted, and the major alternatives illustrated. The exercises following begin the process of integrating an appraisal of all these indicators into a single composite appraisal. They have been carefully sequenced, and chosen from a wide variety of source models so as to maximize exposure to the many different types of detail likely to be found in the process of European and international financial statement appraisal.

Table 15.5 Consolidated source and application of funds for William Morrison Supermarkets plc (52 weeks ended 2 February 1991).

	1991 £000's	1991 £000's	1990 £000's	1990 £000's
Source of funds				
Profit before taxation		50.278		37.007
Adjustment for items not involving movement of funds				
Depreciation	12.317		9.928	
Tax on interest capitalised	(2.015)		(1.305)	
Profit on sale of tangible fixed assets	(78)		(233)	
Share in profit of associated company	(153)		(144)	
Pension scheme provision	1.000		800	
		11.071		9.046
Funds from other sources				
Share issues (net of costs)	1.088		602	
Received from associated company	29		3	
Proceeds from disposal of fixed assets	935		924	
		2.052		1.529
		63.401		47.582
Application of funds				
Dividends paid	(4.987)		(4.655)	
Tax paid	(10.890)		(7.709)	
Purchase of tangible fixed assets	(79.197)		(77.049)	
Loan redemption fund	(7)		(6)	
		(95.081)		(89.419)
		(31.680)		(41.837)
Movements in working capital				
Stocks	305		(161)	
Debtors	294		2.096	
Cash in hand	368		472	
Creditors	(12.001)		(10.392)	
Uncleared banking items	(4.463)		(1.608)	
		(15.497)		(9.593)
Movements in net liquid funds				
Commercial paper programme	16.500		(8.500)	
Multi option facility	18.000		(18.000)	
Bank loans and overdrafts	12.313		(11.144)	
Bank deposits	(2.996)	43.817	5.400	(32.244)
		28.320		(41.837)
Syndicated term loan		(60.000)		—
		(31.680)		(41.837)

Table 15.6 **Consolidated cash flow statement for William Morrison Supermarkets plc (52 weeks ended 1 February 1992).**

	1992 £000's	£000's	1991 £000's	£000's
Operating activities				
Cash received from customers	1,121.863		913.014	
Cash payments to suppliers	(880.232)		(718.964)	
Cash paid to and on behalf of employees	(101.187)		(76.796)	
Other cash payments	(47.267)		(32.284)	
Net cash inflow from operating activities		93.177		84.970
Returns on investments and servicing of finance				
Interest and dividends received	1.288		1.143	
Interest paid	(9.915)		(13.350)	
Interest element of finance lease payments	(38)		(5)	
Received from associated undertaking	—		30	
Dividends paid	(5.472)		(4.987)	
Net cash outflow from returns on investments on servicing of finance		(14.137)		(17.169)
Taxation				
UK corporation tax paid	(14.776)		(10.890)	
Certificate of tax deposit	238		(1.000)	
Tax paid		(14.538)		(11.890)
Investing activities				
Purchase of tangible fixed assets	(98.381)		(78.152)	
Purchase of subsidiary undertakings	(596)		—	
Sale of tangible fixed assets	1.280		840	
Sale of equity investments	161		95	
Loan redemption policy	(6)		(7)	
Net cash outflow from investing activities		(97.542)		(77.224)
Net cash outflow before financing		(33.040)		(21.313)
Financing				
Issue of ordinary share capital	(98.636)		(1.088)	
Capital subscribed by minority interest	(980)		—	
Loan from minority interest	(490)		—	
Capital element of finance lease payments	169		53	
Syndicated term loan	—		(60.000)	
Commercial paper programme	—		16.500	
Multi option facility	30.000		18.000	
Bills of exchange	—		10.000	
Net cash inflow from financing		(69.937)		(16.535)
Increase in cash and cash equivalents		36.897		(4.778)
		(33.040)		(21.313)

Table 15.7 **Reconciliation of operating profit to net cash inflow from operating activities.**

	1992 £000's	1991 £000's
Operating profit	68.418	57.062
Profit sharing scheme	(2.985)	(2.335)
Depreciation	17.123	12.317
Loss on sale of plant. equipment and vehicles	58	185
Increase in stocks	(2.589)	(305)
Movement in operating debtors and creditors	10.547	17.046
Pension scheme provision	2.429	1.000
Stocks. debtors and creditors on purchase of subsidiary undertakings	176	—
Net cash flow from operating activities	93.177	84.970

EXERCISES

15.1 The simplified financial statements of two companies, P and Q, are shown below. Assuming that interest is charged on the long-term loan at 10% per annum, calculate the following ratios and comment on the results:

$$\frac{\text{gross profit}}{\text{turnover}} \; ; \; \frac{\text{net operating profit}}{\text{turnover}} \; ;$$

$$\frac{\text{net profit}}{\text{owner's equity}} \; ; \; \text{ROCE} \; ; \; \text{gearing}.$$

	P	Q
Income statement for 19X1		
Sales	45,000	40,909
Less Cost of sales	(36,000)	(32,727)
Gross profit	9,000	8,182
Less Depreciation	(3,500)	(2,917)
Other expenses	(1,500)	(1,364)
Net profit	4,000	3,901

Balance sheet as at 31 December 19X1

Equipment at cost	35,000	29,167
Less Depreciation	(3,500)	(2,917)
	31,500	26,250
Inventory at cost	10,500	10,000
Net monetary current assets	2,000	2,000
Less Long-term loan	(10,000)	(10,000)
	34,000	28,250
Share capital	25,000	25,000
Retained profits	4,000	3,901
Exchange differences	5,000	(651)
	34,000	28,250

15.2 'The great advantage of a cash flow statement is that, apparently unlike any other accounting statement, it is objective and cannot be manipulated.' Discuss.

15.3 The draft income statement and source and application of funds statement of M is set out below for the year ended 30 November 19X5.

M
Draft income statement
Year ended 30 November 19X5

	ecu	ecu
Credit sales		20,000
Opening inventory	3,000	
Purchases	4,000	
	7,000	
Closing inventory	2,000	
Cost of goods sold		5,000
Gross profit		15,000
Depreciation	2,000	
Loss on sale of asset	1,500	
Wages	5,000	
		8,500
Net profit		6,500
Taxation		3,000
		3,500
Dividends		3,000
Retained profit		500

M
Draft source and application of funds statement
Year ended 30 November 19X5

	ecu	ecu
Adjusted profit (6,500 + 2,000 + 1,500)		10,000
Proceeds on sale of asset		2,000
		12,000
Loan		4,000
		16,000
Purchase of machine	3,000	
Taxation	4,000	
Dividends	2,000	
		9,000
		7,000
Increase/(decrease) in working capital		
Decrease in inventory	(1,000)	
Increase in debtors	5,000	
Decrease in creditors	2,000	
	6,000	
Closing cash 2,400		
Opening cash 1,400		
	1,000	
		7,000

(a) Prepare a detailed cash flow statement for the year ended 30 November 19X5.
(b) Comment on the usefulness of both cash flow statements and source and application of funds statements in financial reporting.

15.4 The summarized balance sheets of R Co. at the end of two consecutive financial years were as shown below, in 000s ecu.

19X1	Summarized balance sheets as at 31 March	19X2
	Fixed assets (at written-down values)	
50	Premises	48
115	Plant and equipment	196
42	Vehicles	81
207		325

		Current assets		
86		Inventory	177	
49		Debtors and prepayments	62	
53		Bank and cash	30	
188			269	
		Current liabilities		
72		Creditors and accruals	132	
20		Proposed dividends	30	
92			162	
	96	*Working capital*		107
	303	*Net assets employed*		432
		Financed by		
250		Ordinary share capital	250	
53		Reserves	82	
	303	Shareholders' funds		332
	–	Loan capital: 7% debentures		100
	303			432

Turnover was 541,000 and 675,000 for the years ended 31 March 19X1 and 19X2 respectively. Corresponding figures for cost of sales were 369,000 and 481,000, respectively.

At 31 March 19X0, reserves had totalled 21,000. Ordinary share capital was the same throughout.

Calculate the following ratios for both years and comment briefly on the results:

Gross profit/Turnover
Net profit/Turnover
Turnover/Net assets employed
Net profit/Net assets employed
Current assets/Current liabilities
Quick assets/Current liabilities

15.5 Attached are summarized balance sheets and income statements for F Co. for 19X1 and 19X2.

F Co.
Summarized balance sheets at year end (million ecu)

		19X2		19X1
Fixed assets				
Tangible – not yet in use		49		41
– in use		295		237
		344		278
Investments		1		1
Loan redemption fund		1		1
			346		280
Current assets				
Inventory		42		41
Debtors – trade	4		4	
– other	4		4	
		8		8
Bank		2		5
Cash		2		2
		54		56
Creditors – due within one year				
– trade	60		60	
– other	87		112	
		147		172
Net current liabilities			93		116
Total assets *less* current liabilities			253		164
Creditors – due between one and five years			61		1
Provision for liabilities and charges			4		3
Net assets			188		160
Capital and reserves				
Ordinary shares of 0.1 ecu each			19		19
Preference shares of 1 ecu each			46		46
Share premium			1		1
Profit and loss account			122		94
			188		160

F Co.
Summarized income statements for the year (million ecu)

	19X2		19X1	
Sales		910		775
Raw materials and consumables		730		633
		180		142
Staff costs	77		64	
Depreciation of tangible fixed assets	12		10	
Other operating charges	38		30	
		127		104
		53		38
Other operating income		4		3
		57		41
Net interest payable		5		4
		52		37
Profit sharing – employees		2		1
		50		36
Taxation		17		12
		33		24
Preference dividends		2		2
		31		22
Ordinary dividends		3		2
		28		20

Note

Net interest payable:		
interest payable	12	9
interest receivable	(1)	(1)
interest capitalized	(6)	(4)
	5	4

(a) Prepare a table of ratios, covering all aspects of interpretation as far as the information allows, for each year.

(b) It has been suggested to you that the situation of the business has got worse, and that anyone owning ordinary shares in F Co. would be advised to sell them as soon as possible. Write a report explaining fully whether you agree or disagree, and why.

CHAPTER 16

Valuation and analysis

> **OBJECTIVES**
>
> - To outline alternative approaches to valuing businesses
> - To consider the effects of accounting policy issues discussed in Part III on the interpretation of financial statements
> - To practice, through exercises, comparative financial statement analysis through time and between businesses

16.1 Introduction

Part III of this book, in its exploration of key issues in financial reporting, discusses the valuation of individual items in financial statements. Here these considerations are extended to consider the valuation of the business as a whole. The chapter then moves towards an integration of much that has gone before, by considering the effects and importance of different accounting policy treatments when comparing the results of a business over time, or when comparing the results of different businesses. These interconnections are developed and explored through exercises involving different accounting policies. This process leads on to the final stage of complexity implied by cross-national analysis. This is developed in Chapter 17, which concludes with a series of international case studies.

16.2 The balance sheet

The balance sheet is often described as a statement of financial position at a point in time. It shows the resources of the business, as well as its sources of finance. Much time has been spent in earlier chapters in exploring how the figures which will appear in a balance sheet have been arrived at.

If viewed as a complete financial picture of the business, balance sheets suffer from several significant drawbacks:

1. *Absence of items.* In general, under the many measurement and cost conventions, only those items acquired through external transactions will appear in a balance sheet at all. Resources created within the business and resources which do not have clearly related costs, such as the collective experience of a project team or workforce, will not be included.
2. *Historical valuation of items.* Most resources are recorded in balance sheets at figures based on their original purchase price. It is difficult to argue that such a basis provides the most relevant information about the business as at the date of the balance sheet.
3. *Effect of matching convention.* Given the logical and mathematical interconnections between the income statement and the balance sheet, accountants have to choose between the alternative approaches of either:

   (a) calculating the figures for the income statement under defined and logical procedures and formulae, and putting whatever number is left over in the balance sheet, or

   (b) calculating the figures in the balance sheet under defined and logical procedures and formulae, and putting whatever number is left over in the income statement.

   In general, accountants adopt the first approach to dealing with particular items much more often than they do the second. Emphasis is put on the income statement calculation (consider depreciation, for example) and the resulting balance sheet number is a residual, often of doubtful meaning.
4. *Flexibility of accounting policy.* The different and often conflicting implications of the common accounting conventions, and the significant degree of subjectivity involved in both choice of accounting policy and detailed application of accounting policy, lead to great flexibility of accounting numbers.

Notwithstanding all the above problems, a balance sheet is the nearest that accountants get to providing a statement of business position and resources for general usage. As such it is not useless, provided that the bases on which it is prepared are understood. It can generally be regarded as showing, for each of the recorded resources, the lower of:

(a) the cost, i.e. the money put into the resource (or some proportion thereof in the case of a depreciated fixed asset);
(b) the benefit, i.e. the proceeds expected to be derived from the resource in the ordinary course of business.

The balance sheet figures can therefore be regarded as providing a worst-case valuation for many of the recorded items, and therefore (remembering that there are usually unrecorded resources that are in a sense included at nil) as a very conservative or prudent picture of the business as a whole. There is one important proviso to this statement, however, the phrase 'proceeds expected to be derived from the resource *in the ordinary course of business*'. This means that the figures follow the going concern convention, and are not prepared to take account of the possibility of imminent closure of the business. Any such sudden closure would probably result in a 'break-up' value for the business far smaller than implied by published financial statements.

Within the limitations inherent in the above discussion, the balance sheet figures, usually known as book values, can be used as partial indicators of business size and financial strength. Net assets, at book value, could be calculated per share, for example. Taking the Bread Co. balance sheets (Table 14.2), and assuming that the share capital consists of ordinary shares of 1 ecu nominal value, net assets per share at book value would be:

$$19X1: \frac{94}{70} = 1.34 \text{ ecu per share}$$

$$19X2: \frac{106}{76} = 1.39 \text{ ecu per share}$$

The absolute figures may not mean very much, but the trend, particularly over a longer period, may well be informative.

16.3 Valuation through expectations

The key words 'value' and 'valuation', in their everyday connotations, imply some element of future orientation. The real value of something might be seen as the amount of benefit expected to be derived from it (not necessarily in money terms), or possibly the amount of sacrifice necessary in order to obtain it. Pursuing this, the value of a business can be related to the benefits which are expected to flow from ownership of the business and the value of a share in a business can be related to the benefits that are expected to flow from ownership of the share.

It is generally agreed that the correct theoretical approach to the valuation of a share in a business is to consider some defined future flows, and to discount the anticipated figures to give present value, i.e. to use the principles of discounted cash flow (DCF). Possible flows to use would include:

- stream of future earnings, from the income statement
- stream of future net cash flows, from cash flow statements
- stream of future dividends (and other cash receipts, e.g. proceeds of sale of shares), i.e. of actual cash receipts by an investor.

In each case there is the problem, not only of predicting the size of the flows, but also of choosing a rational discount rate. This latter will embrace estimates of ruling interest rates, risk positions of the business concerned and attitude to risk of the individual investor and, at least indirectly, estimates of market and economy developments, such as inflation rates and taxation policies.

In the long run, it can be suggested that the above three possibilities reduce to the same thing. Earnings are in a sense nothing more than cash flows adjusted and smoothed through accounting practices – in the long run, total earnings should equal total net cash flow. And, remembering that the stream of future dividends involves the 'final' distribution when the firm is liquidated, the total dividend stream should also equal the total net cash flow stream. The timing may, of course, be very different, and for the individual shareholder it is the capital amount expected for the share when eventually sold on the stock market, rather than a final liquidation dividend, which represents the final item in the dividend stream.

Although techniques such as the above may be useful in revealing the implications of any particular set of assumptions, the assumptions necessary are obviously extremely uncertain and subjective. Recognition of this leads on to the third possible approach to valuation of a business, i.e. market values.

16.4 Valuation through market values

Suppose you own 10 shares in a company with 1m issued shares, and the market value of 1 share as reported in the press of today's date is 6 ecu. This means that the 10 shares you own have a value of 60 ecu, and also that 'the market' values the entire firm at 6m ecu. Such statements assume that the market values parcels of shares of different sizes on a strictly pro rata basis, which is not the case, as a parcel large enough to give influence or control (see Chapter 12) is likely to command extra value.

It can also be argued that the price of a share on a stock market on any particular day is influenced by all kinds of factors which are extraneous to the particular business under consideration, such as general economic, political or exchange rate considerations. However, despite all these difficulties, the quoted market value in a stock market at a date does have one enormous advantage. It actually and demonstrably exists. The market value *is* (allowing for transaction costs between buyer and seller) the money benefit to be derived from selling a share, and the money sacrifice necessary to acquire a share. It may or may not be a fact logically justified by rational appraisal and analysis, but it is still a fact.

It can be argued that in a perfect world with perfect knowledge and foresight, the market value would exactly equal values calculated by discounting expected flows. This would be consistent with the Efficient Markets Hypothesis in its 'strong' form, which assumes in effect that everybody knows everything. More realistically, it can at least be suggested that active participants in public share markets will have taken account of all available published information. At minimum, it can be suggested that the market value of quoted shares provides the one starting point that is objective for working out the worth of a business or of an investment in it.

16.5 Accounting policies and financial appraisal

However, the market may rely partly on analysis of accounting information to establish its value. This leads back to ratio analysis, for which a number of limitations can be suggested including:

- differences in accounting policies
- the historical nature of accounting statements
- changes in the value of money
- hidden short-term fluctuations between financial statements
- the absence of comparable data
- differences in the environments of periods or firms being compared
- other non-monetary factors, excluded from the accounts completely.

Most of these difficulties can be adjusted for when undertaking real financial statement appraisal. Some of them, particularly the later ones in the list, obviously involve both highly subjective and non-financial considerations. Adjustment for such matters will need to be qualitative rather than quantitative. However, many difficulties can be analyzed through an understanding of financial accounting practices, ideas and techniques, and adjustments can be made to improve comparability and the information content of figures and ratios.

This final part of the chapter sets out to illustrate the general approach to be adopted in tackling such considerations and adjustments. The scope for detailed application of the approach is enormous. All of the issues discussed in Part III, and alternative mixtures of the general conventions discussed in Part I, can lead to differences in the financial statements, therefore to differences in ratios and analysis, and therefore to differences in the *apparent* message of the statements and analyses.

Consider the following simple example. Companies A and B are in the same industry. Last year both companies spent 100,000 ecu on new fixed assets. Both companies depreciate such fixed assets at 25% p.a., Company A using the straight-line method and Company B using the reducing balance method. What differences will arise in the financial statements for the two companies, and which ratios will be affected?

Company A will have depreciation charges of 25,000 ecu in years 1 and 2, and a balance sheet figure of $100,000 - (25,000 + 25,000) = 50,000$ ecu at the end of year 2. Company B will have a depreciation charge of 25,000 ecu in year 1, a depreciation charge of 25% of $(100,000 - 25,000) = 18,750$ ecu in year 2, and a balance sheet figure of $100,000 - (25,000 + 18,750) = 56,250$ ecu at the end of year 2.

Companies A and B have different earnings in year 2. They have different balance sheet figures for fixed assets, and therefore for total assets and for net assets. They have different balance sheet figures for reserves, and therefore for owners' equity, for capital employed and for gearing. So most ratios will be affected.

The exercises and cases provided give plenty of practice at investigating and allowing for the effects of accounting policies and accounting policy change. Despite this,

VALUATION AND ANALYSIS

however comprehensive we attempt to be, the real world is always capable of providing some other problem we have not covered. It is therefore the technique and way of thinking that needs to be developed, not an encyclopedic set of examples. A wide-ranging but not excessively complicated illustration of the various skills follows.

EXAMPLE 16.1

Table 16.1 gives summarized balance sheets for Eegrek Co. for the years 19X1 and 19X2. Table 16.2 gives summarized income statements for the same two years. Table 16.3 gives one possible arrangement of a statement of changes in financial position for Eegrek for the year 19X2 under 'funds flow' thinking and Table 16.4 gives an alternative cash flow presentation in accordance with the revised IAS 7. The requirements are as follows:

1. Calculate the following ratios for Eegrek for 19X1 and 19X2:

    Return on capital employed (ROCE)
    Return on owners' equity (ROOE)
    Debtors turnover
    Creditors turnover
    Current ratio
    Quick assets ratio
    Gross profit percentage
    Net profit percentage
    Dividend cover
    Gearing ratio

2. Comment briefly on difficulties of comparing the two sets of ratios.
3. Comment briefly on developments within the business over the two years.

Notes towards a solution

1. Suggested ratio calculations are shown in Table 16.5.
2. There is one significant inconsistency between the sets of information for the two years which is that the land is shown at cost in year 19X1, but at a valuation 20,000 ecu greater in 19X2 (it is clear that the increase in land from 43,000 ecu to 63,000 ecu represents revaluation, as a revaluation reserve of 20,000 has appeared). Since the land does not seem to have been depreciated, there is no effect on earnings, but there is certainly an effect on reserves and therefore on ROCE and ROOE, in each case increasing the denominator for 19X2 and reducing the ratio as calculated.

    More speculatively, there are probably dangers in the averaging assumptions made. The fixed assets shown in the balance sheet at the end of 19X1 may or may

Table 16.1 Balance sheets of Eegrek (ecus).

	19X1 Balance sheet			19X2 Balance sheet		
	Cost	Depn	Net	Cost	Depn	Net
Plant	10,000	4,000	6,000	11,000	5,000	6,000
Building	50,000	10,000	40,000	90,000	11,000	79,000
			46,000			85,000
Investments at cost			50,000			80,000
Land			43,000			63,000
Inventory			55,000			65,000
Debtors			40,000			50,000
Bank			3,000			—
			237,000			343,000
Ordinary shares 1 ecu each			40,000			50,000
Share premium			12,000			14,000
Revaluation reserve			—			20,000
Profit and loss account			25,000			25,000
10% Debentures			100,000			150,000
Creditors			40,000			60,000
Proposed dividend			20,000			20,000
Bank			—			4,000
			237,000			343,000

Table 16.2 Income statements of Eegrek (ecus).

	19X1	19X2
Sales	200,000	200,000
Cost of sales	100,000	120,000
	100,000	80,000
Expenses	60,000	60,000
	40,000	20,000
Dividends	20,000	20,000
	20,000	—
Balance of profit from before	5,000	25,000
Balance of unappropriated profit	25,000	25,000

Table 16.3 **Funds flow statement of Eegrek (ecus).**

Sources			
Funds from operations profit		20,000	
Add back depreciation		2,000	22,000
Issue of debentures			50,000
Issue of shares			12,000
Increase in creditors			20,000
			104,000
Applications			
Purchase of investments			30,000
Purchase of machinery			1,000
Purchase of buildings			40,000
Increase in inventory			10,000
Increase in debtors			10,000
Dividend paid			20,000
			111,000
Net applications			7,000
Bank movement:	1986	3,000	
Less	1987	(4,000)	
			7,000

Table 16.4 **Cash flow statement of Eegrek (ecus).**

Cash flows from operating activities		
Cash receipts from customers	190,000	
Cash payments to suppliers	(110,000)	
	80,000	
Cash payments for operating expenses	(43,000)	
Interest paid	(15,000)	
		22,000
Cash flows from investing activities		
Purchase of investments	(30,000)	
Purchase of buildings	(40,000)	
Purchase of machinery	(1,000)	
		(71,000)
Cash flows from financing activities		
Proceeds from share issue	12,000	
Proceeds from debenture issue	50,000	
Dividends paid	(20,000)	42,000
Net reduction in cash and cash equivalents		(7,000)
Cash and cash equivalents at beginning of year		3,000
Cash and cash equivalents at end of year		(4,000)

Table 16.5 **Ratios of Eegrek.**

	19X1		19X2	
ROCE	$\dfrac{40 + 10}{177}$	= 28%	$\dfrac{20 + 15}{259}$	= 14%
ROOE	$\dfrac{40}{77}$	= 52%	$\dfrac{20}{109}$	= 18%
Debtors' turnover	$\dfrac{200}{40}$	= 5 times	$\dfrac{200}{50}$	= 4 times
Creditors' turnover	$\dfrac{100}{40}$	= $2\frac{1}{2}$ times	$\dfrac{120}{60}$	= 2 times
Current ratio	$\dfrac{98}{60}$	= 1.6:1	$\dfrac{115}{84}$	= 1.4:1
Quick assets	$\dfrac{43}{60}$	= 0.7:1	$\dfrac{50}{84}$	= 0.6:1
Gross profit percentage	$\dfrac{100}{200}$	= 50%	$\dfrac{80}{200}$	= 40%
Net profit percentage	$\dfrac{40}{200}$	= 20%	$\dfrac{20}{200}$	= 10%
Dividend cover	$\dfrac{40}{20}$	= 2 times	$\dfrac{20}{20}$	= 1 times
Gearing ratio	$\dfrac{100}{177}$	= 56%	$\dfrac{150}{259}$	= 58%

not be representative of the average fixed assets in use through 19X1 as a whole. However, it is extremely unlikely that the fixed assets shown in the balance sheet at the end of 19X2 are representative of the average fixed assets in use through that year. The 19X2 balance sheet figures would only be representative if all the additions shown in Table 16.3 had occurred on 1 January 19X2, which is extremely unlikely.

Other general points could obviously be raised as well, such as uncertainty about rates of inflation, non-monetary unrecorded items, and so on.

3. Briefly, even allowing for the distortions mentioned in (2) above, developments in 19X2 appear adverse and potentially dangerous. Rapid expansion of the asset base has not led to extra earnings, so profitability (ROCE and, especially, ROOE) is very sharply reduced. The amount of dividend has been maintained (though presumably not the rate, as there are

more shares in 19X2) despite the worsening scenario. Is the firm at the worst point of the investment cycle – resources poured in, returns not yet begun – or is it overspending to no good purpose? Higher cost of sales but static sales is a distinctly discouraging sign.

SUMMARY

This chapter has discussed approaches towards the valuation of businesses based on traditional balance sheets, on attempts to quantify and evaluate future expectations, and on current market values. Useful valuation must be related to future expectations if it is to help effective decision-making.

The chapter then introduced the importance of considering the effects of accounting policies on financial statements. In particular, changes in policy over time, or differences in policies between different enterprises, must be allowed for when using accounting numbers as the basis for investigation and comparison. A simple illustration explored the ways of thinking necessary in the integration of accounting policy issues and interpretation and appraisal.

EXERCISES

16.1 Attached is an extract from a real set of published accounts, of a Dutch company, of a few years ago.

(a) For each year, calculate return, using both operating profit and net profit, on stockholders' (i.e. shareholders') equity, and a gearing ratio, under each basis.

(b) Write a brief explanation, clear to a non-accountant, about the differences between the figures under the two bases. Which basis should be used for analysis of the group's performance?

Supplementary data based on current value

The consolidated financial statements of Naamloze Vennootschap DSM are drawn up on the basis of historical cost.

Below, supplementary data on the basis of current value are given. Since there is no generally accepted method yet for presenting such data, the bases of valuation and determination of income on the basis of current value are explained insofar as they diverge from those used for the consolidated financial statements.

Fixed assets

The current value of land is generally based on appraisals, that of other tangible fixed assets is determined using price indices from external sources, making allowance for technological developments. Where lower, the recoverable value is used for valuation purposes. The value of tangible fixed assets owned by non-consolidated companies has also been restated using price indices; the effect on the equities of these companies, commensurate with the percentage of participation, is accounted for in the balance sheet.

Current assets

A revaluation is made where current inventory values diverge from the valuation in the consolidated balance sheet.

Stockholders' equity

Equity according to the consolidated balance sheet is increased by the revaluation of tangible fixed assets and inventories, after deduction of relevant deferred tax commitments and minority interests.

Operating profit

The operating profit according to the consolidated statement of income is adjusted for the additional depreciation on tangible fixed assets based on current value and for revaluation of inventories.

Net profit

The same adjustments are applied to the net profit as to the operating profit, additionally allowing for minority interests and the gain realized through loan financing. The tax burden is not adjusted. The financing gain corresponds to the part of the revaluation adjustments in the consolidated statement of income that relates to tangible fixed assets and inventories, insofar as financed with loan capital.

For calculation of the gain realized through loan financing, use is made of the ratio of Group equity to equity invested in tangible fixed assets and inventories. This ratio is determined on the basis of the consolidated balance sheet of Naamloze Vennootschap DSM at the end of the preceding financial year. In calculating the ratio, Group equity is never put at less than 25% of total assets. The difference between the net result calculated on historical cost basis and the current value net result is regarded as adjustment for capital maintenance.

Consolidated Statement of Income

million	1989		1988	
Net sales	10,772		10,121	
Other operating income	397		243	
Total operating income		11,169		10,364
Amortization and depreciation	−602		−627	
Other operating costs	−9,184		−8,530	
Total operating costs		−9,786		−9,157
Operating profit		1,383		1,207
Financial income and expense		−40		−82
Profit on ordinary activities before taxation		1,343		1,125
Tax on profit on ordinary activities		−407		−417
Results of non-consolidated companies		98		83
Profit on ordinary activities after taxation		1,034		791
Extraordinary result after taxation		345		−174
Group result after taxation		1,379		617
Minority interests' share in result		1		5
Net profit		1,380		622

Abridged consolidated balance sheet

million	1989 historical cost	1989 current value	1988 historical cost	1988 current value
fixed assets	**5,070**	**5,925**	4,358	5,235
current assets	**4,624**	**4,625**	3,988	4,000
total assets	**9,694**	**10,550**	8,346	9,235
stockholders' equity	**3,819**	**4,375**	3,074	3,790
minority interests in consolidated companies	**86**	**95**	79	85
current and long-term liabilities	**5,789**	**6,080**	5,193	5,360
total liabilities	**9,694**	**10,550**	8,346	9,235

Consolidated statement of income, restated on the basis of current value

million	1989	1988
operating profit		
on historical cost basis	**1,383**	1,207
– additional depreciation on current value basis	**–115**	–105
– difference between current value and historical cost of inventories	**20**	–65
on the basis of current value	**1,288**	1,037
net profit		
on historical cost basis	**1,380**	622
– additional depreciation on current value basis	**–115**	–105
– difference between current value and historical cost of inventories	**20**	–65
– gain through loan financing	**35**	50
on the basis of current value	**1,320**	502

The adjustment for capital maintenance, calculated with application of DSM's customary system, was £60 million, £75 million being accounted for by tangible fixed assets, –£15 million by inventories. The profit retained largely exceeds the amount of the adjustment for capital maintenance.

16.2 The following details relate to D Co.

Summary balance sheet

	31.12.X7 Actual 000 ecu	31.12X8 Budget 000 ecu	31.12.X8 Actual 000 ecu
Fixed assets			
Tangible assets	957	1,530	1,620
Current assets			
Inventory	205	290	325
Debtors	305	720	810
Cash and bank balances	175	70	—
	685	1,080	1,135
Creditors: Amounts due within one year			
Trade creditors	175	505	545
Other creditors	187	325	310
Bank overdraft	—	—	80
	362	830	935
Net current assets	323	250	200

Creditors: Amounts due in more than one year	—	360	360
	1,280	1,420	1,460
Capital and reserves			
Called-up share capital	800	800	800
Share premium account	200	200	200
Revenue reserves	280	420	460
	1,280	1,420	1,460

Income statements

	19X7 Actual 000 ecu	19X8 Budget 000 ecu	19X9 Actual 000 ecu
Turnover	2,560	4,500	5,110
Cost of sales	(1,700)	(3,150)	(3,580)
Gross profit	860	1,350	1,530
Admin. and distribution costs	(655)	(880)	(1,084)
Operating profit	205	470	446
Interest payable	—	(20)	(35)
	205	450	411
Taxation	(95)	(200)	(185)
	110	250	226
Extraordinary items	9	(2)	3
	119	248	229
Dividends	(82)	(108)	(49)
Retained earnings	37	140	180

Note: The opening inventory figures were 135,000 ecu 19X7 actual and 210,000 ecu 19X8 budget.

Using the above information and appropriate ratios prepare an analyzed financial report on the above company.

16.3 Repeat Exercise 1.4 from Chapter 1.

CHAPTER 17

International analysis

> **OBJECTIVES**
>
> - To examine some international dimensions of the analysis of financial statements
> - To focus on differences caused by language and institutional arrangements
> - To look at ways in which large companies can help analysis
> - To introduce ways of adjusting accounts to an international benchmark

17.1 Purposes and problems

The analysis discussed in the preceding three chapters is hard enough within one country, because of the complexity of the economic world and the incentives that some preparers of accounts have to mislead the users. When trying to compare companies internationally, the difficulties multiply, including differences under the following headings:

- Language problems
- Differences in financial culture
- Interpretation difficulties
- Availability of published accounting data
- Extent and type of audit
- Valuation of assets
- Measurement of profits
- Formats of financial statements
- Frequency of reports
- Quantity of data disclosed
- Different currencies
- Biases in the accounting data
- User-friendliness of annual reports

International comparative analysis might be undertaken by many users of accounts, including:

- brokers, investment analysts and journalists on behalf of shareholder investors;
- bankers and other creditors when deciding on lending;
- multinational companies when appraising existing or potential subsidiaries or competitors.

If analysts are unaware of the international differences, they will make the wrong investment decisions. If they try to make adjustments, this will be time-consuming and expensive. If they restrict themselves to their own home market, they will miss out on valuable opportunities for investment and the spreading of risk.

Several of the areas of difficulty listed above have been discussed in Parts II and III of this book. This chapter examines the first three; and then addresses potential solutions for interpreters of financial statements.

17.2 Language

Language is very obvious as a problem for international comparisons. This might be thought to be trivial in the sense that:

- many people can read more than one language,
- many large companies provide translations,
- experts can always be hired to translate (and they are a lot cheaper than accountants or financiers).

Indeed, compared to some of the other problems mentioned above, language *is* comparatively easy. Nevertheless, there are many pitfalls to be avoided.

Starting with 'English', we should be aware that the accounting jargon used in the United Kingdom and the United States differs considerably. Furthermore, there is great variety within both countries, particularly in the United States. A few examples of UK/US jargon will illustrate the scope for misunderstanding:

US term	*UK term*
Common stock	Ordinary shares
Inventories	Stocks
Treasury stock	Own shares
Receivables	Debtors
Reserve for doubtful accounts	Provision for bad debts
Included in equity	Taken to reserves
Notes	Bills
Bills	Notes

The problem is, of course, not just that the language is different (largely because American is seventeenth century English) but that the words that exist in both languages often mean something different. There is less scope for this sort of confusion when translating from Japanese!

The importance of this problem is not confined to English-speaking countries. Many EC companies produce translations, usually into approximately American English. However, these accounts may have unreliable or misleading translations, partly because the work is often carried out by those who are not expert in accounting. At worst, the English version may be little more than a marketing document. Such translated accounts are, of course, not the real statutory accounts, nor do they have to obey UK or US rules, so they may be extracts or manipulations of the original.

Some examples of translation problems will help to illustrate these points. The accounts of Total Oil (for France) and AEG (for Germany) are used for this purpose (see Examples 17.1–17.3). There is no suggestion that these companies are worse than any others, indeed they are better than many; it is merely that language is a complex problem in a technical area like accounting.

EXAMPLE 17.1

The following is an extract from the English-version annual report of Total Oil:

> Foreign currency balance sheets are converted into French francs on the basis of exchange rates at 31 December 1991. The conversion is applied to fixed assets as well as to monetary assets and liabilities. Gains or losses on translation of their balance sheets at the end of the previous year are dealt with...

This extract shows the word 'conversion' being used interchangeably with 'translation' because the two accounting terms are the same in French (*conversion*). In English the former means a physical act of exchange, whereas the latter (which would be correct here) means an accounting calculation.

EXAMPLE 17.2

A further extract, as found in earlier years of Total Oil reports:

> However, as concerns newly acquired companies the excess of the TOTAL Group's investment in such companies... is capitalized in the consolidated balance sheet and is not amortized.... These surplus values are depreciated on a straight line basis....

The expression 'surplus values' is a translation of *survaleurs*. The English accounting expression would have been 'goodwill'.

EXAMPLE 17.3

When matters get complicated, a translation often becomes opaque or misleading. AEG's note on consolidation techniques is very difficult to understand. It is shown below with our interpretation.

Published translation

Capital consolidation is performed using the 'book value method'. Under this method, the book values of the affiliated companies are netted against the underlying equity in these companies at the time of acquisition or initial consolidation.

Where the book values exceed underlying equity, the difference is allocated to the respective assets or liabilities according to their real value. A difference remaining after the allocation is shown as goodwill or disclosed as a reduction from the reserves. If the book values fall below the underlying equity, the difference is recorded as 'reserve arising from consolidation'.

Authors' suggestion

Full consolidation is performed using a version of fair value accounting. Under this method, the first stage is to compare the cost of the consolidated companies with the book value of the group's share of their net assets. Generally this is done at the date of acquisition, but for existing subsidiaries that have been consolidated for the first time this year, the year end values are used.

Where cost exceeds net assets, the difference is allocated to the subsidiary's assets and liabilities up to and in proportion to their fair values. Any excess remaining is goodwill, which is either shown as an asset or written off against reserves.

Where the initial exercise leads to a negative difference, this is shown as a 'reserve arising from consolidation'.

These examples are illustrations of the point that, although the language may be of good quality, the translation is often not done by accountants, perhaps because bilingual accountants are very expensive to hire. For example, there are no such terms in English as 'surplus values' (Example 17.2) or 'capital consolidation' or 'book value method' (Example 17.3). Of course, none of this should be read as implying a lack of gratitude for translations: it is a very rare US or UK company that bothers at all, presumably because there is no commercial need to do so and because it would, therefore, not be obvious which language to choose.

17.3 Financial culture

It is not just accounting terms and accounting practices that must be disentangled before successful international comparison is possible. There are also different social, cultural and economic backgrounds. Let us take two examples.

1. Because of the long history of debt finance in Germany, it is normal for German companies to have a high gearing ratio compared to US or UK norms. However, not only is this traditional, it is also safer in Germany because of the long-run nature of bank interests in German industry. Bankers might be expected to pump money *into* an ailing company rather than to try to be the first to 'pull the plug'.

    So a high gearing ratio is more normal and less dangerous in Germany. It has been shown in earlier chapters that accounting differences probably make German ratios look higher as well.

2. Table 17.1 shows how the accounting treatment of supplementary employee remuneration influences the computation of the interesting total 'funds generated from operations' for three companies (one British, one Italian and one French).

    We start in column one with the British company which places all pension provisions with a financial institution so that the 'funds' in question leave the company. For a company operating in France, there is a statutory requirement that part of the company's profits be allocated for the benefit of employees, with reinvestment in external assets within two years. In the short-term, we could consider that there is an element in Funds Generated from Operations (+ F.800 in the example) which relates to the allocation for the current period, while the only outflow is the cash placed in external investments (− F.700).

Table 17.1 **The impact of different remuneration schemes on funds generated from operations.**

	UK	France	Italy
	(£)	(Francs)	(Lire)
Earnings	100	1,000	100,000
Add back			
Depreciation of fixed assets	250	2,500	250,000
Provision for employee pensions	80	—	—
less funds applied in the current year	(80)	—	—
Share of profits attributable to employees	—	800	—
less funds applied in the current year	—	(700)	—
Deferred employee remuneration	—	—	80,000
less funds applied in the current year			(30,000)
Funds generated from operations	350	3,600	400,000

Source: S. J. McLeay, in C. W. Nobes and R. H. Parker (eds), *Comparative International Accounting*, Prentice Hall, Hemel Hempstead, 1991, Chapter 17.

Now compare these two approaches with the situation in Italy, where employees are entitled on leaving a company to one month's salary (at current rates of pay) for each year in service. There is no requirement for the company to place these funds in earmarked investments, although the appropriate provisions must be made. Thus, Funds Generated from Operations includes the provision (+ L.80,000) net of the payment to retiring employees (− L.30,000).

Of course, there are many ways of constructing a Cash Flow Statement, and the example is not uncontentious. However, the example shows that, when we compare the funds generated by companies in different countries, part of the explanation of the variability in levels of self-financing lies in the different social systems within which the companies operate.

17.4 Interpretation difficulties

Some more examples of differences that create difficulties of interpretation follow.

Swedish reserves

In Sweden, Finland and, to some extent, Germany special untaxed reserves are an important feature. For example, as the Annual Report from Electrolux (1988, Note 20) shows:

> Fiscal legislation in Sweden... permits allocations to untaxed reserves in order to defer tax payments. Changes in untaxed reserves are reported in the income statement... US GAAP do not permit deduction of such allocations from income.
>
> | | | |
> |---|---|---|
> | Income adjustment: | as reported | SEK 1693 |
> | | allocation | SEK + 969 |
> | Shareholders' equity: | as reported | SEK 11440 |
> | | untaxed reserves | SEK + 5059 |
> | | related deferred tax | SEK − 2529 |

Such untaxed reserves could be seen as partly shareholders' funds and partly deferred tax. They are being reduced in importance in Sweden and Norway, from 1992. A Norwegian example from Norsk Hydro (1991, p. 64) is shown in Table 17.2.

Continental extraordinary items

Listed companies in many countries are required to disclose their 'earnings per share', from which a 'price/earnings ratio' can be calculated. Earnings may exclude extraordinary items. In most continental European countries, there is no standard definition and no requirement to show earnings, although some listed companies volunteer the disclosure.

Table 17.2 **Untaxed reserves in the accounts of Norsk Hydro, 1991.**

	Millions of Krone
Shareholders' equity in the US GAAP financial statements	19,156
Prepaid expenses and other current assets	(63)
Property, plant and equipment – Capitalized costs (a) (b) (d)	(7,839)
Prepaid pension (c)	(2,287)
Other non-current assets	(47)
Dividends payable (f)	(719)
Unrealized exchange gains – current and long-term (e)	(2,349)
Accrued pension liability (c)	(16)
Other long-term liabilities	127
Deferred tax liabilities (g)	14,946
Untaxed reserves (h)	(14,853)
Shareholders' equity in the Norwegian GAAP financial statements	6,056

The definition of 'extraordinary' in the EC Fourth Directive is 'otherwise than in the course of the company's ordinary activities'. However, in practice, the use of the term varies in Europe for several reasons:

1. The Directive is not in force in some countries: such as Austria, Switzerland, Sweden, etc.
2. Some countries add glosses to the definition: e.g. in the United Kingdom (FRS 3), extraordinary items must also be material and not expected to recur. Certain items are specifically defined as not extraordinary, e.g. gains and losses on the sale of fixed assets and investments.
3. Exactly what is 'ordinary activities' varies. For example, in the United Kingdom the sale of a shop by a stores group would not be thought to be extraordinary whereas it probably would be by a French stores group.

Table 17.3 shows the example of a public company in Denmark. Of the extraordinary expenses shown, only the second appears to fit the UK definition, and even that would not be extraordinary if it were related to a continuing segment. Of the gains, the sale of tangible assets may well have been not extraordinary by UK standards. From mid-1993, none of these items would fit the UK definition.

In Greece, the nearest analogous term would be translated as non-trading; in Portugal as non-operating.

In the United Kingdom, until 1993, the definition of 'earnings' excluded extraordinary items. From 1993, extraordinary items are included. Nevertheless analysts in various countries may wish to exclude certain items in order to measure sustainable profit. They will be frustrated by these differences of definition.

A further complication is the use in the United Kingdom of the term 'exceptional items'. These are amounts which are *not* thought to be outside ordinary activities

Table 17.3 **Extraordinary items from FLS Smidth & Co., Denmark**

	K(M)
Note 5. Extraordinary income	
Profit on sale of site	144
Profits on sale of shares	50
Profits on sale of tangible assets	24
Other income	16
	234
Note 6. Extraordinary expenses	
Extraordinary losses on completed orders	44
Redundancy payments	35
Extraordinary write-offs on stocks and work in progress, etc.	31
Losses on sale of tangible assets	14
Losses on sale of properties	4
Other expenses	24
	152

Note The profit before extraordinaries was K 71M

but are abnormal in size or incidence. In French, both extraordinary and exceptional are translated as '*exceptionnel*', which hardly helps international analysis.

In the United Kingdom, extraordinary items are shown after 'profit on ordinary activities after taxation'. That is, tax is split between the amounts charged on ordinary and that on extraordinary profit. Table 17.4 shows a typical UK profit and loss account; the tax on extraordinary items could have been shown on the face of the account but is normally shown in a note. By contrast, in most other countries, extraordinaries are shown gross of taxation and above the tax charge (see Table 17.5 for Denmark, and Table 17.6 for Spain).

Dividends

In Tables 17.5 and 17.6, no dividends are shown as being paid. This is generally the case in continental Europe. In the United Kingdom and Ireland, a provision is made at the end of the year for the dividends proposed by the directors to be paid from the year's profits. This has to be approved at the Annual General Meeting (AGM), but normally this is a formality. Therefore, the matching convention suggests an accrual. In the accounts of a French company (though not necessarily of a group), there are often two columns in a balance sheet, showing 'before allocation' (or 'before AGM decisions') and after.

Table 17.4 Profit and loss account of Cadbury Schweppes plc, 1990.

	1990 £m	1989 £m
Sales	3,146.1	2,776.7
Cost of sales	(1,738.4)	(1,596.9)
Gross Profit	1,407.7	1,179.8
Distribution costs, including marketing	(798.1)	(673.1)
Administration expenses	(276.6)	(234.4)
Other operating income/(charges)	0.9	0.3
Trading Profit	333.9	272.6
Share of profits of associated undertakings	2.9	2.8
Net interest	(57.2)	(31.1)
Profit on Ordinary Activities Before Taxation	279.6	244.3
Tax on profit on ordinary activities	(78.0)	(69.5)
Profit on Ordinary Activities After Taxation	201.6	174.8
Profit attributable to minority interests	(22.2)	(17.0)
Profit Before Extraordinary Items	179.4	157.8
Extraordinary items	—	15.2
Profit Attributable to Shareholders	179.4	173.0
Dividends	(83.6)	(76.3)
Profit Retained For The Year	95.8	96.7
Retained by:		
Cadbury Schweppes plc	53.2	(3.7)
Subsidiary undertakings	41.2	99.2
Associated undertakings	1.4	1.2
	95.8	96.7
Earnings Per Ordinary Share of 25p		
Net basis	25.29p	24.22p

17.5 Help by multinationals

It is often cheaper for the company than the report readers to do something about the problems of interpreting international differences. Companies wishing to raise money on the international markets may volunteer, or be forced in the case

Table 17.5 Profit and loss account of East Asiatic Company, Denmark, 1989.

	1,000 DKK
Net sales	17,737,507
Cost sales	13,665,948
Gross profit	4,071,559
Share of earnings before tax in associated companies	138,074
	4,209,633
Selling and distribution expenses	2,191,093
Administrative expenses	1,013,177
Amortization of goodwill	31,658
Other operating expenses	4,153
Other operating income	117,480
	3,122,601
Operating profit	1,087,032
Dividends from associated companies	
Income from other investments	16,028
	16,028
Profit before financing expenses	1,103,060
Financing income	725,607
Financing expenses	928,414
	202,807
Profit on ordinary activities	900,253
Extraordinary income	365,507
Extraordinary expenses	324,665
	40,842
Profit before taxes	941,095
Provision for income taxes	113,730
Share of tax on earnings in associated companies	68,029
	181,759
	759,336
Allocation to surplus reserve	200,000
Profit before minority interests	559,336
Minority interests	120,190
Net profit	439,146

Table 17.6 Debit side of income statement of Compañía Española de Petróleos SA 1991 (millions of pesetas).

Expenses	
Procurements (Note 19)	224,914
Decrease in finished product and work-in-process inventories	3,174
Personnel expenses	17,207
Period depreciation and amortization	6,225
Variation in operating provisions	6,674
Other operating expenses	44,357
	302,551
Operating income	**12,672**
Financial expenses on debt to Group and associated companies	2,862
Financial expenses on debt to third parties and similar expenses	4,489
Variation in financial investment provisions	10
Exchange losses	1,883
	9,244
Financial income	**2,467**
Ordinary income	**15,139**
Variation in fixed asset provisions	1,753
Losses on fixed assets	663
Extraordinary expenses	258
Prior years' expenses	—
	2,674
Extraordinary income	**0**
Income before taxes	**13,144**
Corporate income tax	1,418
Net income for the year	**11,726**

of some stock exchange rules, to help the readers in one or more of the following ways:

1. Where possible, they choose accounting policies for statutory domestic purposes that are most in line with international practices; for example, some Swiss companies volunteer to consolidate or to capitalize leases. At the extreme, Royal Dutch/Shell tries to comply with US, UK and Dutch rules simultaneously. Companies may also volunteer for an Anglo-American audit when this is not legally necessary.
2. Providing versions of the annual report which translate only the language, although this may raise the problems discussed above. This is common for European companies translating into English.
3. They provide reports in another currency, e.g. some Japanese companies (e.g. Fujitsu, NTT) provide dollar and yen figures; International Thomson organization provides accounts in sterling although it is of Canadian registration. These are sometimes called 'convenience statements', and the year-end translation rate is normally applied to all items.
4. They provide reconciliation statements of net income or net assets from the company's domestic rules to another set. This is most obviously found in the case of companies obeying some SEC rules, when a reconciliation to US GAAP is shown as a supplementary statement (e.g. Electrolux, British Airways, etc.).
5. They may carry out 'limited restatement' of some accounting policies or formats of presentation, presumably as a supplement to domestic reports; this is quite normal for Japanese companies towards US practices.
6. Publishing a substantial reworking and retranslation of the annual report into another set of practices and terms (e.g. Philips). This amounts to secondary financial statements.

17.6 A benchmark for international comparisons

Despite the help of multinationals, interpretation remains a problem for analysts, brokers, bankers, managers, etc. This chapter has shown that there are deep-seated causes for European accounting differences. These are very resistant to change, and they will continue for many years to make international comparisons very difficult. The worst error for analysts is not to realize that the differences are great. The next error is to suppose that they can be adjusted for by simple multipliers or rules of thumb. This book has shown that the world is more complex than that. For example, although German profit numbers are often smaller than UK accountants would have calculated, the degree of understatement varies, and sometimes German profit numbers may be larger.

The only reliable approach is to become well informed about the international differences, and then to adjust for the major items line-by-line. Of course, help can be found in this endeavour. This book has tried to help with the former problem (education), and it now makes preliminary efforts to address the second problem (adjustments).

In order to appraise companies, it is normal to place special emphasis on a few accounting aggregates and ratios. In many ways this is particularly dangerous because the commercial world and the companies in it are more complex than can reasonably be encapsulated in a few simple numbers or ratios. For example, the fixation by some analysts on 'earnings' gives rise to efforts by companies to try to absorb losses in provisions or to take losses to reserves, and to take some subsidiary companies 'off balance sheet'. All these efforts will not be directly connected to the underlying reality of transactions. Despite the fact that the transactions may be well documented in the notes to the financial statements, an analyst who concentrates on a few standard totals and ratios will be misled. Of course, the scope for confusion increases dramatically in multinationals and in international comparisons.

Nevertheless, standard ratios are widely used, and emphasis here will be placed upon adjustments to 'earnings' and 'net assets'. Other figures are either fairly easy to determine (such as the total of current assets, the number of shares outstanding or the market share price) or may be easily derived from the above two key aggregates (such as cash flow or shareholders' equity). In the case of Germany, the Association of Investment Analysts (*Deutsche Vereinigung für Finanzanalyse und Anlageberatung*, DVFA) tries to adjust for the discretionary items in German accounts. Its objective is particularly to adjust earnings, not to an international benchmark of course, but to a more comparable German basis. Some of the main adjustments to German published net profit figures are:

(a) exclusion of all extraordinary and prior year items (even gains and losses on the sale of fixed assets which would be 'exceptional items' in the United Kingdom);
(b) elimination of excess depreciation due to tax rules or for other reasons;
(c) removal of the effects of changes to long-term provisions which are largely discretionary;
(d) elimination of currency gains and losses on non-trading activities.

Our task is to go beyond national comparisons. It is necessary to take account of the major differences examined earlier. A list of some of these differences in the sphere of measurement and valuation (in addition to those mentioned already in this chapter) is as follows.

1. Strict historical cost or *ad hoc* revaluations for fixed assets.
2. Use of percentage-of-completion or completed-contract method for long-term contracts.
3. Use of year-end or transaction rates for translation of foreign currency debtors and creditors in an individual company's accounts.
4. Capitalization (or not) of interest on construction.
5. Revaluation and depreciation (or not) of investment properties.
6. Basing bad debt provisions on tax rules (or not).

7. Basing depreciation charges on tax rules (or not).
8. Valuing current asset marketable securities at market (or not).
9. Using the current rate method or the temporal method for translation.
10. Proportional or equity consolidation for joint ventures.
11. Calculating goodwill by reference to fair values (as opposed to book values).
12. Amortizing goodwill or writing it off against reserves.
13. Using the merger accounting method (or not).

One initial action in preparing for adjustment is to achieve a classification such as that shown in Figure 4.1 and Table 4.6 in Chapter 4. All the European countries in this table, except for the United Kingdom, Ireland, Denmark and the Netherlands, are shown on the right. For accounts from those right-hand countries, the following are some of the adjustments that may be necessary if one wished to move to UK-style numbers.

Action

1.	Conservatism	INCREASE net asset values
2.	Historical cost	INCREASE net asset values
4.	LIFO	INCREASE inventory values for some
4.	Translation	EXTRACT translation adjustments from German and other users of the 'temporal' method
5.	Consolidation	BEWARE lack of consolidation
6.	Associated companies	INCREASE net assets and profit in cases of non-use of equity method
7.	R&D	DECREASE net assets by any capitalized amounts; adjust profits
8.	Leases	INCREASE fixed assets and liabilities where leases are not capitalized
9.	Pensions	EXAMINE carefully. EXTRACT any pension provisions from shareholders' funds
10.	Provisions	INCREASE shareholders' funds by portion of general provisions
11.	Tax	DECREASE depreciation where caused by tax.

In more detail, a possible benchmark towards which one might wish to work for international purposes could have the following features:

1. Earnings:
   (a) after depreciation, interest, tax and preference dividend, minority profits,
   (b) including extraordinary items,
   (c) historical cost numbers,
   (d) provisions for risks or contingencies not charged against profit,
   (e) tax-based provisions and depreciation not charged,
   (f) all subsidiaries included,
   (g) excluding differences on translation of foreign financial statements, but including exchange differences on transactions, loans, etc.,

(h) excluding amortization of goodwill,
(i) including share of profits of associated companies (20–50%),
(j) excluding depreciation of set-up costs and R&D which should be charged in one year,
(k) interest expenses not capitalized,
(l) deferred tax not accounted for, except when expected to be paid soon.
2. Net assets:
   (a) standardize on historical cost for most assets but, if possible, current value of property,
   (b) FIFO not LIFO,
   (c) exclude capitalized goodwill, set-up costs, interest, R&D,
   (d) deferred tax treated as part of reserves unless expected to be paid soon, when it is a provision,
   (e) minorities included,
   (f) all subsidiaries included,
   (g) closing rate translation,
   (h) associates treated by equity method,
   (i) tax-based provisions and those for risks or contingencies treated as reserves,
   (j) finance leases capitalized.

Of these various adjustments, some will be simple from published accounts and some will be capable of estimation. However, some problems will not be soluble from published information, although analysts may find that the above list raises useful questions to be asked at meetings with companies.

In conclusion, it is likely to remain impossible for many years to achieve precise international comparisons of earnings or net assets figures. However, this does not mean that users of financial statements should just give up and pretend that all companies are using the same rules. Approximate adjustments and informed questions will lead to better decision-making. Experts will be better at it than amateurs.

SUMMARY

There are many reasons for analysts to try to carry out international comparative analysis. However, it has all the problems of domestic analysis plus several others.

Language difficulties may be severe for some analysts and some countries, but translations do not solve all the problems. Differences in financial culture and presentation are also hard to adjust for in the areas of pensions, tax reserves, extraordinary items and dividends.

Multinational companies can make several types of adjustment to assist international analysis. However, it is nearly always necessary for the analyst to do further work before international comparisons of earnings, net assets, etc., are meaningful.

German analysts have an organized means of adjusting German results on to a standardized basis. This approach could be adopted internationally by inventing an international benchmark for comparisons, and then applying it to any particular company.

EXERCISES

17.1 This exercise uses a German set of financial statements, and asks for accounting comparisons with the practices of other countries. Extracts from the 1992 Annual Report of Daimler-Benz follow. Use them to attempt the following questions.

1. What language is being used in the translation? (e.g. British, American, etc.). What does Daimler mean by 'fixed assets' (p. 340); 'affiliated companies' (p. 341); 'treasury stock' (p. 343)?
2. Is Daimler accounting for deferred tax? How can 'deferred taxes' be assets (p. 340)?
3. What are 'minority interests' (p. 340)? Are they part of shareholders' funds?
4. Do the accounting rules really lead to 'international practice' as claimed in the 1989 accounts?
   (a) Provisions for pensions (p. 343).
   (b) Writing off goodwill to reserves (p. 342).
   (c) Special tax-deductible depreciation allowances (p. 342).
   (d) Depreciation methods (p. 342).
   (e) Discounting of receivables (p. 342). Why are liabilities not discounted?
   (f) Treatment of foreign receivables and payables (p. 344).
   (g) Exchange rates used for subsidiaries' fixed assets and depreciation (p. 344).
5. Consolidation method and goodwill calculation (p. 343): are these like the practices in France, United Kingdom, etc. (insert your own country)?
6. Is it possible to revalue investments upwards (p. 345)? Does this not seem unusual for German accounting?
7. Are leased assets capitalized (p. 340, 345)? Would you expect this in Germany?
8. How are joint ventures accounted for (p. 343)? Compare with other countries.
9. How are dividends paid accounted for compared with UK practice?
10. How exact would be the calculation of 'reversal of provisions...DM 1,519 million' (p. 349)?
11. Is the income statement vertical/horizontal? *Par nature* or *par destination*? How does this compare with other countries?

Financial Statements
Consolidated Balance Sheet

ASSETS	Notes	December 31, 1992 In Millions of DM	December 31, 1991 In Millions of DM
Non-Current Assets			
Intangible Assets	(1)	611	774
Fixed Assets	(2)	19,254	16,574
Financial Assets	(3)	3,991	3,758
Leased Equipment	(4)	9,777	8,092
		33,633	29,198
Current Assets			
Inventories	(5)	23,138	20,732
Advance Payments Received	(6)	(5,549)	(5,827)
		17,589	14,905
Receivables from Leasing and Sales Financing	(7)	6,166	4,255
Other Receivables	(8)	14,771	12,370
Other Assets	(9)	3,503	5,528
Securities	(10)	6,089	5,725
Cash	(11)	2,968	2,010
		51,086	44,793
Prepaid Expenses and Deferred Taxes	(12)	1,465	1,723
		86,184	75,714

STOCKHOLDER'S EQUITY AND LIABILITIES			
Stockholders' Equity	(13)		
Capital Stock	(14)	2,330	2,330
Paid-In Capital	(14)	2,117	2,117
Retained Earnings	(15)	13,440	13,182
Minority Interests	(16)	1,228	1,214
Unappropriated Profit of Daimler-Benz AG		604	605
		19,719	19,448
Provisions			
Provisions for Old-Age Pensions and Similar Obligations	(17)	12,217	10,790
Other Provisions	(18)	22,478	17,239
		34,695	28,029
Liabilities			
Liabilities from Leasing and Sales Financing	(19)	10,971	8,113
Accounts Payable Trade	(20)	6,517	7,015
Other Liabilities	(21)	13,725	12,600
		31,213	27,728
Deferred Income		557	509
		86,184	75,714

Consolidated Statement of Income

	Notes	1992 In Millions of DM	1991 In Millions of DM
Sales	(22)	98,549	95,010
Increase in Inventories and Other Capitalized In-House Output	(23)	2,330	3,556
Total Output		100,879	98,566
Other Operating Income	(24)	4,506	3,545
Cost of Materials	(25)	(49,084)	(49,456)
Personnel Expenses	(26)	(32,003)	(29,372)
of which for Old-Age Pensions DM 1,539 million (1991: DM 1,511 million)			
Amortization of Intangible Assets, Depreciation of Fixed Assets and of Leased Equipment	(27)	(7,085)	(5,977)
Other Operating Expenses	(28)	(15,254)	(13,824)
Income from Affiliated, Associated and Related Companies	(29)	118	56
Interest Income	(30)	577	623
Write-Downs of Financial Assets and of Securities	(31)	(121)	(134)
Results from Ordinary Business Activities		2,533	4,027
Extraordinary Result	(32)	—	(544)
Income Taxes	(33)	(586)	(1,039)
Other Taxes	(33)	(496)	(502)
Net Income	(34)	1,451	1,942
Profit Carried Forward from Previous Year		2	8
Transfer to Retained Earnings		(816)	(1,275)
Income Applicable to Minority Shareholders		(184)	(99)
Loss Applicable to Minority Shareholders		151	29
Dividend (1991: Unappropriated Profit) of Daimler-Benz AG		604	605

Notes to the Consolidated Financial Statements

Principles and Methods

The consolidated financial statements have been prepared in accordance with regulations set forth in the Commercial Code; the amounts are shown in millions of D-marks. The items, which are summarized in the balance sheet and the statement of income, are separately shown in the notes and, where necessary, explained.

Deviating from the previous year, we additionally show in the consolidated financial statements — apart from the caption "leased vehicles and equipment" — the captions "receivables from sales financing" and "liabilities from leasing and sales financing", in order to accomodate (sic) the pecularities of the financial services business.

Accounting Principles and Valulation Methods

During the year under review, we have continued to apply the same accounting principles and valuation methods. Assets and liabilities presented in the consolidated balance sheet — in identical group circumstances — are uniformly valued. In 1992, as in previous years, provisions for approved conversion, reconstruction and maintenance projects have been set up, or have been systematically updated.

Intangible assets are valued at acquisition costs and are written off over the respective useful lives. Goodwill resulting from the capital consolidation, if derived from the extension of the group, is in principle amortized over five years; goodwill relating to the restructuring of the group is charged to retained earnings. Goodwill which arose from the creation of strategic alliances, is split. The portion relating to the group's expansion is written off over the relevant useful life, the one relating to the restructuring is charged to retained earnings.

Fixed assets are valued at acquisition or manufacturing costs. The self-constructed facilities comprise direct costs and applicable materials and manufacturing overheads, including depreciation allowances.

The acquisition/manufacturing costs for fixed assets are reduced by scheduled depreciation charges. The opportunities for special tax-deductible depreciation allowances were fully utilized, i.e. in connection with Section 7d of the Income Tax Act (environmental protection investment), Section 6b of the Income Tax Act, Section 4 of the Regional Development Law and Subsection 35 of the Income Tax Guidelines.

Scheduled fixed asset depreciation allowances are calculated generally using the following useful lives: 17 to 50 years for buildings, 8 to 20 years for site improvements, 3 to 20 years for technical facilities and machinery, and 2 to 10 years for other facilities and factory and office equipment. Facilities used for multishift operations are depreciated using correspondingly lower useful lives. Buildings are depreciated using straight-line depreciation rates — and where allowable under the Tax Codes — declining rates. Movable property with a useful life of four years or more is depreciated using the declining-balance method. For movable property, we change from the declining-balance method to the straight-line method of calculating depreciation allowances when the equal distribution of the remaining net book value over the remaining useful life leads to higher depreciation amounts. Depreciation allowances on additions during the first and second half of the year are calculated using the full year or half-year rates, respectively. Low-value items are expensed in the year of acquisition.

Investments in *related companies*, and in *other long-term financial assets* are valued at the lower of cost or market; non-interest bearing or low-interest bearing receivables are shown at their present value. Major *investments in associated companies* are valued according to the book value method at equity.

Leased equipment is valued at acquisition or manufacturing costs, and is depreciated using the declining-balance method. We change from the declining-balance method to the straight-line method of calculating depreciation allowances when the equal distribution of the remaining net book value over the remaining useful life leads to higher depreciation amounts. The opportunities for tax-deductible depreciation allowances were fully utilized, i.e. in connection with Subsection 35 of the Income Tax Guidelines.

Raw materials and supplies as well as *goods purchased for resale* are valued at the lower of cost or market. *Finished goods* are valued at manufacturing costs which comprise, apart from direct material and direct labor, applicable material and manufacturing overheads including depreciation charges.

To the extent that inventory risks are determinable, i.e. for reduced usability after prolonged storage or after design changes, reasonable deductions are made, which are calculated based on a loss-free valuation.

Receivables and other assets — if non-interest bearing — are reduced to their present value at the balance sheet date, and are valued taking into account all known risks. A lump-sum allowance for doubtful accounts on a country-specific scale is deducted from the receivables in recognition of the general risk inherent in receivables.

Treasury stock is valued at the expected selling price to employees of the Daimler-Benz group. *Securities* are valued at the lower of cost or market value at the balance sheet date.

Provisions for old-age pensions and similar obligations are actuarially determined on the basis of an assumed interest rate of 6% using the Entry Age Actuarial Cost Method. The regulations of the 1992 Pension Reform Act have been taken into account in calculating the provision amount.

Provisions for taxes and *other provisions* are determined on the basis of fair and reasonable business judgements. The obligations in the personnel and social area are reflected in the financial statements at non-discounted values expected to be paid in the future as benefits are vested.

Liabilities are shown at their repayment amounts.

Companies Included in Consolidation

The companies included in consolidation encompass, apart from Daimler-Benz AG, 271 (1991: 255) domestic and foreign subsidiaries and 7 joint venture companies.

During the year under review, 26 companies have, for the first time, been added to consolidation. Moreover, one joint venture company was included pro rata, for the first time, pursuant to Section 310 of the Commercial Code. A total of 10 subsidiaries and one joint venture company were deleted from consolidation.

Deutsche Aerospace Airbus GmbH and its subsidiaries were fully consolidated in the consolidated accounts effective January 1, 1992. Up to 1991, Deutsche Aerospace Airbus GmbH was only consolidated at equity in conformity with Section 296, Subsection 1, Paragraph 1 of the Commercial Code. After the transfer by the Kreditanstalt für Wiederaufbau of its 20% stake in Deutsche Aerospace Airbus GmbH to DASA, this limitation with respect to exercising its rights no long applies, which, on account of agreements with the Federal Republic of Germany and of rules in the bylaws, had existed up to that point.

The first-time consolidation of the Deutsche Aerospace Airbus group effected both the consolidated balance sheet and the consolidated statement of income. These effects are explained under the relevant balance sheet and statement of income captions.

In 1991, only the balance sheet items of the Eurocopter companies were proportionally included in consolidation because of their relatively short affiliation with the group; in 1992, they were included in the statement of income as well.

Because income and expense items relative to the German helicopter activities were still included in the 1991 accounts, comparability of group financial statements with the previous year is not materially affected.

Not included are 248 subsidiaries, whose effect on the assets, liabilities, financial position and results of operations of the group is not material (their total sales volume is less than 1% of consolidated sales), and 11 companies administering pension funds whose assets are subject to restrictions.

Principles of Consolidation

Capital consolidation was effected according to the book value method where the parent's acquisition costs are eliminated against the relevant share capital and retained earnings at the time of acquisition or first-time inclusion in consolidation. This applies analogously to the joint venture companies that were included pro rata.

The differences resulting from the capital consolidation (debit balance) are, as far as possible, allocated to the relevant balance sheet items and are written off to income over their useful lives. For the treatment of the remaining differences (goodwill), see explanations under "accounting principles and valuation methods". The remaining goodwill resulting from the addition of the *joint venture companies* of the Eurocopter group is shown under "intangible assets"; the portion applicable to the group's expansion will be amortized over a useful life of 10 years. The other portion was charged to retained earnings in 1992, without affecting income.

A difference (credit balance) resulting from the capital consolidation is shown under the balance sheet caption "other provisions" earmarked as "difference from capital consolidation with reserve characteristics".

Profits earned by subsidiaries after the date of acquisition are added to consolidated retained earnings. The unappropriated profit shown in the financial statements corresponds to the dividend payout proposed by Daimler-Benz AG. For this reason we have charged the income-affecting consolidation adjustments and the profits earned by our subsidiaries to consolidated retained earnings.

The consolidated financial statements included 127 *associated companies*.

At year-end, 13 associated companies have been included in our consolidated financial statements according to the *book value method* at equity.

The remaining associated companies are shown under investments in affiliated companies at acquisition costs — as they are not material to the consolidated assets, liabilities, financial position and results of operations.

The 34% stake in Sogeti S. A., Grenoble which was acquired by Daimler-Benz AG in December of 1991, was transferred to debis AG in October 1992. As of December 31, 1992, Sogeti was included in consolidation at equity according to the book value method. However, only the 1991 accounts were used because Sogeti's 1992 financials had not been available at the time the Daimler-Benz consolidated financial statements were prepared. The goodwill of DM 355 million will be amortized over 15 years.

Intercompany receivables and payables have been eliminated; the differences resulting from *debt consolidation* have been charged or credited to income.

All material *intercompany profits* resulting from the intercompany sales of goods and services have been eliminated, except items of minor importance. This also applies to sales of goods and services by associated companies to companies included in consolidation.

Intercompany sales and other intercompany earnings have been eliminated against the relevant costs, or reclassified to "capitalized in-house output" or to "increase in inventories", respectively.

Deferred taxes (debit balance) shown in the consolidated balance sheet result from income-affecting consolidation adjustments.

Curreny (sic) Translation

Foreign currency receivables are translated in the individual financial statements at the bid price on the day they are recorded or at the spot rate on the balance sheet date if lower. Foreign currency payables are translated at the asked price on the day they are recorded or at the spot rate on the balance sheet date if higher.

The accounts of all foreign companies are translated to D-marks on the basis of historial exchange rates for non-current assets, and at year-end exchange rates for current assets, borrowed capital, and unappropriated profit. Stockholders' equity in D-marks is the remaining difference between translated assets less translated liabilities and unappropriated profit. The difference resulting from the translation of balance sheet items is recorded in consolidated retained earnings.

Expense and income items are essentially translated at average annual exchange rates. To the extent that they relate to fixed assets (fixed asset depreciation, profit or loss from disposal of fixed assets), they are translated at historical costs. Net income, additions to retained earnings, and the unappropriated profit are translated at year-end rates. The difference resulting from the translation of annual net income, between annual average rates and the exchange rates at the balance sheet date, is reflected in other operating income (1991: other operating expenses).

The adjustments made in the income statements by our subsidiaries in Brazil for monetary devaluations have been retained in the consolidated statement of income without change, effectively preventing reflection of inflationary profits. The income taxes, which were aredly geared to the balance sheet date in the national financial statments, have been translated at year-end rates.

Items from inflation-adjusted income statements of our Argentinian companies are translated at year-end exchange rates. Fictitious profits/losses resulting from the divergence between the inflationary trend and the changes in the currency's value have been eliminated.

Notes to the Consolidated Balance Sheet

1 Intangible Assets

Intangible assets, amounting to DM 611 million (1991: DM 774 million) comprise goodwill arising from the capital consolidation and from individual company financial statements, acquired EDP software, patents and, to a lesser extent, advance payments made. The decrease against the previous year is largely due to amortizations of goodwill charged to income and to the write-off of Eurocopter's goodwill to retained earnings.

2 Fixed Assets

The increase in property, plant and equipment by DM 2,680 million to DM 19,254 million is derived from additions of DM 7,829 million, of which DM 1,410 million represent net book values that are to be included within the scope of the first-time full consolidation of the Deutsche Aerospace Airbus group. These additions are reduced by re-classifications of DM 17 million, disposals of DM 433 million, and depreciation allowances of DM 4,699 million. Special tax-deductible depreciation allowances amount to DM 163 million (1991: DM 77 million); depreciation allowances in excess of scheduled depreciation amount to DM 21 million (1991: DM 39 million).

3 Financial Assets

A complete listing of our stock ownership will be filed with the commercial registry office at the county court house in Stuttgart under the number HRB 15,350.

Unscheduled write-downs, largely of investments in associated companies and of other long-term receivables totaling DM 83 million (1991: DM 115 million) had to be made.

Investments in non-current assets should have been written up by DM 7 million in accordance with the value appreciation doctrine (reinstatement of original values, Section 280 of the Commercial Code). However, such a write-up was omitted for tax reasons.

4 Leased Equipment

The increase in lease equipment – almost exclusively vehicles – by DM 1,685 million to DM 9,777 million, pertains largely to Mercedes-Benz Credit Corporation, Norwalk, U.S.A., and to Mercedes-Benz Leasing GmbH, Stuttgart. About 85% of the balance sheet total pertains to these two companies. Special tax-deductible depreciation allowances amount to DM 3 million (1991: DM 10 million).

5 Inventories

In millions of DM	12/31/1992	12/31/1991
Raw materials and manufacturing supplies	3,342	3,041
Work in progress	8,836	8,160
Finished goods, parts and goods purchased for resale	9,694	8,557
Advance payments for suppliers	1,266	974
	23,138	20,732

Mercedes-Benz and Deutsche Aerospace account for the majority of consolidated inventories. The increase over last year is, with roughly DM 1,150 million, derived from the Mercedes-Benz corporate division, particularly from Mercedes-Benz AG and its foreign sales companies and with about DM 1,250 million from the DASA corporate division and DM 1,650 million as a result of the first-time, full consolidation of the Deutsche Aerospace Airbus group.

6 Advance Payments Received

Advance payments received amounting to DM 5,549 million (1991: DM 5,827 million) were almost exclusively for projects and long-term contracts at AEG, DASA AG, Dornier, Eurocopter and MTU; they were deducted from inventories.

7 Receivables from Sales Financing

This caption pertains to accounts receivable from customers totaling DM 6,166 million (1991: DM 4,255 million), of which DM 2,804 million (1991: DM 2,699 million) mature after more than one year

8 Receivables
9 Other Assets

In millions of DM	12/31/1992	12/31/1991
Receivables from sales of goods and services of which maturing after more than one year DM 491 (1991: 225) million	11,916	10,625
Receivables from affiliated companies of which maturing after more than one year DM 59 (1991: 11) million	1,178	335
Receivables from related companies of which maturing after more than one year DM 58 (1991: 596) million	1,677	1,410
Total receivables of which maturing after more than one year DM 608 (1991: 832) million	14,771	12,370
Other assets of which maturing after more than one year DM 394 (1991: 1,377) million	3,503	5,528

Approx. DM 0.4 billion (1991: DM 0.3 billion) of the receivables from related companies pertain mainly to fixed-interest debt instruments and securities.

Other assets include investments of liquid funds in debt instruments not traded on stock exchanges. They amount to DM 437 million (1991: DM 2,564 million).

10 Securities

In millions of DM	12/31/1992	12/31/1991
Treasury stock	33	16
Other securities	6,056	5,709
	6,089	5,725

During the year under review, we purchased 225,511 common shares (par value DM 11.3 million = 0.48% of the total outstanding share capital) at an average price of DM 709 a share.

In November of 1992, we sold 145,990 shares to our employees (par value DM 7.3 million = 0.31% of the total outstanding share capital) at a preferential price of DM 469 for each share (in the event that one share was purchased) or DM 520 for each share (in the event that two shares were purchased).

We owned 122,287 common shares on the balance sheet date (par value DM 6.1 million = 0.26% of the total outstanding share capital).

Other securities pertain mainly to fixed interest securities.

Within "current assets" there would have been a revaluation of DM 26 million necessary under the revaluation obligation. This did not take place due to tax law.

11 Cash

Cash amounting to DM 2,968 million (1991: DM 2,010 million) consists of deposits in financial institutions, cash on hand, deposits at the Bundesbank (German Federal Bank), in post office accounts, and checks on hand.

Liquid funds, shown among various balance sheet captions, total DM 9.8 billion (1991: DM 10.6 billion).

12 Prepaid Expenses and Deferred Taxes

Deferred taxes on income-affecting elimination entries amount to DM 1,329 million (1991: DM 1,596 million).

Deferred taxes — a debit balance overall — as shown in the consolidated individual balance sheets are not included.

13 Stockholders' Equity

The changes in stockholders' equity are as follows:

	In millions of DM
Balance at 12/31/1991	19,448
Dividends paid by Daimler-Benz AG for 1991	(603)
Amount transferred from 1992 net income to retained earnings	816
Write-off of goodwill	(173)
Unappropriated profit of Daimler-Benz AG 1992	604
Change in stock ownership of minority shareholders	14
Difference from currency translation	(180)
Other changes	(207)
Balance at 12/31/1992	19,719

14 Capital Stock and Paid-in Capital

Capital stock and paid-in capital pertain to Daimler-Benz AG.

15 Retained-Earnings

Retained earnings comprise retained earnings allocated under statute of DM 160 million, retained earnings allocated for treasury stock of DM 33 million, and other retained earnings of Daimler-Benz AG of DM 8,534 million. Also reflected here are the company's share in the retained earnings and results of operations of consolidated subsidiaries, insofar as they have been earned by them since their affiliation with the group. Additionally, this caption takes into account the cumulative results from the elimination of intercompany earnings and from debt consolidation, as well as the difference arising from currency translations.

16 Minority Interests

The stock ownership of outside third parties in the subsidiaries included in consolidation pertain mostly to Daimler-Benz Luft- und Raumfahrt Holding AG, AEG, Mercedes-Benz of South Africa, Dornier, MTU and Eurocopter.

17 Provisions for Old-Age Pensions and Similiar Obligations

Pension provisions rose to Dm 12,217 million (1991: DM 10,790 million). DM 499 million of the DM 1,427 increase pertains to the change in the circle of consolidated companies.

When the assets of the provident funds are added to the provisions for old-age pensions, the company's pension obligations are fully covered.

18 Other Provisions

In millions of DM	12/31/1992	12/31/1991
Provisions for taxes	1,655	1,248
Difference from capital consolidation with reserve characteristics	21	44
Other provisions	20,802	15,947
	22,478	17,239

The provisions for taxes include DM 764 million (1991: 645 million) which pertain, to a large extent, to Daimler-Benz AG for open years awaiting final assessment.

The difference amount with reserve characteristics resulting from the capital consolidation originates from the first-time consolidation of one subsidiary; this amount will be available to offset potential extraordinary expenses during the start-up years.

Apart from existing warranty obligations, other provisions take into account, above all, obligations in the personnel and social area, risks for losses inherent in pending business transactions, and risks arising from contractual liabilities and pending litigation.

Additional provisions exist for expenditures which are based on approved change-over, alteration and some development projects, for possible additional costs in connection with completed contracts, and for maintenance which had been planned for the year under review but had to be deferred until the following year. In addition, provisions have been recorded for future obligations in connection with restructuring activities.

The DM 5,239 million increase pertains with DM 4,028 to the Deutsche Aerospace Airbus Group which was consolidated via DASA.

24 Other Operating Income

The income amount included in this caption for the reversal of provisions total DM 1,519 million. (1991: DM 893 million). Additional income is derived from exchange profits in connection with ongoing purchase and payment transactions, mostly earned abroad; exchange losses against such income are shown under other operating expenses. In addition, income is derived from costs charged to third parties, from security sales, and from rentals and leases.

Altogether, DM 2,226 million of other operating income is attributable to prior years.

25 Cost of Materials

In millions of DM	1992	1991
Cost of raw materials and supplies as well as of goods purchased for resale	43,951	44,340
Cost of services purchased	5,133	5,116
	49,084	49,456

In relation to a total output of DM 100,879 million (1991: DM 98,566 million), the ratio of cost of materials amounted to 49% (1991: 50%).

26 Personnel Expenses/Employment

In millions of DM	1992	1991
Wages and salaries	26,138	23,813
Social levies and expenses for old-age pensions	5,865	5,559
	32,003	29,372
Employment (weighted annual average)	Number	Number
Wage earners	216,023	221,216
Salaried employees	150,650	144,101
Trainees/apprentices	15,960	16,194
	382,633	381,511

The 1992 employment figures for the first time include the employees of Deutsche Aerospace Airbus GmbH and its subsidiary.

In addition, 12,072 people are employed in the joint venture company Eurocopter.

17.2 The best case study of all is probably the real-world situation. This allows you to:

(a) choose situations which are topical,
(b) choose countries about which you are both knowledgeable and interested,
(c) see just how difficult interpretation of financial statements in a pan-European context can be.

Therefore:

1. Obtain the published financial statements, in languages you read well, of two companies or groups of companies, from different European countries, for the same year or, if possible, series of years.
2. Analyze them in detail and produce a report on their relative strengths and weaknesses. Your analysis will involve, among other things:

    (a) reading the information in full, several times,
    (b) carefully considering any language issues,
    (c) noting inconsistent accounting policies and different accounting treatments, and attempting to adjust for them to give greater comparability,
    (d) preparing ratios, as consistently as possible,
    (e) producing a report, which includes proper recognition of the weaknesses in the available information.

Look out carefully for deliberately 'creative' accounting!

APPENDIX

The EC Fourth Directive on company law

Article 1

1. The coordination measures prescribed by this Directive shall apply to the laws, regulations and administrative provisions of the Member States relating to the following types of companies:

— in Germany:
die Aktiengesellschaft, die Kommanditgesellschaft auf Aktien, die Gesellschaft mit beschränkter Haftung;
— in Belgium:
la société anonyme/de naamloze vennootschap, la société en commandite par actions/de commanditaire vennootschap op aandelen, la société de personnes à responsabilité limiteé/de personenvennootschap met beperkte aansprakelijkheid;
— in Denmark:
aktieselskaber, kommanditaktieselskaber, anpartsselskaber;
— in France:
la société anonyme, la société en commandite par actions, la société à responsabilité limitée;
— in Greece:
η ανώνυμη εταιρία, η εταιρία περιορισμένης ευθύνης, η ετερόρρυθμη κατά μετοχές εταιρία;
— in Ireland:
public companies limited by shares or by guarantee, private companies limited by shares or by guarantee;
— in Italy:
la società per azioni, la società in accomandita per azioni, la società a responsabilità limitata;
— in Luxembourg:
la société anonyme, la société en commandite par actions, la société à responsabilité limitée;
— in the Netherlands:
de naamloze vennootschap, de besloten vennootschap met beperkte aansprakelijkheid;

— in the United Kingdom:
public companies limited by shares or by guarantee, private companies limited by shares or by guarantee.

2. Pending subsequent coordination, the Member States need not apply the provisions of this Directive to banks and other financial institutions or to insurance companies.

SECTION 1

General provisions

Article 2

1. The annual accounts shall comprise the balance sheet, the profit and loss account and the notes on the accounts. These documents shall constitute a composite whole.
2. They shall be drawn up clearly and in accordance with the provisions of this Directive.
3. The annual accounts shall give a true and fair view of the company's assets, liabilities, financial position and profit or loss.
4. Where the application of the provisions of this Directive would not be sufficient to give a true and fair view within the meaning of paragraph 3, additional information must be given.
5. Where in exceptional cases the application of a provision of this Directive is incompatible with the obligation laid down in paragraph 3, that provision must be departed from in order to give a true and fair view within the meaning of paragraph 3. Any such departure must be disclosed in the notes on the accounts together with an explanation of the reasons for it and a statement of its effect on the assets; liabilities, financial position and profit or loss. The Member States may define the exceptional cases in question and lay down the relevant special rules.
6. The Member States may authorize or require the disclosure in the annual accounts of other information as well as that which must be disclosed in accordance with this Directive.

SECTION 2

General provisions concerning the balance sheet and the profit and loss account

Article 3

The layout of the balance sheet and of the profit and loss account, particularly as regards the form adopted for their presentation, may not be changed from one financial year to the next. Departures from this principle shall be permitted in exceptional cases. Any such departure must be disclosed in the notes on the accounts together with an explanation of the reasons therefor.

Article 4

1. In the balance sheet and in the profit and loss account the items prescribed in Articles 9, 10 and 23 to 26 must be shown separately in the order indicated. A more detailed subdivision of the items shall be authorized provided that the layouts are complied with. New items may be added provided that their contents are not covered by any of the items prescribed by the layouts. Such subdivision or new items may be required by the Member States.
2. The layout, nomenclature and terminology of items in the balance sheet and profit and loss account that are preceded by Arabic numerals must be adapted where the special nature of an undertaking so requires. Such adaptations may be required by the Member States of undertakings forming part of a particular economic sector.
3. The balance sheet and profit and loss account items that are preceded by Arabic numerals may be combined where:
(a) they are immaterial in amount for the purposes of Article 2 (3); or
(b) such combination makes for greater clarity, provided that the items so combined are dealt with separately in the notes on the accounts. Such combination may be required by the Member States.
4. In respect of each balance sheet and profit and loss account item the figure relating to the corresponding item for the preceding financial year must be shown. The Member States may provide that, where these figures are not comparable, the figure for the preceding financial year must be adjusted. In any case, non-comparability and any adjustment of the figures must be disclosed in the notes on the accounts, with relevant comments.
5. Save where there is a corresponding item for the preceding financial year within the meaning of paragraph 4, a balance sheet or profit and loss account item for which there is no amount shall not be shown.

Article 5

1. By way of derogation from Article 4 (1) and (2), the Member States may prescribe special layouts for the annual accounts of investment companies and of financial holding companies provided that these layouts give a view of these companies equivalent to that provided for in Article 2 (3).
2. For the purposes of this Directive 'investment companies' shall mean only:
(a) those companies the sole object of which is to invest their funds in various securities, real property and other assets with the sole aim of spreading investment risks and giving their shareholders the benefit of the results of the management of their assets;
(b) those companies associated with investment companies with fixed capital if the sole object of the companies so associated is to acquire fully paid shares issued

by those investment companies without prejudice to the provisions of Article 20 (1) (h) of Directive 77/91/EEC.

3. For the purposes of this Directive 'financial holding companies' shall mean only those companies the sole object of which is to acquire holdings in other undertakings and to manage such holdings and turn them to profit without involving themselves directly or indirectly in the management of those undertakings, the aforegoing without prejudice to their rights as shareholders. The limitations imposed on the activities of these companies must be such that compliance with them can be supervised by an administrative or judicial authority.

Article 6

The Member States may authorize or require adaptation of the layout of the balance sheet and profit and loss account in order to include the appropriation of profit or the treatment of loss.

Article 7

Any set-off between asset and liability items, or between income and expenditure items, shall be prohibited.

SECTION 3

Layout of the balance sheet

Article 8

For the presentation of the balance sheet, the Member States shall prescribe one or both of the layouts prescribed by Articles 9 and 10. If a Member State prescribes both, it may allow companies to choose between them.

Article 9

Assets

A. **Subscribed capital unpaid**

of which there has been called

(unless national law provides that called-up capital be shown under 'Liabilities'. In that case the part of the capital called but not yet paid must appear as an asset either under A or under D (II) (5)).

B. **Formation expenses**
as defined by national law, and in so far as national law permits their being shown as an asset. National law may also provide for formation expenses to be shown as the first item under 'Intangible assets'.

C. **Fixed assets**

  I *Intangible assets*
  1. Costs of research and development, in so far as national law permits their being shown as assets.
  2. Concessions, patents, licences, trade marks and similar rights and assets, if they were:
     (a) acquired for valuable consideration and need not be shown under C (I) (3); or
     (b) created by the undertaking itself in so far as national law permits their being shown as assets.
  3. Goodwill, to the extent that it was acquired for valuable consideration.
  4. Payments on account.

  II *Tangible assets*
  1. Land and buildings.
  2. Plant and machinery.
  3. Other fixtures and fittings, tools and equipment.
  4. Payments on account and tangible assets in course of construction.

  III. *Financial assets*
  1. Shares in affiliated undertakings.
  2. Loans to affiliated undertakings.
  3. Participating interests.
  4. Loans to undertakings with which the company is linked by virtue of participating interests.
  5. Investments held as fixed assets.
  6. Other loans.
  7. Own shares (with an indication of their nominal value or, in the absence of a nominal value, their accounting par value) to the extent that national law permits their being shown in the balance sheet.

D. **Current assets**

  I. *Stocks*
  1. Raw materials and consumables.
  2. Work in progress.
  3. Finished goods and goods for resale.
  4. Payments on account.

II. *Debtors*
(Amounts becoming due and payable after more than one year must be shown separately for each item.)
1. Trade debtors.
2. Amounts owed by affiliated undertakings.
3. Amounts owed by undertakings with which the company is linked by virtue of participating interests.
4. Other debtors.
5. Subscribed capital called but not paid (unless national law provides that called-up capital be shown as an asset under A).
6. Prepayments and accrued income (unless national law provides for such items to be shown as an asset under E).

III. *Investments*
1. Shares in affiliated undertakings.
2. Own shares (with an indication of their nominal value or, in the absence of a nominal value, their accounting par value) to the extent that national law permits their being shown in the balance sheet.
3. Other investments.

IV. *Cash at bank and in hand*

E. **Prepayments and accrued income**
(unless national law provides for such items to be shown as an asset under D (II) (6)).

F. **Loss for the financial year**
(unless national law provides for it to be shown under A (VI) under 'Liabilities').

Liabilities

A. **Capital and reserves**

I. *Subscribed capital*
(unless national law provides for called-up capital to be shown under this item. In that case, the amounts of subscribed capital and paid-up capital must be shown separately).

II. *Share premium account*

III. *Revaluation reserve*

IV. *Reserves*
1. Legal reserve, in so far as national law requires such a reserve.
2. Reserve for own shares, in so far as national law requires such a reserve, without prejudice to Article 22 (1) (b) of Directive 77/91/EEC.

3. Reserves provided for by the articles of association.
4. Other reserves.

V. *Profit or loss brought forward*

VI. *Profit or loss for the financial year*
(unless national law requires that this item be shown under F under 'Assets' or under E under 'Liabilities').

B. **Provisions for liabilities and charges**
1. Provisions for pensions and similar obligations.
2. Provisions for taxation.
3. Other provisions.

C. **Creditors**
(Amounts becoming due and payable within one year and amounts becoming due and payable after more than one year must be shown separately for each item and for the aggregate of these items.)
1. Debenture loans, showing convertible loans separately.
2. Amounts owed to credit institutions.
3. Payments received on account of orders in so far as they are not shown separately as deductions from stocks.
4. Trade creditors.
5. Bills of exchange payable.
6. Amounts owed to affiliated undertakings.
7. Amounts owed to undertakings with which the company is linked by virtue of participating interests.
8. Other creditors including tax and social security.
9. Accruals and deferred income (unless national law provides for such items to be shown under D under 'Liabilities').

D. **Accruals and deferred income**
(unless national law provides for such items to be shown under C (9) under 'Liabilities').

E. **Profit for the financial year**

(unless national by provides for it to be shown under A (VI) under 'Liabilities').

Article 10

A. **Subscribed capital unpaid**

of which there has been called

(unless national law provides that called-up capital be shown under L. In that case, the part of the capital called but not yet paid must appear either under A or under D (II) (5)).

B. **Formation expenses**

as defined by national law, and in so far as national law permits their being shown as an asset. National law may also provide for formation expenses to be shown as the first item under 'Intangible assets'.

C. **Fixed assets**

  I. *Intangible assets*
   1. Costs of research and development, in so far as national law permits their being shown as assets.
   2. Concessions, patents, licences, trade marks and similar rights and assets, if they were:
      (a) acquired for valuable consideration and need not be shown under C (I) (3); or
      (b) created by the undertaking itself, in so far as national law permits their being shown as assets.
   3. Goodwill, to the extent that it was acquired for valuable consideration.
   4. Payments on account.

  II. *Tangible assets*
   1. Land and buildings.
   2. Plant and machinery.
   3. Other fixtures and fittings, tools and equipment.
   4. Payments on account and tangible assets in course of construction.

  III. *Financial assets*
   1. Shares in affiliated undertakings.
   2. Loans to affiliated undertakings.
   3. Participating interests.
   4. Loans to undertakings with which the company is linked by virtue of participating interests.
   5. Investments held as fixed assets.
   6. Other loans.
   7. Own shares (with an indication of their nominal value or, in the absence of a nominal value, their accounting par value) to the extent that national law permits their being shown in the balance sheet.

D. **Current assets**

  I. *Stocks*
   1. Raw materials and consumables.
   2. Work in progress.

3. Finished goods and goods for resale.
4. Payments on account.

II. *Debtors*

(Amounts becoming due and payable after more than one year must be shown separately for each item.)
1. Trade debtors.
2. Amounts owed by affiliated undertakings.
3. Amounts owed by undertakings with which the company is linked by virtue of participating interests.
4. Other debtors.
5. Subscribed capital called but not paid (unless national law provides that called-up capital be shown under A).
6. Prepayments and accrued income (unless national law provides that such items be shown under E).

III. *Investments*
1. Shares in affiliated undertakings.
2. Own shares (with an indication of their nominal value or, in the absence of a nominal value, their accounting par value) to the extent that national law permits their being shown in the balance sheet.
3. Other investments.

IV. *Cash at bank and in hand*

E. **Prepayments and accrued income**
(unless national law provides for such items to be shown under D (II) (6)).

F. **Creditors: amounts becoming due and payable within one year**
1. Debenture loans, showing convertible loans separately.
2. Amounts owed to credit institutions.
3. Payments received on account of orders in so far as they are not shown separately as deductions from stocks.
4. Trade creditors.
5. Bills of exchange payable.
6. Amounts owed to affiliated undertakings.
7. Amounts owed to undertakings with which the company is linked by virtue of participating interests.
8. Other creditors including tax and social security.
9. Accrual and deferred income (unless national law provides for such items to be shown under K).

G. **Net current assets/liabilities**
(taking into account prepayments and accrued income when shown under E and accruals and deferred income when shown under K).

H. **Total assets less current liabilities**

I. **Creditors: amounts becoming due and payable after more than one year**
   1. Debenture loans, showing convertible loans separately.
   2. Amounts owed to credit institutions.
   3. Payments received on account of orders in so far as they are not shown separately as deductions from stocks.
   4. Trade creditors.
   5. Bills of exchange payable.
   6. Amounts owed to affiliated undertakings.
   7. Amounts owed to undertakings with which the company is linked by virtue of participating interests.
   8. Other creditors including tax and social security.
   9. Accruals and deferred income (unless national law provides for such items to be shown under K).

J. **Provisions for liabilities and charges**
   1. Provisions for pensions and similar obligations.
   2. Provisions for taxation.
   3. Other provisions.

K. **Accruals and deferred income**
   (unless national law provides for such items to be shown under F(9) or I(9) or both).

L. **Capital and reserves**

   I. *Subscribed capital*
      (unless national law provides for called-up capital to be shown under this item. In that case, the amounts of subscribed capital and paid-up capital must be shown separately).

   II. *Share premium account*

   III. *Revaluation reserve*

   IV. *Reserves*
      1. Legal reserve, in so far as national law requires such a reserve.
      2. Reserve for own shares, in so far as national law requires such a reserve, without prejudice to Article 22 (1) (b) of Directive 77/91/EEC.
      3. Reserves provided for by the articles of association.
      4. Other reserves.

   V. *Profit or loss brought forward*

   VI. *Profit or loss for the financial year*

Article 11

The Member States may permit companies which on their balance sheet dates do not exceed the limits of two of the thee following criteria:
— balance sheet total: 1 000 000 EUA,
— net turnover: 2 000 000 EUA,
— average number of employees during the financial year: 50
to draw up abridged balance sheets showing only those items preceded by letters and roman numerals in Articles 9 and 10, disclosing separately the information required in brackets in D (II) under 'Assets' and C under 'Liabilities' in Article 9 and in D (II) in Article 10, but in total for each.

Article 12

1. Where on its balance sheet date, a company exceeds or ceases to exceed the limits of two of the three criteria indicated in Article 11, that fact shall affect the application of the derogation provided for in that Article only if it occurs in two consecutive financial years.
2. For the purposes of translation into national currencies, the amounts in European units of account specified in Article 11 may be increased by not more than 10%.
3. The balance sheet total referred to in Article 11 shall consist of the assets in A to E under 'Assets' in the layout prescribed in Article 9 or those in A to E in the layout prescribed in Article 10.

Article 13

1. Where an asset or liability relates to more than one layout item, its relationship to other items must be disclosed either under the item where it appears or in the notes on the accounts, if such disclosure is essential to the comprehension of the annual accounts.
2. Own shares and shares in affiliated undertakings may be shown only under the items prescribed for that purpose.

Article 14

All commitments by way of guarantee of any kind must, if there is no obligation to show them as liabilities, be clearly set out at the foot of the balance sheet or in the notes on the accounts, and a distinction made between the various types of guarantee which national law recognizes; specific disclosure must be made of any valuable security which has been provided. Commitments of this kind existing in respect of affiliated undertakings must be shown separately.

SECTION 4

Special provisions relating to certain balance sheet items

Article 15

1. Whether particular assets are to be shown as fixed assets or current assets shall depend upon the purpose for which they are intended.
2. Fixed assets shall comprise those assets which are intended for use on a continuing basis for the purposes of the undertaking's activities.
3. (a) Movements in the various fixed asset items shall be shown in the balance sheet or in the notes on the accounts. To this end there shall be shown separately, starting with the purchase price or production cost, for each fixed asset item, on the one hand, the additions, disposals and transfers during the financial year and, on the other, the cumulative value adjustments at the balance sheet date and the rectifications made during the financial year to the value adjustments of previous financial years. Value adjustments shall be shown either in the balance sheet, as clear deductions from the relevant items, or in the notes on the accounts.
   (b) If, when annual accounts are drawn up in accordance with this Directive for the first time, the purchase price or production cost of a fixed asset cannot be determined without undue expense or delay, the residual value at the beginning of the financial year may be treated as the purchase price or production cost. Any application of this provision must be disclosed in the notes on the accounts.
   (c) Where Article 33 is applied, the movements in the various fixed asset items referred to in subparagraph (a) of this paragraph shall be shown starting with the purchase price or production cost resulting from revaluation.
4. Paragraph 3 (a) and (b) shall apply to the presentation of 'Formation expenses'.

Article 16

Rights to immovables and other similar rights as defined by national law must be shown under 'Land and buildings'.

Article 17

For the purposes of this Directive, 'participating interest' shall mean rights in the capital of other undertakings, whether or not represented by certificates, which, by creating a durable link with those undertakings, are intended to contribute to the company's activities. The holding of part of the capital of another company shall be presumed to constitute a participating interest where it exceeds a percentage fixed by the Member States which may not exceed 20%.

Article 18

Expenditure incurred during the financial year but relating to a subsequent financial year, together with any income which, though relating to the financial year in question, is not due until after its expiry must be shown under 'Prepayments and accrued income'. The Member States may, however, provide that such income shall be included in 'Debtors'. Where such income is material, it must be disclosed in the notes on the accounts.

Article 19

Value adjustments shall comprise all adjustments intended to take account of reductions in the values of individual assets established at the balance sheet date whether that reduction is final or not.

Article 20

1. Provisions for liabilities and charges are intended to cover losses or debts the nature of which is clearly defined and which at the date of the balance sheet are either likely to be incurred, or certain to be incurred but uncertain as to amount or as to the date on which they will arise.
2. The Member States may also authorize the creation of provisions intended to cover charges which have their origin in the financial year under review or in a previous financial year, the nature of which is clearly defined and which at the date of the balance sheet are either likely to be incurred, or certain to be incurred but uncertain as to amount or as to the date on which they will arise.
3. Provisions for liabilities and charges may not be used to adjust the values of assets.

Article 21

Income receivable before the balance sheet date but relating to a subsequent financial year, together with any charges which, though relating to the financial year in question, will be paid only in the course of a subsequent financial year, must be shown under 'Accruals and deferred income'. The Member States may, however, provide that such charges shall be included in 'Creditors'. Where such charges are material, they must be disclosed in the notes on the accounts.

SECTION 5

Layout of the profit and loss account

Article 22

For the presentation of the profit and loss account, the Member States shall prescribe one or more of the layouts provided for in Articles 23 to 26. If a Member State prescribes more than one layout, it may allow companies to choose from among them.

Article 23

1. Net turnover.
2. Variation in stocks of finished goods and in work in progress.
3. Work performed by the undertaking for its own purposes and capitalized.
4. Other operating income.
5. (a) Raw materials and consumables.
   (b) Other external charges.
6. Staff costs:
   (a) wages and salaries;
   (b) social security costs with a separate indication of those relating to pensions.
7. (a) Value adjustments in respect of formation expenses and of tangible and intangible fixed assets.
   (b) Value adjustments in respect of current assets, to the extent that they exceed the amount of value adjustments which are normal in the undertaking concerned.
8. Other operating charges.
9. Income from participating interests, with a separate indication of that derived from affiliated undertakings.
10. Income from other investments and loans forming part of the fixed assets, with a separate indication of that derived from affiliated undertakings.
11. Other interest receivable and similar income, with a separate indication of that derived from affiliated undertakings.
12. Value adjustments in respect of financial assets and of investments held as current assets.
13. Interest payable and similar charges, with a separate indication of those concerning affiliated undertakings.
14. Tax on profit or loss on ordinary activities.
15. Profit or loss on ordinary activities after taxation.
16. Extraordinary income.
17. Extraordinary charges.
18. Extraordinary profit or loss.
19. Tax on extraordinary profit or loss.
20. Other taxes not shown under the above items.
21. Profit or loss for the financial year.

Article 24

A. **Charges**
   1. Reduction in stocks of finished goods and in work in progress:

2. (a) raw materials and consumables;
   (b) other external charges.
3. Staff costs:
   (a) wages and salaries;
   (b) social security costs with a separate indication of those relating to pensions.
4. (a) Value adjustments in respect of formation expenses and of tangible and intangible fixed assets.
   (b) Value adjustments in respect of current assets, to the extent that they exceed the amount of value adjustments which are normal in the undertaking concerned.
5. Other operating charges.
6. Value adjustments in respect of financial assets and of investments held as current assets.
7. Interest payable and similar charges, with a separate indication of those concerning affiliated undertakings.
8. Tax on profit or loss on ordinary activities.
9. Profit or loss on ordinary activities after taxation.
10. Extraordinary charges.
11. Tax on extraordinary profit or loss.
12. Other taxes not shown under the above items.
13. Profit or loss for the financial year.

B. **Income**
1. Net turnover.
2. Increase in stocks of finished goods and in work in progress.
3. Work performed by the undertaking for its own purposes and capitalized.
4. Other operating income.
5. Income from participating interests, with a separate indication of that derived from affiliated undertakings.
6. Income from other investments and loans forming part of the fixed assets, with a separate indication of that derived from affiliated undertakings.
7. Other interest receivable and similar income, with a separate indication of that derived from affiliated undertakings.
8. Profit or loss on ordinary activities after taxation.
9. Extraordinary income.
10. Profit or loss for the financial year.

Article 25

1. Net turnover.
2. Cost of sales (including value adjustments).
3. Gross profit or loss.
4. Distribution costs (including value adjustments).

5. Administrative expenses (including value adjustments).
6. Other operating income.
7. Income from participating interests, with a separate indication of that derived from affiliated undertakings.
8. Income from other investments and loans forming part of the fixed assets, with a separate indiction of that derived from affiliated undertakings.
9. Other interest receivable and similar income, with a separate indication of that derived from affiliated undertakings.
10. Value adjustments in respect of financial assets and of investments held as current assets.
11. Interest payable and similar charges, with a separate indication of those concerning affiliated undertakings.
12. Tax on profit or loss on ordinary activities.
13. Profit or loss on ordinary activities after taxation.
14. Extraordinary income.
15. Extraordinary charges.
16. Extraordinary profit or loss.
17. Tax on extraordinary profit or loss.
18. Other taxes not shown under the above items.
19. Profit or loss for the financial year.

Article 26

A. **Charges**
1. Cost of sales (including value adjustments).
2. Distribution costs (including value adjustments).
3. Administrative expenses (including value adjustments).
4. Value adjustments in respect of financial assets and of investments held as current assets.
5. Interest payable and similar charges, with a separate indication of those concerning affiliated undertakings.
6. Tax on profit or loss on ordinary activities.
7. Profit or loss on ordinary activities after taxation.
8. Extraordinary charges.
9. Tax on extraordinary profit or loss.
10. Other taxes not shown under the above items.
11. Profit or loss for the financial year.

B. **Income**
1. Net turnover.
2. Other operating income.
3. Income from participating interests, with a separate indication of that derived from affiliated undertakings.

4. Income from other investments and loans forming part of the fixed assets, with a separate indication of that derived from affiliated undertakings.
5. Other interest receivable and similar income, with a separate indication of that derived from affiliated undertakings.
6. Profit or loss on ordinary activities after taxation.
7. Extraordinary income.
8. Profit or loss for the financial year.

Article 27

The Member States may permit companies which on their balance sheet dates do not exceed the limits of two of the three following criteria:
— balance sheet total: 4 million EUA,
— net turnover: 8 million EUA,
— average number of employees during the financial year: 250
to adopt layouts different from those prescribed in Articles 23 to 26 within the following limits:
(a) in Article 23: 1 to 5 inclusive may be combined under one item called 'Gross profit or loss';
(b) in Article 24: A (1), A (2) and B (1) to B (4) inclusive may be combined under one item called 'Gross profit or loss';
(c) in Article 25: (1), (2), (3) and (6) may be combined under one item called 'Gross profit or loss';
(d) in Article 26: A (1), B (1) and B (2) may be combined under one item called 'Gross profit or loss'.
Article 12 shall apply.

SECTION 6

Special provisions relating to certain items in the profit and loss account

Article 28

The net turnover shall comprise the amounts derived from the sale of products and the provision of services falling within the company's ordinary activities, after deduction of sales rebates and of value added tax and other taxes directly linked to the turnover.

Article 29

1. Income and charges that arise otherwise than in the course of the company's ordinary activities must be shown under 'Extraordinary income and extraordinary charges'.

2. Unless the income and charges referred to in paragraph 1 are immaterial for the assessment of the results, explanations of their amount and nature must be given in the notes on the accounts. The same shall apply to income and charges relating to another financial year.

Article 30

The Member States may permit taxes on the profit or loss on ordinary activities and taxes on the extraordinary profit or loss to be shown in total as one item in the profit and loss account before 'Other taxes not shown under the above items'. In that case, 'Profit or loss on ordinary activities after taxation' shall be omitted from the layouts prescribed in Articles 23 to 26.

Where this derogation is applied, companies must disclose in the notes on the accounts the extent to which the taxes on the profit or loss affect the profit or loss on ordinary activities and the 'Extraordinary profit or loss'.

SECTION 7

Valuation rules

Article 31

1. The Member States shall ensure that the items shown in the annual accounts are valued in accordance with the following general principles:
(a) the company must be presumed to be carrying on its business as a going concern;
(b) the methods of valuation must be applied consistently from one financial year to another;
(c) valuation must be made on a prudent basis, and in particular:
   (aa) only profits made at the balance sheet date may be included,
   (bb) account must be taken of all foreseeable liabilities and potential losses arising in the course of the financial year concerned or of a previous one, even if such liabilities or losses become apparent only between the date of the balance sheet and the date on which it is drawn up,
   (cc) account must be taken of all depreciation, whether the result of the financial year is a loss or a profit;
(d) account must be taken of income and charges relating to the financial year, irrespective of the date of receipt or payment of such income or charges;
(e) the components of asset and liability items must be valued separately;
(f) the opening balance sheet for each financial year must correspond to the closing balance sheet for the preceding financial year.
2. Departures from these general principles shall be permitted in exceptional cases. Any such departures must be disclosed in the notes on the accounts and the reasons for them given together with an assessment of their effect on the assets, liabilities, financial position and profit or loss.

Article 32

The items shown in the annual accounts shall be valued in accordance with Articles 34 to 42, which are based on the principle of purchase price or production cost.

Article 33

1. The Member States may declare to the Commission that they reserve the power, by way of derogation from Article 32 and pending subsequent coordination, to permit or require in respect of all companies or any classes of companies:
(a) valuation by the replacement value method for tangible fixed assets with limited useful economic lives and for stocks;
(b) valuation by methods other than that provided for in (a) which are designed to take account of inflation for the items shown in annual accounts, including capital and reserves;
(c) revaluation of tangible fixed assets and financial fixed assets.

Where national law provides for valuation methods as indicated in (a), (b) and (c), it must define their content and limits and the rules for their application. The application of any such method, the balance sheet and profit and loss account items concerned and the method by which the values shown are calculated shall be disclosed in the notes on the accounts.

2. (a) Where paragraph 1 is applied, the amount of the difference between valuation by the method used and valuation in accordance with the general rule laid down in Article 32 must be entered in the revaluation reserve under 'Liabilities'. The treatment of this item for taxation purposes must be explained either in the balance sheet or in the notes on the accounts.

   For purposes of the application of the last subparagraph of paragraph 1, companies shall, whenever the amount of the reserve has been changed in the course of the financial year, publish in the notes on the accounts *inter alia* a table showing:
   — the amount of the revaluation reserve at the beginning of the financial year,
   — the revaluation differences transferred to the revaluation reserve during the financial year,
   — the amounts capitalized or otherwise transferred from the revaluation reserve during the financial year, the nature of any such transfer being disclosed,
   — the amount of the revaluation reserve at the end of the financial year.

   (b) The revaluation reserve may be capitalized in whole or in part at any time.
   (c) The revaluation reserve must be reduced to the extent that the amounts transferred thereto are no longer necessary for the implementation of the valuation method used and the achievement of its purpose.

   The Member States may lay down rules governing the application of the revaluation reserve, provided that transfers to the profit and loss account from the revaluation reserve may be made only to the extent that the amounts transferred have been entered as charges in the profit and loss account or reflect increases in value which have been actually realized. These amounts must be disclosed separately in the profit and loss account. No part of the revaluation reserve may be distributed, either directly or indirectly, unless it represents gains actually realized.

(d) Save as provided under (b) and (c) the revaluation reserve may not be reduced.

3. Value adjustments shall be calculated each year on the basis of the value adopted for the financial year in question, save that by way of derogation from Articles 4 and 22, the Member States may permit or require that only the amount of the value adjustments arising as a result of the application of the general rule laid down in Article 32 be shown under the relevant items in the layouts prescribed in Articles 23 to 26 and that the difference arising as a result of the valuation method adopted under this Article be shown separately in the layouts. Furthermore, Articles 34 to 42 shall apply *mutatis mutandis*.

4. Where paragraph 1 is applied, the following must be disclosed, either in the balance sheet or in the notes on the accounts, separately for each balance sheet item as provided for in the layouts prescribed in Articles 9 and 10, except for stocks, either:

(a) the amount at the balance sheet date of the valuation made in accordance with the general rule laid down in Article 32 and the amount of the cumulative value adjustments; or

(b) the amount at the balance sheet date of the difference between the valuation made in accordance with this Article and that resulting from the application of Article 32 and, where appropriate, the cumulative amount of the additional value adjustments.

5. Without prejudice to Article 52 the Council shall, on a proposal from the Commission and within seven years of the notification of this Directive, examine and, where necessary, amend this Article in the light of economic and monetary trends in the Community.

Article 34

1. (a) Where national law authorizes the inclusion of formation expenses under 'Assets', they must be written off within a maximum period of five years.

   (b) In so far as formation expenses have not been completely written off, no distribution of profits shall take place unless the amount of the reserves available for distribution and profits brought forward is at least equal to that of the expenses not written off.

2. The amounts entered under 'Formation expenses' must be explained in the notes on the accounts.

Article 35

1. (a) Fixed assets must be valued at purchase price or production cost, without prejudice to (b) and (c) below.
   (b) The purchase price or production cost of fixed assets with limited useful economic lives must be reduced by value adjustments calculated to write off the value of such assets systematically over their useful economic lives.
   (c) (aa) Value adjustments may be made in respect of financial fixed assets, so that they are valued at the lower figure to be attributed to them at the balance sheet date.
      (bb) Value adjustments must be made in respect of fixed assets, whether their useful economic lives are limited or not, so that they are valued at the lower figure to be attributed to them at the balance sheet date if it is expected that the reduction in their value will be permanent.
      (cc) The value adjustments referred to in (aa) and (bb) must be charged to the profit and loss account and disclosed separately in the notes on the accounts if they have not been shown separately in the profit and loss account.
      (dd) Valuation at the lower of the values provided for in (aa) and (bb) may not be continued if the reasons for which the value adjustments were made have ceased to apply.
   (d) If fixed assets are the subject of exceptional value adjustments for taxation purposes alone the amount of the adjustments and the reasons for making them shall be indicated in the notes on the accounts.
2. The purchase price shall be calculated by adding to the price paid the expenses incidental thereto.
3. (a) The production cost shall be calculated by adding to the purchasing price of the raw materials and consumables the costs directly attributable to the product in question.
   (b) A reasonable proportion of the costs which are only indirectly attributable to the product in question may be added into the production costs to the extent that they relate to the period of production.
4. Interest on capital borrowed to finance the production of fixed assets may be included in the production costs to the extent that it relates to the period of production. In that event the inclusion of such interest under 'Assets' must be disclosed in the notes on the accounts.

Article 36

By way of derogation from Article 35 (1) (c) (cc) the Member States may allow investment companies within the meaning of Article 5 (2) to set off value adjustments to investments directly against 'Capital and reserves'. The amounts in question must be shown separately under 'Liabilities' in the balance sheet.

Article 37

1. Article 34 shall apply to costs of research and development. In exceptional cases however the Member States may permit derogations from Article 34 (1) (a). In that case they may also provide for derogations from Article 34 (1) (b). Such derogations and the reasons for them must be disclosed in the notes on the accounts.
2. Article 34 (1) (a) shall apply to goodwill. The Member States may, however, permit companies to write goodwill off systematically over a limited period exceeding five years provided that this period does not exceed the useful economic life of the asset and is disclosed in the notes on the accounts together with the supporting reasons therefor.

Article 38

Tangible fixed assets, raw materials and consumables which are constantly being replaced and the overall value of which is of secondary importance to the undertaking may be shown under 'Assets' at a fixed quantity and value, if the quantity, value and composition thereof do not vary materially.

Article 39

1. (a) Current assets must be valued at purchase price or production cost, without prejudice to (b) and (c) below.
   (b) Value adjustments shall be made in respect of current assets with a view to showing them at the lower market value or, in particular circumstances, another lower value to be attributed to them at the balance sheet date.
   (c) The Member States may permit exceptional value adjustments where, on the basis of a reasonable commercial assessment, these are necessary if the valuation of these items is not to be modified in the near future because of fluctuations in value. The amount of these value adjustments must be disclosed separately in the profit and loss account or in the notes on the accounts.
   (d) Valuation at the lower value provided for in (b) and (c) may not be continued if the reasons for which the value adjustments were made have ceased to apply.
   (e) If current assets are the subject of exceptional value adjustments for taxation purposes alone, the amount of the adjustments and the reasons for making them must be disclosed in the notes on the accounts.
2. The definitions of purchase price and of production cost given in Article 35 (2) and (3) shall apply. The Member States may also apply Article 35 (4). Distribution costs may not be included in production costs.

Article 40

1. The Member States may permit the purchase price or production cost of stocks of goods of the same category and all fungible items including investments to be calculated either on the basis of weighted average prices or by the 'first in, first out' (FIFO) method, the 'last in, first out' (LIFO) method, or some similar method.
2. Where the value shown in the balance sheet, following application of the methods of calculation specified in paragraph 1, differs materially, at the balance sheet date, from the value on the basis of the last known market value prior to the balance sheet date, the amount of that difference must be disclosed in total by category in the notes on the accounts.

Article 41

1. Where the amount repayable on account of any debt is greater than the amount received, the difference may be shown as an asset. It must be shown separately in the balance sheet or in the notes on the accounts.
2. The amount of this difference must be written off by a reasonable amount each year and completely written off no later than the time of repayment of the debt.

Article 42

Provisions for liabilities and charges may not exceed in amount the sums which are necessary.

The provisions shown in the balance sheet under 'Other provisions' must be disclosed in the notes on the accounts if they are material.

SECTION 8

Contents of the notes on the accounts

Article 43

1. In addition to the information required under other provisions of this Directive, the notes on the accounts must set out information in respect of the following matters at least:
   (1) the valuation methods applied to the various items in the annual accounts, and the methods employed in calculating the value adjustments. For items included in the annual accounts which are or were originally expressed in foreign currency, the bases of conversion used to express them in local currency must be disclosed;
   (2) the name and registered office of each of the undertakings in which the company, either itself or through a person acting in his own name but on the company's behalf, holds at least a percentage of the capital which the Member

States cannot fix at more than 20%, showing the proportion of the capital held, the amount of capital and reserves, and the profit or loss for the latest financial year of the undertaking concerned for which accounts have been adopted. This information may be omitted where for the purposes of Article 2 (3) it is of negligible importance only. The information concerning capital and reserves and the profit or loss may also be omitted where the undertaking concerned does not publish its balance sheet and less than 50% of its capital is held (directly or indirectly) by the company;

(3) the number and the nominal value or, in the absence of a nominal value, the accounting par value of the shares subscribed during the financial year within the limits of an authorized capital, without prejudice as far as the amount of this capital is concerned to Article 2 (1) (e) of Directive 68/151/EEC or to Article 2 (c) of Directive 77/91/EEC;

(4) where there is more than one class of shares, the number and the nominal value or, in the absence of a nominal value, the accounting par value for each class;

(5) the existence of any participation certificates, convertible debentures or similar securities or rights, with an indication of their number and the rights they confer;

(6) amounts owed by the company becoming due and payable after more than five years as well as the company's entire debts covered by valuable security furnished by the company with an indication of the nature and form of the security. This information must be disclosed separately for each creditors item, as provided for in the layouts prescribed in Articles 9 and 10;

(7) the total amount of any financial commitments that are not included in the balance sheet, in so far as this information is of assistance in assessing the financial position. Any commitments concerning pensions and affiliated undertakings must be disclosed separately;

(8) the net turnover within the meaning of Article 28, broken down by categories of activity and into geographical markets in so far as, taking account of the manner in which the sale of products and the provision of services falling within the company's ordinary activities are organized, these categories and markets differ substantially from one another;

(9) the average number of persons employed during the financial year, broken down by categories and, if they are not disclosed separately in the profit and loss account, the staff costs relating to the financial year, broken down as provided for in Article 23 (6);

(10) the extent to which the calculation of the profit or loss for the financial year has been affected by a valuation of the items which, by way of derogation from the principles enunciated in Articles 31 and 34 to 42, was made in the financial year in question or in an earlier financial year with a view to obtaining tax relief. Where the influence of such a valuation on future tax charges is material, details must be disclosed;

(11) the difference between the tax charged for the financial year and for earlier financial years and the amount of tax payable in respect of those years,

provided that this difference is material for purposes of future taxation. This amount may also be disclosed in the balance sheet as a cumulative amount under a separate item with an appropriate heading;
(12) the amount of the emoluments granted in respect of the financial year to the members of the administrative, managerial and supervisory bodies by reason of their responsibilities, and any commitments arising or entered into in respect of retirement pensions for former members of those bodies, with an indication of the total for each category;
(13) the amount of advances and credits granted to the members of the administrative, managerial and supervisory bodies, with indications of the interest rates, main conditions and any amounts repaid, as well as commitments entered into on their behalf by way of guarantees of any kind, with an indication of the total for each category.
2. Pending subsequent coordination, the Member States need not apply paragraph 1 (2) to financial holding companies within the meaning of Article 5 (3).

Article 44

The Member States may permit the companies referred to in Article 11 to draw up abridged notes on their accounts without the information required in Article 43 (1) (5) to (12). However, the notes must disclose the information specified in Article 43 (1) (6) in total for all the items concerned.

Article 12 shall apply.

Article 45

1. The Member States may allow the disclosures prescribed in Article 43 (1) (2):
(a) to take the form of a statement deposited in accordance with Article 3 (1) and (2) of Directive 68/151/EEC; this must be disclosed in the notes on the accounts;
(b) to be omitted when their nature is such that they would be seriously prejudicial to any of the undertakings to which Article 43 (1) (2) relates. The Member States may make such omissions subject to prior administrative or judicial authorization. Any such omission must be disclosed in the notes on the accounts.
2. Paragraph 1 (b) shall also apply to the information prescribed by Article 43 (1) (8).

The Member States may permit the companies referred to in Article 27 to omit the disclosures prescribed by Article 43 (1) (8). Article 12 shall apply.

SECTION 9

Contents of the annual report

Article 46

1. The annual report must include at least a fair review of the development of the company's business and of its position.
2. The report shall also give an indication of:
(a) any important events that have occurred since the end of the financial year;
(b) the company's likely future development;
(c) activities in the field of research and development;
(d) the information concerning acquisitions of own shares prescribed by Article 22 (2) of Directive 77/91/EEC.

SECTION 10

Publication

Article 47

1. The annual accounts, duly approved, and the annual report, together with the opinion submitted by the person responsible for auditing the accounts, shall be published as laid down by the laws of each Member State in accordance with Article 3 of Directive 68/151/EEC.

The laws of a Member State may, however, permit the annual report not to be published as stipulated above. In that case, it shall be made available to the public at the company's registered office in the Member State concerned. It must be possible to obtain a copy of all or part of any such report free of charge upon request.

2. By way of derogation from paragraph 1, the Member States may permit the companies referred to in Article 11 to publish:
(a) abridged balance sheets showing only those items preceded by letters and roman numerals in Articles 9 and 10, disclosing separately the information required in brackets in D (II) under 'Assets' and C under 'Liabilities' in Article 9 and in D (II) in Article 10, but in total for all the items concerned; and
(b) abridged notes on their accounts without the explanations required in Article 43 (1) (5) to (12) However, the notes must disclose the information specified in Article 43 (1) (6) in total for all the items concerned.

Article 12 shall apply.

In addition, the Member States may relieve such companies from the obligation to publish their profit and loss accounts and annual reports and the opinions of the persons responsible for auditing the accounts.

3. The Member States may permit the companies mentioned in Article 27 to publish:
(a) abridged balance sheets showing only those items preceded by letters and roman numerals in Articles 9 and 10 disclosing separately, either in the balance sheet or in the notes on the accounts:
  — C (I) (3), C (II) (1), (2), (3) and (4), C (III) (1), (2), (3), (4) and (7), D (II) (2), (3) and (6) and D (III) (1) and (2) under 'Assets' and C (1), (2), (6), (7) and (9) under 'Liabilities' in Article 9,
  — C (I) (3), C (II) (1), (2), (3) and (4), C (III) (1), (2), (3), (4) and (7), D (II) (2), (3) and (6), D (III) (1) and (2), F (1), (2), (6), (7) and (9) and (I) (1), (2), (6), (7) and (9) in Article 10,
  — the information required in brackets in D (II) under 'Assets' and C under 'Liabilities' in Article 9, in total for all the items concerned and separately for D (II) (2) and (3) under 'Assets' and C (1), (2), (6), (7) and (9) under 'Liabilities',
  — the information required in brackets in D (II) in Article 10, in total for all the items concerned, and separately for D (II) (2) and (3);
(b) abridged notes on their accounts without the information required in Article 43 (1) (5), (6), (8), (10) and (11). However, the notes on the accounts must give the information specified in Article 43 (1) (6) in total for all the items concerned.
This paragraph shall be without prejudice to paragraph 1 in so far as it relates to the profit and loss account, the annual report and the opinion of the person responsible for auditing the accounts.
Article 12 shall apply.

Article 48

Whenever the annual accounts and the annual report are published in full, they must be reproduced in the form and text on the basis of which the person responsible for auditing the accounts has drawn up his opinion. They must be accompanied by the full text of his report. If thy person responsible for auditing the accounts has made any qualifications or refused to report upon the accounts, that fact must be disclosed and the reasons given.

Article 49

If the annual accounts are not published in full, it must be indicated that the version published is abridged and reference must be made to the register in which the accounts have been filed in accordance with Article 47 (1). Where such filing has not yet been effected, the fact must be disclosed. The report issued by the person responsible for auditing the accounts may not accompany this publication, but it must be disclosed whether the report was issued with or without qualification, or was refused.

Article 50

The following must be published together with the annual accounts, and in like manner:
— the proposed appropriation of the profit or treatment of the loss,
— the appropriation of the profit or treatment of the loss,
where these items do not appear in the annual accounts.

SECTION 11

Auditing

Article 51

1. (a) Companies must have their annual accounts audited by one or more persons authorized by national law to audit accounts.
   (b) The person or persons responsible for auditing the accounts must also verify that the annual report is consistent with the annual accounts for the same financial year.
2. The Member States may relieve the companies referred to in Article 11 from the obligation imposed by paragraph 1.
   Article 12 shall apply.
3. Where the exemption provided for in paragraph 2 is granted the Member States shall introduce appropriate sanctions into their laws for cases in which the annual accounts or the annual reports of such companies are not drawn up in accordance with the requirements of this Directive.

SECTION 12

Final provisions

Article 52

1. A Contact Committee shall be set up under the auspices of the Commission. Its function shall be:
(a) to facilitate, without prejudice to the provisions of Articles 169 and 170 of the Treaty, harmonized application of this Directive through regular meetings dealing in particular with practical problems arising in connection with its application;
(b) to advise the Commission, if necessary, on additions or amendments to this Directive.
2. The Contact Committee shall be composed of representatives of the Member States and representatives of the Commission. The chairman shall be a representative of the Commission. The Commission shall provide the secretariat.

3. The Committee shall be convened by the chairman either on his own initiative or at the request of one of its members.

Article 53

1. For the purposes of this Directive, the European unit of account shall be that defined by Commission Decision No 3289/75/ECSC of 18 December 1975. The equivalent in national currency shall be calculated initially at the rate obtaining on the date of adoption of this Directive.
2. Every five years the Council, acting on a proposal from the Commission, shall examine and, if need be, revise the amounts expressed in European units of account in this Directive, in the light of economic and monetary trends in the Community.

Article 54

This Directive shall not affect laws in the Member States requiring that the annual accounts of companies not falling within their jurisdiction be filed in a register in which branches of such companies are listed.

Article 55

1. The Member States shall bring into force the laws, regulations and administrative provisions necessary for them to comply with this Directive within two years of its notification. They shall forthwith inform the Commission thereof.
2. The Member States may stipulate that the provisions referred to in paragraph 1 shall not apply until 18 months after the end of the period provided for in that paragraph.
   That period of 18 months may, however, be five years:
   (a) in the case of unregistered companies in the United Kingdom and Ireland;
   (b) for purposes of the application of Articles 9 and 10 and Articles 23 to 26 concerning the layouts for the balance sheet and the profit and loss account, where a Member State has brought other layouts for these documents into force not more than three years before the notification of this Directive;
   (c) for purposes of the application of this Directive as regards the calculation and disclosure in balance sheets of depreciation relating to assets covered by the asset items mentioned in Article 9, C (II) (2) and (3), and Article 10, C (II) (2) and (3);
   (d) for purposes of the application of Article 47 (1) of this Directive except as regards companies already under an obligation of publication under Article 2 (1) (f) of Directive 68/151/EEC. In this case the second subparagraph of Article 47 (1) of this Directive shall apply to the annual accounts and to the opinion drawn up by the person responsible for auditing the accounts;
   (e) for purposes of the application of Article 51 (1) of this Directive.

Furthermore, this period of 18 months may be extended to eight years for companies the principal object of which is shipping and which are already in existence on the entry into force of the provisions referred to in paragraph 1.

3. The Member States shall ensure that they communicate to the Commission the texts of the main provisions of national law which they adopt in the field covered by this Directive.

Article 56

1. The obligation to show in annual accounts the items prescribed by Articles 9, 10 and 23 to 26 which relate to affiliated undertakings, as defined by Article 41 of Directive 83/349/EEC, and the obligation to provide information concerning these undertakings in accordance with Articles 13 (2), and 14 and point 7 of Article 43 (1) shall enter into force on the date fixed in Article 49 (2) of that Directive.

2. The notes on the accounts must also disclose:
(a) the name and registered office of the undertaking which draws up the consolidated accounts of the largest body of undertakings of which the company forms part as a subsidiary undertaking;
(b) the name and registered office of the undertaking which draws up the consolidated accounts of the smallest body of undertakings of which the company forms part as a subsidiary undertaking and which is also included in the body of undertakings referred to in (a) above;
(c) the place where copies of the consolidated accounts referred to in (a) and (b) above may be obtained provided that they are available.

Article 57

Notwithstanding the provisions of Directives 68/151/EEC and 77/91/EEC, a Member State need not apply the provisions of this Directive concerning the content, auditing and publication of annual accounts to companies governed by their national laws which are subsidiary undertakings, as defined in Directive 83/349/EEC, where the following conditions are fulfilled:
(a) the parent undertaking must be subject to the laws of a Member State;
(b) all shareholders or members of the subsidiary undertaking must have declared their agreement to the exemption from such obligation; this declaration must be made in respect of every financial year;
(c) the parent undertaking must have declared that it guarantees the commitments entered into by the subsidiary undertaking;
(d) the declarations referred to in (b) and (c) must be published by the subsidiary undertaking as laid down by the laws of the Member State in accordance with Article 3 of Directive 68/151/EEC;
(e) the subsidiary undertaking must be included in the consolidated accounts drawn up by the parent undertaking in accordance with Directive 83/349/EEC;

(f) the above exemption must be disclosed in the notes on the consolidated accounts drawn up by the parent undertaking;
(g) the consolidated accounts referred to in (e), the consolidated annual report and the report by the person responsible for auditing those accounts must be published for the subsidiary undertaking as laid down by the laws of the Member State in accordance with Article 3 of Directive 68/151/EEC.

Article 58

A Member State need not apply the provisions of this Directive concerning the auditing and publication of the profit-and-loss account to companies governed by their national laws which are parent undertakings for the purposes of Directive 83/349/EEC where the following conditions are fulfilled:
(a) the parent undertaking must draw up consolidated accounts in accordance with Directive 83/349/EEC and be included in the consolidated accounts;
(b) the above exemption must be disclosed in the notes on the annual accounts of the parent undertaking;
(c) the above exemption must be disclosed in the notes on the consolidated accounts drawn up by the parent undertaking;
(d) the profit or loss of the parent company, determined in accordance with this Directive, must be shown in the balance sheet of the parent company.

Article 59

1. A Member State may require or permit that participating interests, as defined in Article 17, in the capital of undertakings over the operating and financial policies of which significant influence is exercised, be shown in the balance sheet in accordance with paragraphs 2 to 9 below, as sub-items of the items "shares in affiliated undertakings" or "participating interests" as the case may be. An undertaking shall be presumed to exercise a significant influence over another undertaking where it has 20% or more of the shareholders' or members' voting rights in that undertaking. Article 2 of Directive 83/349/EEC shall apply.
2. When this Article is first applied to a participating interest covered by paragraph 1, it shall be shown in the balance sheet either:
(a) at its book value calculated in accordance with Articles 31 to 42. The difference between that value and the amount corresponding to the proportion of capital and reserves represented by the participating interest shall be disclosed separately in the balance sheet or in the notes on the accounts. That difference shall be calculated as at the date as at which the method is applied for the first time; or
(b) at the amount corresponding to the proportion of the capital and reserves represented by the participating interest. The difference between that amount and the book value calculated in accordance with Articles 31 to 42 shall be disclosed separately in the balance sheet or in the notes on the accounts. That

difference shall be calculated as at the date as at which the method is applied for the first time.

(e) A Member State may prescribe the application of one or other of the above paragraphs. The balance sheet or the notes on the accounts must indicate whether (a) or (b) above has been used.

(d) In addition when applying (a) and (b) above, a Member State may require or permit calculation of the difference as at the date of acquisition of the participating interest referred to in paragraph 1 or, where the acquisition took place in two or more stages, as at the date as at which the holding became a participating interest within the meaning of paragraph 1 above.

3. Where the assets or liabilities of an undertaking in which a participating interest within the meaning of paragraph 1 above is held have been valued by methods other than those used by the company drawing up the annual accounts, they may, for the purpose of calculating the difference referred to in paragraph 2 (a) or (b) above, be revalued by the methods used by the company drawing up the annual accounts. Disclosure must be made in the notes on the accounts where such revaluation has not been carried out. A Member State may require such revaluation.

4. The book value referred to in paragraph 2 (a) above, or the amount corresponding to the proportion of capital and reserves referred to in paragraph 2 (b) above, shall be increased or reduced by the amount of the variation which has taken place during the financial year in the proportion of capital and reserves represented by that participating interest; it shall be reduced by the amount of the dividends relating to the participating interest.

5. In so far as a positive difference covered by paragraph 2 (a) or (b) above cannot be related to any category of asset or liability, it shall be dealt with in accordance with the rules applicable to the item "goodwill".

6. (a) The proportion of the profit or loss attributable to participating interests within the meaning of paragraph 1 above shall be shown in the profit-and-loss account as a separate item with an appropriate heading.

    (b) Where that amount exceeds the amount of dividends already received or the payment of which can be claimed, the amount of the difference must be placed in a reserve which cannot be distributed to shareholders.

    (c) A Member State may require or permit that the proportion of the profit or loss attributable to the participating interests referred to in paragraph 1 above be shown in the profit-and-loss account only to the extent of the amount corresponding to dividends already received or the payment of which can be claimed.

7. The eliminations referred to in Article 26 (1) (c) of Directive 83/349/EEC shall be effected in so far as the facts are known or can be ascertained. Article 26 (2) and (3) of that Directive shall apply.

8. Where an undertaking in which a participating interest within the meaning of paragraph 1 above is held draws up consolidated accounts, the foregoing paragraphs shall apply to the capital and reserves shown in such consolidated accounts.

9. This Article need not be applied where a participating interest as defined in paragraph 1 is not material for the purposes of Article 2 (3).

Article 60

Pending subsequent coordination, the Member States may prescribe that investments in which investment companies within the meaning of Article 5 (2) have invested their funds shall be valued on the basis of their market value.

In that case the Member States may also waive the obligation on investment companies with variable capital to show separately the value adjustments referred to in Article 36.

Article 61

A Member State need not apply the provisions of point 2 of Article 43 (1) of this Directive concerning the amount of capital and reserves and profits and losses of the undertakings concerned to companies governed by their national laws which are parent undertakings for the purposes of Directive 83/349/EEC:
(a) where the undertakings concerned are included in consolidated accounts drawn up by that parent undertaking, or in the consolidated accounts of a larger body of undertakings as referred to in Article 7 (2) of Directive 83/349/EEC; or
(b) where the holdings in the undertakings concerned have been dealt with by the parent undertaking in its annual accounts in accordance with Article 59, or in the consolidated accounts drawn up by that parent undertaking in accordance with Article 33 of Directive 83/349/EEC.

Article 62

This Directive is addressed to the Member States.
Done at Brussels, 25 July 1978.

For the Council
The President
K. von DOHNANYI

Glossary of terms

> This glossary is primarily written in British English, although there are many cross-references to American English. Many continental European companies translate their financial statements into a form of mid-Atlantic English.
>
> Terms used in an entry that are themselves defined elsewhere in the glossary are shown in small capitals.

A

accelerated depreciation   DEPRECIATION which is either at a faster rate than would be suggested by an asset's expected life or using methods which charge proportionately more depreciation in earlier years. This is most commonly found in the context of tax concessions designed to encourage investment. For the calculation of taxable income in such cases, businesses would be allowed to depreciate certain assets (like energy-saving devices or assets in depressed regions) more quickly than accountants otherwise would. This occurs in many countries.

account   a record of all the bookkeeping entries relating to a particular item. For example, the wages account would record all the payments of wages. An account in the double entry system has a debit side (left) and a credit side (right). Often accounts are referred to as T-accounts, because of the rulings on the page that divide the left from the right and underline the title. Of course, pages have now generally been replaced by spaces on a computer disk. A business may have thousands of accounts, including one for each debtor and creditor.

In the early days of accounting, there were only personal accounts (for people who owed and were owed money). Later, there were 'real' accounts for property of various sorts; and 'nominal' accounts for impersonal, unreal items like wages and electricity. Accounts may be collected together in groups in ledgers or books of account.

'Accounts' may also mean financial statements, such as BALANCE SHEETS and PROFIT AND LOSS ACCOUNTS.

accountability the major original purpose of accounting; so that the owners of resources (now shareholders, for example) can check up on the managers or stewards of those resources (now boards of directors, for example).

accountancy and accounting These terms are used interchangeably by many people. However, in the United Kingdom it tends to be, for example, the *accountancy* profession, but management *accounting*. That is, the former tends to be associated with the profession, and the latter with the subject matter, particularly in the context of education or theory. In the United States, the word 'accountancy' is rarer.

accounting policies the detailed methods of valuation and measurement which a particular company has chosen from those generally accepted by law, accounting standards or commercial practice. These policies must be used consistently.

accounting principles The word 'principles' is a slight problem in accounting. In the United States it tends to mean conventions of practice, whereas in the United Kingdom it means something more fundamental and theoretical. Thus, the American 'GENERALLY ACCEPTED ACCOUNTING PRINCIPLES' encompasses a wide range of broad and detailed accounting rules of practice. In the United Kingdom, the detailed rules are often called practices, policies or bases; and broader matters like ACCRUALS or CONSERVATISM were traditionally referred to as concepts or conventions. So, in the United Kingdom, GAAP may mean 'generally accepted accounting practices'.

accounting standards technical accounting rules of valuation, measurement and disclosure set by committees of accountants. The exact title of accounting standards varies from country to country. The practical use of the words seems to originate officially with the Accounting Standards Steering Committee (later the Accounting Standards Committee) in the United Kingdom in 1970.

accounts payable US expression for CREDITORS in the United Kingdom. These are amounts owed by the business, usually as a result of purchases in the normal course of trade from suppliers who allow the business to pay at some point after purchase. Discounts will often be allowed for early payment of such accounts. The total of accounts payable at the period end form part of CURRENT LIABILITIES on a balance sheet.

accounts receivable US expression for DEBTORS in the United Kingdom. These are the amounts to be paid to the business by outsiders, normally as a result of sales to customers who have not yet settled their bills. Accounts receivable are valued at the amount of the accounts, less an allowance ('provision' in UK terminology) for any amounts thought likely to be uncollectable. Those which are fairly certain to be uncollectable are bad debts; and there may also be allowances for specific amounts expected to be uncollectable, and general allowances against the total of accounts receivable. The general allowances would be calculated in the light of past experience with bad debts. In certain countries, the size of provisions is, in effect, controlled by the amounts allowed for tax purposes. All these allowances reflect the perceived need for CONSERVATISM, particularly in the valuation of such CURRENT ASSETS. After taking into account these provisions, the total of accounts receivable will be part of current assets on a balance sheet.

accruals convention an expression sometimes used to describe the standard practice of concentrating on the period to which an expense or revenue relates rather than on the period in which cash is paid or received. It is also known as the MATCHING principle, particularly in North America. More details are given under that heading.

accrued expenses (or accruals) expenses which relate to a year but for which a bill will not be received until the following year. Recognition of accrued expenses results from the need regularly to draw up financial statements at a fixed time (for example, at the end of a company's year).

During a year, electricity will be used or properties will be rented, yet at the year end the related bills may not have been received. Thus, at the year end, 'accrued' expenses are charged against income by accountants even though cash has not been paid nor the bills even received. The double entry for this is the creation of a CURRENT LIABILITY on the balance sheets. This practice may apply also to wages and salaries, taxes, and so on. An allocation of amounts to 'this year' and 'next year' may be necessary where a supplier's account straddles two accounting years. The practice is an example of the use of the MATCHING concept.

Similarly, some accounts of suppliers which are paid in any year may be wholly or partly paid on behalf of the activities of the next year. In this case, the relevant expenses for the year will have to be adjusted downwards by the accountant, and a CURRENT ASSET called 'prepayments' recorded on the balance sheet. Thus, payments of property taxes and insurance premiums may be partly prepayments.

accumulated depreciation the total amount by which the accounting value of a fixed asset has so far been reduced to take account of the fact that it is wearing out or becoming obsolete (see DEPRECIATION).

acid test name sometimes given to a ratio of some of a business's liquid assets to some of its short-term debts. It is thus one test of the likelihood of liquidity problems. It is also called the quick ratio.

activity based costing (ABC) a topical expression for the practice of relating as many expenses as possible, often previously regarded as overheads, to particular production activities.

allowances US expression for PROVISIONS, i.e. amounts charged against profit in anticipation of reductions in value.

amortization a word used, particularly in North America, to refer to DEPRECIATION of intangible assets.

annual general meeting (AGM) the meeting at which shareholders may question directors on the contents of the ANNUAL REPORT and financial statements; vote on the directors' recommendation for dividends; vote on replacement for retiring members of the board; and conduct other business within the ARTICLES OF ASSOCIATION.

articles of association a document drawn up at the foundation of a company, setting out the rights and duties of the shareholders and directors, and the relationship between the one class of shareholders and another (see, also, MEMORANDUM).

asset generally, something owned that has future economic benefits. However, it turns out that to define exactly what an accountant means by an 'asset' is exceptionally difficult. A definition would be contained as part of a CONCEPTUAL FRAMEWORK, perhaps: a resource controlled by an enterprise, as a result of past events, from which future economic benefits are expected to flow to the enterprise.

associated company A British term for a company over which another has significant influence. The term is not so well known in the United States. According to the EC Seventh

Directive, a company will be presumed to be an associated company if it is owned to the extent of 20% or more and is not a subsidiary or joint venture (see CONSOLIDATED FINANCIAL STATEMENTS). Companies held as joint ventures will be treated as associated companies in many countries.

auditing standards rules for the practice of auditors, formalized in a similar way to the technical rules of ACCOUNTING STANDARDS. The rules contain ethical guidelines as well as detailing the work to be covered by an audit and the standard practice for the audit report.

authorized share capital the maximum amount of a particular type of share in a particular company that may be issued. The amount is laid down in the company's MEMORANDUM (in the case of the United Kingdom). It may be interesting information to shareholders as it puts a limit on the number of co-owners.

average cost (AVCO) in the context of INVENTORY valuation, a method of determining the historical cost of a particular type of inventory. As its name suggests, the cost of any unit of inventory or material used is deemed to be the average of the unit costs at which the inventory was bought. The average can be worked out at set intervals or each time there is a further purchase. AVCO is allowed by the EC Fourth Directive and is a minority practice in some countries. See FIFO and LIFO.

B

balance sheet a snapshot of the accounting records of assets, liabilities and capital of a business at a particular moment, most obviously the accounting year end. The balance sheet is the longest established of the main financial statements produced by a business. As its name suggests, it is a sheet of the balances from the double entry system at a particular time. It is important to note that it is probably neither a snapshot of what the business is *worth* nor of what the separate assets are worth. This is because not all the business' items of value are recognized by accountants as ASSETS, and because the asset valuation methods used are normally based on past costs rather than on present market values.

Big Six (formerly Big Eight) an expression used to describe the world's largest accounting firms, which have offices virtually throughout the world.
The Big Six (in alphabetical order):

Arthur Andersen
Coopers & Lybrand
Deloitte Touche Tohmatsu
Ernst & Young
Klynveld Peat Marwick Goerdeler (KPMG)
Price Waterhouse

Business combinations acquisitions or mergers involving two or more companies.

C

capital allowances a system of DEPRECIATION used in the determination of taxable income that is unique to the British Isles. This tends to be more generous than the depreciation that accountants charge for financial accounting purposes.

capital employed the aggregate finance used by a business. Sometimes the expression is used to refer to the total of all liabilities and capital; sometimes it means 'net capital employed', that is it excludes current liabilities.

cash flow sometimes used to refer very loosely to the amount of cash coming into or out of a business in a particular period. However, it can be used as a more precise accounting term, particularly in North America, to refer to NET INCOME with DEPRECIATION charges added back. The latter will have been deducted in the calculation of the former but is not of course a cash payment of the period in question. Thus, profit plus depreciation gives an impression of cash generated by trading operations. This is not very exact, particularly because of changes in INVENTORY (stocks) and because of outstanding credit sales and purchases that have been included in the calculation of profit but will not yet have led to cash movements. However, as a quick measure it may have its uses.

cash flow statements annual financial statements that are compulsory in several countries. They concentrate on the movement of cash in the year.

closing rate method UK term for the world's most common method of foreign currency translation. The US term is current rate method.

common stock US term for the ordinary shares in a corporation. Normally a majority of the ownership capital will comprise issues of common stock, though PREFERENCE/PREFERRED SHARES are also issued.

conceptual framework a theoretical structure to underlie the technical rules in accounting. Several Anglo-Saxon standard setting bodies have published such frameworks since the mid-1970s.

conservatism the fundamental and ancient accounting concept that accountants should, when in doubt, show the worse picture rather than the better. Conservatism requires that assets should be shown at the lowest of all reasonable values; that all foreseeable losses should be accounted for immediately, but that profits should never be recorded until they become REALIZED PROFITS.

consistency the concept that a company should use the same rules of measurement and valuation from year to year in its financial statements. This is now well established in most developed countries. A company may be allowed to change in special circumstances, such as an alteration in ACCOUNTING STANDARDS, but the change should always be disclosed in the annual report. The purpose of consistency is to enable a better comparison of a year's profits and values with those of previous years. The concept that different *companies* should use the same rules to assist intercompany comparisons might be called UNIFORMITY.

consolidated financial statements a means of presenting the position and results of a parent and its subsidiary companies as if they were a single entity. Consolidation ignores the separation of parents and subsidiaries due to legal and geographical factors; it accounts for the group of companies as if they were a single entity. Approximately, the financial statements of all the companies in the group are added together, with adjustments to extract intra-group trading and indebtedness.

contingent liabilities possible liabilities. As part of CONSERVATISM, accountants recognize all reasonably probable losses in advance. Some losses are contingent upon some event, like the loss of a law case or a debtor defaulting on a bill of exchange which the company has guaranteed. If these contingencies are improbable or are impossible to quantify, they are not accounted for, in the sense of adjusting the financial statements, but are explained in the notes to the BALANCE SHEET.

creditors A creditor is a 'truster', someone to whom a business owes money. The US expression is ACCOUNTS PAYABLE. Creditors are created by purchases 'on credit' or loans of various sorts. Short-term creditors are included under 'current liabilities' on a balance sheet; they are expected to be paid within the year. If credit purchases are the cause, the title used might be 'trade creditors'.

Long-term creditors are those who are not expected to be paid within the year. These might be trade creditors but would more likely be holders of bonds or debentures. The latter would normally be entitled to receive interest, whereas trade creditors are not. However, trade creditors often offer discounts for prompt payment, which is an implied way of charging interest.

CREDITORS of all sorts are shown in a balance sheet at the amounts which a business expects to pay. Particularly in the case of long-term loans, this may be different from the amount originally borrowed or from the amount that would have to be paid to redeem the loan at the balance sheet date.

current assets By convention, an ASSET on a BALANCE SHEET is 'current' if it is not intended for continuing use in the business. Such assets include INVENTORIES, ACCOUNTS RECEIVABLE (US)/DEBTORS (UK), and cash. Also, a BALANCE SHEET may include current asset investments.

current cost accounting (CCA) one of many possible systems designed to adjust accounting for changing prices. It is often included under the generic heading INFLATION ACCOUNTING, although its normal form does not involve adjustments for inflation, but for specific price changes relating to the business' assets. CCA is particularly associated with the United Kingdom, Australia and New Zealand.

current liabilities those amounts on a BALANCE SHEET that are expected to be paid by the business within a year. Thus they will include trade CREDITORS (UK)/ACCOUNTS PAYABLE (US), certain tax liabilities, and proposed dividends. Bank overdrafts are included on the grounds that they fluctuate in size and are technically recallable at short notice.

Current liabilities are generally valued at their 'face value', the amount that is expected to be paid.

Current purchasing power accounting (CPP) a UK term for the method of adjusting HISTORICAL COST ACCOUNTING financial statements to take account of inflation. The US equivalent is GENERAL PRICE LEVEL ADJUSTED or CONSTANT DOLLAR.

current rate method the US term for a method of foreign currency translation. The UK term is CLOSING RATE METHOD.

D

debtors In a BALANCE SHEET, debtors are usually mostly trade debtors, i.e. customers who have not yet paid cash. The US terminology is ACCOUNTS RECEIVABLE. Such amounts are shown as CURRENT ASSETS because they are generally expected to be paid within the year.

In a balance sheet, debtors are valued at what they are expected to pay to the business, bearing in mind the principle of CONSERVATISM. Thus, BAD DEBTS are written off, and PROVISIONS (ALLOWANCES in US terminology) are made for doubtful debts. The PROVISIONS can be both specific (against suspected debts) and general (based on the average experience of bad debts).

deferred tax caused by timing differences between when an amount is recognized for accounting income purposes and when it is recognized for taxable income. For example, suppose that depreciation for tax purposes is more rapid than for accounting purposes; in such a case, in the early years of an asset's life, tax depreciation will be larger than accounting DEPRECIATION (and vice versa later). Thus there are reversing timing differences.

depreciation a charge against the profit of a period to represent the wearing out, usage or consumption of FIXED ASSETS in that period. So, machinery and equipment, vehicles and buildings are generally depreciated, though land normally is not. The technique of depreciation means that accountants do not charge the whole cost of a fixed asset against the profit of the year of purchase, but they charge it gradually over the years of the use and wearing out of the asset. This fits with the MATCHING concept.

deprival value a term for the amount by which a business would be worse off if it were deprived of a particular asset. This is sometimes referred to as its 'value to the business' or 'value to the owner'.

development expenditure may be distinguished from research expenditure in that the former has a practical application in mind.

Directives of the EC on company law blueprints for laws that must be enacted throughout the European Community. This is part of the process of harmonization of company law and accounting. The Commission drafts Directives, which are then adopted by the Council of Ministers, and implemented into national laws. The most important Directives for accounting are the Fourth and the Seventh.

discounted cash flow (DCF) future cash flows, adjusted to take account of their timing. Such 'discounted' cash flows are used when making investment choices between competing projects. The most reliable method of deciding which project is best and whether any particular one is worth doing is to work out each project's net present value (NPV) by adding up all the discounted expected net cash flows. The NPV calculation will include the outflow of the initial investment. A project with a positive NPV is worth doing; the project with the highest NPV is the best.

In financial reporting, discounting is rare.

E

earnings a technical accounting term, meaning the amount of profit (normally for a year) available to the ordinary shareholders (UK)/common stockholders (US). That is, it is the profit after all operating expenses, interest charges, taxes and dividends on PREFERRED/PREFERENCE stock.

earnings per share exactly what its name suggests: the most recent year's total EARNINGS divided by the number of ordinary/common shares. Of course, there can be complications, for example, when the number of shares has changed during the year.

efficient market hypothesis an elegant and important theory, usually applied to the price of shares on large stock exchanges, that all publicly available information is immediately taken into account in the price of shares. In markets like the New York or London Stock Exchanges there are many buyers and sellers of shares, the prices are well known, and much other information is freely available. In such cases, one would expect that new relevant information about a company would very rapidly affect its price.

equity method a method used, particularly as part of the preparation of CONSOLIDATED FINANCIAL STATEMENTS, for ASSOCIATES (those companies over which a group has 'significant influence' but not a controlling interest).

exceptional items A UK expression for those items in a profit and loss account that are within the ordinary activities of the business, but are of unusual size. The treatment for these is to disclose them separately in the account or the notes to it. Such items are to be distinguished from EXTRAORDINARY ITEMS.

exposure drafts documents that precede the issue of ACCOUNTING STANDARDS. They are intended to attract response from companies, auditors, academics, investment analysts, financial institutions, etc.

extraordinary items gains or losses which are outside the ordinary activities of the business, are of material size, and are not expected to recur. The narrowness of interpretation of this expression differs greatly internationally.

F

fair value a term particularly used in group accounting. Assets and liabilities of new subsidiaries are brought into consolidated accounts in the United States or the United Kingdom at fair values rather than book values. This is designed to be an estimate of their cost to the group at the date of acquisition of the subsidiary. Fair value is usually measured by net current replacement cost.

FEE the Fédération des Experts Comptables Européens, a Brussels-based body of European professional accountancy institutes.

FIFO (first-in, first-out) a common assumption for accounting purposes about the flow of items of raw materials or other INVENTORIES. It need not be expected to correspond with physical reality, but may be taken for accounting purposes. The assumption is that the first units to be received as part of inventories are the first ones to be used up or sold. This means that the most recent units are deemed to be those left at the period end. When prices are rising, and assuming a reasonably constant purchasing of materials, FIFO leads to a fairly up-to-date closing inventory figure. However it gives an out-of-date and therefore low figure for the cost of sales. This leads to what many argue is an overstatement of profit figures, when prices are rising.

fiscal year US expression for the period for which companies prepare their annual financial statements. The majority of US companies use December 31 as the fiscal year end, which corresponds with the year end for tax purposes. In the United Kingdom, the expression 'fiscal year' means tax year.

fixed assets the assets that are to continue to be used in the business, such as land, buildings and machines. The opposite are CURRENT ASSETS. An equivalent US expression is 'property, plant and equipment'.

FRS an abbreviation for Financial Reporting Standard, that is an ACCOUNTING STANDARD issued in the United Kingdom from 1990 onwards by the Accounting Standards Board.

G

gearing a measurement of the degree to which a business is funded by loans rather than SHAREHOLDERS' EQUITY. The US expression is LEVERAGE.

generally accepted accounting principles (GAAP) a technical term, particularly used in the United States, to include the ACCOUNTING STANDARDS of the Financial Accounting Standards Board, and extant rules of predecessor bodies. Also included are some of the rules of the SECURITIES AND EXCHANGE COMMISSION (SEC).

general price level adjusted accounting (GPLA) a US term for a system of adjusting historical cost accounting by price indices to take account of inflation. It is also called CONSTANT DOLLAR ACCOUNTING or, in the United Kingdom, CURRENT PURCHASING POWER ACCOUNTING.

going concern an important underlying concept in accounting practice. The assumption for most businesses is that they will continue for the foreseeable future. This means that, for most purposes, the break-up or forced-sale value of the assets is not relevant.

goodwill In the United States and the United Kingdom, the amount paid for a company in excess of the FAIR VALUE of its net assets at the date of acquisition. A slightly different definition is used in some countries. Goodwill exists because a GOING CONCERN business is usually worth more than the sum of the accounting values of its identifiable NET ASSETS. This may be looked upon as its ability to earn future profits above those of a similar newly formed company or it may be seen as the 'goodwill' of customers, the established network of contacts, loyal staff, skilled management, and so on.

group accounts UK expression for CONSOLIDATED FINANCIAL STATEMENTS.

H

historical cost accounting the conventional system of accounting, widely established throughout the world, except in some countries where inflation is endemic and high. Even in the latter countries, the GENERAL PRICE LEVEL ADJUSTED system is a set of simple adjustments carried out annually from historical cost records.

holding company a company that owns or controls others. In the narrow use of the expression, it implies that the company does not actively trade but operates through various subsidiaries.

I

income statement the most common US name for the statement of revenues and expenses of a particular period, leading to the calculation of net income or net profit. The format of the income statement is either 'vertical'/'statement' form or 'horizontal'/'two-sided'/ 'account' form.

The equivalent UK statement is the PROFIT AND LOSS ACCOUNT.

inflation accounting usually interpreted as encompassing all sorts of systems that might adjust or replace HISTORICAL COST ACCOUNTING to take account of changing prices. Many such systems are poorly described by the term, because they do not involve a recognition of general price level movements. Systems that do adjust for *inflation* are called CURRENT

PURCHASING POWER ACCOUNTING (UK), GENERAL PRICE LEVEL ADJUSTED accounting (US) or CONSTANT DOLLAR ACCOUNTING (US).

intangible assets ASSETS that are not physical or tangible, such as goodwill or patents.

interim dividend dividend payment based on the profits of less than a full accounting period.

interim reports a half-yearly or more frequent report generally from companies listed on a stock exchange.

International Accounting Standards Committee (IASC) an organization composed of representatives of over 90 professional accountancy bodies from different countries. It was formed in 1973 and has its headquarters in London. Its purpose is to devise and promulgate international standards in order to reduce the variation of practices in financial reporting throughout the world. Its member bodies have promised to use their best endeavours to ensure compliance with standards. The standards bear a close relationship to US and UK practices.

International Federation of Accountants (IFAC) a body comprising representatives from the accountancy professions of many nations. It was formed in 1977, and is based in New York. Its largest task is the organization of the four-yearly World Congresses of Accountants. It also has committees that promote international harmonization of auditing and management accounting. However, it leaves the area of accounting standards to the IASC (see preceding entry).

inventories raw materials, work-in-progress and goods ready for sale. In the United Kingdom, the word 'stocks' is generally used instead.

investment properties properties held by a business for investment or rental income, rather than for owner occupation.

L

leverage US term for the degree to which a business is funded by loans rather than by shareholders' equity. In a profitable highly levered company, a percentage increase in trading profit will be magnified by the time it reaches the stockholders, because the return to the lenders is a fixed amount of interest. The equivalent UK expression is GEARING.

liabilities present obligations of an enterprise, arising from past events, the settlement of which is expected to result in an outflow of resources (usually cash). Most liabilities are of known amount and date. They include long-term loans, bank overdrafts and amounts owed to suppliers. There are current and non-current liabilities. The former are expected to be paid within a year from the date of the BALANCE SHEET on which they appear. Most measures of liquidity include knowing the total of current liabilities; NET CURRENT ASSETS is the difference between the current assets and the current liabilities.

Liabilities are valued at the amounts expected to be paid at the expected maturity date. In some cases, amounts that are not quite certain will be included as liabilities (CONTINGENCIES); they will be valued at the best estimate available. The convention of CONSERVATISM suggests that amounts that are reasonably likely to be liabilities should be treated thus. Less likely amounts are noted.

LIFO (last-in, first-out) one of the methods available for the calculation of the cost of INVENTORIES, in those frequent cases where it is difficult or impossible to determine exactly which items remain or have been used. When prices are rising, LIFO will lead to more up-to-date values for the use of inventory in cost of sales and, thus, lower profits. Therefore, it is popular with many companies in Italy and the United States, where it is allowed for tax purposes.

However, the inventory value shown in the BALANCE SHEET may be seriously misleading as it will be based on very old prices.

M

matching a convention that the expenses and revenues measured in order to calculate the profit for a period should be those that relate to the period, rather than those where cash has been paid or received. This is sometimes called the ACCRUALS CONVENTION.

materiality a very strong concept in Anglo-Saxon accounting that rules should not be strictly applied to unimportant amounts. For example, some companies may have very small amounts of a particular revenue, expense, asset or liability; if such an account would normally be shown in the financial statements, it nevertheless need not be if it is immaterial in size. This will help to make the statements clearer, by omission of trivial amounts. Materiality is also to be seen at work in the extensive rounding of numbers in financial statements.

Similarly, a strictly correct measurement or valuation method may be ignored for immaterial items. For example, the fitting of new and improved door locks on an office building is strictly an enhancement of the building and should lead to that asset being shown at a higher cost in the balance sheet. However, the cost will be immaterial in the context of the building, and capitalization would complicate future depreciation charges. Thus, it would be normal to treat the new locks as an expense.

There is no precise definition of what is material. However, an item is immaterial if omission or mistreatment of it would not alter a reader's assessment of the financial statements. As a rule of thumb, this might be expressed as a few per cent of sales or profit.

memorandum of association a legal document drawn up as part of the registration of a company in the United Kingdom. The memorandum includes a record of the company's name, its registered office, its purposes and its AUTHORIZED SHARE CAPITAL.

The other document drawn up at the birth of a UK company is the ARTICLES OF ASSOCIATION. These are rules concerning the relationships of the company to the shareholders, the shareholders to each other, and so on.

Merger accounting a method of accounting for a business combination. In the United States it is in fairly common use, under the name of POOLING OF INTERESTS, under which heading more details may be found.

minority interests the capital provided by group shareholders who are not parent company shareholders. Many subsidiary companies are not fully owned by the parent company. This means that they are partly owned by 'minority' shareholders outside the group. In the preparation of CONSOLIDATED FINANCIAL STATEMENTS, accountants bring in 100% of all assets, liabilities, expenses and revenues of subsidiaries. This is because the group fully *controls* the subsidiary, even if it does not fully own it. In such financial statements, the subsidiary is submerged into the rest of the group, and the capital provided by the minority shareholders is separately recognized as part of the capital of the group called 'minority interests'. This amount grows each time the relevant subsidiary makes a profit which is not distributed.

In the consolidated profit and loss account, the share of the group profit owned by minorities is also shown as 'profit attributable to minorities'.

N

net assets the worth of a business in accounting terms, as measured from its BALANCE SHEET. That is, it is the total of all the recorded ASSETS, less the LIABILITIES that are owed to outsiders. Naturally, this total equals the SHAREHOLDERS' EQUITY.

However, in reality, a business is nearly always worth more than its net assets, because accountants will generally have been using HISTORICAL COST ACCOUNTING as a measurement basis, and because important assets like the goodwill of customers will have been excluded due to the CONSERVATISM and money measurement conventions. Thus, the market capitalization of a company will nearly always be greater than its accounting 'net assets'.

net current assets the net current assets or working capital of a business is the excess of the CURRENT ASSETS (such as cash, INVENTORIES and DEBTORS/ACCOUNTS RECEIVABLE) over the CURRENT LIABILITIES (such as trade creditors and overdrafts).

This is a measure of the extent to which the business is safe from liquidity problems. See also CURRENT RATIO.

net income normal US expression for NET PROFIT in UK terminology.

net profit normal UK expression for the excess of all the revenues over all the expenses of a business for a period. The PROFIT AND LOSS ACCOUNT of a business will show the net profit before tax and the net profit after tax. The profit is then available for distribution as dividends (assuming there is sufficient cash) or for transfer to various RESERVES. After any dividends on PREFERENCE SHARES have been deducted, the figure may be called EARNINGS.

net realizable value (NRV) the amount that could be raised by selling an asset, less the costs of the sale. Normally, NRV implies a sale in the normal course of trade; thus, there would also be a deduction for any costs to bring the asset into a saleable state.

nominal value Most shares have a nominal or PAR VALUE. This is little more than a label to distinguish a share from any of a different value issued by the same company. Normally, the shares will be currently exchanged at above the nominal value, and the company will consequently issue any new shares at approximately the market rate.

Dividends may be expressed as a percentage of nominal value; and share capital is recorded at nominal value, any excess being recorded as SHARE PREMIUM.

O

off-balance sheet finance One important example of off-balance sheet finance is the existence of capital or finance leases that are not treated as ASSETS and LIABILITIES (capitalized). Suppose that a business has decided to lease most of its plant and equipment rather than buying it. Suppose, too, that it does not capitalize its leases, because it or its leases fall outside the rules or because it is in a country where capitalization is not required. Now, let us compare this company with a similar one that has borrowed money and bought all its assets. The lessee has few assets and few loans, whereas the buying company has many assets and many loans. Thus, the lessee will appear to have a much better GEARING/LEVERAGE position and a better return on capital. This is despite the fact that it is using the same amount of assets, and has contracted to make lease payments for many future years.

In several countries, it is now necessary for 'capital' or 'finance' leases to be capitalized as though owned, and for an equal liability to be created. This adjusts for the otherwise misleading off-balance sheet finance. It expresses SUBSTANCE OVER FORM. There are many other ways of achieving off-balance sheet finance. In the context of CONSOLIDATED FINANCIAL STATEMENTS, it may be possible to exclude companies which are substantially subsidiaries.

ordinary shares as the name suggests, the normal type of shares, called COMMON STOCK in the United States. They can be distinguished from PREFERENCE SHARES.

own shares shares in a company bought back by the company from its shareholders. In the United States, own shares are called TREASURY STOCK.

P

paid-in surplus US expression for SHARE PREMIUM.

par value the normal US expression for NOMINAL VALUE.

pay-back method a popular technique for appraising the likely success of projects, or for choosing between projects. It involves the analysis of their expected future net cash inflows, followed by a calculation of how many years it will take for the original capital investment to be recovered. It seems to be popular because it is simple to use and, perhaps more importantly, simple to explain to non-financial managers.

pooling of interests a method of accounting for business combinations that is fairly common in the United States, and in occasional use in the United Kingdom, where it is known as MERGER ACCOUNTING. The method has several attractions to companies and it is therefore necessary for there to be rules to control its use. In the United States, these rules are to be found in APB Opinion 16, and they include that the merger should be accomplished by the exchange of shares only, so that no cash leaves the group of companies.

Most business combinations do not fit within the rules, and so the normal 'acquisition' or 'purchase' method of preparing CONSOLIDATED FINANCIAL STATEMENTS is used.

preferred stock/preference shares Some shares in some companies are issued as preference shares (UK) or preferred stock (US). These shares normally have preference over ORDINARY SHARES/COMMON STOCK for dividend payments and for the return of capital if a company is wound up. That is, ordinary/common dividends cannot be paid in a particular year until the preference/preferred dividend (generally including arrears), which is usually a fixed percentage, has been paid.

private company a company that is not allowed to create a market in its securities. Such 'private limited companies' have special designatory letters after their names, such as Ltd, GmbH, Sarl, BV, Srl. They are to be distinguished from PUBLIC COMPANIES. In most countries where this distinction exists, private companies are much more numerous than public companies. Rules of disclosure, audit, profit distribution, etc., may be less onerous for private companies.

profit and loss account the UK expression for the financial statement that summarizes the difference between the revenues and expenses of a period. Such statements may be drawn up frequently for the managers of a business, but a full audited statement is normally only published for each accounting year. The equivalent US expression is INCOME STATEMENT.

proportional consolidation a technique used in some countries as part of the preparation of CONSOLIDATED FINANCIAL STATEMENTS for a group of companies. It brings into the consolidated financial statements the group's share of all the assets, liabilities, revenues and expenses of the partly owned company. The method is virtually unknown in the United Kingdom and the United States, but is used by companies in France and the Netherlands for dealing with investments in companies that are held on a joint venture basis with one or more other investing companies.

provisions and reserves Unfortunately, there is some vagueness about the use of these two words. However, a provision in the United Kingdom usually means an amount charged against profit to reduce the recorded value of an asset or to cover an expected loss, even if the exact amount or timing of the liability is uncertain. A reserve, on the other hand, is an amount voluntarily or compulsorily set aside out of profit (after it has been calculated), often in order to demonstrate that the amount is not to be distributed as dividends.

However, US usage of the words is loose. For example, it is not unknown for accountants and others to talk about a 'bad debt reserve'; and in some continental European countries there may be very large 'provisions for contingencies' that Anglo-Saxon practice would treat as reserves. In US terminology, 'allowance' is often used instead of 'provision', and an amount set aside to cover an expected liability would often be called a reserve.

prudence a concept that is very strong in the accounting practices of nearly all countries. As the term suggests, it implies being cautious in the valuation of assets or the measurement of profit. It means always taking the lowest reasonable estimate of the value of assets, always anticipating losses but never anticipating profits.

In the United States, 'CONSERVATISM' is the word generally used for this concept.

public company a company whose securities (shares and loan stock) may legally be publicly traded. In the United Kingdom, the legal form of such a company is set out in the Companies Acts. The company must have 'public limited company' (or plc) as part of its name. There are equivalents to this form in other European countries (e.g. SA, AG, NV, SpA), but in the United States the nearest equivalent is a corporation that is registered with the SECURITIES AND EXCHANGE COMMISSION. Often the expression 'public company' is used loosely to mean companies which actually do have traded shares.

Q

quarterly reporting Companies registered with the SECURITIES AND EXCHANGE COMMISSION in the United States (the approximate equivalent of public companies in the United Kingdom) are required to do more than present lavish disclosures in their annual reports. They also have to make quarterly reports on turnover and on gross and net profit.

R

realization convention a well-established principle of conventional accounting, that gains or profits should only be recognized when they have been objectively realized by some transaction or event. This is consistent with the all-pervasive concept of CONSERVATISM, which anticipates losses but never profits.

receivables the US expression for amounts of money due to a business; often known as ACCOUNTS RECEIVABLE. The UK term is 'DEBTORS'.

reducing balance depreciation a technique of calculating the depreciation charge, usually for machines, whereby the annual charge reduces over the years of an asset's life. A fixed percentage DEPRECIATION is charged each year on the cost (first year) or the undepreciated cost (subsequent years).

Registrar of Companies a government official who is charged with the collection, organization and granting of public access to the financial statements of companies.

replacement cost accounting a system of preparing financial statements in which all ASSETS (and expenses relating to them, such as DEPRECIATION) are valued at current replacement costs.

reserves UK term for amounts notionally set aside out of profits (after the latter have been calculated), often to register the fact that they are voluntarily or compulsorily undistributable. The US equivalent is an appropriation of retained earnings. Reserves should be distinguished from PROVISIONS. In the United Kingdom, the latter are charged in the calculation of profit, and represent reductions in the value of ASSETS or anticipation of LIABILITIES. Of course, neither reserves nor provisions are amounts of cash. A provision relates to an accounting expense, and a reserve is an accounting allocation of undistributed profit from one heading to another. Reserves belong to shareholders and are part of a total of shareholders' equity, which also includes share capital. This total is represented by all the assets of the business, less the liabilities owed to outsiders.

It should be noted that this terminology is used somewhat loosely by some accountants. In the United States, 'reserve' is used to cover some of the meanings of 'provision' in the United Kingdom.

restricted surplus a US expression for amounts of past profit that are unavailable for distribution to shareholders. The UK equivalent would be 'undistributable reserves'.

retained profit/earnings amounts of profit, earned in the preceding year and former years, that have not yet been paid out as dividends. 'Retained earnings' is a typical US expression for such amounts, though it would also be understood in the United Kingdom. 'Retained profit' is a more usual UK expression.

revaluation Conventional accounting uses HISTORICAL COST as the basis for the valuation of assets. However, in some countries, it is acceptable to revalue fixed assets, either annually or from time to time. These revaluations can be done on the basis of current replacement cost or NET REALIZABLE VALUE. It is quite normal for large companies in some European countries to show land and buildings at revalued amounts in their balance sheets. Clearly, the purpose of this is to avoid a seriously misleading impression of their worth, when prices have risen substantially.

S

sale-and-leaseback a method of raising funds by a company without immediately depleting resources or incurring LIABILITIES. If a company owns and uses FIXED ASSETS, it may find it advantageous, for tax or other reasons, to sell them to a financial institution (the lessor) who then leases them back to the company.

The assets do not physically move as part of this process; so the company's business is not interrupted. The company receives a lump sum, which it may need for various purposes, and agrees to make future lease payments. Legally, it no longer owns the assets, nor does it have a legal liability. However, since the real substance of the situation is not well represented by the legal form it has now become accounting practice for certain leases in several countries to be recorded as both an asset and a liability in the lessee's balance sheet.

sales The figure for sales recorded in the financial statements for a period will include all those sales agreed or delivered in the period, rather than those that are paid for in cash. The sales figure will be shown net of sales taxes (VAT, etc.).

In the United Kingdom, the word TURNOVER is used in the financial statements, although 'sales' is generally used in the books of account.

secret reserves various means by which a company, particularly a financial institution, can make its true financial strength unclear in its financial statements. The purpose of this is to build up resources in case of future difficulty. If that future difficulty eventually emerges, it may be possible to hide it completely by merely absorbing it with the secret reserves. This may avoid a dangerous loss of confidence in the bank or other company concerned.

Secret reserves may be created by deliberately allowing FIXED ASSETS or INVENTORIES to be undervalued, or by creating unnecessary PROVISIONS.

The problem with such accounting practices is that they do indeed obscure the true financial position of a company from its shareholders and lenders. Thus, deliberate creation of secret reserves has gradually been outlawed in most countries.

Securities and Exchange Commission (SEC) US government agency set up in 1934 after the Wall Street Crash of 1929. Its function is to control the issue and exchange of publicly traded shares. Companies with such shares must register with the SEC, and then obey a mass of detailed regulations about disclosure and audit of financial information. An SEC-registered company in the United States is the nearest equivalent to a PUBLIC LIMITED COMPANY in Europe. In both countries, not all such companies are listed on a stock exchange.

segmental reporting an analysis of sales, profit or assets by line of business or by geographical area.

shareholders' funds the total of the shareholders' interest in a company. This will include the original share capital, amounts contributed in excess of the PAR VALUE of shares (i.e. SHARE PREMIUM or PAID IN SURPLUS), and retained profits. In the United States, this total is sometimes called Stockholders' Equity or Owners' Equity.

share premium amounts paid into a company (by shareholders when they purchased shares from the company) in excess of the NOMINAL VALUE of the shares. Shares are recorded at nominal values. However, share premium may be treated for most purposes exactly as if it were share capital. Both are included in SHAREHOLDERS' FUNDS.

In the United States there are many equivalent expressions, e.g. 'paid-in surplus'.

SSAP an abbreviation for Statement of Standard Accounting Practice, that is an ACCOUNTING STANDARD set for the United Kingdom and Ireland between 1970 and 1990.

stock US term for securities of various kinds; for example, COMMON STOCK or PREFERENCE STOCK (equivalent to ordinary and preference shares in UK terminology). However, the word 'share' is also understood in the United States, so that 'stockholder' and 'shareholder' are interchangeable.

In the United Kingdom this meaning survives, particularly in the expressions 'Stock Exchange' and 'Loan Stock'.

A source of great confusion in Anglo-American conversation is the British use of the word 'stocks' for what are called INVENTORIES in the United States.

stockholders' equity US expression for SHAREHOLDERS' FUNDS.

straight-line depreciation a system of calculating the annual DEPRECIATION expense of a FIXED ASSET. This method charges equal annual instalments against profit over the useful life of the asset. In total, the cost of the asset less any estimated residual scrap value is depreciated. This method is simple to use and thus very popular.

substance over form the presentation in financial statements of the underlying economic substance of a particular transaction, rather than the superficial legal or technical form of it. This is a fundamental idea in the world of Anglo-Saxon accounting. For example, when plant is leased by a lessee from a lessor there is no transfer of legal ownership or creation of legal liabilities. However, in many cases, the transaction is very similar to a purchase of assets and borrowing of money by the lessee. The plant will be at the lessee's premises, and the lessee will have contracted to pay a series of future lease payments. To concentrate on the legal form of the transaction would ignore the economic reality.

This method of thinking is taken the furthest in the United States. Another example there is the 'correction' of interest receipts or payments on loans which have a non-commercial rate of interest.

T

tangible assets ASSETS with physical existence, such as property, plant or equipment.

temporal method the principal method of foreign currency translation used in the United States between 1975 and 1981. It is now only to be used in particular circumstances in US or UK rules, but is fairly common in Germany.

timing difference a difference between the accounting year when certain expenses and revenues are recorded in the calculation of profit as opposed to when they are treated as deductions or increases in the calculation of taxable income. For example, accelerated DEPRECIATION for tax purposes will allow plant and machinery to be charged for tax purposes over a shorter period than that used by accountants as the useful life for depreciation in financial statements.

Such timing differences may lead to the need to account for DEFERRED TAX.

treasury stock US expression for a company's shares that have been bought back by the company and not cancelled. The shares are held 'in the corporate treasury'. They receive no dividends and carry no votes at company meetings.

The UK equivalent term is 'own shares'. The term 'treasury stock' is confusing to a UK reader because it might appear to refer to government bonds.

true and fair view the overriding legal requirement for the presentation of financial statements of companies in the United Kingdom, most of the Commonwealth and the European Community. The nearest US equivalent is 'fair presentation'.

turnover the UK expression used in profit and loss accounts for the SALES revenue of an accounting period. This is shown net of value added tax.

U

undistributable reserves amounts, paid in by shareholders or notionally allocated out of profits, that are not available for distribution to the shareholders as dividends. The US term is 'restricted surplus'.

Undistributable reserves would include SHARE PREMIUM and reserves on the REVALUATION of assets.

uniformity the use of the same rules of accounting or financial statement presentation from one company to another. Improvements in uniformity are encouraged by the setting of ACCOUNTING STANDARDS. One reason for this is to improve comparability between the financial statements of different companies.

unusual items US term for amounts that are not outside the ordinary course of the business, but are unusual in size or incidence. The approximate UK equivalent is EXCEPTIONAL ITEMS.

W

window dressing the manipulation of figures in financial statements in order to make them appear better (or perhaps worse) than they otherwise would be. A company might wish to do this in order to affect the actions of existing or potential shareholders or lenders, the government, or other readers of financial statements.

working capital the difference between CURRENT ASSETS and CURRENT LIABILITIES. This total is also known as NET CURRENT ASSETS, under which entry there are more details.

Annotated bibliography

This bibliography includes some writings in English with a European dimension. Desirable further reading depends on the aspect that readers wish to develop. Many will undoubtedly wish to study the regulatory framework of their own countries. Such books are best written by national authors, almost certainly in the native language concerned. The reader can relate the contents of these books to the wider framework developed here.

Quite a different matter is the consideration of international accounting in its general and comparative aspect. Three possibilities here are as follows (with greater or less European concentration):

C. W. Nobes and R. H. Parker, *Comparative International Accounting*, third edition, Prentice Hall, London, 1991.

F. D. S. Choi and G. G. Mueller, *International Accounting*, second edition, Prentice Hall, London, 1992.

D. Alexander, *International Comparative Accounting*, Academic Press, London (forthcoming).

None of the three are explicitly European in their focus. Of interest here is the *FEE European Survey of Published Accounts 1991*, Routledge, London.

Further surveys are expected at approximately two-yearly intervals (they are expensive). For detailed surveys of the EC countries there is the twelve-volume *European Financial Reporting* series, edited by S. McLeay and S. Archer, Routledge, London (1992 and later).

This is still gradually emerging – detailed, expensive, in English but usually with local expert authorship involved. A more convenient but rather less detailed alternative to the twelve-volume series is:

D. Alexander and S. Archer, *The European Accounting Guide*, first edition, Academic Press, London, 1992.

Regular updated editions are expected. This covers non-EC European countries also. It it expensive in hardback, but a cheap paperback edition is currently available.

Coopers & Lybrand Europe have produced a series of books on European accounting practices compared with the United Kingdom:
Accounting Comparisons: UK/Europe (1992 and later).

A book concentrating on group accounting in Europe is:
International Group Accounting edited by S. J. Gray, A. G. Coenenberg and P. D. Gordon, Routledge, London, 1993.

A more detailed work is FEE's
Seventh Directive Options and their Implementation, Routledge, London, 1993.

Feedback on exercises

Use of exercises

We have attempted to provide a wide variety of exercises without excessive volume or uninteresting repetition. Suggested numerical solutions, and outline feedback to discussion points, are provided in all cases. The exercises and feedback should be regarded as very much part of the text. They develop many of the points made in the chapters themselves, and provide an opportunity to develop the flexible and critical thinking which is so necessary for the understanding and improvement of European accounting practice.

Readers with a particular focus on interpreting financial statements, rather than preparing them, may sensibly omit some of the longer technical exercises.

It is obviously desirable to tackle an exercise thoroughly before looking at our own suggestions. Equally, the feedback given should be regarded as an input into the thinking and the discussion. It should never be regarded as automatically correct, and should never be used to stifle alternative viewpoints.

The best and most realistic case study in this area, however, is the one you provide yourself, or come up against in real life. Obtain the accounting statements for two or three companies from two or three countries, preferably for at least two or three years. Explore the differences, and analyze them for yourself.

Note on formats of financial statements

In general, these exercises use the vertical, *par destination*, form of the income statement. This is used, for example, in the United Kingdom, the United States, the Netherlands, by some German companies and, in France, for many group income statements. The other formats found in Europe are mentioned from time to time in the text (e.g. in the Appendix to Chapter 5, and in Figure 6.1).

For balance sheets, the book has used both horizontal and vertical types.

Outline feedback

Chapter 1

1.1 Theoretically, certainly. It can provide useful information and therefore lead to more efficient and effective decision-making. However, it is only justified in practice if:

   (a) the information is actually useful;
   (b) the information is actually used;
   (c) the costs of producing and circulating the information do not exceed its benefits.

1.2 Pointers towards the various likely information needs are given in the text. Significant differences of need or emphasis are easy to suggest. One solution would be just to provide more and more information, but this leads to acute problems of confusion and misunderstanding (as well as cost). Separate reports for different purposes? A general report ideal for nobody? Note that managers *are* usually considered separately, via management accounting.

1.3 Decisions are by definition about the future. You can decide what to eat tomorrow, but you cannot decide what to eat yesterday. Accounting information is usually based on past events. More reliable but less relevant?

1.4 Perhaps it all depends what 'reasonably' means. The needs of different users are certainly different (illustrate), but greater relevance from multiple reports would need to be set against:

   (a) costs of preparation;
   (b) danger of confusion and the difficulties of user education.

1.5 Open discussion. We suspect not. It is possible that users can specify the decision that they need to make, though even that is likely to be doubtful. The chances that the average accounts' user can actually specify the particular information characteristics relevant to his own needs seems extremely small. This suggests that the accountant will have to tell the user what the user's own needs are.

1.6 We cannot help much here. Discussion would be beneficial, and note and consider likely contextual explanations for differences.

1.7 As 1.6 but more so. Do any national patterns emerge?

Chapter 2

2.1 (a) F company balance sheets (in ecu)

	31.12.X3	31.12.X4
Freehold shop	135,000	135,000
Delivery vans	10,000	10,000
Inventory of goods	32,000	29,000
Amounts owed by customers	35,000	34,000
Cash at bank	19,000	36,000
Cash in till	500	2,000
	231,500	246,000
Capital	154,200	174,000
Loans	50,000	50,000
Amounts owed to supplier	26,500	21,250
Wages owed to staff	800	750
	231,500	246,000

The missing item was the capital at the relevant date.

(b) For 19X3, the opening capital was 150,000 ecu and the closing capital was 154,200 ecu. The increase presumably represents the profit for the year of 4,200 ecu. Similarly for 19X4, the profit would appear to be $174,000 - 154,200 = 19,800$ ecu. Note that the capital figure is cumulative. Its total increase from 150,000 to 174,000 represents the combined profits of the two years.

(c) The 31.12.X3 capital figure would be the net figure *after* deducting the dividend paid. This gives:

$$150,000 + \text{profit} - 15,000 = 154,200$$

The conclusion would therefore be that profits for the year 19X3 must have been 19,200 ecu.

(d) In several possible senses the delivery vans could be expected to be less good resources as they become older. It could be argued that some of the original new vans must have been used up during the operations of the two years. This might suggest that the assets figure, particularly for 19X4, is overstated. This would mean that the profit figure is also overstated. Think of possible ways of allowing for this, before the problem is considered more formally later.

2.2 Suggested adjustments are shown in Figure F2.1. Alternative answers are not necessarily wrong. For example, it is generally argued that revaluation gains are different from profits, but for some purposes the distinction may not be

		(a)	(b)	(c)	(d)	(e)	(f)	(g)	(h)
Revaluation								+12,000	
Shares	50,000								
Retained profit	7,000	+1,200	−400				+300		−1,000
Creditors	12,000			−8,000					+1,000
	69,000								
Premises	20,000							+12,000	
Equipment	9,000							−400	
Vehicle	7,000				−7,000				
Inventory	15,500	−2,800							
Debtors	2,500	−1,000				−2,500			
Bank	14,700		−400	−5,000	+7,000	+2,000			
Cash	300	+3,000		−3,000		+500	+700		
	69,000								

Figure F2.1 Adjustments to the balance sheet for G company.

necessary. A more important example, and an early introduction to the possibilities for lack of harmonization in financial accounting, is adjustment (h). It can be argued that G company has not yet done anything, merely indicated a future intention. If nothing has been done, and the formal process of 'declaring' the dividend has not yet happened, then perhaps no entries should be made.

This argument is regarded as logical in many countries, and in some cases, e.g. Germany, it would be normal practice not to make any adjustment at all for situation (h). In others, e.g. the United Kingdom, the adjustment shown is normal practice.

2.3 Solution to Kings Cross Company quadrant.

Applications				Sources			
Assets				*Capital and Liabilities*			
Land and buildings	110,000	+40,000	150,000	Share capital	150,000		150,000
Machinery	50,000	−5,000	45,000	Revaluation		+40,000	40,000
				Retained profits	5,000	+26,000	
Vehicles	25,000	−2,500	22,500			−13,000	18,000
Inventory at end of year	30,000		30,000				
Debtors	35,000		35,000	Loans (10%)	20,000		20,000
Prepayments		+3,000	3,000				
				Creditors	50,000	+1,000	
Cash at bank	10,000		10,000			+1,500	
						+2,000	
						+13,000	67,500
	260,000		295,500		225,000		295,500

Expenses				Revenues			
Cost of goods sold	90,000		90,000	Sales	160,000		160,000
Wages	20,000		20,000				
Interest		+2,000	2,000				
Rent, insurance, sundry expenses	15,000	+1,000					
		−3,000					
		+1,500	14,500				
Depreciation		+5,000					
		+2,500	7,500				
			134,000				
Profit			26,000				
	125,000		160,000		160,000		160,000

2.4 This question introduces a more practical treatment of the inventory and cost of goods sold. It has been assumed so far that every time a sale is made the business knows the exact cost of the actual items or units that have been sold. In the context of large-scale operations in the real world this assumption is both impractical and unnecessary. All that is really needed is to determine the cost of the inventory in hand at the beginning and at the end of the year. This can be done in two ways, either by physically counting inventory at each year end date and calculating the cost of those items only, or by keeping continuous inventory records in quantity terms (which can be compared with actual inventory holdings from time to time as and when convenient or necessary to ensure accuracy), and reading off the year-end figures.

The logic of this method is to assume that all the purchases in the year are expenses, and during the year to forget about inventory for this purpose. The inventory at the end of the previous year was obviously an asset. This is the same as the inventory at the beginning of the current year, so this too is clearly an asset, to be recorded in the assets section of the balance sheet. The purchases are treated as expenses and recorded in the expenses section of the recording system.

At the end of the year we will have arrived at the wrong answer. Our closing inventory, determined by one of the two methods just described will not in reality be the same as our opening inventory. If the actual closing inventory is higher than the opening inventory this will have been caused by some of the purchases in the year being added to inventory and therefore not sold. Such items need to be removed from expenses and added to assets. If the actual closing inventory is lower than the opening inventory this will have been covered by the total items sold in the year being greater than the total items purchased in the year, the difference being the reduction in inventory levels. Such items need to be removed from assets and added to expenses.

We suggest that the most logical and sure way of dealing with this is as follows:

opening inventory	opening goods available for sale
+ purchases	+ additional goods available for sale
= total goods available for sale	= total goods available for sale
− closing inventory	− total goods available for sale which were not sold
= cost of sales	= total goods (available for sale which were) sold

The recommended process is thus:

(a) opening inventory is in the assets quadrant
(b) purchases are in the expenses quadrant
(c) transfer opening inventory to purchases
(d) transfer closing inventory from purchases
(e) figure remaining in the expenses quadrant is cost of sales.

In practice the net difference between opening and closing inventory is often presented as a single figure.

Applications				Sources			
Assets				Capital and Liabilities			
Land and buildings	60,000		60,000	Share capital	150,000		150,000
Plant and machinery	40,000	−4,000	36,000				
				Retained profits	6,000	+37,000	
Vehicles	30,000	−6,000	24,000			−30,000	13,000
Inventory at start of year	20,000	−20,000		Creditors	37,000	+500	
		+25,000	25,000			+30,000	67,000
Debtors	20,000		20,000				
Shares in listed company	40,000		40,000				
Cash at bank and in hand	25,500		25,500				
	235,500		230,500		193,000		230,500
Expenses				Revenues			
Purchases (adjusted to cost of sales)	50,000	+20,000 +25,000	45,000	Sales	147,500		147,500
Depreciation		+4,000		Dividends from listed investment	2,000		2,000
		+6,000	10,000				
Wages and salaries	41,000		41,000				149,500
Salesmen's commission	6,000		6,000				
Rent, insurance, sundry expenses	8,500		8,500				
Cash discounts allowed	1,500		1,500				
Audit fees		+500	500				
	107,000		112,500		149,500		
Profit			37,000				
	342,500		149,500		342,500		149,500

2.5 Solution to Kingsad quadrant

Applications				Sources			
Assets				*Capital and Liabilities*			
Land and buildings	100,000	+50,000	150,000	Share capital	100,000		100,000
Plant and machinery	50,000	−5,000	45,000				
				Retained profits	46,000	+13,500	
						−5,000	54,500
Inventory at 1 Jan. 1994	30,000	−30,000		Revaluation reserve		+50,000	50,000
		+20,000	20,000	Creditors	30,000	+5,000	35,000
Debtors	25,000	−1,000	24,000				
Prepayments		+500	500				
	205,000		239,500		176,000		239,500

Expenses				*Revenues*			
Purchases (adjusted to cost of sales)	70,000	+30,000		Sales	150,000		
		−20,000	80,000	less returns	1,000		149,000
Depreciation		+5,000	5,000				
Wages and salaries	40,000		40,000				
General expenses	10,000	−500	9,500				
Bad debt		+1,000	1,000				
			135,500				
Profit			+13,500				
	120,000		149,000		149,000		149,000
	325,000				325,000		

2.6

Rent

19X1			19X1		
	Cash	300	Dec. 31 Income Statement		400
Dec. 31 Balance c/d		100			
		400			400
			Dec. 31 Balance b/f		100

Taxes

19X1			19X1		
Jan. 1	Balance b/d	80	Dec. 31 Income Statement		350
19X1	Cash	360	Dec. 31 Balance c/d		90
		440			440
Dec. 31 Balance b/f		90			

Sections of balance sheet at 31 December 19X1

Current Assets		*Current Liabilities*	
Taxes paid in advance	90	Rent owing	100

2.7

Income Statement for year ended 30 September 19X2 (in ecu)

Inventory	4,400	Sales	31,219
Purchases	21,435		
	25,835		
Less Inventory	7,200		
Cost of Goods Sold	18,635		
Gross Profit c/d	12,584		
	31,219		31,219
Wages	4,399	Gross Profit b/f	12,584
Insurance	242	Rents received	500
Light and Heat	185		
Sundry Expenses	319		
Selling Expenses	532		
Net Profit	7,407		
	13,084		13,084

Balance sheet as at 30th September 19X2

Land and buildings	7,700	Capital	12,920
Equipment	1,400	Net profit	7,407
Vehicles	1,500		20,327
Office furniture	2,816		
Inventory	7,200	Bank overdraft	323
Debtors	2,926	Creditors	2,829
Insurance prepayment	32	Wages owing	95
	23,574		23,574

2.8

Income statement for year ended 31st December 19X7 (in ecu)

Inventory	9,274	Sales	81,742
Purchases	62,101		
	71,375		
Less Inventory	9,884		
Cost of goods sold	61,491		
Gross profit	20,251		
	81,742		81,742
Rent and property taxes	840	Gross profit	20,251
Light and heat	331		
Salaries and wages	8,268	Rent received	1,000
Insurances	90		
Motor expenses	1,190		
General expenses	933		
Net profit	9,599		
	21,251		21,251

Balance sheet as at 31st December 19X7

Premises	10,000	Capital	24,447
Motor vans	8,000	Net profit	9,599
Office furniture	2,148		34,046
Inventory	9,884		
Debtors	7,689	Creditors	5,462
Bank	1,582	Light and heat due	85
Property taxes in advance	40		
Rent due	250		
	39,593		39,593

Chapter 3

3.1 There is scope for wide differences of view, and considerable debate. We suspect that objectivity and prudence are likely to come higher up the 'importance' scale for accountants and auditors than they are up the 'useful' scale. This would lead to discussion of whether the user matters more or the producer matters more!

3.2 It is really much less objective than people often claim. Examples of 'unobjectivity' include:

problem of determining purchase cost
overhead allocation
depreciation calculation
provisions and their estimation
prudence (a subjective bias by definition).

3.3 Completeness requires the inclusion of all relevant contents. The monetary measurement convention requires that that which is not measurable is not recorded, even if it is clearly relevant. Discuss the conflict.

3.4 See the definition in text and the following discussion.
   The whole process is subjective in principle, and often arbitrary in practice (e.g. the date the invoice happened to get typed), and the answer to (c) is surely 'no'.

3.5 This is about the balance sheet equation. Resources equals claims. Revenue recognition increases claims (i.e. profits) and therefore increases resources, for example, stock at cost may be replaced by debtors at selling price.

3.6 (a) (i) The *historical cost convention* is that transactions are recorded in the accounts at the original price. An item then remains in the accounting records at that original figure until disposal. Assets, and therefore expenses, are recorded and evaluated at original cost, and profit is calculated as revenues less original cost of resources used.

   (ii) The *going concern convention* is the assumption, in the absence of evidence to the contrary, that the business will continue to trade in the normal way into the foreseeable future. This enables the accountant to assume that inventory will eventually be sold, that fixed assets will continue to be used, and so on.

(b) No, traditional financial accounting based on the historical cost convention does not make the going concern convention unnecessary. Traditional and current practice relies heavily on the going concern convention. Inventory is evaluated on the assumption that it will eventually be sold in the ordinary course of business. Fixed assets are depreciated over their estimated useful life to the business, and this requires the assumption that the business will continue to operate over the period of that useful life. Prepayments assume that the firm will operate and use the service acquired. Indeed the whole basis of the accruals convention is that the business is a continuing operation and the going concern convention is, therefore, crucial to current accounting practice even though that practice is based on the historical cost convention.

(c) The reason why a shareholder needs a report at all is because he wishes to use the report to influence some future action or decision on his part. If this is not so, then he has no use for the report whatever its contents. However, the above does not strictly answer the question. The shareholder may well find a report on the past events extremely useful as a guide to predicting future outcomes and future trend. Equally, however, the shareholder may find management's estimate of future events to be directly useful to him. Perhaps the short answer to the question, is 'both'!

3.7 There are a number of possible treatments.

Write off the whole amount in 19X1. This could be justified on the grounds of *prudence* – any return being highly speculative.

Write off the amount in strict proportion to the expected benefits. This would be supported by the *matching* convention, i.e. to allocate the expenses over the period of benefit in proportion to that benefit. This would imply expenses of 0 in 19X1 (as benefit does not commence in 19X1), 6,000 in 19X2 and 4,000 in 19X3.

The conflict between prudence and matching is usually resolved through compromise though, in areas of real doubt, some accountants or rule-makers in some countries believe that prudence should prevail and be given greater emphasis. A reasonable compromise in this case might well be to charge all the 10,000 as an expense in 19X2 – any return in 19X2 being much more speculative than those expected in 19X3.

This suggested compromise is, however, a highly debatable (indeed subjective!) proposition and its validity would depend on the particular circumstances, advice of advertising and industry experts, earlier treatment of similar items (*consistency* is an important accounting convention) and also on the *materiality* of the amounts concerned. If the amounts concerned are small in relation to your results as a whole, then it is pointless to spend time and money in a lengthy and detailed investigation.

We should perhaps also consider the users of the accounting reports. For example, a *trade creditor* will be particularly interested in the assets and liability position. From this point of view, an asset which exists because of the speculative expectation of higher sales next year is not exactly a safe 'near-cash' security. On the other hand, a *shareholder* will be concerned with the future trend of profits, and application of the matching convention is arguably an essential requirement for showing a fair indication of present profit and current and future trends.

3.8 See text, but avoid the unthinking use of technical phrases and formal definitions. Discussion and mutual criticism would be useful here.

3.9 See Chapters 1 and 3. Importance of (and conflict between?) relevance, reliability, etc. Specific uses might include profitability and liquidity appraisal, assessment of managers and directors, invest/disinvest decisions and so on.

3.10 There is certainly a conflict between these two conventions. Perhaps, though, this does not stop them both being beneficial ideals to bear in mind as part of a desirable context for accounting thought and action. Or does it? Scope for discussion here.

3.11 The proposition as stated is certainly defensible. On the other hand it could be suggested that:

(a) past information is not irrelevant if it improves the quality of estimates about the future;
(b) management cannot be allowed to produce its own estimates because of lack of neutrality, and accounts must therefore seek to confine themselves to 'facts'.

3.12 This is quite a complicated issue. Terms need to be defined, as in the text, and then explained in common sense non-technical terms (not so easy). Perhaps the fundamental idea behind the problem here can be highlighted by posing another question. If a uniform accounting treatment is imposed for some particular transaction or type of contract is this:

(a) good, because uniformity automatically leads to comparability, or
(b) bad, because the information given is likely to be irrelevant to the *particular* situations involved, and therefore the information cannot adequately allow comparison between those situations?
Scope for discussion.

3.13 Again, much scope for discussion. If accounting statements are about the communication of complicated and subjective concepts between unpredictable and all-too-human human beings (assumption 1), and a coherent overall framework is interpreted in a pseudo-scientific sense as containing logically coherent interrelationships and allowing prediction of the so-far unknown from that which is already established (assumption 2), then the suggested statement is certainly correct.

But how valid are assumptions 1 and 2 here?

Chapter 4

Detailed feedback would be superfluous in this area.
   The crucial requirements are:

(a) wide and free-thinking ideas and discussion;
(b) recognition by readers of the restricting influences on their own attitudinal starting-points.

Chapter 5

5.1 There is scope for much diversity of detail here. Issues to consider perhaps include harmonization/standardization, nationalism and natural lethargy,

418   FEEDBACK ON EXERCISES

and the deep and significant contextual differences which militate against successful harmonization. If the European Community and the IASC are not working in the same direction could this be because each body is no more than the sum of the nationalistic influences pressurizing it?

5.2 Optionality is undoubtedly *very* great, though the trend in both cases is for gradual reduction. Maybe it is, or at least was, inevitable in order to obtain any progress at all. Perhaps differences caused by different business and cultural environments cannot be changed without changing the environments? Usefulness – better than nothing, and a move in the right direction, etc. (?).

5.3 A company operating in a local environment should perhaps be allowed to prepare accounts as determined by that environment. However, a company quoted on any European stock exchange should perhaps be required to produce reports useful to any European citizen. Against the first proposition, does 'operate' mean 'obtain investment', or does it include normal trading operations with customers and suppliers? If the latter, surely nobody operates in a local environment. Against the second proposition is it possible in practice? Scope for general discussion.

Chapter 6

6.1 (a) One definition of assets that has been suggested is that they are 'probable future economic benefits obtained or controlled by a particular entity as a result of past transactions or events'. The essential words and phrases in this definition are:

  (i) *probable* – although accounts may be historical in nature it is necessary when preparing financial statements to take into account the future, and thus any benefits need to be probable;
  (ii) *future* – the definition of an asset should mention that the benefits provided by assets relate to more than one accounting period into the future;
  (iii) *economic benefits* – the benefit to be derived from an asset should be economic (this would exclude non-economic benefits; for example, the pleasure derived from owning a rare book) and the ownership should be beneficial, which distinguishes it from a liability;
  (iv) *obtained or controlled* – an asset may be owned or the entity may have control over it, for example, an asset which is subject to a financial lease may be capitalized because an entity has control over that asset, although it has no legal ownership;
  (v) *entity* – assets may be found in any financial statement and not just businesses, and therefore the word entity is appropriate.
  (vi) *past transactions or events* – before an entry can be made in the books of account, there must have been a transaction which can be supported by documentation, or an economic event.

(b) Fixed asset expenditure may be distinguished from other types of expenditure insofar as it results in an asset with all of the following characteristics:

(i) it is intended to be held by an entity for use in the production or supply of goods and services on a continuing basis;
(ii) it is intended to have a life of more than one accounting period;
(iii) it is not intended for sale in the ordinary course of business.

6.2 (a) Machine 1 is an operating lease as there is no transfer of the risks or rewards of ownership.
(b) Machine 2 involves a total payment of 12,000 ecu. Since this is much greater than 8,000 ecu, it implies that rewards of ownership are transferred. So, it is a finance lease.
(c) Machine 3 involves a total payment of 7,200 ecu which, on present value terms, will never equate to anything approaching 8,000. Therefore it is an operating lease.

6.3 Machine 1 will cause a simple expense at the rate of 250 ecu per month, with corresponding reductions in the bank balance.
   Machine 2 will involve an opening entry:

Dr Leasehold machine	8,000	
Cr Lease liability		8,000

Each payment of 1,500 ecu will contain some interest and some repayment of the liability. Thus:

Dr Interest expenses	X	
Dr Lease liability	X	
Cr Bank		1,500

Additionally there will be an annual depreciation charge based on the 8,000 ecu cost figure.
   Machine 3, being an operating lease like Machine 1, will involve an expense charge of the amounts due.

6.4 Briefly, there is no legal ownership of the tangible asset, but there is legal ownership of the right to use it. There is ownership and control over an economic resource. Are financial statements supposed to be about economic or legal situations? In the end, this question requires a consensus answer, because there is no theoretical one.

6.5 Scope for discussion, perhaps related ultimately to relevance vs. reliability, and the needs/importance of different users. We would suggest that the statement in the question is correct but is tautological in the sense that words like 'intention' and 'reasonably' are used throughout, and are not defined.

Chapter 7

7.1 The cost figure should be the total cost of making the fixed asset usable or improving it, excluding all costs of actually using it or repairing it. This gives:

$$11{,}000 + 100 + 200 + 500 = 11{,}800 \text{ ecu}$$

Note the difference in treatment between the additional component and the replacement parts.

7.2 (a) Annual charge $= \dfrac{12{,}000 - 2{,}000}{400}$

$\qquad\qquad\qquad\; = 2{,}500$ ecu

(b)
Year 1	Cost	12,000	ecu
	Depreciation (40%)	4,800	
	NBV	7,200	
Year 2	Depreciation (40%)	2,880	
	NBV	4,320	
Year 3	Depreciation (40%)	1,728	
	NBV	2,592	
Year 4	Depreciation (40%)	1,037	
	NBV	1,555	ecu

(c) If reducing balance had been used, then an asset recorded at 1,555 ecu is sold for 2,000 ecu, giving a gain of 445 ecu. This is a realized gain, and is in a sense merely a correction to the estimated depreciation charges of earlier years. Under the straight line method, in this example, no correction is needed.

The effects on reported profit can be summarized as follows:

	Straight line			Reducing balance		
Year 1	Reduction	2,500	ecu	Reduction	4,800	ecu
Year 2		2,500			2,880	
Year 3		2,500			1,728	
Year 4		2,500			1,037	
Year 5		Nil		Increase	445	
Total effect		10,000	ecu		10,000	ecu

7.3 (a) The essential point is that depreciation is an *allocation* process following the logic of the matching convention. It gives, perhaps, the (historical) cost of the benefit derived from and using the asset during the year.

(b) The simple, and perhaps only safe, answer is that it is the unallocated part of the original figure. This does not sound very useful from the viewpoint of readers of a balance sheet. NBV is *not* a value in any economic sense.

7.4 Arguments for the capitalization of interest:

(a) Interest on funds borrowed to create an asset is not different in nature from the other costs associated with the asset. If there is a time lag between commencing the development, and receiving earnings from the asset, the interest paid on borrowed funds during this period may fairly be treated as part of the cost of the asset.

(b) If interest on borrowings used to develop an asset is charged against revenue before the asset starts to earn, the measurement of income for that period will be distorted as a direct consequence of acquiring the asset. Similarly, unless the full cost of the development is measured and amortized against its earnings when they commence, an overstated profit figure will result.

(c) Capitalization of interest will show the true cost of the development for accurate comparison with assets purchased on the open market.

Arguments for treating interest as a charge to income without regard to the purpose of the borrowings are:

(a) Borrowed funds finance the whole of the activities of the business and cannot be associated with individual assets unless some form of arbitrary allocation is applied.

(b) All funds have a cost. Thus it is illogical to capitalize interest on borrowed funds and ignore internally generated funds which may also be used to finance capital developments.

(c) Interest is calculated on a time basis and should thus be treated as a period cost. This treatment enables a more accurate indication of past and future cash flows to be derived from the accounts.

7.5 See text. Note significance of allocation over the useful life in proportion to the benefit, i.e. the pattern of benefit is crucial. The relevance or otherwise of other ancillary expenses in this particular matching process is also important.

7.6 Debatable of course, but if the matching convention is accepted at all, then it is surely better to have depreciation vaguely right, rather than not there or precisely wrong.

Chapter 8

8.1 The inventory figure for production cost of manufactured items can certainly never be reliable in an economic sense. However, it can be precisely determined and precisely calculated, once the necessary arbitrary assumptions about overhead behaviour have been made. Such precision could be suggested as improving comparability, and therefore relevance. However, can figures based on simplistic and arbitrary assumptions ever be truly relevant to any particular user?

8.2 (a) **Violas.** Since the inventory is reduced to nil by 30th September then profits under all assumptions will be the same, as differences in calculated profit arise only because of different assumptions about usage.

	ecu
Sales	2,700
Cost of sales	1,750
Gross profit	950
Value of closing inventory	250

However under replacement cost:

Operating profit	1,050
Holding loss realized	100
Gross profit	950

Cellos

(i) FIFO

		ecu
Sales		3,200
Opening inventory	1,200	
Purchases	2,400	
	3,600	
Closing inventory		
(1 @ 800)		
(1 @ 900)	1,700	1,900
Gross profit		1,300

(ii) LIFO

Sales		3,200
Opening inventory	1,200	
Purchases	2,400	
	3,600	
Closing inventory		
(1 @ 600)		
(1 @ 900)	1,500	2,100
Gross Profit		1,100

(iii) Weighted average

$$\begin{array}{lll} \text{Inventory} \\ 2\ @\ 600 & = 1{,}200 \\ 1\ @\ 700 & = \underline{\ \ 700} \\ 3 & \ 1{,}900 \end{array}$$

30th June Weighted average = 633 (i.e. 1,900 ÷ 3)

$$\begin{array}{lll} 2\ @\ 633 & = 1{,}266 \\ 1\ @\ 800 & = \underline{\ \ 800} \\ 3 & \ 2{,}066 \end{array}$$

30th September weighted average = 689 (i.e. 2,066 ÷ 3)

$$\begin{array}{lll} 1\ @\ 689 & = 689 \\ 1\ @\ 900 & = \underline{\ \ 900} \\ 2 & \ \underline{1{,}589} \text{ closing inventory} \end{array}$$

Sales	3,200
Cost of sales	
1 @ 633	
2 @ 689	2,011
Gross profit	1,189

(iv) Replacement cost

As at 30th June: replacement cost of inventory	= 3 × 700	= 2,100
Profit on sale		= 300
Holding gains		= 200
As at 30th September: replacement cost of inventory	= 3 × 800	= 2,400
Profit on sale		= 600
Holding gains		= 200
As at 30th November: replacement cost of inventory	= 2 × 900	= 1,800
Holding gain		= 100
Total operating profit		= 900
Total holding gains		= 500

(b) Discussion.

(i) FIFO seems to produce more up-to-date costs in the balance sheet.

(ii) LIFO seems to produce more up-to-date expense figures in the income calculation.
(iii) Weighted average achieves neither of the above, or a bit of both, depending on your attitude.
(iv) Replacement cost achieves both, at the cost of more complexity and perhaps more subjectivity, though this last point is debatable.

8.3 It can certainly be validly argued that failure to use the percentage of completion method, if paragraph 43 is satisfied, would result in a failure to report, or even to attempt to report, the economic substance of position and performance (if that is what financial statements are supposed to do). However, there is always some uncertainty involved (what does 'reliably estimated' mean?). The usual discussion(!).

Chapter 9

9.1 Logically, of course, the statement is perfectly correct. However, it is clear from earlier chapters that there is no possibility of getting the balance sheet 'right' in any coherent objective sense, and it is clear from this chapter that there is no possibility of getting the liabilities 'right' in such a sense either. So in the real world the owners' equity can never be right

9.2 The point is almost certainly overstated in the question, but the general direction of the argument is surely correct. Human attitude will always be a factor, but 'whim' can be influenced and perhaps controlled by the creation of professional norms and practices. Some would argue that legal or centrally inspired accounting plans can remove the human element, but others might reply that such plans are purely arbitrary, and are indeed themselves created by human whim. Scope for debate here.

9.3 This should cause a bit of thought. Depreciation provisions? Provisions for possible bad debts? Receipts for sales already received where the sale has not been made yet? The first two of these are likely to be shown as deductions on the asset side of the balance sheet, but the third one is not. Any more?

Chapter 10

10.1 See text. Discussion should include reference to the tax effects of dividend policies, and economic implications.

10.2 (a)

	Year				
	1	2	3	4	Total
Accounting profit (after depreciation charge)	100	100	100	100	400
Accounting depreciation	20	20	20	20	80
Tax allowance for depreciation	80	—	—	—	80
Taxable profit	40	120	120	120	400
Profit before tax	100	100	100	100	400
Taxation	20	60	60	60	200
Profit after actual tax	80	40	40	40	200
Profit before tax	100	100	100	100	400
Taxation charge if calculated on accounting profits	50	50	50	50	200
Profit after accounting tax	50	50	50	50	200

The profit after tax figures, which are used for the e.p.s and P/E ratio (see Part IV) would indicate that in year 2 the performance of the company halved. However, has the firm, has the management, been half as successful? Arguably not! Over the four-year period the firm has made the same accounting profit with the same resources each year. Thus the profit after accounting tax figures provide a better guide to the performance of the company.

(b)

	Year				
	1	2	3	4	Total
Profit before tax	100	100	100	100	400
Taxation payable for year	20	60	60	60	200
Additional charge (credit) to deferred tax account	30	(10)	(10)	(10)	0
Total tax charge	50	50	50	50	200
Profit after tax	50	50	50	50	200

Deferred tax account

Balance c/d 31.12.01	30	Appropriation account 31.12.01	30
	30		30
Appropriation a/c 31.12.02	10	Balance b/d 1.1.02	30
Balance c/d 31.12.02	20		
	30		30
Appropriation a/c 31.12.03	10	Balance b/d 1.1.03	20
Balance c/d 31.12.03	10		
	20		20
Appropriation a/c 31.12.04	10	Balance b/d 1.1.04	10
	10		10

10.3

	Year				
	1	2	3	4	Total
Accounting profit	100	100	100	100	400
Depreciation charged	20	20	20	20	
Depreciation charged		25	25	25	
Depreciation charged			30	30	
Depreciation charged				55	
Profit before depreciation	120	145	175	230	670
assets (∴ 100% tax depreciation)	80	100	120	220	520
Taxable profit	120 − 80 = 40	145 − 100 = 45	175 − 120 = 55	230 − 220 = 10	670 − 520 = 150
Income statements					
Profit before tax	100	100	100	100	400
Taxation: payable for year	20	22.5	27.5	5	75
plus Additional charge (credit) to deferred tax account: 50% of	(80 − 20)[a] = 30	(100 − 45)[a] = 27.5	(120 − 75)[a] = 22.5	(220 − 130)[a] = 45	125
Total tax charge	50	50	50	50	200
Profit after tax	50	50	50	50	200

[a] i.e. the assets purchased less the cumulative depreciation

Comparing 10.2 and 10.3, we see that the total position over the four years is no longer the same. The total tax charge is increased by 125 ecu. This is not surprising, as it equals the liability provided for at the end of year 4 on the deferred tax account. The transfer to the deferred tax account can be seen to be the result of an amalgam of positive originating timing differences relating to capital allowances, and negative reversing timing differences relating to depreciation. The resultant figure of profit after tax, 50 per annum, reflects the underlying profitability of the company. It does not give an impression of improved profitability because of the effect of tax allowances related to asset acquisitions.

Deferred tax account

Balance c/d 31.12.01	30	Appropriation account 31.12.01	30
	30		30
		Balance b/d 1.1.02	30
Balance c/d 31.12.02	57.5	Appropriation a/c 31.12.02	27.5
	57.5		57.5
		Bal. b/d 1.1.03	57.5
Bal. c/d 31.12.03	80	Appropriation a/c 31.12.03	22.5
	80		80
		Bal. b/d 1.1.04	80
Bal. c/d 31.12.04	125	Appropriation a/c 31.12.04	45
	125		125
		Bal. b/d 1.1.05	125

10.4 An interesting proposition! Is there, for example, an 'expected outflow of resources'? If not, there is no liability. If no provision for deferred tax is made, the effect is to increase ownership equity by the full amount of the provision not made. However, this is not consistent with the *deferral* of tax due, and, ultimately its payment must be expected unless legislation changes. If present values are used, this would suggest a present value that is very low, perhaps immaterial. They are not usually considered though. Scope for much discussion.

Chapter 11

11.1 (a)

Historical cost accounting

	Income statements for the years:			Balance sheets at year ends:		
	19X0	19X1		19X0		19X1
Sales	3,000	3,600	Inventory			
Cost of sales	(2,000)	(2,000)	@ 1,000 (4)	4,000	(2)	2,000
Gross profit	1,000	1,600	@ 1,200 (2)	2,400	(2)	2,400
Expenses (rent)	(600)	(700)	@ 1,400 (0)	0	(2)	2,800
Net profit	400	900		6,400		7,200
Tax	(200)	(450)				
Retained profit	200	450	Cash	3,800		3,450
				10,200		10,650
			Capital	10,000		10,000
			Retained profits	200		650
				10,200		10,650

(b)

Replacement cost accounting

	Income statements for the years:			Balance sheets at year ends:		
	19X0	19X1		19X0		19X1
Sales	3,000	3,600	Inventory			
Cost of sales	(2,200)	(2,600)	@ 1,300 (6)	7,800	(0)	0
Gross profit	800	1,000	@ 1,400 (0)	0	(6)	8,400
Expenses (rent)	(600)	(700)				
Operating profit	200	300	Cash	3,800		3,450
Tax paid	(200)	(450)		11,600		11,850
Profit/(loss)	0	(150)				
Realized holding gain						
(2 × 100)	200 (2 × 300)	600	Capital	10,000		10,000
Historic cost profit	200	450	Realized holding			
			gain	200		800
				10,200		10,800
			Distributable profits	0		(150)
			Unrealized holding			
			gain	1,400		1,200
				11,600		11,850

(c) The figures show that, given an intention to continue the operations of the business at the current level, the historical cost profit figure is entirely mythical – indeed in the second year the business has an operating loss on this basis.

11.2 (a)

Duck Co. balance sheet as at 31 December 19X0

				ecu			ecu
Fixed assets:				12,600	Shareholders' interest:		
less depreciation				1,260	Shares		10,000
				11,340			
Current assets:					Profit		(20)
Inventory			4,000		Holding gains	3,600	
Cash	10,000					950	4,550
	8,000						14,530
	47,900				Loan		8,000
	(9,000)				Current liabilities:		
	(35,550)				Creditors		960
	(13,200)	8,150		12,150			
				23,490			23,490

Income statement for the year to 31 December 19X0

			ecu			ecu
Purchases	8,000			Sales	7,200	
	8,250				10,800	
	8,500				15,600	
	10,800	35,550			14,300	47,900
Holding gains		950				
		36,500				
Closing inventory (40 × 100)		4,000				
		32,500				
Gross profit c/f		15,400				
		47,900				47,900
General expenses		13,200		Gross profit b/d		15,400
Loan interest		960				
Depreciation		1,260		Net loss c/f		20
		15,420				15,420

Inventory holding gains are calculated as follows:

1 March	$100 - 60 = 40 \times (-5) =$	(200)
1 June	$210 - 150 = 60 \times 10 \;=$	600
1 September	$310 - 280 = 30 \times 5 \quad\;\;=$	150
1 December	$430 - 390 = 40 \times 10 \;=$	400
		950

(b) Holding gains are those gains, or credit balances, caused by increases in the recorded figures of resources over the period during which they are held by a business. They cause an increase in the ownership claims on the business, but have not arisen as the result of a transaction.

Whether or not any particular holding gains are to be regarded as distributable is a function of the capital maintenance assumption adopted. As discussed in the text, the numerical increase in resources represented by the holding gain will need to be used in the replacement of the original resources once they have been used. If, therefore, the capital maintenance concept being used is the maintenance of the current operating capability of the business then the holding gains are not available for distribution as dividend. Note that this logic follows whether or not the holding gains are 'realized' through the sale of the original resource.

11.3

	ecu		ecu	
Exit value income statements				
Sales	20,000		25,000	
Cost of sales	11,000		12,000	
	9,000		13,000	
'Depreciation'	4,000	(1)	2,000	(2)
	5,000		11,000	
Less Operating gain included in previous year	—		500	(3)
	5,000		10,500	
Add Unrealized operating gain	500	(4)	800	(5)
Realizable income	5,500		11,300	
Exit value balance sheets				
Fixed assets	6,000		4,000	
Inventory	2,500		3,800	
Cash	12,000	(6)	24,000	(7)
	20,500		31,800	
Capital	15,000		15,000	
Realizable income	5,500		16,800	
	20,500		31,800	

Notes
1. 10,000 − 6,000
2. 6,000 − 4,000
3. Included as realized in the 11,000 but already included, as unrealized, in the 5,500 for year 1.
4. 2,500 − 2,000
5. 3,800 − 3,000
6. 15,000 − 10,000 + 20,000 − (11,000 + 2,000)
7. 12,000 + 25,000 − (12,000 + 1,000)

The unrealized gain on inventory is here calculated on an annual basis, inventory during the year being left at cost. It would be possible, although more complicated, to record such unrealized gains more frequently – even daily if desired. Care must be taken, however, to ensure that a previously recorded unrealized gain is not again added into 'realizable income' when it is realized.

11.4

Person	Deprival value	Reason
A	2	Cost of replacement
B	6	Cost of replacement
C	11	Economic value not received
D	14	Realizable value not received
E	19	Cost of replacement
F	22	Cost of replacement

11.5 **Stage 1**. Convert the historical figures at the beginning of the year into ecu of current purchasing power at the beginning of the year.

			31.12.X7 000 ecu
Fixed assets			
Cost	500 × 220/180		611
less Depreciation	300 × 220/180		366
			245
Current assets			
Inventory	100 × 220/215	102	
Debtors		200	
Bank		150	
		452	
less			
Current liabilities			
Creditors		300	
			152
Share capital and reserves (balancing figure)			397

Stage 2. Convert the historical figures at the end of the year into ecu of current purchasing power at the end of the year.

			31.12.X8 000 ecu
Fixed assets			
Cost	500 × 240/180		666
Depreciation	400 × 240/180		533
			133
Current assets			
Inventory	150 × 240/235	153	
Debtors		300	
Bank		350	
		803	
less			
Current liabilities			
Creditors		400	
			403
Share capital and reserves (balancing figure)			536

Stage 3. Update the share capital and reserves figure calculated in Stage 1 from 31.12.X7 ecu of current purchasing power into 31.12.X8 ecu of purchasing power.

	31.12.X8 000 ecu
Share capital and reserves 397 × 240/220	433
Profit for year is 536,000 − 433,000 = 103,000	

Stage 4. Let us now prepare the income statements for the year ended 31.12.X8

	Historical cost 000 ecu			CPP 000 ecu
Sales		1,850	× 240/230	1,931
Cost of goods sold				
opening inventory	100		× 240/215	112
purchases	1,350		× 240/230	1,409
	1,450			1,521
less closing inventory	150		× 240/235	153
		1,300		1,368
Gross profit		550		563
Expenses	300		× 240/230	313
Depreciation	100		× 240/180	133
Loss on net monetary items	—		(see note)	14
		400		460
Net profit		150		103

The loss on net monetary items is calculated as follows:

	000s ecu
Net monetary items, 31.12.X7	50
Net monetary items, 31.12.X8	250
Increase in year	200

Since 50 has been held throughout the year, this represents a purchasing power loss of:

$$50 \times \frac{20}{220} = 5$$

The increase of 200 is assumed to have accrued evenly throughout the year, and therefore represents a purchasing power loss of:

$$200 \times \frac{10}{230} = \frac{9}{14}$$

Tutorial note. You may find that your answer does not agree with the above answer by the odd ecu or so because of the rounding of figures.

11.6 For explanation and illustration, see text. The key point is that replacement cost accounting splits up the historical cost profit into two different elements: the current operating profit and the holding gains. These elements have different causes and different effects, and reporting the split facilitates separate analysis and interpretation.

11.7 An interesting one. Replacement cost accounting, given rising cost levels, leads to a lower operating profit figure, which is more prudent. It also leads to higher asset figures in the balance sheet, which is less prudent. These two effects considered together will lead to much lower profitability and return on resource ratios, which perhaps sounds more prudent!

11.8 Arguably, the suggestion would give an income statement with a useful long-run operating perspective (note that this would perhaps be even more relevant if based on future RC rather than on current RC figures) and at the same time a balance sheet of current cash equivalents, i.e. meaningful current market values. Discuss the advantages of both of these. Against this, there would be a loss of internal consistency in the reporting package which seems significant. Discuss this, too.

11.9 In essence, CPP adjustments attempt to update financial measurements for changes in the value of the measuring unit, without altering or affecting the underlying basis of valuation – usually, but not necessarily, historical cost. They do it by using general averaged index adjustments, usually, but again not necessarily, by means of a retail price index.

11.10 Note the generality of the wording of the question, no particular valuation mechanism is mentioned. Perhaps, as authors and teachers, we should not give our own views. In the end it may come back to relevance vs. reliability. Is a general index relevant to anybody or anything?

Chapter 12

12.1 See text, but briefly:

A subsidiary implies control through shareholding or dominant influence.
A joint venture implies joint control by two or more parties.
An associate implies significant influence, without control or dominant influence.
An investment in shares implies a relatively passive role with no material influence.

With a subsidiary, the usual approach is consolidation, including complete combination of individual company accounting statements, with the necessary recognition of minority interests. With an associate, the usual approach is equity accounting, where the investment figure is increased by the appropriate proportion of the success of the associate, i.e. in effect, a one-line proportional consolidation. With an investment in shares, no benefits are taken in the consolidated accounts except for dividends.

Note the possibility of a more general use of proportional consolidation where joint ventures are concerned. Note also the practical difficulties of differentiation which underlie the above apparently straightforward distinctions.

12.2 Consolidated balance sheet as at 30.6.X2

	000 ecu
Assets	
Goodwill (Note 1)	50
Land and Plant	1,200
Inventory (1,000 – 10)	990
Debtors (240 – 2)	238
	2,478
Liabilities	
Creditors (46 – 2)	44
	2,434
Represented by	
Ordinary 1 ecu shares	1,000
Reserves (Note 2)	1,280.5
	2,280.5
Minority interest (Note 3)	153.5
	2,434

Note 1

Cost of investment in B		275
less ordinary shares acquired	75	
reserves acquired 75% × 200	150	225
Goodwill on acquisition		50

Note 2

Reserves A	1,045
reserves post acquired B	
75% (524 – 10 – 200)	235.5
	1,280.5

Note 3

Minority interest	
25% ordinary shares	25
25% reserves = 25% × 514	128.5
	153.5

438 FEEDBACK ON EXERCISES

12.3 (a)

	Cost of control	35
	Shares of net assets	
	75% (50−3)	35.25
	Negative goodwill	0.25

(b)

Intra-group transfer of machine − unrealized profit	1,500
excess depreciation charges 20% × 1,500	300
B's accounts unrealized profit	1,200

(c)

Intra-group stock transfer − unrealized profit	3,000
33 − 1/3% × 9,000 ecu	
Reduction in value	1,000
A's accounts unrealized profit	2,000

Consolidated balance sheet as at 30 June 19X4

		000s
Fixed assets		
Land and buildings		120
Plant and machinery		52.8
		172.8
Current assets		
Inventory	50	
Debtors	69	
Bank	28	
	147	
Creditors <1 year		
Creditors	146	1
		173.8
Represented by		
Ordinary 1 ecu shares		100
Capital reserves		10.25
Revenue reserves		
(36 − 2 + 75%(19 − 1.2))		47.35
		157.6
Minority interest		16.2
(25%(66 − 1.2))		173.8

12.4

	Acquisition ecu		Merger ecu
Plant and machinery	14,000		13,000
Goodwill on acquisition	13,500	(Note 4)	—
	27,500		13,000
Net current assets	7,500		7,000
	35,000		20,000
Issue ordinary shares (1 ecu)	15,000	(Note 1)	15,000
Share premium	18,000	(Note 2)	—
Revenue reserves	2,000	(Note 3)	5,000
	35,000		20,000

Notes
1. Based on a one-for-one exchange, A will need to issue a further 6,000 1 ecu shares (i.e. 9,000 + 6,000 = 15,000).
2. Issued at a price of 4 ecu per share the share premium on the issue of A shares for acquisition accounting purposes will be 3 ecu per share (i.e. 6,000 × 3 = 18,000).
3. For acquisition accounting purposes (but not for merger accounting) the reserves of M of 3,000 as at the date of acquisition are not group reserves and are set off in the goodwill calculation.
4. Cost of investment (i.e. 6,000 shares at 4 ecus each)   24,000
   Less fair value of net assets acquired (i.e. 8,000 + 2,500)   (10,500)
                                                                 13,500

Despite the simplicity of this example the differences are amply illustrated:

1. Under acquisition accounting, a non-distributable share premium account arises.
2. Under merger accounting, the reserves of M at the date of acquisition are regarded as reserves of the group.
3. For acquisition accounting the assets of M are recorded at fair values, whereas for merger accounting purposes book values prevail.
4. Under merger accounting there is no goodwill on acquisition.

12.5 (a) Goodwill may be defined as the difference between the value of a business as a whole, and the aggregate of the value of its separable net assets. The net assets are usually valued at fair value, but sometimes book values are used in some countries.

(b) (i) Goodwill regarded as an asset which is no different from any other.
(ii) Goodwill will be maintained through normal trading activities, purchased goodwill being substituted by non-purchased goodwill.
(iii) Elimination of an asset incapable of valuation (and whose length of life is indeterminate).

The preferences require open discussion!

Chapter 13

13.1 (a)

Loan – Debtor

Year 1	10,000	Loss on loan	500
		Bal. c/d	9,500
	10,000		10,000
Year 2 bal. b/f	9,500		
Gain	1,000	Bal. c/d	10,500
	10,500		10,500
Year 3 bal. b/f	10,500	Cash	10,600
Gain	100		
	10,600		10,600

(b) Year 1, loss of 500 ecu taken to income statement.
Year 2, gain of 1,000 ecu taken to income statement (?).
Year 3, gain of 100 ecu taken to income statement.

(c) The year 1 treatment is supported by both matching and prudence.

The year 2 treatment proposed here is much more debatable. It is supported by the matching convention and also by the consistency convention, but it obviously goes against prudence. A middle approach would be to take 500 ecu of the year 2 gain to the income statement (to reverse the loss in year 1) and to take the remaining 500 to reserves. Different approaches are allowed in different countries, and they can all be both defended and criticized.

The year 3 treatment is surely generally acceptable, as the whole thing is now history. The gain is fully realized under any criteria.

13.2 (a) Closing rate method

Income statement for year 31 December X0

	rate	
Net profit	2	150
Taxation	2	75
		75
Dividend	2	30
		45

Balance sheet as at 31 December X0

	rate		
Fixed assets	2		165
Inventory	2	180	
Debtors	2	120	
		300	
Creditors	2	120	180
			345
Ordinary share capital	3		200
Retained profits (from above)			45
Reserves – exchange difference			100
			345

(b) Temporal rate method

Income statement for year 31 December X0

	rate		
Sales	2.5		600
Opening inventory	3	80	
Purchases	2.5	480	
		560	
Closing inventory	2	180	380
			220
Depreciation	3		40
			180
Taxation	2		75
			105
Dividends	2		30
			75
Gain on exchange (from balance sheet)			15
			90

Balance sheet as at 31 December X0

Fixed assets	3		110
Inventory	2	180	
Debtors	2	120	
		300	
Creditors	2	120	180
			290
Ordinary share capital	3		200
Retained profits (75 + balance 15)			90
			290

13.3 It is very easy to demonstrate differences, both in terms of theoretically possible alternatives, and by a survey of European practice. The resulting differences in the published financial statements can sometimes be very large. Whether this situation is likely to continue for a long time is a more open question. Given the deep-seated cultural and historical basis for many national attitudes in this as in other areas, it is perhaps difficult to foresee rapid movement towards significantly greater harmonization.

Chapter 15

15.1

	P		Q	
$\dfrac{\text{gross profit}}{\text{turnover}}$	$\dfrac{9{,}000}{45{,}000}$	= 20%	$\dfrac{8{,}182}{40{,}909}$	= 20%
$\dfrac{\text{net operating profit}}{\text{turnover}}$	$\dfrac{5{,}000}{45{,}000}$	= 11%	$\dfrac{4{,}901}{40{,}909}$	= 12%
$\dfrac{\text{net profit}}{\text{owners' equity}}$	$\dfrac{4{,}000}{34{,}000}$	= 12%	$\dfrac{3{,}901}{28{,}250}$	= 14%
ROCE	$\dfrac{5{,}000}{44{,}000}$	= 11%	$\dfrac{4{,}901}{38{,}250}$	= 13%
gearing	$\dfrac{10{,}000}{34{,}000}$	= 29%	$\dfrac{10{,}000}{28{,}250}$	= 35%

Although P and Q appear somewhat similar in overall profile, Q shows itself to be more efficient in its operations and use of resources through the second, third and fourth ratios. On the other hand Q has a higher gearing ratio which would tend to make potential future lenders slightly more wary of Q than of P, other things being equal.

The diligent reader may recognize these figures. They are taken directly from Table 13.1, in which these summary accounts were presented as alternative translations of the results of one particular foreign subsidiary. If considered in the original currency as presented in Table 13.1, the above differences would be entirely spurious. Always look behind the numbers!

15.2 It may be true that the receipt or payment of cash is an objective fact. However, a cash flow statement is derived from the conventional annual accounts by a series of adjustments, so some of the inherent subjectivity remains. Also, the cash flow statement requires that the cash movements are analyzed under appropriate headings, and some subjectivity comes in here. Perhaps more importantly from an interpretative point of view, management can push through cash transactions, or time cash transactions, in such a way as to influence the picture given by the resulting cash flow statement.

15.3 (a)

M Cash flow statement for year ended 30 November 19X5

	ecu	ecu
Sales (20,000 − 5,000)		15,000
Purchases (5,000 + 2,000 − 1,000)	6,000	
Wages	5,000	
	11,000	
		4,000
Proceeds of sale of assets		2,000
		6,000
Loan		4,000
		10,000
Machine	3,000	
Taxation	4,000	
Dividends	2,000	
		9,000
		1,000
Closing cash	2,400	
Opening cash	1,400	
		1,000

(b) Solvency and liquidity can be achieved without profitability, and profitability can be achieved without liquidity and solvency, at least in the short term. Information about both aspects is therefore desirable. As between cash flows and funds flows, cash flow statements are better focused, not surprisingly in a sense, on the actual money movement.

15.4

	19X1		19X2	
	000 ecu		000 ecu	
Workings				
Turnover	541		675	
Less Cost of sales	369		481	
Gross profit	172	(derived)	194	(derived)
GP/T%	(172 × 100)/541 = 31.8%		(194 × 100)/675 = 28.7%	
Closing reserves	53		82	
Dividends proposed	20		30	
	73		112	
Less Opening reserves	21		53	
Net profit	52	(derived)	59	(derived)
NP/T%	(52 × 100)/541 = 9.6%		(59 × 100)/675 = 8.7%	
T/NAE	541/303 = 1.8 ×		675/432 = 1.6 ×	
NP/NAE%	(52 × 100)/303 = 17.2%		(59 × 100)/432 = 13.7%	
CA/CL	188/92:1 = 2.0:1		269/162:1 = 1.7:1	
QA/CL	102/92:1 = 1.1:1		92/162:1 = 0.6:1	

GP/T%   The deterioration could be due to a rise in purchase prices not passed on in increased selling prices and/or a change in sales mix, etc.

NP/T%   Roughly in line with the decline in GP/T%. Could also be caused by high administration and/or sales expenses.

T/NAE   The full year effect of the increased investment has not yet materialized. In addition, year-end inventories have doubled possibly indicating a build-up for a promotional drive.

NP/NAE%   The decline is attributable to the combined effects of the two preceding ratios.

CA/CL   Working capital has increased, notably due to inventory and debtors. The inventory build-up, partly financed by an increase in creditors, has been noted above and this may be coupled with a planned (or lax) credit control.

QA/CL   The increased investment has produced a liquidity problem.

15.5 (a) Some possible ratio calculations:

F Co.

	19X2	19X1
Current ratio	$\frac{54}{147} = 36.7\%$	$\frac{56}{172} = 32.6\%$
Acid test ratio	$\frac{12}{147} = 8.2\%$	$\frac{15}{172} = 8.7\%$
ROCE	$\frac{57}{249} = 22.9\%$	$\frac{41}{161} = 25.5\%$
ROOE	$\frac{33}{188} = 17.5\%$	$\frac{24}{160} = 15.0\%$
e.p.s.	$\frac{31}{190} = 0.163$ ecu	$\frac{22}{190} = 0.116$ ecu
Trade debtors' turnover	$\frac{4}{910} \times 365 = 2$ days	$\frac{4}{775} \times 365 = 2$ days
Trade creditors' turnover	$\frac{60}{730} \times 365 = 30$ days	$\frac{60}{633} \times 365 = 35$ days
Gross profit %	$\frac{180}{910} = 19.8\%$	$\frac{142}{775} = 18.3\%$
Operating profit %	$\frac{57}{910} = 6.3\%$	$\frac{41}{775} = 5.3\%$
Inventory turnover	$\frac{42}{730} \times 365 = 21$ days	$\frac{41}{663} \times 365 = 23$ days
Gearing	$\frac{61}{188} = 32.4\%$	$\frac{1}{160} = 0.6\%$

(b) The company has a number of features which appear at first sight to be unusual. The most obvious is that there are hardly any debtors. On the other hand the company seems to have over 2 m ecu permanently as cash, as well as positive bank balances The inventory turnover period is also short. In one sense this demonstrates a remarkably efficient organization. Inventory is sold quickly, sales are paid for very quickly indeed – and creditors appear willing to wait for their money. The effect of this on the balance sheet is to produce a total of current assets which is very much lower than the current liabilities, which gives the impression of a very illiquid business.

(c) However, the positive aspects of this situation surely outweigh the negative ones. Much of the company's activities are being financed, presumably interest free, by the creditors! If we take the given figures literally, it appears that the company buys inventory, sells it and makes its profit 21 days later. It actually receives the sales proceeds 23 days after the purchase, but does not have to pay for its original purchases for another seven days after that. Gearing has risen by 5,400%, but this figure is quite meaningless as it was virtually zero in 19X1. Gearing is still low, there are enormous fixed assets which are presumably available as security for any further required borrowings, and the company has a large and apparently regular positive flow of funds from its trading operations. In reality the company seems to have cash available on tap whenever it wants it.

From a profitability point of view, the position also seems very sound indeed. Profit to sales may not be all that high, but the sales volume is clearly great, and profit to capital is good. It is important to note that the ROCE and ROOE figures given could be misleading if not interpreted carefully. The ROCE is before tax and the ROOE is after tax. Further, the ROOE relates to all shareholders. The enquiry here explicitly relates to an ordinary shareholder. A return on ordinary shareholders' interest should perhaps be calculated. This might be:

$$\frac{31}{142} = 21.8\%$$

As an overall comment, the company, probably in the retail or cash-and-carry sector, seems in a very strong position and there seems no reason at all to rush out and sell ordinary shares.

Chapter 16

16.1 (a)

	1989	1988
Historical cost basis		
$\dfrac{\text{operating profit}}{\text{owners' equity}}$	$\dfrac{1{,}383}{3{,}819} = 36\%$	$\dfrac{1{,}207}{3{,}074} = 39\%$
$\dfrac{\text{net profit}}{\text{owners' equity}}$	$\dfrac{1{,}380}{3{,}819} = 36\%$	$\dfrac{622}{3{,}074} = 20\%$
gearing	$\dfrac{3{,}819}{9{,}694} = 39\%$	$\dfrac{3{,}074}{8{,}346} = 37\%$
Current value basis		
$\dfrac{\text{operating profit}}{\text{owners' equity}}$	$\dfrac{1{,}288}{4{,}375} = 29\%$	$\dfrac{1{,}037}{3{,}790} = 27\%$
$\dfrac{\text{net profit}}{\text{owners' equity}}$	$\dfrac{1{,}320}{4{,}375} = 30\%$	$\dfrac{502}{3{,}790} = 13\%$
gearing	$\dfrac{4{,}375}{10{,}550} = 41\%$	$\dfrac{3{,}790}{9{,}235} = 41\%$

(b) It can be argued that the current value figures give a truer economic comparison with other currently available alternatives. For two of the three ratios, the trends, perhaps more useful than the absolute amounts, are different. From 1988 to 1989, operating profit to owners' equity falls on a historical cost basis and rises on a current value basis. Gearing worsens on a historical cost basis and stays constant on a current value basis. Note also, as an aside, but as a point of major significance, the effects of the extraordinary items in the two years. Their existence tends to suggest that the operating profit ratio is a much better long-term indicator than the net profit ratio. This makes the difference in trend direction for the operating profit ratio under the two bases all the more significant. Perhaps a much longer time series is needed.

16.2 A wide variety of ratios may be calculated. Those attached are a longer list than one is likely to prepare in practice. On the other hand, other ratios may be just as helpful as the ones suggested here.

Briefly, it is clear that major changes were budgeted for. A major expansion was intended. Sales were to be encouraged by a planned fall in the gross profit margin. However, a sharp reduction (in percentage terms) in the expenses and overheads of running the business was planned, so that the net profit percentages, and the earnings ratios, would rise substantially.

The financing of this rapid expansion was to be achieved partly by a planned reduction (equals 'worsening') in the working capital position, as evidenced by the current, debtors and creditors ratios, and partly by long-term borrowing as evidenced by the gearing ratio.

In the outcome, the plans have been achieved to a considerable extent. The net profit before interest and tax as a percentage of turnover has risen by less than budget, but the asset turnover ratio has risen by more than budget. The net effect of these two movements is that net profit before interest and tax as a percentage of net assets (= ROCE) has risen very significantly, though not quite up to budget. Earnings as a percentage of equity has nearly doubled compared with the previous year.

The only area of uncertainty seems to be on the financing side. Gearing has followed the plan, but liquidity ratios are slightly below budget, and an unexpected bank overdraft has appeared. The budgeted dividend has been sharply cut, presumably because of the cash shortage.

Gross profit as a percentage of turnover
19X7 Actual	$860/2{,}560 \times 100 =$	33.6%
19X8 Budget	$1{,}350/4{,}500 \times 100 =$	30.0%
19X8 Actual	$1{,}530/5{,}110 \times 100 =$	29.9%

Admin. and distribution costs as a percentage of turnover
19X7 Actual	$655/2{,}560 \times 100 =$	25.6%
19X8 Budget	$880/4{,}500 \times 100 =$	19.6%
19X8 Actual	$1{,}084/5{,}110 \times 100 =$	21.2%

Net profit before interest and tax as a percentage of turnover
19X7 Actual	$205/2{,}560 \times 100 =$	8.0%
19X8 Budget	$470/4{,}500 \times 100 =$	10.4%
19X8 Actual	$446/5{,}100 \times 100 =$	8.7%

Net profit before interest and tax as a percentage of net assets
19X7 Actual	$205/1{,}280 \times 100 =$	16.0%
19X8 Budget	$470/(1{,}420 + 360) \times 100 =$	26.4%
19X8 Actual	$446/(1{,}460 + 360) \times 100 =$	24.5%

Asset turnover ratio
19X7 Actual	$2{,}560/1{,}280 =$	2.0:1
19X8 Budget	$4{,}500/1{,}780 =$	2.5:1
19X8 Actual	$5{,}110/1{,}820 =$	2.8:1

Current ratio
19X7 Actual	$685/362 =$	1.9:1
19X8 Budget	$1{,}080/830 =$	1.3:1
19X8 Actual	$1{,}137/935 =$	1.2:1

Quick assets ratio
19X7 Actual	$(685 - 205)/362 =$	1.3:1
19X8 Budget	$(1{,}080 - 290)/830 =$	1.0:1
19X8 Actual	$(1{,}135 - 325)/935 =$	0.9:1

Debtors' average collection period[1]
19X7 Actual	$305 \times 365/2{,}560 =$	43 days
19X8 Budget	$720 \times 365/4{,}500 =$	58 days
19X8 Actual	$810 \times 365/5{,}110 =$	58 days

Creditors' average settlement period[2]
19X7 Actual	$175 \times 365/1{,}770 =$	36 days
19X8 Budget	$505 \times 365/3{,}230 =$	57 days
19X8 Actual	$545 \times 365/3{,}700 =$	54 days

Inventory ratio (using average inventory − see Workings 2)
19X7 Actual	$1{,}700/170 =$	10 times
19X8 Budget	$3{,}150/250 =$	12.6 times
19X8 Actual	$3{,}580/265 =$	13.5 times

Gearing ratio
19X7 Actual	none	
19X8 Budget	$360/1{,}420 \times 100 =$	25.3
19X8 Actual	$360/1{,}460 \times 100 =$	24.7

Earnings as a percentage of equity (see Workings 3)
19X7 Actual	$110/1{,}261.5 \times 100 =$	8.7%
19X8 Budget	$250/1{,}350 \times 100 =$	18.5%
19X8 Actual	$226/1{,}370 \times 100 =$	16.5%

Dividend cover
19X7 Actual	$119/82 =$	1.5 times
19X8 Budget	$248/108 =$	2.3 times
19X8 Actual	$229/49 =$	4.7 times

---

[1] Assuming all sales are on credit and that the debtors figure represents trade debtors only.
[2] Assuming all purchases are on credit and that the creditors figure represents purchase creditors only (see Workings 1).

Workings
1. Calculation of purchases figures

	19X7 Actual 000 ecu	19X8 Budget 000 ecu	19X8 Actual 000 ecu
Opening inventory	135	210	205
Purchases (by difference)	1,770	3,230	3,700
	1,905	3,440	3,905
Less closing inventory	205	290	325
Cost of sales	1,700	3,150	3,580

2. Calculation of average inventory   000 ecu

19X7 Actual $(135 + 205)/2 =$ 170
19X8 Budget $(210 + 290)/2 =$ 250
19X8 Actual $(205 + 325)/2 =$ 265

3. Calculation of average equity (assuming no shares issued in 19X7)
   000 ecu

19X7 Actual
$(1,280 - 37) + 37/2 =$ 1,261.5
19X8 Budget $1,280 + 140/2) =$ 1,350
19X8 Actual $1,280 + 180/2 =$ 1,370

16.3 Have your views changed?

Chapter 17

17.1 (1) The translation, like many others from continental Europe, uses a mixture of US and UK terms.

'Fixed assets' should be written as 'tangible assets' (UK) or 'Property, plant and equipment' (US). In the UK, 'Fixed assets' would mean all the non-current assets.

'Affiliated companies' is a vague US expression, which here means subsidiaries, but sometimes means associates.

'Treasury stock' is a US expression for a company's own shares bought back by the company.

(2) Daimler is accounting for certain aspects of deferred tax, but little would be expected to arise in Germany. They are accounting for the deferred tax that results from eliminating profits during the consolidation process.

(3) Minority interests are the parts of the group owned by shareholders other than the parent or other subsidiaries. In most countries, these elements would not be considered as shareholders' funds (because there is a concentration on *parent company* shareholders). In Germany, however, minority interests are considered part of (total) shareholders' funds.

(4) It is not clear what 'international' means. However, taking the word to mean the United States or the United Kingdom:

  (a) German pensions are provided internally on the basis of tax rules. US/UK pensions are funded externally on the basis of the best estimates of actuaries.

  (b) US practice is to capitalize and amortize over 40 years. UK practice is to write off immediately to reserves. Daimler uses a mixture in one company.

  (c) and (d) US/UK practice is to make an estimate of wearing out, then to use a consistent method. Daimler maximizes depreciation for tax (and, therefore, accounting) purposes. This includes being inconsistent in its methods.

  (e) Some receivables are discounted to net present value. This is a way of reducing their size (and tax value). This is not US/UK practice. Of course, liabilities are not reduced. It would not be prudent (or tax efficient).

  (f) Foreign monetary items are translated at the worse of the year end and transaction rates. This gives lower debtors and higher creditors than using the US/UK closing rate method. It also avoids recognizing gains (but not losses) until settlement.

  (g) Daimler uses historical rates in order to keep to historical cost in Deutschmarks. US/UK practice is to use closing rates.

(5) The goodwill calculation uses book values and then allocates the differences on the basis of fair values. The US/UK method uses fair values from the start.

(6) Normally, it is not possible in Germany (or usual anywhere) to revalue long-term investments upwards. However, where they had been reduced in value before, and the reason no longer applies, they should be revalued to 'cost'. However, the tax law allows this not to be done.

(7) Leases are seldom capitalized in Germany. It would alter the tax calculations and it would override the legal form of arrangements. In this case, the assets *belong* to Daimler, and are being leased *out* to others.

(8) Joint ventures are proportionally consolidated. This is optional in Germany, Spain or the Netherlands; compulsory in France; not allowed

in the United Kingdom (except for non-company joint ventures). If the proportional method is not used, then equity accounting should be.

(9) Dividends are not charged in the income statement (of any year). At the year end, the dividend is not legally approved, so it is not accounted for in Germany (or France, Spain). When it is paid, it is shown as a reserve movement (see note 13).

In the United Kingdom, proposed dividends are accounted for as an appropriation of profit and a current liability.

(10) This is an ironic question. The vast amount of provision movement appears to be very much an estimate. Therefore, from a US/UK point of view, the resulting profit figure is difficult to interpret.

(11) The income statement is vertical *par nature*. In France (except groups), Spain or Italy it would be horizontal *par nature*. In the United Kingdom and for some French groups, it would be vertical *par destination* (as it is for some German companies).

Note: In 1993, Daimler-Benz made major changes to accounting as part of its agreement with the SEC of the United States.

Index

accountancy profession,
  accountancy bodies, 6, 74 Table
  international differences, 73–5
  regulation, 6–8
accounting,
  definitions, 3, 4 Table, 385
  financial compared with management, 5
  purposes and users, 3–6
  regulation, 6–8
accounting period, 46
accounting policies and financial appraisal, 314–19, 385
accounting theory, international differences, 76
accruals convention, *see* matching convention
accruals and deferred income, 357, 360, 363, 386
acid test, 291, 386
AICPA, depreciation accounting, 146
amortization, meaning of term, 143, 386
annual report, 376–8
asset turnover ratios, 277–8
assets, 12, 58–60, 386
  see also current assets; fixed assets; intangible assets
associated company, definition, 246, 386–7
audit, 106, 378
auditing, 5–6, 387
Australia, public accountancy bodies, 74
  classiffication, 81
average cost, 168, 387

balance sheet,
  abridged, 97, 98, 361, 377
  business valuation, 310–12
  consolidated accounts, basis for translation, 265 Table
  dating, 37
  debtors, 15, 16
  description and contents, 11–17, 387
  EC Fourth Directive format, 99–102, 115, 352–4, 354–63
  inventory, 14, 15
  purchases, 13, 14
  wages, 14, 16
  worked examples, 12–15
Belgium,
  accounting and taxable income, 211
  classification, 81
  company names, 96
  deferred tax, 210
  depreciation, 158
  fixed assets, valuation, 127, 129
  goodwill on consolidation, 251
  inflation, 217
  inventory valuation, 174
  legal system, 67
  long-term contracts, 175
  R&D accounting, 137, 138
  tax system, 199, 203, 205
  true and fair concept, 105
book value per share, 284
brands, valuation, 136, 138
business entity, 45
business valuation, 310–23
  accounting policies and financial appraisal, 314–19
  balance sheet, 310–12
  market values, 313
  through expectations, 312–13

Canada, public accountancy body, 74
  classification, 81
capital,
  definition, 13, 45
  subscribed, 356, 360
capital allowances, 71, 387
capital gains, 196
capital and liabilities, 184–91
capital maintenance, 220–4
capital reserves, 187
capitalization,
  leases, 132–4
  R&D, 136
cash at bank and in hand, 356, 359

455

cash and funds flow statements, 294-301, 302-4, 388
cash ratio, 291
classification of international accounting practice, 77-84, 84-5
  change from 1980, 82, 84
  early classifications, 78-9
  Nobes two group classification, 80, 81 Fig
  using clustering, 79-80
common size statements, 272
company names, EC countries, 95, 96 Table
concessions, 135
conservatism, 48, 50, 107, 388
consistency, 48-9, 388
consolidated financial statements, *see* group accounting
construction contracts, inventory valuation, 172, 175-81
contingent liabilities, 185, 388-9
continuity, 48, 50, 53
Contact Committee, EC, 378-9
control,
  definition, 237
  see also parent/subsidiary relationship
conversion, definition, 257
cost price, 46
credit, meaning of, 26, 27
creditors, 357, 359, 360, 374
creditors turnover ratio, 293
currency translation, *see* foreign currency translation
current asset investments, example, 140
current assets,
  definition, 59, 389
  Fourth Directive, 355-6, 358-9, 372-3
  valuation, 372-3
current cost, description, 121
current cost accounting, 226-9, 231, 389
current operating performance, 285
current purchasing power, 220, 224, 389
current ratio, 291
current replacement cost, 225-6
current value accounting, 122, 175, 181, 224-6

debenture, types of, 187-8
debit, meaning of, 26, 27
debtors, 15, 16, 356, 359, 389
debtors turnover ratio, 292, 293
deferred tax, 71, 205-12
  changes in tax rates, 212
  depreciation, 206-8
  description, 205, 390
  disclosure, comparison of EC countries, 210 Table
  revaluation, 206
Denmark,
  accounting and taxable income, 211
  classification, 81

company names, 96
deferred tax, 210
depreciation, 158
extraordinary items, 330, 331, 333
fixed assets, revaluation, 230
fixed assets, valuation, 127, 129
goodwill on consolidation, 251
inflation, 217
inventory valuation, 174
long-term contracts, 175
R&D accounting, 137, 138
tax system, 199, 203
translation of financial statements, 264, 265, 266
true and fair concept, 105
depreciation, 71, 143-61, 218
  allocation methods, 151-4
  basic concept, 143-6
  criticisms, 156-7
  declining charge methods, 151-3
  deferred tax, 206-8
  definition, 146, 390
  double entry, 149, 152
  EC Fourth Directive, 146
  effect on assets of not charging, 149, 150 Table
  funds flow statements, 297
  IAS definition, 146
  intangibles, 159-60
  land and buildings, 157, 158 Table
  mid-year purchases, 155-6
  plant and machinery, 157, 158 Table
  reducing balance method, 152-3, 398
  and replacement, 149-51, 231
  residual value and disposal, 155
  revaluation, 153-4, 156
  straight-line method, 145 Fig, 153 Table, 157, 400
  sum of digits method, 152
  tax bases, 195-6
  useful economic life, 154-5
  usage methods, 153, 154 Table
  and valuation, 147-8
developing countries, IASC, 111-12
development of accounting, international nature, 65-6
discounted cash flow (DCF), 312, 390
dividend cover, 288
dividend yield, 288
dividends, 186, 331
  double taxation, 199-200
  methods to mitigate, 200-5
dividends received, 197
double entry bookkeeping, 24-37
  advantages, 29-31
  justification, 25-9
dual standards, 113-15
duality, 45

INDEX

earnings, 284–6
  definition, 286, 390
earnings per share (e.p.s.), 286–8, 329
EC Common Industrial Policy, 91
EC company (*Societas Europea* (SE)), 95
EC Directives,
  corporate accounting, 93 Table
  description, 92, 390
  implementation as laws, 95 Table
  procedure for setting, 92
EC Fourth Directive, 92, 94, 117
  accounting principles, 103–6
  annual report, 98, 376–8
  balance sheet,
    abridged, 97, 98, 361, 377
    format, 99–102, 115, 352–4, 354–63
  contents survey, 96–8
  Contact Committee, 378–9
  current assets, 355–6, 358–9, 372–3
  deferred taxation, 212
  definition of annual accounts, 96–7
  depreciation, 146
  extraordinary items, 330
  fixed assets, 125–6, 135, 141, 355, 358, 362, 371–2
  format of financial statements, 97
  formation expenses, 355, 370
  goodwill on consolidation, 250
  introduction of, 92
  inventory valuation, 170–2
  liabilities, 185, 356–7
  medium-sized companies, 98
  notes on the accounts, 373–6
    abridged, 375, 377
  parent/subsidiary companies, 380–1
  profit and loss account formats, 97, 102–3, 115–16, 352–4, 363–7
  revaluation of assets, 97
  small companies, 97
  true and fair concept, 103, 104 Table, 105, 106
  unpaid capital, 354, 357–8
  valuation rules, 97, 125–6, 135, 141, 170–2, 368–73
  when applicable, 351–2
EC harmonization, 91–6, 91, 107
EC Regulations, 92, 93 Table
EC Second Directive, 94–5
EC Seventh Directive, 102, 117, 237, 238
economic value, 122
employees, 374
  loans and emoluments to, 375
England,
  legal system, 67–8
  see also UK
entity concept of group, 236–7
equity, definition, 58, 185
equity accounting, 247–9

equity instrument, definition, 189
exceptional items, 330, 391
expenses, 18, 60, 197
expenses to sales ratio, 275–6
extraordinary items, 285–6, 329–31, 367, 391

fair presentation, 50
Fédération des Experts Comptables Européens (FEE), 7, 112, 391
(FIFO), *see* first-in, first-out
finance providers, international differences, 68–70
Financial Accounting Standards Board (FASB), conceptual framework, 51
financial culture, differences in, 328–9
financial liability, definition, 188
financial statements,
  information requirements, 53–8
  translation, *see* translation of financial statements
finished goods, 164
Finland, untaxed reserves, 329
first-in, first-out (FIFO), 168–9, 170, 373, 391
fixed assets,
  definition, 59, 391
  depreciation, *see* depreciation
  intangibles, examples, 138–40
  valuation, 107, 121–42
    adjustments, 363
    brands, 136, 138
    charging diminutions in value, 126
    historical cost, 123
    intangibles, 134–40; Fourth Directive, 135, 141, 355, 358
    investment properties, 131
    investments, 140
    land and buildings, 126, 127 Table, 128
    leasing, 131–4
    plant and machinery, 128, 129 Table
    R&D, 135–6
    summary, 122 Fig, 141
    tangibles, Fourth Directive and IASC rules, 125–6, 141, 355, 358, 362, 371–2
    taxation, 72
    variation in European balance sheets, examples, 128–31
foreign currency translation, 257–68
  definitions and terms, 257–8
  financial statements, *see* translation of financial statements
  transactions, 258–60
formation expenses, 355, 370
formats, 106, 115–16
France,
  accountancy bodies, 74, 75
  accounting practice, 76
  accounting and taxable income, 211
  asset values, changing, 192

458 INDEX

France (*continued*)
  business licence tax, 198
  classification, 81
  COB, 70
  commissaires aux comptes, 7
  company names, 96
  consolidated accounts, tax rules, 72
  deferred tax, 210
  depreciation, 158, 195
  development of accounting, 65
  dividends, 197, 331
  enforcement of IASC standards, 110
  expenses, 197
  experts comptables, 7
  fixed assets, valuation, 123, 126, 127, 128, 129
  goodwill on consolidation, 250, 251
  inflation, 217, 219
  intangible assets, 139
  inventory valuation, 174
  legal system, 67
  long-term contracts, 175
  operating loss reliefs, 197
  proportional consolidation, 246
  R&D accounting, 137, 138, 139
  R&D capitalization, 136
  raising finance, 68
  remuneration schemes impact on generation of funds, 328
  revaluation of assets, 72, 229
  security market control, 70
  tax system, 203, 204
  taxation and group accounts, 84
  translation of financial statements, 264, 265, 266
  true and fair concept, 105
fund management ratios, *see* liquidity analysis, fund management ratios

gains, definition, 60
gearing, 281–2, 392
gearing ratio, calculating, 281
general price-level adjusted systems (GPLA systems), 224, 392
Germany,
  accountancy training, 73
  accounting practice, 76
  accounting and taxable income, 211
  Aktiengesetz, 94, 98, 99, 100, 102–3
  audits, 73
  capital gains, 196
  capitalizing leases, 132
  classification, 81
  company names, 96
  corporate taxation, 194
  deferred tax, 209, 210
  depreciation, 71–2, 147, 157, 158, 159, 192, 195
  development of accounting, 65
  dividends received, 197
  enforcement of IASC standards, 110
  expenses, 197
  fixed assets, valuation, 123, 126, 127, 129
  gearing ratio, 328
  goodwill on consolidation, 250, 251
  GPLA systems, 224
  inflation, 217, 219
  inventory valuation, 174
  legal system, 67
  long-term contracts, 175
  Massgeblichkeitsprinzip, 71
  net profit, 336
  operating loss reliefs, 197
  profit and loss account, 102–3
  proportional consolidation, 246
  R&D accounting, 137, 138
  R&D capitalization, 136
  raising finance, 68–9
  tax experts (*Steuerberater*), 73
  tax systems, 203, 204–5
  taxes, 198
  translation of financial statements, 261, 264, 265, 266
  true and fair concept, 105
  untaxed reserves, 329
  Vereidigte Buchprüfer, 73
going concern, 48, 50, 53, 392
goodwill, 135, 372, 392
  on consolidation, 241–2, 250–2
Greece,
  accounting and taxable income, 211
  company names, 96
  deferred tax, 210
  depreciation, 158
  extraordinary items, 330
  fixed assets, valuation, 127, 129
  goodwill on consolidation, 251
  inflation, 217
  inventory valuation, 174
  legal system, 67
  R&D accounting, 137, 138
  revaluation of assets, 72, 229
  tax system, 203, 205
  true and fair concept, 105
gross profit, 31–2
gross profit margin, 170, 274–5
group accounting, 236–56, 380, 392
  consolidated accounts, 252–3, 388
  entity concept of group, 236–7
  establishment of parent/subsidiary relationship, 237–9
  goodwill on consolidation, 241–2, 250–2
  intercompany transactions, 249
  investments in other non-controlled companies, 246–9
    equity accounting, 247–9, 391
  merger accounting, 249

group accounting (*continued*)
  minority interests, 243–5
  parent company approach, 236, 239–43
  proportional consolidation, 245–6
Group d'Etudes, *see* FEE
guarantees, 361

harmonization,
  benefits, 116
  definition, 87
  EC, *see* EC harmonization
  measurement, 90
  obstacles to, 89–90
  reasons for, 88–9
historical cost, 46, 121–2, 181, 392
historical rates of exchange, *see* translation of financial statements, temporal method
history of corporate tax, 193
hybrid securities, 188–9

IASC, 107–12, 116
  benefits, 111
  board members, 107, 108 Table
  cash and funds flow statements, 295, 300
  definition of equity, 185
  definition of liability, 184
  depreciation, 154–5
  developing countries, 111–12
  enforcement, 110–11
  financial statements,
    elements of, 58–60
    objectives, 52–3
    translation, 264
  Framework for Preparation and Presentation of Financial Statements, 5, 51–8
  goodwill on consolidation, 250
  history and purpose, 8, 107–8, 393
  inventory valuation, 170–2
  R&D, 108–9
  recognition of accounting elements, 60–1
  standards, 108–10
  valuation of fixed assets, 125–6
income,
  definition, 60
  differences between accounting and taxable income, 211 Table
income statement, 17–23
  definition, 392
  inventory purchase and sale, 19–20, 21
  preparation, 18–23
  translation, 260, 266 Table
  wages payment, 20, 21
index of retail prices, 215–17
inflation,
  definition, 215
  in EC, 217 Table
  index of retail prices, 215–17
  international differences, 75

  measurement, 215–17
  see also price changes, accounting for
intangible assets,
  definition, 135, 393
  depreciation, 159–60
  examples, 138–40
  valuation, 134–40
intercompany transactions, 249
interest cover, 292
interest payments, 198, 371
International Accounting Standards Committee, *see* IASC
international analysis, 324–50
  benchmark for comparisons, 335–8
    earnings, 337–8
    net assets, 338
  financial culture, 328–9
  interpretation difficulties, 329–92
    dividends, 331
    extraordinary items, 329–31
    help by multinationals, 332, 335
    untaxed reserves, 329, 330
  language problems, 325–7
International Federation of Accountants (IFAC), 7, 112–13, 393
inventory,
  accruals and prepayments, 34–7
  buying and selling, 13, 14, 15, 17
  sale and purchase, 19–21
inventory turnover ratio, 293–4
inventory valuation, 162–83, 170
  construction contracts, 175–81
  continuous stock-taking (perpetual inventory), 165
  current value accounting, 175
  disclosure of method, 171
  Fourth Directive and IASC rules, 170–2
  input values, 166–7, 373
    historical cost, 167–70; average cost, 168; FIFO, 168–9, 170, 373; LIFO, 169, 170, 373; retail inventory and gross profit margin, 170; specific or unit cost, 167–8; standard cost, 169–70
  output values, 165–6
  relationship with profit, 163 Table
  stock-takes (periodic counts), 164–5
  summary, 181, 182 Fig
  work-in-progress, comparative survey of EC countries, 173, 174 Tables
investment properties, valuation, 131
investment ratios, *see* profitability analysis, investment ratios
investments, 140, 356, 359
Ireland,
  accounting and taxable income, 211
  classification, 81
  company names, 95, 96
  current cost accounting, 226

Ireland (*continued*)
  deferred tax, 210
  depreciation, 158
  dividends, 331
  fixed assets,
    revaluation, 230
    valuation, 127, 129
  goodwill on consolidation, 251
  inflation, 217
  inventory valuation, 174
  long-term contracts, 175
  R&D accounting, 137, 138
  tax systems, 203–4
  translation of financial statements, 265, 266
  true and fair concept, 105
Italy,
  accounting practice, 76
  audits, 73
  capitalizing leases, 132
  classification, 81
  company names, 96
  CONSOB, 70
  corporate taxation, 194
  deferred tax, 210
  development of accounting, 65
  enforcement of IASC standards, 110
  fixed assets,
    revaluation, 72, 229
    valuation, 127, 128, 129
  inflation, 217
  inventory valuation, 174, 230
  R&D accounting, 137
  raising finance, 68, 69
  remuneration schemes impact on generation of funds, 328, 329
  security market control, 70
  tax system, 203
  taxation, 198, 219
  true and fair concept, 105

Japan,
  capital gains, 196
  classification, 81
  depreciation, 195
  development of accounting, 66
  dividends received, 197
  legal system, 67
  operating loss reliefs, 197
  public accountancy body, 74
joint venture, 245

labour, capitalization, 123
land and buildings,
  depreciation, 157, 158 Table
  valuation, 126, 127 Table, 128
language problems, international analysis, 325–7
last-in, first-out (LIFO), 169, 170, 230, 393–4
leases, capitalizing, 132–4

leasing, valuation, 131–4
legal systems, international differences, 67–8
leverage, 281–2, 393
liabilities, 58–60
  current, definition, 60, 389
  definition, 58, 184, 393
  determining existence, 59
  long-term, definition, 60
licences, 135
LIFO, *see* last-in first out
liquidity analysis, 290–309
  cash flow statements, 294–5, 299–301, 303–4 Tables
  funds flow statements, 294–8, 295–8, 302 Table
    worked example, 297–8
  fund management ratios, 292–4
    creditors turnover ratio, 293
    debtors turnover ratio, 292, 293
    inventory turnover ratio, 293–4
  interest cover, 292
  liquidity ratios, 290–1
    acid test, 291
    cash ratio, 291
    current ratio, 291
loan capital, 68
loans to employees, 375
long-term borrowing, 282–3
long-term contracts, valuation, survey of EC countries, 174, 175 Table
losses, taxation, 196, 197 Table
Luxembourg,
  accounting and taxable income, 211
  company names, 96
  deferred tax, 210
  depreciation, 158
  fixed assets, valuation, 127, 129
  goodwill on consolidation, 251
  inflation, 217
  inventory valuation, 174
  R&D accounting, 137, 138
  tax system, 199, 203
  true and fair concept, 105

market value per share, 284
matching convention, 47–8, 50, 53, 394
materiality convention, 49, 394
materials, capitalization, 123
merger accounting, 249, 394
mid-year purchases, depreciation, 155–6
monetary items, gains and losses, 218
monetary measurement, 45–6
money, as asset, 13
Mueller, Prof. G., 78–9
mutual recognition, 90–1

Nair and Frank, 79–80
net book value (NBV), 147–8

net contributions of asset, 148
net profit, 275, 395
net realizable value, 122, 225, 395
net turnover, 374
Netherlands,
  accounting and taxable income, 211
  balance sheets, 99
  capital gains, 196
  capitalizing leases, 132
  classification, 81
  company names, 95, 96
  deferred tax, 71, 209, 210
  depreciation, 147, 158, 195, 231
  development of accounting, 65
  dividends received, 197
  expenses, 197
  fixed assets,
    revaluation, 156, 230
    valuation, 126, 127, 129, 130
  goodwill on consolidation, 251
  GPLA systems, 224
  inflation, 217
  inventory valuation, 174
  long-term contracts, 175
  operating loss reliefs, 197
  profit and loss account, 103
  proportional consolidation, 246
  public accountancy body, 74
  R&D accounting, 137, 138
  shares in subsidiaries and associated
    companies, 140
  stock exchange, 69–70
  tax system, 199, 203, 205
  taxation, 71, 72, 147
  translation of financial statements, 265, 266
  true and fair concept, 105
New Zealand, public accountancy body, 74
  classification, 81
Nobes, C.W., 80, 81 Fig, 82, 83 Table
Norway,
  translation of financial statements, 265, 266
  untaxed reserves, 329, 330
notes on the accounts, 373–6
  abridged, 375, 377

objectivity convention, 49, 50
OECD, 113

parent company concept, 236
parent/subsidiary relationship, 237–9, 380–1
participating interests, 381–3
payments, 135
payments on account, 135, 355
payroll tax, 198
plant and machinery,
  depreciation, 157, 158 Table
  valuation, 128, 129 Table

Portugal,
  company names, 96
  extraordinary items, 330
  inflation, 217
  legal system, 67
  tax system, 203
prepayments and accrued income, 356, 359, 363
price changes, effect on accounting, 218–19
price changes, accounting for, 215–35
  ad libidum revaluations, 230
  current cost accounting, 226–9, 231
  current value accounting, 224–6
    current replacement cost, 225–6
    economic value, 225
    net realizable value, 225
  European disagreement, 219–20
  general price-level adjusted systems (GPLA
    systems), 224
  general or specific adjustment, 220–4, 231
  government-controlled revaluations, 229
  replacement cost depreciation, 231
  special reserves, 230
  summary, 231–2
  see also LIFO
price/earnings (P/E) ratio, 288–9, 329
profit, tax adjustments to accounting profit, 208,
  209 Fig
profit and loss account, 33–4, 381, 396
  formats, 102–3, 115–16, 197, 352–4, 363–7
profitability analysis, 271–89
  finance ratios, 278–83
    return on capital employed (ROCE),
      279–83
    return on owners' equity (ROOE), 279,
      283
  investment ratios, 284–9
    book value per share, 284
    dividend cover, 288
    dividend yield, 288
    earnings, 284–6
    earnings per share (e.p.s.), 286–8
    market value per share, 284
    price/earnings (P/E) ratio, 288–9, 329
  profit ratios, 272–6
    expenses to sales, 275–6
    gross profit margin, 274–5
    net profit margin, 275
  profitability ratios, 276–8
    asset turnover ratios, 277–8
    non-financial resource ratios, 278
proportional consolidation, 245–6, 397
proposed dividends, 185
provisions, 360, 373, 397
prudence, 55–6, 397
  see also conservatism
publication of accounts, 106

quick assets ratio, *see* acid test

R&D,
  capitalization, 136
  comparison of European accounting methods, 137 Table
  definition, 135
  IASC standards, 108–9
  valuation, 135–6, 372
raw materials, 164, 355, 358
realization of revenue, 46–7
registered office, 373–4
remuneration schemes, impact on generation of funds, 328–9
replacement cost, 122, 398
reserves, 187, 230, 356, 357, 398
residual value and disposal, 155
retail inventory, 170
return on capital employed (ROCE), 279–83
return on owners' equity (ROOE), 279, 283
revaluation, 60, 72, 156, 206, 229, 398
revaluation reserve, 187, 356, 357, 369–70
revenue, definition, 60
revenue reserves, 187

Sandilands Committee, 227
Scandinavia, legal system, 67
secret reserves, 189, 399
share capital, 68, 356, 361, 374
  types of, 186–7
share premium account, 187, 356, 360, 399
significant influence, definition, 246
social security tax, 198
Societas Europea (SE), 95
South America,
  fixed assets, valuation, 123
  GPLA systems, 224
Spain,
  accounting practice, 76
  capitalizing leases, 132
  cash and funds flow statements, 295
  classification, 81
  company names, 96
  deferred tax, 210
  extraordinary items, 334
  fixed assets, valuation, 126, 127, 128, 129
  goodwill on consolidation, 250
  inflation, 217
  intangible assets, 138–9
  inventory valuation, 174
  legal system, 67
  R&D accounting, 137, 138–9
  R&D capitalization, 136
  revaluation of assets, 72, 229
  tax system, 203
  translation of financial statements, 260, 261
  true and fair concept, 105
specific or unit cost, 167–8
standard cost, 169–70
standardization, definition, 87

stock,
  comparative usage of term, 164 Table, 399
  Fourth Directive, 355, 358–9
  see also inventory
stock exchanges, international differences, 69 Table
subsidiary, *see* parent/subsidiary relationship
Sweden,
  classification, 81
  depreciation, 158
  fixed assets, valuation, 127, 129
  translation of financial statements, 265, 266
  untaxed reserves, 329
Switzerland,
  fixed assets, valuation, 127, 129, 130–1
  intangible assets, 139–40
  translation of financial statements, 265, 266

tax bases, 193, 195–8
  capital gains, 196
  depreciation, 195–6
  dividends received, 197
  expenses, 197
  interest payments, 198
  losses, 196, 197 Table
  summary, 212–13
tax systems, 193–4, 199–205
  classical systems, 199–200
  imputation systems, 200–4
  split-rate systems, 204–5
  summary, 213
taxation, 107, 212–13, 374–5
  dividends, imputation systems, 200–4
  economic double taxation of dividends, 199–200, 213
  harmonization, 205
  inflation, 219
  international differences, 70–3
  timing of payment, 194
  see also deferred tax
trade marks, 135
trading account, 31–2
transactions translation, definition, 257
translation of financial statements, 260–7
  basis, comparison of countries, 265–6 Tables
  closing rate method, 261, 262–4, 368
  current rate method, 261, 369
  definition, 257
  summary 264–5
  temporal method, 261–2, 262–4
true and fair view, 50, 57, 103, 104 Table, 105–6, 400
turnover, net, 367

UEC, *see* FEE
UK,
  accounting practice, 76–7
  accounting and taxable income, 211

UK (*continued*)
  balance sheets, 99, 100, 101
  capital allowance, 71, 146, 147
  capital gains, 196
  classification, 81
  company names, 95, 96
  current cost accounting, 226
  current purchasing power accounting, 224
  deferred tax, 71, 206, 209, 210, 212
  depreciation, 71, 146, 158, 159, 195, 206
  development of accounting, 65, 66
  dividends, 197, 331
  enforcement of IASC standards, 110
  exceptional items, 330
  expenses, 197
  extraordinary items, 330, 331
  fixed assets,
    revaluation, 156, 230
    valuation, 123, 126, 127, 129
  goodwill on consolidation, 250, 251
  index of retail prices, 216, 217
  inflation, 217
  inventory valuation, 174
  leases, capitalization, 132, 133
  long-term contracts, 175
  operating loss reliefs, 197
  profit and loss account, 103
  property rates, 198
  proportional consolidation, 246
  public accountancy bodies, 74
  R&D accounting, 137, 138
  R&D capitalization, 136
  raising finance, 68
  remuneration schemes impact on generation of funds, 328
  tax systems, 199, 200–3, 204
  taxation, 71, 72, 219
  terminology compared with USA, 325–6
  translation of financial statements, 260, 261, 264, 265, 266
  true and fair concept, 105
  see also England
unpaid capital, 354, 357–8
untaxed reserves, 189, 191, 329, 330
USA,
  capital gains, 196
  capitalizing leases, 132
  classification, 81
  deferred tax, 71, 209
  depreciation, 146–7, 195
  development of accounting, 66
  dividends received, 197
  economic crisis 1920s–1930s, 76
  enforcement of IASC standards, 110–11
  expenses, 197
  GPLA systems, 224
  LIFO inventory valuation, 230
  operating loss reliefs, 197
  public accountancy body, 74
  R&D capitalization, 136
  raising finance, 68
  Securities and Exchange Acts, 76
  tax system, 199, 205
  taxation, 71, 72, 146–7
  terminology compared with UK, 325–6
  translation of financial statements, 260, 261
useful economic life, 144, 154–5

valuation rules, Fourth Directive, 97, 368–73
valuation, *see* business valuation; current assets; fixed assets; inventory valuation
vehicles, depreciation, 123

wages payment, 14, 16, 20, 21
work-in-progress, 164, 173, 174 Tables, 355, 358–9